Blindness and Early Childhood Development

2nd Edition, Revised

by David H. Warren

University of California at Riverside

AFB

American Foundation for the Blind

BLINDNESS AND EARLY CHILDHOOD DEVELOPMENT
2nd edition, revised
by David H. Warren

ISBN 0-89128-123-1
L.C. No. 84-16796

Library of Congress Cataloging in Publication Data

Warren, David H.
Blindness and early childhood development.

Bibliography: p.
Includes index.
1. Children, Blind. 2. Child development. I. Title.
HV1596.2.W37 1984 155.4'511 84-16796
ISBN 0-89128-123-1 (pbk.)

2nd printing 1989

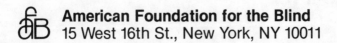

American Foundation for the Blind
15 West 16th St., New York, NY 10011

Table of Contents

Introduction and Acknowledgments to the Second Edition

In a letter to me in June, 1973, Zofja Jastrzembska noted that there was a great need to gather together what is known and understood about various facets of the development of children with visual impairment, to point out where the knowledge and understanding are lacking or incomplete in significant ways, and, to the extent possible, to draw implications of the research literature for practice. With a good deal of apprehension, I agreed to undertake the project, and the first edition of *Blindness and Early Childhood Development,* published in 1977, was the result. In this second edition, I have incorporated work that has become available in the meantime.

Most simply stated, my goal is to provide a review of the available knowledge about the effects of visual impairment on child development, encompassing most of the areas that would ordinarily be considered in a text on child development: motor and locomotor development, perceptual development, language and cognitive development, social, emotional, and personality development. The large body of literature on formal educational programs is omitted because it forms an entity sufficiently self-contained to be treated elsewhere as a unit.

The book contains nine chapters. The first seven are content chapters, each containing review sections and attempts to integrate the knowledge in a substantive area. Chapters 1 covers the infancy period, roughly birth to two years of age. Chapter 2 surveys the literature on perceptual and motor development. Chapter 3 treats the development of cognitive functions such as classification and imagery. Chapter 4 is on intelligence and IQ testing. Chapter 5 includes the literature on language development. Chapter 6 is concerned with socialization and social development, and Chapter 7 covers personality development and emotional factors. Chapter 8 has two parts. The first is a brief summary of the definite conclusions that may be drawn about the effects of visual handicap on the various areas of development. The second part is more lengthy and has as its goal the delineation of areas that are in critical need of more research attention. I consider Chapter 9 to be perhaps the most important of all. In it I have discussed some of the most serious methodological shortcomings of the available research literature. Not wishing to be critical without offering constructive alternatives, I take the liberty of suggesting both specific and general ways in which future research might be designed. I would like to emphasize the need for a more integrative and multileveled research format. I believe that one of the major reasons we do not presently know more about the effects of visual impairment on development is that research has tended to be conducted in a piecemeal fashion, without adequate regard to either the vertical or the horizontal relationship of the behavior under study to the larger picture of human behavior.

Although the book is organized in a topical manner, there is a need to consider the overall developmental picture of the blind child. For example, language development obviously does not proceed independently of cognitive development. An experiential program designed to foster language development without taking cognitive development into account would necessarily fail. Another relationship is that between motor and perceptual development. There are less obvious examples, though, that are equally important. Perceptual development, especially auditory functioning, is a critical component of the development of social interaction, and the one should not be considered without the other. It is unfortunate that the interrelatedness of the various aspects of development tends to play havoc with an organization that is based on topics rather than age levels. Yet the topical approach seems to be the most useful way of organizing the work.

Four questions are posed in each of the content chapters. *First,* in what ways are blind children similar to sighted children of the same age, and in what ways are they different? What differences are there between early blind and late blind children? *Second,* what are the factors that produce differences in development between blind and sighted children or between types of blind children? If blind children are slower to begin to crawl or walk, what are the reasons for the lag? *Third*, what can be done to produce optimal developmental progression in the various areas? For example, how might the child's experience be structured so as to eliminate or minimize the developmental lag in crawling? Consideration of this question involves another: to what extent is it desirable for a specific developmental lag to be minimized? It may be that, because the information available to the blind child is restricted, it is desirable for him to progress more slowly in a given area in order to attain the best possible eventual level of behavior. The other side of this coin is the question of "critical period." It may be that in some area a critical chronological age is involved, so that acquisition of a skill or characteristic is much more difficult after that time. *Fourth,* what can be done to remediate delays that have already occurred? If a child has grown to the age of five without adequate language skills, what types of remedial experience are useful in helping him to acquire these skills?

Note that the first question asks a comparative question (comparing blind with sighted children), and that despite the fact that the subsequent questions only refer directly to the blind, they are all addressed to aspects of the comparative question through their concern with developmental lag. Much of the research literature is, in fact, designed to compare blind and sighted children. Therefore, it may be argued, the best summary of such a research literature is one that takes the same approach. However, there are some inherent dangers in this approach. I would like to suggest some perspective and some caution on the issue of comparison of sighted and visually impaired children, and to ask the reader to keep this in mind as he or she reads this book or any other comparatively oriented work.

Students of comparative psychology are commonly told that there is a right way to think about comparisons among species, say rats and humans, and a wrong way. The commonly offered justification for studying the rat is that we learn things about rats that we can generalize to humans. So far so good, but at this point we can begin to distinguish the right way and the wrong way. Take the study of aggressive behavior, for example. The wrong way is to study aggression in the rat and how it varies with a factor, such as social crowding, draw a conclusion about the relationship between these variables based on the rat, and then conclude that the same relationship must hold for other animals, including humans. The flaw in this approach is the false assumption that aggression plays the same role for humans as it does for rats, that social crowding is the same phenomenon, and that therefore the meaningful relationship between social crowding and aggression is the same. In fact, of course, many other factors besides social crowding affect aggression in rats as well as in humans. The interrelationships of these various factors may make the functional relationship between crowding and aggression very different for rats and humans; therefore straightforward generalization is almost never warranted.

Does this mean that comparative studies of rats and humans are worthless? Not at all—there is the right way. The right way requires the aggression of the rat to be studied within the larger context of the rat's behavior and environment. Aggression plays an important role in the rat's total existence, and it is influenced by many factors in the rat's world. The functional role of aggression for the rat must be evaluated and studied within this entire context. From that sort of study, we learn about the relationships among many variables for the rat: we learn how the whole picture fits together. This kind of picture can be very instructive in guiding research with human aggression, helping to identify possibly important variables and to guide hypothesis formulation. But then, with our interest turned to humans, again aggression must be studied with a keen eye to the role that it plays in the spectrum of human behavior, and to how it is related to the many other factors that operate to influence human behavior. The study of the rat's behavioral system, in all of its intricacies, is valuable, as is the study of the human's behavioral system. And the comparison of the systems is valuable. But isolated comparisons of simple variables, taken without regard to how the variables may differ in their ecological importance for rats and humans, are worthless and indeed dangerous in their tendency to lead us to false conclusions.

Let us turn now to the blind and the sighted child. No matter how much we may wish it otherwise, the worlds of the two are different. Not as different as those of the human and the rat, to be sure, but different nevertheless, and the same cautions should be observed in drawing comparisons. There are several specific dangers in doing research that compares the blind with the sighted. First, the ecologies of the children are different in complex ways. To take the most obvious and indeed tautological example, the visual system serves a different purpose for the two; it plays a different role in the reception of information about the world. So too, because of the differences in visual systems, do the other senses serve purposes that are not identical for the blind and the sighted child. So the first danger is that what may superficially look like the same characteristic for the two is really different. If it is studied as if it were the same, and if conclusions are drawn based on that (false) assumption, our conclusions are wrong.

Second, there are methodological problems in designing research to make comparisons. I have made these arguments extensively elsewhere (Warren, 1978a,b) and will summarize only briefly here. Take the study of a classification skill, for example, in which the child is presented with a group of objects and is asked to place them into subgroups. The sighted child is typically tested on this ability with vision available, but the blind child obviously cannot be and is thus tested with tactually discriminable materials. Is it suitable to compare his tactual performance with the sighted child's visual performance? Probably not. But should we instead test the sighted child under blindfold with only tactile cues available, and make the comparison with the blind? This procedure would be more defensible, but it too has its shortcomings—the sighted child is now being asked to perform a task using a sense that he does not ordinarily have to rely on for such a task, and it is doubtful that we would obtain a valid picture of his classification skills in this way. Methodologically, then, the comparative approach is dangerous, for what seems on the face of it to be a natural and straightforward comparison is not, on closer scrutiny.

Third, even if the methodological problems were solved and we did draw conclusions that were not flawed, we would be likely to use the results to reach what I consider to be a faulty rationale for practice. Consider what our goal in working with the visually impaired child should be. Should it be to make the child reach developmental milestones at the same age as the sighted child, or should we instead seek to optimize the developmental course of the visually impaired child? Comparative research tends to lead us toward the first goal. I argue that it is the second goal that we should take as a guiding principle.

Part of the desire for equality for the visually impaired child no doubt stems from the goals of social equality that became so crystallized in the 1960s. But let us examine what equality means. All of us, I am sure, are committed to the goal of equal opportunity for the visually impaired child. By "equal opportunity" I mean the opportunity to develop to his fullest capacity and to lead the richest life possible, participating in the highest possible levels of education, vocation, and recreation. This is just what we wish for the sighted child, and I do not see this point as arguable. But it is certainly a leap to suggest that the index of success in this quest, speaking now of how to prepare the visually impaired child best to achieve his optimal level, should be the achievement of the developmental norms for the sighted child. It may well be that in some areas of development, optimizing the situation to allow the visually impaired child to reach his optimal level will lead to equality of developmental norms. If so, fine, but it is the optimization that should be the criterion of success, not the equalization of the norms.

To the extent that research comparing blind and sighted children leads us to the false goal of attempting to equate developmental norms, this research is counterproductive to what our goal should be—it should be to achieve the kind of environment for the blind child in which he will be able to reach the highest levels of which he is capable. I urge the reader to bear this goal in mind.

One of my key goals is the identification of areas which are in need of more or better research. No major developmental areas have been totally neglected by researchers, and in some areas there is enough good information to make reasonable statements about what the developmental picture is and what should be done to optimize the development of blind children. In many areas, though, there are major gaps. I hope that it will be of benefit to the field to point to these gaps and to suggest both specific and general ways of attacking them. I attempt this in Chapter 8.

There are several difficulties in writing a review such as this, and two of these deserve specific mention at the outset. First, the population of children defined as blind or visually impaired is extremely heterogeneous and must often be subdivided in order to make any meaningful statement. Second, the literature on blind children is tremendously varied in quality and type.

Two dimensions of variation in visual status that are most commonly recognized in the literature are the age of onset of blindness and the severity of impairment. There is a wealth of evidence that careful attention must be paid to the age of onset. This dimension is perhaps most obvious when writers speak of a "visualization" ability of the later blind, and of the absence of the ability to visualize in the early blind. The distinction seems particularly important in spatial abilities, but it extends to many other areas of development as well. In fact, the simple distinction between blind at birth and later blind is inadequate. Some writers group together all children blinded before five years and compare them to those blinded later. While this rough distinction may be adequate for some comparisons, it is an oversimplification when dealing with areas such as spatial behavior, language development, or socialization. In these areas a much finer age-at-onset division is required.

The existence or absence of a period of early vision is not the only factor in age of onset. There may be differences created by complications attendant to the onset of blindness itself, such as hospitalization that may occur at critical development periods. Too, determination of the age of onset may be difficult for several reasons. Records may be inexact or unavailable, or the onset may have been gradual. For this and other reasons, it is probably desirable to know not only the age at onset, but also the cause of blindness. In retinoblastoma the onset is typically gradual, while blindness resulting from an accident is often, although not always, sudden.

Even within the category of children who become blind very early, some subdivision is usually necessary to avoid lumping together children with quite different characteristics. A high proportion of children used in the blind-at-birth research over the past three decades have been retrolental fibroplasia (RLF) children. Strictly speaking, these children are not blind at birth. Rather, they become blind within a few months as a result of the oxygen-rich environment that is characteristic of the incubator treatment of prematurity. To be sure, the incidence of RLF has decreased dramatically since its cause was isolated in the early 1950s, but this fact only highlights the necessity for close attention to etiology. Other causes of early blindness may be even more important to differentiate. An obvious example is Rubella blindness, which is quite often associated with hearing difficulties and other central nervous system involvement. Although research seldom groups Rubella children indiscriminately with other blind children, groupings that make equally little sense have often been made. It is especially important to distinguish among various types of multiply handicapped blind children from the point of view of both treatment and research.

I will attempt to draw a line between overgeneralizing across varied types and etiologies of blindness on the one hand, and boring the reader with needless detail on the other. This line, though, must be drawn differently depending on the area under consideration, and whenever a difficult choice has to be made it is my conviction that it should be toward including too much rather than too little detail.

The second major difficulty in reviewing the literature is the variety of the literature itself. Available material falls roughly into three categories: research reports, case studies, and "personal experience" reports.

Research reports differ widely in quality. From the purist's point of view, most of the research is not experimental; that is, conditions are not manipulated by the experimenter and subjects are not randomly assigned to experimental conditions. Much of the research should instead be called evaluative, since it is designed to determine performance levels of subjects with various status characteristics (blind vs. sighted children) on a given measure. The primary independent variable is a visual characteristic such as degree of residual vision or age at onset, variables that are not under the experimenter's control. The quality of the report has nothing to do with whether the research is evaluative or experimental. Research quality has to do with adequacy of definitions, with control in the testing situation, with statistical treatment, and with the rigor of logical inferences and conclusions. It is in these areas that too much of the research on blindness is inadequate. To be sure, there are inherent characteristics of the subject population that create difficulties for researchers. The heterogeneity of the blind population is one such characteristic. If subjects are obtained from a residential school, the children of a given age are likely to have varying degrees of residual vision, varying etiologies, and varying incidence and severity of additional handicaps. To obtain a large enough sample for statistical treatment, it is often necessary either to group together subjects of widely differing visual histories or to group together subjects over a wider age range than would be acceptable in research with sighted children. Neither option is desirable in most research, but the difficulty remains. The emerging use of multivariate design and analysis techniques may prove of immense help in solving the research problems that are inherent in this subject population.

It is frustrating to find a report with an interesting title, one that might have been useful if the writer had specified characteristics of the subject sample such as age of onset, degree of blindness, or even subjects' ages. It is unfortunate, when this information is not available, that the time of the children has been taken up without gain, and that resources have been devoted to a study without useful payoff. That the subject population is a difficult one to work with from a research design and statistical point of view is no excuse for the failure to specify operational definitions adequately, to describe the sample, to describe testing conditions, or to provide appropriate statistical summaries.

These criticisms apply to a substantial portion of the blindness literature but by no means to all of it. There are in every area studies that are well done and well reported.

The second category of report in the literature is the case study. These reports are often very useful in formulating initial hypotheses about relationships among variables, although they cannot in general be used to test hypotheses in any rigorous way. The great advantage is that vast detail about the subject's characteristics may be provided, and his behavior may be described to give a much fuller picture than can be provided by numerical results. This "full picture" approach, even with very limited numbers of subjects, is of special value to a review such as this one which is intended to provide an overall view, ranging across a number of different but interrelated facets of development. A large number of the case study reports appear in psychoanalytically oriented journals. To the nonanalytically oriented developmental psychologist, these reports often use terms that seem to lack specificity of referent. For example, the notion of the differentiation of self from world seems to make intuitive sense, but it is a rare report that discusses what this notion means in operational terms. It is correspondingly difficult, therefore, to fit the concept into a theoretical system of sufficient rigor to allow empirical test. To be sure, more experimentally oriented researchers often use terms without being able to specify exactly what the terms mean. Both experimental research and case studies should make every attempt to provide operational definitions of terms so that the reader may understand the usage of the terms. It is this level of definition, often lacking in case reports, that results in work that is difficult to evaluate.

This is a relatively mild complaint, and it does not override the value of the case study approach. The case reports are often based on very careful obervations taken repeatedly on the same children. The psychoanalytic reports are of particular value because of their regard for the importance of the early years of life, a period which has unfortunately been almost totally neglected by the researcher.

"Personal experience" reports are those which draw conclusions based on personal, practical, or clinical involvement. They are perhaps the most difficult for the reviewer to evaluate. Lest it appear that I regard this to be a second-class category, I should note that many such reports contain very useful material for the purposes of building intervention or remedial programs. Although this material is perhaps less satisfying to the researcher and theoretician, one cannot lightly dispute the collective experience of a number of practitioners when they agree on some conclusion. When consensual support exists for some point, even without research support, I will use the point freely as a building block, typically appending a verbal asterisk. As the conclusions of various writers begin to differ, however, the material rapidly loses its usefulness. I will allude to some of these differences of opinion, but my bias against the material will not easily be hidden.

The difficulties created for my task by the nature of the literature are not insuperable, nor are they a valid reason for avoiding the task. I am convinced of the need for the work, and of the need to make the best of what is available.

Since I finished reviewing the research literature for publication of the first edition, in 1977, there has been a good deal of material published bearing on the visually impaired child. In fact, the second edition contains more than 200 new references, bringing the total bibliography list to more than 650 items. However, despite the volume of new material that has become available, there have been few breakthroughs of the sort that necessitate a change in the basic conclusions that I drew in 1977, or that have led the field in significant new directions. For the most part, the conclusions are the same, though in many areas buttressed by new facts or better demonstrations of old ones. In some respects this is an unfortunate statement to have to make—one would hope that the field would move further forward in a seven year period. On the other hand, it is also evidence that in some areas the research available through 1977 was so thorough and conclusive that little could be added to it, except to flesh out some of the details. While this may be true for some areas, in most areas of research it is hardly true that we know all that we need to know. One hopes that the next seven years will show great research activity that explores vital areas, making use of new research paradigms that will fill in the significant gaps that remain in our knowledge system about the effects of visual impairment on the development of children.

One area in which there has been significant new research with new paradigms is language development, particularly in the meaning of words and the nature of the social use of language. The conclusion that I drew from the language development literature in 1977 was, briefly, that there were few significant differences between blind and sighted children's development. The evidence was that the blind child acquires language pretty much as the sighted child does, with few important differences in timing or quality of acquisition. Because of more sophisticated methodologies that have since been applied in this area, we now not only realize that there are significant differences in the nature of the child's acquisition of meaning and in the use of language for social interchange, but we also know that there are very good reasons that this is so. The language environment of the visually impaired child is typically different from that of the sighted child, apparently because of the tendency of parents to "take account of" the child's handicap in speaking with him. This new and important material will be reviewed in Chapter 5.

Another area which has seen significant progress concerns the cognitive bases for spatial behavior and mobility. Here it is not so much that the new methodologies have produced evidence at odds with what we had before as it is the reconceptualization of the issues and the development of new methodologies to deal with those recast issues. This material is covered in Chapter 2 in a new section entitled "Spatial Cognition."

Another new section appears in Chapter 2, entitled "Sensory Aids." Although there were by 1977 sporadic reports of the use of various sensory aids with visually impaired children, there was not sufficient material to warrant a review and summary. Now there is more, and the use of aids with infants in particular raises several issues that are worthy of discussion.

Finally, a word about terminology. There is some disagreement about the use of the terms "blindness," "visual impairment," and "visual handicap." I have avoided the use of the latter term because of my conviction that visual loss need not result in a handicapped individual, at least not in the sense that he or she can do things less well than people without a visual loss. Often the term "blindness" is used to denote total visual loss, or loss of all but light perception (LP), while "visual impairment" is used to denote lesser degrees of visual loss. I have not maintained this distinction with any degree of rigor, primarily because I find that it is a somewhat cumbersome one that does not really accomplish the finer distinctions that are needed in analyzing the research literature. Instead, I have tried to use finer distinctions wherever appropriate, giving detail about the cause and duration of visual loss as well as about the severity.

Acknowledgments

I have been very gratified by the extremely positive responses that I have received from my colleagues in the field about the first edition of this book. I have been especially pleased by comments from students who have found it useful in guiding their graduate studies. These comments, in fact, played a very important motivating factor in my decision to bring the work up to date in a second edition, rather than simply having the first edition reprinted in its original form. I hope that the second edition will be useful for new generations of students, as well as for others who may find occasion to read it.

I wish to thank a number of people for their contributions to various aspects of the project that became the first edition of *Blindness and Early Childhood Development* in 1977. Joe and Joanie Kocon assisted in the first phase of the literature search. In the initial stages of the work, a group of seminar students provided a valuable forum for discussion. This group included Linda Anooshian, Janet Bollinger, Gary Dickerson, Anne Fulgoni, Michael Haberman, Tricia Jordan, Shirley Judy, Ted Knipe, Terry Schmitt, and Mel Widawski. Diana Ketterman assisted me with some of the material in the chapter on cognitive development. A special note of thanks is due Janice Harrington Matthews, who provided an analysis of play and creativity. In addition, Janice spent many painstaking hours checking my accuracy in reporting the details of the literature, and at the same time she helped to make my often dry writing somewhat more readable. All of these people are or have been my students, and I would like to take this opportunity to extent to all of them my gratitude for the intellectual stimulation that they have provided and continue to provide for me.

I am indebted to Emerson Foulke, Milton Gottesman, Lewis Petrinovich, and Robert Welch for consenting to read and comment on various parts of the manuscript. Leslie Clark has, in this project and others, helped me nurture a perspective on visual impairment, and I have found his wisdom and good sense extremely valuable. Zofja Jastrzembska made her own vast knowledge and the library resources of the American Foundation for the Blind available to me, and she has provided a valuable sounding board for my emerging ideas and analyses of the literature. I am most indebted to her for her support and encouragement throughout the project.

In the past several years I have found immense benefit from my association with my colleage, Dr. Edward Strelow, who has collaborated effectively with me in our joint research program and who has, just as importantly, provided a source of ideas and a sounding board for my own. Dr. Strelow deserves special thanks.

Finally, I wish to express thanks to my wife, Lynda, and my son, Michael, for the support that they have given me throughout the writing of both books. They have many times fallen asleep to the distant tune of a typewriter, but they have realized how important the project has been to me and have given nothing but support.

David H. Warren
April, 1984

1
Infancy

The term infancy generally is used to refer to the first two years of life. During this period, the child normally accomplishes vast progress in several areas. He changes from an asocial being whose behavior is not at all responsive to the requirements of the social surroundings to a child who is responsive to others and who modifies his behavior at least to some extent in accordance with their wishes. (The parent of any two-year-old knows the limitations of this easy generalization, however!) His language develops to support a basic level of verbal social interchange. His perceptual skills change from rudimentary capabilities for processing simple sensory stimuli to more mature abilities to organize volumes of sensory information into complex perceptual events. He develops a fundamental understanding of the "rules" of the physical world, although this is far from complete by two years of age. The advances in cognition depend critically on the developing capabilities for processing complex sets of perceptual information, and reciprocally, cognitive advances allow more efficient perceptual processing. In the area of motor development, he changes from a neonate with very little control over gross or fine musculature to a two-year-old with relatively good command of gross motor behavior and a rapidly developing fine motor control. Whereas at birth his motor behavior appeared random and uncontrolled, at two he can not only crawl, but walk and manipulate objects with some dexterity and much intentionality. The development of motor behavior is closely tied to the other areas of development in infancy, particularly perception and cognition.

In this chapter I will first discuss early sensory stimulation, then move from early perceptual development to motor development, then to cognitive development and finally to socialization. It is important to note that the literature discussed in this chapter concerns primarily those infants who have been visually impaired since birth — there is very little differentiation in the literature of the first two years between congenital and acquired visual impairment. By contrast, the literature to be discussed in later chapters will cover those children who have been visually impaired since birth as well as those who have become visually impaired after some period of visual experience.

Much of the advance in the literature has depended critically on the development of methodologies that are appropriate for the study of infants. This is particularly true for the study of perceptual development. During the past decade or two, research methods have been developed which allow the evaluation of sensory discriminative abilities in young infants. Although these methods, such as habituation-dishabituation, have the potential for revealing the precise discriminative abilities of infants, the methods are extremely tedious to use. As a result, information about the tactile, auditory, olfactory and gustatory discriminations of sighted infants is sparse. There has been little if any application of these research methods to blind infants, and thus information about the sensory discriminative abilities of blind infants is almost nonexistent. The information that is available about the abilities of blind infants has been obtained primarily through the use of observational rather than interventive methods. Observational techniques, however, allow only rough assessment of the precision of sensory and perceptual abilities, and less can be learned about these abilities than might be by other techniques.

The successful use of observational techniques depends on the subject's ability (and willingness!) to produce observable behavior. The development of motor behavior constitutes a set of questions in its own right, however, and in infants the study of perceptual abilities is intertwined with the study of motor development. Often a firm conclusion cannot be made about a perceptual ability. For example, if one sets out to evaluate some aspect of auditory perception in infants and plans to use a motor response indicator, such as reaching out for a sound producer, what can be concluded if an infant does not produce the response? It may be that the infant can perceive the stimulus but that he cannot (or does not want to) reach for it. If so, a conclusion of perceptual inability on the basis of lack of reaching would be mistaken. It is important, in using observational techniques, to follow some general principles. First, one must study the subject's motor capabilities thoroughly enough to know what he can and cannot do, and one must be sensitive to changes in these capabilities over age. Second, one should observe more than one behavioral indicator. For instance, in addition to looking for a reaching response, one might observe any changes in nondirected hand movements, head orientation, sucking behavior, and general body activity.

In studying questions of perceptual development, it is necessary to keep in mind the importance of the nonvisual senses for the blind infant. Vision provides a continuous, rich, consistent, precise, and reliable source of information for the sighted child. He depends on this information to help him orient to and identify objects and people, to regulate his own motor behavior, and to provide an overall organization of space. The question for the blind infant is, then, not only how well the nonvisual senses can perform the functions that they serve for the sighted child, but also to what extent the nonvisual senses can substitute for the functions that vision serves for the sighted child. Can the blind infant identify objects and people, can he direct his motor activity, can he acquire a spatial framework? The answer, briefly summarized, is that most of these functions can be and often are served by other modalities. Sometimes, however, there are deficiencies, and it is possible to point to at least general factors in the experience of blind children that play an important part in determining how well the functions are served.

The Importance of Early Sensory Stimulation

The past two decades have seen a great deal of research directed to the question of the role of early sensory stimulation in the development of perceptual and other systems. A major impetus for work in this area was provided by Riesen's (1947) early research on the effects of visual deprivation in chimpanzees. Riesen found that raising animals in the dark or in unpatterned illumination produced various neurological and behavioral abnormalities. Other researchers have pursued this work into many areas, using many species of animals as subjects. One of the extremely interesting developments in this area of research has been the demonstration that there are emotional and behavioral consequences of early somatosensory stimulation. Denenberg (1964), for example, has found striking differences in rats on indices of emotional reactivity as a result of differences in early handling. DeNelsky and Denenberg (1967a,b) have demonstrated that a simple daily handling procedure early in life can produce enhanced exploratory behavior, expressed specifically in tactile (1967a) and visual (1967b) seeking of stimulus variation.

Studies such as that of DeNelsky and Denenberg (1967b) are important in their demonstration that the effects of stimulation in one sensory modality are not restricted to that modality alone. Related evidence was reported by Riesen (1966), who showed that visual deprivation alone did not produce substantial depression of emotional and learning behavior as long as the animals (cats, monkeys) received normal stimulation of other modalities, especially tactual and auditory. However, when visual deprivation was coupled with restriction of other types of stimulation, the animals proved to be either hyper- or hypoemotional. Other researchers, notably Harlow (1958), have demonstrated the vital role of tactual experience in producing adequate development in emotional and other areas.

Studies such as these clearly carry implications for blind persons. Several writers have discussed the problem. Freedman (1971), in particular, noted that visual deprivation itself may not be the critical factor in producing the developmental lags in locomotion that have been cited by writers such as Fraiberg (1977). Freedman and Cannady (1971) reviewed several case studies characterized by various types of deprivation, including both visual and environmental deprivation (in "environmental deprivation," Freedman and Cannady considered the critical factor to be a lack of early handling). They concluded that more severe lags are found in individuals who have experienced environmental (somatosensory) deprivation than those who have experienced visual deprivation. Freedman (1971), in fact, presented hypothetical developmental curves that suggest that "coenesthetic" (somatosensory, plus diffuse visual and auditory) stimulation is important at an earlier developmental stage than specific visual or auditory stimulation. Another line of evidence in support of the importance of early somatosensory stimulation comes from a research program reported by White and Held (1966), in which relatively deprived institutionalized infants received as little as 20 minutes a day of extra handling by a caretaker, but showed significantly earlier development of visual attentiveness than a control group.

Prescott (1976) provided a review of much of the material from both human and infrahuman subjects bearing on early stimulation. He argued that vestibular stimulation is as important as and should be considered independently from somatosensory stimulation. He emphasized the need to distinguish between effects of deprivation in the somatosensory or the vestibular mode and effects of deprivation in the visual mode, and he pointed out that many of the undesirable effects that have been attributed to visual loss are probably in fact attributable to the other types of deprivation that may easily accompany visual loss. Some corroboration for Prescott's emphasis on vestibular functions is found in a study by Korner and Thoman (1970) in which the effects on visual alertness of vestibular and contact stimulation were assessed. The subjects were sighted infants from two to five days of age. For infants who were crying at the time of intervention, vestibular stimulation alone produced a substantial increase in visual alertness, while contact stimulation alone produced little effect.

How does visual loss imply deprivation of somatosensory, vestibular, or other sensory stimulation? It does not, necessarily, but various writers have noted that in many cases, other types of sensory deprivation do accompany blindness. The tendency for some parents of blind infants to engage in very little body contact with the infant has been mentioned by Burlingham (1967) and Fraiberg, Smith, and Adelson (1969), among others. To the extent that the results of studies such as DeNelsky and Denenberg (1967a) may be generalized to human infants, a lack of early somatosensory and vestibular stimulation may lead to a lesser degree of "stimulus variation seeking" later on when the child becomes able to explore his surroundings. Burlingham (1967), among others, has noted what may be a general consequence of a lack of early somatosensory stimulation—some children "seem to lack any desire for the objects surrounding them and consequently show no sign of a wish to play" (p. 187). Another factor that may contribute to the more passive behavior of young blind children is the parental overprotection syndrome, which has also been cited as a precursor of poor mobility (Warren & Kocon, 1974).

Somatosensory and vestibular deprivation may be especially serious in cases where prematurity or other complications at birth necessitate a substantial period of incubation or other confinement to a hospital. The typical incubator environment may include some auditory and visual isolation, as well as more drastically reduced tactile and vestibular stimulation. Visual isolation is probably the least severe of these aspects of deprivation, since incubator walls are often made of plastic or glass and allow the infant relatively normal visual experience. For the infant who will become blind from retrolental fibroplasia (RLF) as a result of the oxygen-rich environment of the incubator, the visual environment probably makes little difference. In many hospitals, auditory deprivation is probably not serious either, since no attempt is made to soundproof isolettes and the premature infant is exposed to the normal range of nursery sounds. In fact some hospitals make a special effort to provide auditory stimulation. It is undoubtedly in the areas of tactile and vestibular stimulation that the incubator infant's sensory experience is least like that of a normal infant. For reasons of antisepsis, handling of the infant is often kept to a minimum, and the infant does not receive either the tactile contact derived from being held or the vestibular stimulation that accompanies changes in position. (It should be noted that some hospitals have adopted a policy of encouraging nurses and parents to handle the premature infants.) Neither does the incubated premature infant receive the somatosensory and vestibular stimulation that he would be receiving from the mother's activities if he had remained *in utero* until term.

Some of the effects of early sensory deprivation will be further explored in Chapter 7. Suffice it to say that a strong case may be made for the attribution of some emotional disturbances in RLF blind children to early sensory deprivation. Thus sensory deprivation may be a particularly devastating condition, producing deficits not only in exploratory behavior and related learning and cognitive functions but also in the area of emotional development.

Audition

There is no evidence that visual impairment creates a handicap in any of the basic auditory discriminative abilities of pitch, sound quality, or loudness. In some areas where a function that is normally primarily visual has to be served by audition, however, differences may be noted. One example is the identification of environmental events where vision normally plays an important role. Another example, which will be discussed more fully later, is the onset of locomotion, where vision plays an important stimulating role.

Using data from several sources, it is possible to piece together a general timetable for the normative development of the use of and responsiveness to sound by the blind infant. The fact that even such a relatively incomplete developmental picture has to be pieced together from various sources points to the neglect of auditory functioning in the research literature. During the first few months, the infant may smile in response to his parent's voice (Freedman, 1964). At six months, a slight movement toward a clock chime occurs (Burlingham, 1964). At six to eight months, while a hand response occurs in response to the loss of an object handled tactually, no hand response appears to an object experienced only auditorily. At seven months, there is attention to sounds created by actions of the hands in the environment (Burlingham, 1964). At eight months, an aversive response to a stranger's voice may be observed, and from nine to 11 months, the beginnings of coordination of the auditory and tactile modes appear (Fraiberg, Siegel & Gibson, 1966). One relatively precocious infant showed locomotion in a walker toward the sound of the mother at 10 months (Fraiberg & Freedman, 1964), while this same behavior was noted at 14 months in a child who had been three months premature (Wills, 1970). At about 11 months, reaching for an object occurs on the basis of sound cues. Readiness for "reaching to sound" may be indicated by tentative movements of the fingers in the direction of the object (Fraiberg et al. 1966). Fraiberg et al. also reported that the first instances of reaching to sound are often followed within a very few days by the first attempts at crawling, and that at 14 months there is a good ability to track and find an object dragged across a rug.

It is unfortunate that a more detailed chronology of the normal development of auditory function in blind infants is not available. The composite picture presented above is not nearly detailed or reliable enough to serve as a "development chart" against which the progress of a blind infant might be checked. Given the importance of auditory functions for the blind infant, it seems clear that much more effort should be expended in this area.

Relatively little attention has been paid to the development of an auditory developmental chart for sighted infants, and it is thus not possible to make a definitive statement about the possibility of developmental lags of either blind or sighted infants. As was noted at the outset, there is little reason to suggest that a lag might exist in the basic auditory discriminative abilities. There is, however, evidence that orientation to sound sources does not occur as early for blind infants as for sighted. Sighted children make very early oculomotor responses to sounds. Wertheimer (1961), for example, observed a directional orientation of the eyes to sounds within the first minutes of life. Aronson and Rosenbloom (1971) found signs of distress in 30-day-old infants when the apparent visual position of the infant's mother was different from the apparent source of her voice. McGurk and Lewis (1974) and others have cast some doubt on the reliability of the Aronson and Rosenbloom results; even so, it seems reasonable to conclude that visual-auditory coordination of spatial events occurs early for sighted infants. The precise nature of the interaction between audition and vision in localization is not known, but there have been suggestions that vision plays an instructive role with respect to auditory localization. That is, the infant may roughly localize a sound as being off to one side or the other, and by orienting to it visually he gains more precise information about the location of the object and learns to interpret more precisely the patterns of auditory stimulation (Bower, 1974; Warren, 1970).

Considering the apparently spontaneous tendency of the sighted infant to turn his eyes toward a sound source, the function of the visual information that becomes available to him, and the unavailability of that information for the blind infant, it seems reasonable to expect that blind infants might be at a disadvantage in using auditory spatial information. C. Williams (1968) cited a personal communication by Murphy to the effect that "blind children are as much as four months retarded in their ability or preparedness to turn their heads toward a sound source" (p. 738). Similarly, Lairy and Harrison-Covello (1973) noted that "The reactions of orientation to noise, which appear about the second month in the sighted child, are observed only towards the seventh month in the blind child" (pp. 3–4). Evidence for this picture of developmental lag is not unequivocal, though. For example, Freedman (1964) observed that a 14-week-old blind infant turned her eyes toward the source of a sound. Clearly there is disagreement in this literature. Much more systematic observation is necessary, and a detailed study of the eye, head, and hand responses to auditory stimulation might provide valuable information.

Several authors (Fraiberg & Freedman, 1964; Wills, 1970) have noted the surprisingly late occurrence of reaching to a sound stimulus by blind infants. Fraiberg, Siegel, and Gibson (1966) provided more detailed normative information about reaching to sound and concluded that this behavior does not typically occur in blind infants until the last quarter of the first year. The failure of blind infants to reach for sound cues is not generally attributable to difficulties in auditory perception, since, as Fraiberg and Freedman have pointed out, the blind infant does smile selectively in response to his mother's voice by three to five months of age.

Several reports seem to contradict the late reaching to sound reported by Fraiberg and Wills. Bower (1974) cited results of an unpublished study by Urwin (1973), who reported that one infant, born without eyeballs, reached out to grasp noisemaking objects at an age of 16 weeks. This reaching "disappeared by the age of six months, despite considerable reinforcement and practice, and had not reappeared by the age of ten months" (Bower, 1974, p. 169). It may be that this interim reaching period occurs in many blind infants, only to disappear and reoccur toward the end of the first year. It would be surprising, though, if such a period of early reaching had escaped the attention of the Fraiberg group. The issue is an interesting one, and it is important despite the report by Urwin that the reaching disappeared even though attempts were made to maintain it. Unfortunately no follow-up has been reported. Als, Tronick, and Brazelton (1980) reported that, in the case of an infant whose mother was particularly effective in establishing an affective bond with the infant, a great deal of social interaction and perceptual attentiveness and responsiveness occurred within the first few months of life, including the ability to reach to sounds at five months of age.

Interestingly, Correa, Poulson, and Salzberg (1984) reported the elicitation of reach–grasp behavior in three subjects whose developmental age (Griffiths Mental Deficiency Scales) was less than six months, but whose chronological ages were two to four years. The reaching occurred to noise-making toys, as a result of appropriate behavioral contingencies.

It is important to analyze the nature of the developmental lag in reaching to sound. In fact, the lag is in reaching to objects, rather than in reaching to objects on the basis of sound cues. Freedman, Fox-Kolenda, Margileth, and Miller (1969) provided data that indicate that sighted infants do not use sound "as an indicator of the existence of a sound-making object" until the last quarter of the first year; this development is not different from that reported for blind infants by Fraiberg and others, and there is thus no specifically *auditory* lag. The difference between blind and sighted infants occurs by virtue of the fact that sighted infants normally begin reaching to external objects on the basis of *visual* cues during the second quarter of the first year. The lag, then, is not in reaching to sound, but in *reaching to objects.* Auditory cues are not an effective substitute, to the blind infant, for the role that visual cues serve in stimulating reaching to objects for the sighted infant. Fraiberg and her colleagues have devoted considerable effort to attempts to elicit reaching to sound cues earlier, but these attempts have been largely unsuccessful. "We now know that for the totally blind baby, there is no adaptive substitution of sound for vision in intentional reaching until the last quarter of the first year" (Fraiberg, Smith, & Adelson, 1969, p. 129).

Fraiberg (1968) considered the basis for the failure of the blind infant to reach to sound cues to be a cognitive one. The auditory information is not sufficient to allow the development of the object concept, that is, the notion that an object retains its identity from one time and place to another time and place. Both Burlingham (1964) and Wills (1970) have made similar arguments about the infant's difficulty in using auditory information to mediate acquisition of the object concept. It is not the case that the six-month-old infant is cognitively incapable of developing the object concept, though. Several writers, notably Fraiberg et al. (1966), point out that blind infants do show evidence of object constancy when the object is experienced tactually. If they have had an object in their hands, they will reach out in search if the object is removed by about seven months of age.

Two questions arise. The first question concerns the difficulty of establishing the object concept on the basis of auditory cues, in contrast to the apparent effectiveness of tactual cues in mediating the object concept. The second question concerns an apparent discrepancy in the function of auditory cues. Auditory cues are apparently sufficient to allow the infant to distinguish between his parent (a "constant" object) and other people, but they are apparently not sufficient to mediate the constancy of other objects, such as the bell used as a stimulus by Fraiberg et al. (1966). The differential response to the parent's voice indicates that, under certain circumstances, the infant has object constancy quite early, even on the basis of auditory cues. Why, then, is constancy of other objects so difficult to achieve? One possibility was suggested by Burlingham (1964), who noted that some blind infants show withdrawal from auditory stimuli, as though these stimuli evoked fear. This fear may be a result of the fact that the infant has virtually no control over the nature or frequency of most of the sounds in his environment. At the same time, many of these sounds are not readily identifiable by the infant. The young blind infant does not have vision available, he is not receptive to verbal explanations, and he is restricted from tactual identification of much of his environment. A second factor is suggested by Fraiberg and Freedman (1964), who state: "It is apparent, then, that if cathexis of the object is achieved, a mental representation of mother can be formed on the basis of a variety of nonvisual sensory data" (p. 157). That is, constancy develops only for those objects that occupy positions of extreme importance for the infant. The bell that was used by Fraiberg et al. (1966) was apparently not such an important object. It may be, then, that audition-based object constancy for the six-month-old blind infant is not impossible if the object is an important enough one, and presumably if the infant has received prior information about the object via other modalities, such as touch.

Hart (1983) suggested that the delay sequence reported by Fraiberg is not a necessary consequence of early blindness, noting that many children show a developmental progression much more positive than that reported by Fraiberg and her colleagues. Hart did not suggest that the Fraiberg formulation is incorrect, but rather that it is incomplete in an important respect. Simply put, Fraiberg's formulation is that visual impairment produces delay in development of the object concept and thus delay in reaching to objects, and that the delay in reaching causes delay in crawling and walking. Hart agreed that a lag in reaching retards crawling and walking, but she proposed a motor rather than a cognitive basis for the lag in reaching. She noted that a common characteristic of blind infants, particularly those with incubator experience, is resistance to the prone position. Hart further cited evidence linking experience in the prone position to effective development of the motor strength and coordination requisite for reaching. Thus her formulation is the following: resistance to the prone position leads to delay in the motor abilities needed for reaching, which delays reaching and in turn crawling and walking.

Hart's formulation suggests that there is hope for breaking this "delay creates delay" cycle. The hope lies in nurturing an early acceptance of the prone position. She reported success in accomplishing this, and subsequent reaching to objects on a timetable within the sighted range of development.

Hart (1983) cautioned, appropriately, that the research base for her tentative conclusions is as yet incomplete. Nonetheless, the alternative that she presented to Fraiberg's (1977) relatively gloomy conclusions about the apparent immutability of the developmentally delayed sequence is an extremely important one, and it warrants focused research attention. If there is an effective antidote to the early stages of the developmental delays, then the prognosis for the early cognitive and motor development of blind infants is prospectively much more positive than that suggested by Fraiberg's findings and conclusions.

Early Motor Development

There is reasonably uniform agreement in the literature that the motor development of the congenitally blind child in the first few months of life is not markedly different from that of the sighted child. Newborn blind children, like sighted ones, show nondirected gross arm and leg movements. There has not been a great deal of normative work done with the progression through early stages of gross and fine motor abilities. Norris, Spaulding, and Brodie (1957) presented tabular information about the performance of their intensively studied sample of blind infants on the Cattell Infant Intelligence Scale. The items on this test having to do with motor development tend to be related to manual manipulation rather than to larger locomotor activity. In many respects the age results for the blind infants were parallel to the age norms for sighted infants. For example, "raising the head and chest" and "manipulating fingers" were comparable. There was evidence for lag in certain areas, though. In particular, "unilateral reaching" and "persistent reaching" both showed lags of several months. Other items involving fine motor control also showed delay, such as "scissors grasp," manipulation of pegs in holes, and scribbling. Norris et al. concluded that lags occur selectively in those areas where the blind infant's experience has been inadequate. They also note that, within some areas of performance, those infants who had been allowed and encouraged to explore their environment tended to show less deficiency.

Adelson and Fraiberg (1974) reported detailed comparisons of a group of 10 congenitally blind, otherwise normal infants with the Norris et al. (1957) sample and with developmental norms for sighted children. The Adelson and Fraiberg evaluations included more thorough study of the development of gross motor abilities. The infants' performance on various items ranged from the sighted norm to considerably worse than the sighted norm. Items falling within the normal range were "sits alone momentarily," "rolls from back to stomach," "sits alone steadily," "takes stepping movements when hands are held," and "stands alone." Adequate head control was reported for all subjects for whom information was available. The five items on which a substantial proportion of the blind infants showed a developmental lag were "elevates self by arms, in prone," "raises self to sitting position," "pulls to stand," "walks alone, three steps," and "walks alone across the room." Adelson and Fraiberg noted that the items where no lag occurred involve primarily postural skills, while the items showing a deficit involve self-initiated mobility. Within the limits of possible comparisons, the Adelson and Fraiberg group performed similarly to the larger Norris et al. sample, although in the later stages the Norris results showed somewhat greater lags. The Adelson and Fraiberg infants were involved in the ongoing "education" program conducted by Fraiberg, and it seems likely that this experience played a part in avoiding cumulative deficits.

A minor disagreement is evident in the development of grasping. As noted above, Norris et al. found the scissors grasp to be somewhat delayed, while Fraiberg (1968) reported the basic nature of the pincer grasp at 10 months to be similar in blind and sighted infants. Fraiberg did, however, note a marked delay in the coordination of the two hands. She reported a typical failure to bring the two hands together at the midline, and a consequent retardation in the ability to use the two hands in concert to explore and manipulate tactually. Fraiberg, Smith, and Adelson (1969) reported some success in producing more effective midline tactual behavior by placing hanging objects over the infant when he was in a supine position, and by placing the five-month-old infant in a seat at a table on which objects could be found and manipulated by both hands in a relatively constricted space.

Fraiberg and others report a typical lag in the onset of crawling and walking. Fraiberg (1968) found that crawling did not occur until late in the first year, in spite of the fact that other motor indications were that the children were strong enough to crawl well before they actually did, and that they were observed to rest on hands and knees for several months prior to the actual onset of crawling. Fraiberg has hypothesized that this developmental lag is related to the observation that reaching to objects based on sound cues does not occur as early in the blind infant as does reaching to visual cues in sighted infants. Fraiberg and Freedman (1964), for example, have argued that it is the act of reaching out for an object when in the hands and knees position that serves as the first component of crawling. Fraiberg (1968) cited several instances where an infant had for weeks been able to support himself on hands and knees but did not crawl forward. Within a very few days after the onset of reaching to sound, late in the first year, crawling began.

As noted earlier, Fraiberg's group has devoted considerable effort to the attempt to elicit reaching to sound earlier, with the expectation that crawling would then occur with less developmental lag. There are several points in favor of trying to produce reaching to sound earlier than the end of the first year, and at the same time there are arguments against pushing this or any other aspect of development beyond its spontaneous rate. Fraiberg and Freedman (1964) argued that it is important to find an effective substitute for the visual perception of external objects, since "failure to achieve locomotion within a critical period of time may be one of the factors that bring about developmental arrest in the deviant children" (p. 163). I would add that the development of spatial relations concepts is probably at least as critically affected as is locomotor development by the blind infant's failure to respond earlier to events on the basis of their sounds. The sighted infant certainly begins very early to make associations between the visually perceived locations of objects and their sound properties as well as their tactile properties, and it may well be this very early intermodality experience that provides for the effective later use of auditory or tactile information alone. Sufficient information about this intermodality interdependence is not available, but it seems reasonable to assume that the earlier the blind infant begins to receive *effective* correlated auditory and tactile experience, the better basis he would have for the development of adequate spatial relations concepts later.

There are thus several reasons for arguing that efforts should be made to get the blind infant to reach for objects by sound alone, and to experience simultaneously auditory and tactile spatial information. At the same time, there are reasons for avoiding too great a concentration on this area of development. First, although there is little evidence available, there are a number of observations that children often regress in an aspect of development if they are pushed too hard, and that the regression may often generalize to other areas of performance (e.g., Fraiberg et al., 1969). Second, during the first year the blind infant has a vast set of learning tasks before him, and it may be better to let him concentrate his developmental energy in those areas in which he can make spontaneous progress, rather than pushing abilities which are not spontaneously ready to occur. In this connection, Fraiberg (1968) noted that a "readiness signal" may in fact be available: "a fluttering of the fingers, sometimes a grasping, ungrasping motion of the hands, which tells us that the 'graspability' of the object is beginning to register when the sound is heard" (p. 283).

The question remains: what if the developmental lag in crawling does violate a critical period, such that locomotor abilities might suffer permanently if the child does not crawl until he is a year old or so? Although this may be the case, the evidence in favor of it is not strong. In fact, it seems likely that cases of permanent locomotor inadequacy may be better explained by other factors. First, there is good evidence from sighted children that motor restriction during the normal period of crawling or walking (as in the case of packboard children) does not permanently retard those functions. Rather, as soon as the child gets the opportunity (once he is maturationally ready), he crawls and walks, and in fact he tends to develop those functions more quickly than a child who undergoes more normal experience. Second, there are many individuals who have been blind from birth but who have become very effectively mobile and who do not suffer from cognitive or other related handicaps. Either these individuals were provided with some program of experience that led to early reaching and crawling, or they were late in locomotion and still did not suffer permanent "developmental arrest." The first alternative, that these people received some special experience as infants, deserves intensive research attention, since, if such experience is possible, it should be identified and made available for all children who are blind from birth. The second alternative seems quite viable, and the ensuing questions may be stated in a more direct way, that is, to what factors can cases of permanent developmental arrest be attributed? Hart's (1983) identification of resistance to the prone position is pertinent here. She suggested that efforts to have the blind infant accept the prone position have been successful in bringing the infant to a state of earlier physical readiness for reaching and crawling. In addition, as has been argued elsewhere (Warren & Kocon, 1974), it seems quite likely that somewhat later a social factor, parental overprotection, may be implicated. It is likely that a child may receive optimal correlated hand/sound/object experience but still may not become effectively mobile because his parents are afraid to let him venture into potentially dangerous situations. The solution may involve making sure both that certain inhibitory circumstances do not occur and that certain experiences (such as the prone position) do occur.

One additional point should be made here with respect to the onset of reaching. Although some visually impaired infants are in fact totally blind at birth, many are not totally blind. Light perception (LP) cannot by itself impart much information about the identity of objects, but it may be useful in imparting information about their existence, and specifically about their existence independently of the infant's tactual contact with them. Fraiberg (1968) noted that a child with LP in one eye did apparently respond to the shadow produced by holding his hand up in front of that eye, and Fraiberg et al. (1966) stated that they have found that infants with even a small amount of useful vision approximate the developmental norms of sighted children more closely than totally blind infants do. It would seem important to make use of any residual vision at all to provide a mediating bridge between tactual and auditory experience with objects. A sound producing object can be moved back and forth before the eyes, and the process can be repeated with the child's hand on the object. Any constancy that could be attached to objects by such experience might serve to bridge the cognitive gap and produce reaching and (if Fraiberg is right in her hypothesis about the connection between reaching to sound and crawling) crawling much earlier.

The question of how to provide effectively coordinated tactual and auditory experience has received relatively little attention. Spatial relations include concepts of the relationships among objects in external space. Spatial abilities will be more adequate in individuals who have an adequate concept of the existence and structure of space independent of their own bodies. Thus, for the purpose of effective mobility, the structure of external space may be of great importance. It seems likely that any experience designed to produce external spatial relations concepts will automatically produce observer-based spatial concepts, as long as the experience involves active participation by the child. One likely vehicle would be a board, placed laterally in front of the child, with variously shaped levers or buttons protruding from it. Each protrusion would have not only its own characteristic shape, but also a characteristic sound differing from the other sounds. Since the board retains its spatial structure, the child would learn that different sounds occur in different locations and would come to associate the sounds and the locations with the motor movements of the hand necessary to produce the sounds. A variation on this toy might be one with a lever that the child can move back and forth laterally, with a different sound occurring at each of a series of lateral locations. The point of both toys is to provide a distinctive sound in each of a series of specific locations, and to have the child gain experience with the sound-location correspondence via his own manual behavior.

In summary, in the area of motor development there are selective lags, and they are concentrated in areas that involve orientation to the external environment, such as reaching, crawling, and walking. Although there are some areas of disagreement within the literature, there does seem to be support for the theme that adequacy of motor and locomotor development depends somehow on experience, and that inadequacy may often be traced to restricted experience. The relatively general statements about the dependence of development on experience are not very satisfying, since they are rarely stated in sufficient detail to allow effective modifications to be made in the environment of the blind infant. There is a need for normative data based on larger samples of infants than have been studied in detail. Further, these data should be gathered in conjunction with data on the characteristics of the environments that the infants are exposed to. Adequate attention to aspects of the physical and social environment, as well as to the developmental progress of individual infants, should produce a better understanding of the characteristics of the motor and locomotor development of blind infants and of the environmental conditions that are conducive to normal or abnormal development.

Stereotypic Behaviors

There has been a great deal of concern in the blindness literature with the incidence of various stereotypic behavior patterns which are sometimes grouped together under the term "blindisms." (See Eichel [1978] for a useful review.) Since several accounts of stereotypic behaviors make reference to infancy, it is appropriate that the issue be considered here.

The term "blindism" has been used to cover a wide range of behavior, including both small movements of parts of the body, such as eye rubbing, head turning, and hand gestures, and larger body involvement, such as rocking or swaying. The term has also been used to include more complex and involved sequences of movements. The common factor in all uses of the term is the repetitiveness of the behavior that is involved. In fact, the term "blindism" is a misnomer, since these behaviors that often occur in blind children are not discriminable from behaviors observed in some autistic children, or even from behaviors observed in normal children without apparent problems of either a perceptual or an emotional nature. A study by the Indian National Institute for the Visually Handicapped (1981) found the incidence of stereotypic behaviors in sighted children to approximate that for the blind, although the types of behaviors differed considerably. Better names are stereotypic behaviors, or mannerisms, terms which refer to the common element of repetitiveness among these behaviors, and these terms will be used henceforth.

Several general hypotheses have been suggested to explain the occurrence of stereotypic behaviors in blind children. Perhaps the most compelling is the notion that these behaviors represent attempts to increase the general level of sensory stimulation. That is, since the child does not receive extensive visual stimulation, he is motivated to "make up for" the lack by increasing the stimulation available via other sensory modalities, primarily tactual and vestibular. Burlingham (1965, 1967) is an advocate of this viewpoint, as is Curson (1979). Burlingham (1967), for example, hypothesized that "the well-known blindisms, i.e., the rhythmical rocking, swaying, and eye rubbing, are the result of too little stimulation through mutual body play in infancy" (p. 189). Burlingham (1965) also noted that such stereotypies are not limited to blind children, since seeing children may also exhibit them when they are deprived of their normal mobility by parental restriction or hospitalization. Guess (1966) found that sensory deficit and locomotor restraint are associated with stereotypic behavior. He studied groups of blind and sighted, retarded, institutionalized males ranged in age from six to 20. Guess found a negative correlation between ambulatory behavior and self-manipulation, and a positive correlation between ambulatory behavior and manipulation of the environment. Presumably, if the child engages in environmental manipulation, he simply has less time for self-manipulation, and vice versa. The factors that bear on self vs. environmental manipulation were not clarified by the study, although Guess did find less self-stimulatory behavior in the group of sighted children and suggested that visual deficit was implicated in producing a greater incidence of stereotypies.

Thurrell and Rice (1970) studied the incidence of eye rubbing as related to the degree of visual impairment in children in a school for the blind, aged six to 20. Eye rubbing occurred more frequently in the younger children. The subjects were divided into three groups on the basis of severity of loss: no measurable visual function, LP or movement perception, and some useful vision (counting fingers). The LP group showed significantly more eye rubbing than either the totally blind or the useful vision group. Thurrell and Rice discussed the results within a sensory deprivation model, suggesting that in the LP group the visual system was sufficiently functional to allow transmission of the visual stimulation that may be produced by eye rubbing (phosphenes). The visual system of the totally blind group was presumed to be too dysfunctional to allow transmission of any peripheral effects created by eye rubbing. The explanation of the results seems quite reasonable, although it is unfortunate that indices of other stereotypic behaviors, such as rocking, were not included in the study. An argument that clouds the eye rubbing issue appears in a study by Dekaban (1972), who cited evidence suggesting that eye rubbing may be a result of photophobia, rather than a search for additional stimulation of the visual system. Jastrzembska (personal communication) has suggested that eye poking might well be considered separately from other types of stereotypies, since there is anecdotal evidence that eye poking only occurs in young primates that are kept with their parents and in blind children in cultures where the young child spends much of its time carried on the mother's body. A study by the Indian National Institute for the Visually Handicapped (1981) similarly concluded that eye poking may be a manifestation of tension more than other stereotypies are.

Perhaps the most useful support for the sensory stimulation hypothesis comes from studies done with animals. Prescott (1976) cited evidence that visually deprived monkeys and cats show extremely active barpressing responses when visual stimulation is made contingent on barpressing. A similar argument about somatosensory stimulation may be made from the studies of Melzack (Melzack & Thompson, 1956; Melzack & Scott, 1957).

A variation on the sensory stimulation explanation is provided by Burlingham (1965) and others, who have suggested that repetitive behavior is pleasurable because it provides a vehicle for "motor discharge." Conceptually, motor behavior could be thought to be satisfying independently of the sensory stimulation that it provides to the blind, but in practical terms, this notion would seem to be entirely subsumable under the sensory stimulation hypothesis.

As much as the sensory deprivation formulation seems to make sense, most of the evidence that is taken to support it may also be used to support an alternative hypothesis, that stereotypic behaviors are a result of social rather than sensory deprivation. This alternative explanation is particularly suitable for the studies with animals in which the deprivation of sensory input has often also involved deprivation of social contacts with other animals. In fact, Berkson (1973) has demonstrated that stereotypic behaviors that are indistinguishable from those thought to be a result of sensory deprivation may be produced by social isolation even within a relatively rich sensory environment.

For blind infants, it is difficult to separate the sensory stimulation factor from the social stimulation factor. Webster (1983) cited both factors in his discussion of the notable absence of stereotypic behaviors in black South African blind children. A parent who for whatever reason is led to provide an environment that is deficient in social stimulation will also in effect be providing a deprived environment with respect especially to vestibular and somatosensory stimulation. In fact, Schaffer and Emerson (1964) and others have made the argument that the critical aspect of interaction between parent and child in the early months of life is the sensory stimulation that it provides the infant, rather than social or interpersonal stimulation. However difficult the question, it is an important one. Consider, for example, the prematurely born infant who must be restricted to an incubator for a period of several weeks. Vestibular and somatosensory stimulation could presumably be provided for such an infant by mechanical means, while social interaction might be undesirable for medical reasons or impractical for staffing reasons.

Another aspect of the stereotypies question has to do with the situations in which they tend to occur. This topic has been less widely treated, but a generally accepted notion is that stereotypic behavior tends to occur in stressful or novel situations. Knight (1972) argued that even sighted children tend to "regress" to behaviors characteristic of earlier developmental stages when they are placed in stressful situations. Smith, Chethik, and Adelson (1969) viewed stereotypies as regressions to a former safe activity in the face of frustration or excessive demands. Several case reports provide interesting documentation for their notion. One child had held her hands in a peculiar closed fisted posture which had effectively prevented her from using her hands in tactual exploration. Even though therapy was successful in producing more effective use of the hands for exploratory behavior, stressful situations such as the approach of a stranger would cause the child to show the closed fist posture momentarily.

As was noted earlier, the dynamics of the initial acquisition and the subsequent expession of stereotypic behaviors are not well understood. A reasonable formulation would seem to be that certain motor habits are acquired, just as they are in sighted children. There is a tendency for blind children to engage in specific types of motor behavior (such as rocking) because of the vestibular and somatosensory stimulation that they provide; further, this tendency is stronger for blind children because of a need for a higher level of total sensory stimulation that is generally available in the absence of visual function. In both blind and sighted children, stressful situations produce a tendency to regress to familiar behavior patterns, but these patterns are fewer and better practiced in blind children, so they are more obviously interpretable as stereotypic behaviors. Eichel (1979) suggested alternatively that whereas the genesis of stereotypic behaviors may be accounted for by one of the preceding theories, their continuation may be better explained by their selective reinforcement (e.g., by increased attention) by other people, and eventually by the behaviors' becoming self-reinforcing and therefore self-sustaining. Whatever the source of the reinforcement, whether it be increased sensory stimulation, reduction of stress, or attention from others, it is clear that stereotypic behaviors can be regulated by the use of reinforcement contingencies. This issue will be discussed below.

An interesting perspective on stereotypic behavior that does not fit easily into any of the formulations discussed above was provided by Stone (1964). The subjects for his study were institutionalized, retarded, RLF blind children between the ages of five and 16. On the basis of extensive observations, Stone distinguished between two patterns of stereotypies, which he designated withdrawal and alerting. The withdrawal pattern was characterized by rhythmic repetitiveness with a constant frequency of one phase per second. A typical example might involve rocking while simultaneously rubbing the eyes rhythmically. Frequently it was apparent that children engaged in these stereotypic sequences lost some degree of awareness of the environment—thus the appellation "withdrawal." Stone interpreted this type of movement sequence as producing "a rhythmic simultaneous sensory bombardment." Children frequently entered such sequences when they were placed in bed restraints, or in reaction to a contact from another child. The "alerting" type, on the other hand, was less rhythmic, more complex, and more ritualistic. When in such a state, the child was more aware of the external environment and apparently less caught in the sequence of his activity than was the case in the withdrawal state. Often the alerting activity was seen in reponse to discovery of a novel object which had caught the child's attention.

In a subsequent phase of his investigation, Stone studied the patterns of EEG activity that accompanied the two types of stereotypies in three boys. During the "withdrawal blindism," the slow EEG patterns that are characteristic of drowsy states were found. By contrast, the "alerting blindism" was accompanied by the more active EEG characteristic of waking states. Stone suggested that stereotypic behaviors "must represent an important method for the child in the alteration or regulation of his contact with a stressful reality" (p. 18). The "withdrawal blindism" in particular may represent the child's attempt to meet a stressful situation by creating a sequence of rhythmic and intensive sensory stimulation that produces an altered, and specifically a lower, state of consciousness.

Stone's suggestions may, then, be interpreted as attributing to the retarded blind child a fairly active role in the manipulation of his level of consciousness in order to regulate the extent of his contact with the external world. Extension of his observations to the stereotypic behaviors of nonretarded blind children would be of considerable interest.

There are several arguments in favor of trying to prevent excessive stereotypic behavior in blind children. One factor is simply social acceptability. A second is the possible physiological damage that may occur by excessive eye rubbing or poking, or head banging. Perhaps less obvious is the fact that, as Guess (1966) has documented, the frequency of self-manipulative behavior is inversely related to the frequency of environmental manipulation. Freeman (1974) found a greater tendency to engage in stereotypic behavior among lower-IQ blind children. Piaget (1952) has charted the normal developmental progression within the first year from manipulation of self to manipulation of objects. To the extent that the child persists in self-manipulatory habits, he tends not to develop those habits of manipulation of the environment that are critical in his developing understanding of the world. To the extent that stereotypies occur in response to novel situations, a child who shows a great deal of stereotypic behavior will tend not to maintain contact with novel situations, and will therefore be slower to experience the variety that the world has to offer. Several writers (Hoshmand, 1975; Caetano & Kauffman, 1975) have noted the degree to which stereotypic behaviors interfere with the blind child's attention in educational settings.

It is possible to reduce the frequency of stereotypic behavior. Sandler (1963) reported one case of a very active child who did not engage in excessive stereotypic behavior, and whose mother had responded to early indications of eye rubbing by placing objects in the child's hands to divert his activity. Several papers illustrate the effectiveness of behavior modification approaches in reducing or eliminating stereotypic behavior. Caetano and Kauffman (1975) reported cases of nine- and 10-year-old girls, one partially sighted and the other with LP, whose rocking behavior was drastically reduced by the administration of a behavior program in which accumulated points were traded for glass marbles. Miller and Miller (1976) described a very extensive behavior modification program, using candy reinforcers, that was successful in eliminating high frequency "head wagging" behavior in a 13-year-old congenitally blind girl. No recurrence of the behavior was found about a year after the termination of the reinforcement program. In an excellent demonstration of behavior modification research, Blasch (1975) used a combination of positive reinforcement and aversive stimulation and found a significant reduction in frequency of the most common stereotypic behavior for each of six subjects. Furthermore, there was no evidence that the reduction in one kind of stereotypic behavior produced a corresponding increase in another kind (symptom substitution); in fact, other untreated stereotypic behaviors also showed a reduction in four of the six cases. The behaviors were monitored over a ten-day period after the cessation of the program, and the frequencies of stereotypies did not increase during this period.

Williams (1978) reported success in using behavioral intervention techniques to reduce stereotypic behavior in a retarded, deaf–blind child. Clearly, then, behavioral techniques may be used successfully to regulate mannerisms. Hayes and Weinhouse (1978) provided a very useful analysis of the variety of behavior modification techniques applicable to stereotypic behavior, and of the advantages and disadvantages of their use in various situations with various kinds of children. They stressed, in particular, the need for a careful analysis of the nature of the stereotypic behavior, its cause, the reinforcement that sustains it, and the appropriate matching of the behavior modification approach to these particulars.

To the extent that stereotypic behavior increases in response to stress, it is important to be sensitive to situations that may be particularly stressful for the blind child. For example, as noted earlier, types of unfamiliar auditory stimulation may be more stressful for the blind child than for the sighted child. Parental counseling may be especially useful here, in that parents may become more sensitive to potential sources of stress and to indicators of stress that may be provided by the child, and they may be able to learn to provide a temporarily more supportive situation for the child when needed. At the same time, the danger of overprotection must not be forgotten, since too severe a buffering of stressful situations may prevent the child from becoming able to deal with them on his own. Hoshmand (1975) stressed the need for comprehensive research on the developmental variables that affect the early onset and maintenance of stereotypies. She suggested that an experiential developmental learning framework would be useful in such research, with an emphasis on specifics of the parent-child interaction.

Cognitive Development

According to Piaget's theory of cognitive development, the first two years constitute the Sensorimotor Period, during which the infant's behavior progresses from being characterized by simple reflexes to showing an internalized and representational form of problem solving. The Sensorimotor Period is broken down into six stages:

1. Reflexes (birth to one month). The infant's behavior is characterized primarily by reflexive responses to his own body and to some aspects of the external world. Some refinement of reflexive behavior occurs as the infant discovers, for example, that some objects are "suckable" and some are not.
2. Primary Circular Reactions (1 to 4 months). The infant begins to repeat selectively those actions that produce effects that are interesting or satisfying to him. These actions are primarily directed to his own body rather than to external objects.
3. Secondary Circular Reactions (4 to 8 months). The infant reproduces behaviors that produce effects in the external world that are satisfying or interesting to him. This stage marks the beginning of the infant's effective orientation to the external world.
4. Coordination of Secondary Circular Reactions (8 to 12 months). The beginnings of intentionality are seen in the fourth stage, in that the infant begins to coordinate his behavior with respect to the external world in more complex ways. His use of specific means to obtain specific ends demonstrates his increasing organization of the world. He begins to anticipate the effects of his own actions and those of other people.
5. Tertiary Circular Reactions (12 to 18 months). In this stage, the infant's behavior clearly involves active trial and error experimentation on the world. His behavior becomes more flexible in that he can systematically vary his actions to obtain a specific goal. He seems to seek novelty for the sake of learning more about the world.
6. Internalization of Thought (18 months to two years). This stage marks the beginnings of internalized thought. The child needs no longer engage in overt trial and error behavior but rather can think about possible behaviors and the effects that they would have. According to Piaget, this stage is a landmark in that it frees the child from his own perceptions and behaviors. He begins to be able to imagine behaviors and their consequences.

There has been very little direct treatment of the effects of blindness on the infant's progress through the stages of the Sensorimotor Period. Stephens (1972) discussed some implications of visual impairment. She noted Piaget's stress on the importance of the infant's interaction with his environment, as well as the fact that in the normal infant a large measure of that interaction depends on vision. There is some material, primarily from papers in the psychoanalytic literature, that may be brought to bear on the question of the blind infant's progress through Piagetian stages of sensorimotor development.

Since there is not a great deal of critical interaction with the external world until the end of the second stage, it is reasonable to expect that the blind infant would not be delayed in producing the behaviors characteristic of the initial stages. There is some confirmation of this expectation. Sandler (1963), for example, reported that blind and sighted infants show comparable development until about four months of age, and Fraiberg (1968) reported comparable motor development for blind and sighted infants in the early months. During the second stage, though, the sighted infant engages in extensive hand watching (White, 1971) and toward the end of that stage begins to exercise visual direction of his hand movements.

The visual control of manual behavior is an important component of third stage behaviors, and so it might be expected that the developmental patterns of blind and sighted infants would begin to diverge in the third stage, the divergence occurring most strikingly in the failure of the blind infant to begin to reach for objects. This developmental difference has been discussed extensively in Chapter 2, and it does apparently produce a lag in the blind infant's orientation to the external world. Fraiberg (1968) noted that the infant's hands "can give him only a small part of the information he needs for learning about his world, and his hands during this period do not serve intentionality. . ." (p. 284). Sandler (1963) likewise argued that the blind child is delayed in his turning outward to the world. At a time (27-36 weeks) corresponding roughly to the end of the third stage, however, Fraiberg, Siegel, and Gibson (1966) noted hand movements that they interpreted as the beginnings of search for an object. Because of the potential difficulties for the blind infant in the third stage, it might be expected that the coordination of secondary circular reactions and the attendant organization of the external world would be delayed. Sandler (1963), in fact, noted that

> The blind child will nevertheless lack the sensory continuity afforded by visual stimulation. This lack of continuity must inevitably hinder the integration of the child's sensorimotor experiences. . . . Although auditory cues help the blind baby in attaining a degree of spatial orientation . . . , their inconstancy must make the process exceedingly difficult, when compared with the sighted child who has constant visual information at his disposal (p. 354).

However, the blind infant does show evidence of organization of the external world toward the end of the first year. Fraiberg et al. (1966), in discussing the period from 37 to 48 weeks, reported that "The tactile and auditory schemas begin to unite toward the end of this period. . . . Following tactile contact with a sound-making object, he occasionally is able to trace it through sound cues and to recover it'' (p. 343). There is little evidence that bears directly on the developments characteristic of the fifth stage, although it should be noted that the delays in locomotion that have been reported by many writers (see Chapter 2) may serve to restrict the blind infant's application of a varied trial and error experimentation on the world.

There is also little evidence that applies directly to the sixth stage. However, the capacity for mental representation is well represented by the existence of a mature object concept. Fraiberg (1968) noted that the achievement of the object concept is delayed in blind infants until three to five years of age, in contrast to two years for the sighted child. One reason for the delay is the blind child's failure to engage in sustained search behavior. While the sighted child searches actively for hidden objects during much of the second year, Fraiberg reported that ''we have seen only one blind child between the ages of 16 months and three years who will conduct such a search'' (p. 287). It is not clear whether the failure to sustain search produces the observed lag in object concept or whether the child fails to search because he does not have a mature concept of the permanence of objects. Fraiberg apparently considered both causal relationships to be possible. Search fails because the blind child ''cannot deduce the displacements of an object in space. The failure of search leaves the blind child with a temporary handicap in cognitive development; he cannot believe that an object exists when it does not manifest itself to him, and this conceptual problem becomes a temporary barrier to the development of spatial concepts and notions of causality'' (p. 287).

Reynell and Zinkin (1975) reported the development of a set of developmental assessment procedures for use with young children, including infants, with visual impairments. The procedures include sections on motor and cognitive functioning. The assessment instrument is not normed and is intended for rough diagnostic use in the design of early education interventions. Results from the use of the ''sensorimotor understanding'' section of the cognitive assessment material revealed that blind infants begin to lag behind sighted and partially sighted infants within the first year.

Thus, although the development of blind and sighted infants is apparently similar in the earliest months of the sensorimotor period, divergence may be seen at the time the sighted infant normally begins to reach for external objects (three to four months). This and other differences apparently create a definite lag in the later sensorimotor stages. Impairment of vision may produce these effects in at least two ways. First, since perceptual interaction with the environment is necessary for cognitive growth, blindness handicaps the child simply by giving him less total information about the world. The fact that vision normally provides the most detailed and specific information is important, but the continuity of visual experience is perhaps a more critical lack for the blind infant. Second, the blind infant lacks the organizational function that vision normally provides. For the sighted child, vision seems to serve as a means of unifying the perceptual experiences gained via other modalities. This function is especially important in the second half of the first year when the sighted child is actively organizing the world and his experience with it; the totally blind child cannot experience this visual integration and therefore might be expected to show a different developmental pattern.

One of the notable achievements of early cognitive development is the understanding of the basic distinction between the self and the rest of the animate and inanimate world. Scott (1969) offered a perspective on this differentiation of the self from the world:

> The first major differences in development between the blind and sighted child begin to appear when the child's neuromusculature develops to the point where he is capable of controlled body movements. The sighted child is attracted by his environment, as he begins to have direct sensory experience of it. The differentiation between self and environment begins to emerge at this point. By differentiating objects from one another, by manipulating them, and by observing his impact upon them, the child is slowly able to distinguish the boundary between self and non-self. This process is greatly frustrated in the blind child. . . . First, the amount of the environment which he can know and experience directly is limited. . . . Second, that part of his environment which is within his reach does not have the same stimulus value to the blind child that it has for the sighted one. . . . Third, the blind child's appreciation of his impact upon the objects which he manipulates is limited (p. 1030).

A related issue is the extent to which the blind child is capable of making a distinction between his own ideas and thoughts and those of others. Scott (1969) suggested that the maintenance of such a distinction is more difficult for the blind child, and he cited as evidence some material from Helen Keller's experience. In one instance, she submitted an essay which was in fact a close facsimile of a story that had been read to her by a teacher. Keller was unaware of the extent of the influence and was thereafter apparently extremely concerned whether her creations were in fact her own or were unconscious reproductions of material that she had been exposed to. There is apparently no evidence about the extent to which such cognitive confusions may occur in the blind, and the issue has received little attention with sighted children. Scott described a study in which he administered a series of Asch-type tests, where conformity to group pressure may be assessed in the context of making perceptual judgments. The children were from 12 to 16 years old and were congenitally blind. A relatively high proportion of conforming responses was obtained. Scott regarded the data as evidence that "the confusion of self and other among blind children is relatively common" (p. 1038), and he further stressed the extent to which the blind children were unaware of the extent of the influence of the group.

Further research on this type of question would be well worthwhile. Scott's evidence from the study of confederate influence on perceptual judgments is only a partial answer to the question of the extent of cognitive differentiation between self and others. Beyond this very basic question are further issues of self-confidence in cognitive and perceptual judgments, as well as the issue of the susceptibility of self-confidence to structured attempts to strengthen it.

Social Development

Socialization is the term used to denote the child's change from a self-centered being to a social being. The newborn infant does not have to, and does not, take into account the fact that other people have needs; the older child views himself as part of a wider social context and tempers his behavior in consideration of its effect on others. Socialization includes not only the acquisition of skills such as eating, dressing, and toilet control, but also the development of interpersonal behaviors including emotional ties, and participation in small and large groups.

Perhaps as much as for any other area of development, it may be said of socialization that visual deficit does not directly and necessarily create differences between blind and sighted children. Various aspects of the lack of vision may influence the dynamics of socialization, and therefore the tasks of socialization may be somewhat different for the blind child. Perhaps more than for other areas of development it may be said that socialization is an interactive process that involves other people in critical ways. By definition, socialization involves the growing process of interacting with other people and with the demands they impose on the child. Thus, the ways that other people respond to the fact of the child's handicap may play a greater part in socialization than in other areas of development.

It may be useful to consider briefly the role of vision in various categories of socialization, both from the point of view of the child's lack of vision and from that of the reaction of the members of the social environment to that lack. For the sighted child, the acquisition of social skills such as eating and dressing clearly involves vision and visual information. The role of the parent in providing substitute information for the blind child is clear. Toilet training may be one of the most difficult areas, involving as it does certain rituals with physical locations and curious objects, and also involving, as discussed by many personality theorists, a set of crucial ego dynamics. For the sighted child, toilet training is the scene for one of the most important interpersonal developments, one where some of the important bases of the child's response to authority may be established. For the blind child, this may be a doubly difficult period. The role of vision in the interpersonal aspects of socialization is also great. Social attachment is considered to be one of the first real emotional links between infant and parent. For most children, evidence of attachment may be clearly seen toward the middle of the first year, when the relatively nonselective interaction of the younger infant is replaced by an orientation to just one or two members of the family. A fear of strangers often accompanies the development of attachment. Clearly the absence of vision might interfere with this process. It is known that vision is not the only modality on which the sighted child depends in identifying people, but vision does provide a salient source of reliable information. Hearing, touch, and smell remain as sources of information about the identity of people when vision is lost, and these senses all have limitations that vision does not. It might, therefore, be expected that the blind infant would have more difficulty not only in positively identifying attachment targets, but also in excluding strangers.

Thus it should not be surprising to find evidence of slow or abnormal social development in visually impaired infants and children. Nevertheless, Stone and Chesney (1978) found less inappropriate social responsiveness among visually impaired infants than those with other handicaps such as Downs Syndrome and brain injuries. Similarly on the positive side, Als, Tronick, and Brazelton (1980) described in detail the relationship between a mother and a blind infant, in which the mother's sensitivity to the need to balance demandingness and supportiveness led to a wholly positive picture of healthy social development. No doubt many other such examples could be cited.

Tait (1972e) provided an interesting analysis of the socialization process that extends through several years of age. The explanation is within the Eriksonian framework, and segments bear quoting:

> Erikson (1950) presents three stages in the development of the child, each of which, by means of play, must be mastered if a sense of reality and mastery of the environment is to be achieved. The first stage begins with, or centers on, the child's own body. It consists of the exploration by repetition of sensual perceptions, kinesthetic sensations, vocalizations, and similar phenomena. In the next stage, the child plays with available persons and things, primarily his mother's body. . . . Finally, at nursery-school age, playfulness reaches into the world shared with others. The child then discovers what content can be successfully represented only in the world of toys and things, and what content can be shared with others and forced upon them (p. 139).

The progression is from egocentric to limited social to extended social. Tait suggested that during the first stage, blind and sighted children may be on relatively equal terms. In the second, however, the blind child may be at a disadvantage both in being "less attracted to the other-than-self world" and in being less efficient in acquiring information about this world.

As already noted, not all the difficulties of socialization under visual impairment are the child's. Since socialization does involve other people, the reactions of others to the handicap bear importantly in the socialization process. Sommers (1944) reported the results of a study that has been widely cited in subsequent literature. Although the subjects were visually impaired adolescents and their parents, there is no reason to think that the results are not equally applicable to the parents of infants and young children. On the basis of lengthy structured interviews, Sommers distinguished four types of parental attitudes toward visual impairment: (1) viewing the child's blindness as a form of punishment of the parent, (2) fearing that others would think that the child's blindness was a result of the parent's having a social disease, (3) feeling guilty because of negligence or because of having violated some moral or social code, and (4) feeling personally disgraced. Sommers also distinguished five modes of parental adjustment to the child's handicap: (1) acceptance, where the parent is genuinely accepting of the child and realistic and objective about the handicap, (2) denial, where the parent denies the existence or importance of the handicap, failing to admit the fact that the child is in some sense different, (3) overprotection, (4) disguised rejection, where the parent disguises a negative attitude by showing excessive concern with the handicap, and (5) overt rejection, where the parent resents the child and blames anybody available for the handicap.

Endress (1968) provided evidence that there are relationships between mothers' attitudes toward their blind preschool children and various characteristics of their children, including developmental level. Information about developmental level was obtained from the Maxfield–Buchholz Scale (MB). The parents of children with some residual vision (LP) reported stronger feelings of democracy, acceptance, and indulgence that those of totally blind children. In addition, those parents whose children had above-age-level MB scores showed more acceptance than those whose children had below-age-level scores.

Tait (1972e) discussed at length the implications of maternal rejection of the blind child, noting that the adequacy of the parental response to the child's visual handicap depends in large part on the parent's own psychological well-being, including both his personal and his social adjustment. Imamura (1965) reported that the blind child's requests for attention or help tend to be ignored more often than those of the sighted child. Tait (1972e) noted that the frequency of ignoring is not necessarily a good index of parental rejection, however, since it is probable that the sighted child makes fewer such requests, often waiting until he has established eye contact with the parent to do so. Nevertheless, the insensitivity of the blind child to eye contact does subject him to the consequences of a greater "ignoring rate," and it puts a heavier burden on the parent of the blind child to be sensitive to occasions of demand. In particular, "the mother's natural ability to respond to auditory cues rather than visual cues may very well be an important factor in establishing a satisfactory relationship with her blind child" (Tait, 1972e, p. 142). One consequence of the higher ignoring rate for the blind child may be a feeling that he is unable to control his environment. The issue of locus of control will be considered in a later section. It suffices here to point out that a common response to perceived lack of control over the external environment may be the tendency to withdraw from that environment and to invest more energy in the self. In terms of Tait's analysis of the child's progression through the three early stages of socialization, such internal orientation might make it more difficult for the child to shift his focus from himself to the external world.

Another point made by Tait is the importance to the child of being observed by others. Although the parent of the blind child may watch him a great deal, the child cannot be aware of the attentiveness unless it is conveyed by other than visual means. This fact may have implications for exploratory behavior, an important aspect of the child's turning from his internal world to the external world. Since it is known that sighted children engage in more exploratory behavior when they are aware of being observed by the parent (Walters & Parke, 1965), the lower attentiveness perceived by the blind child may result in a weaker sense of security and thus a lesser tendency to engage in environmental exploration. While this situation has obvious implications for the child's cognitive development, it also has implications for his social development. When vision is absent, there may be a greater tendency for the child to remain dependent on the parent in order to feel secure. Coupled with the parent's spontaneous and natural tendency to overprotectiveness, as noted by Sommers (1944), the situation is set for the blind child to become less independent of the parent and thus become less effective in dealing with the world in an independent fashion. As Tait pointed out, the parent's dilemma is "preparing her child for independence in the world while feeling that independence for her child is, if not impossible, at least more difficult. The task is further complicated by the fact that the mother does not really know how to teach this independence to her child who is essentially living in a different dimension" (p. 148).

Telson (1965), in stressing the importance of professional counseling for the parent of the blind child, noted the tendency for the parent, as well as the child, to accrue secondary gain from the child's handicap. Since it is commonly accepted that the parent of the blind child must (to paraphrase Telson) make more sacrifices and formally abdicate his life in favor of the child's, the "social approval, compounded of sympathy and praise for his untiring devotion, gives the parent a unique place in the sun, with all the attendant prestige and honor" (p. 128). While this picture of the glories of being the parent of a blind child may be somewhat distorted, it does suggest a problem, since a parent who sees himself as self-sacrificing might well react more negatively when the child does not cooperate as the parent expects. As Telson points out, it is the rare parent who sees himself as a contributor to the child's overdependency or immaturity. Similar problems were raised by Hill (1951) and by Cohen (1964) in discussions of various aspects of parental responses to visually impaired infants. Cohen noted several characteristics of initial reactions, such as parental denial and guilt (including searching for what they might have "done wrong"). Significantly, these problems need to be met during a time when the parents are also under a variety of other more practical pressures, such as concern about their ability to procure and afford adequate care for the child, and tension between the parents or between them and relatives.

Two conclusions may be drawn from this material. One is that the behavior and characteristics of socialization agents, the people with whom the child interacts in the process of his socialization, are important factors in the socialization process. The outcome of the process may depend just as heavily on their adequacy as it does on the characteristics of the child. The second point is related, and it is that professional counseling for the parents of blind infants may often be desirable.

Social Attachment and Social Responsiveness

Social attachment refers to the development of emotional ties to a small number of people. In the first few months of age, the infant's social responsiveness is often characterized as nonselective. He typically does not object to being held by strangers, although he may give indications, such as differential smiling or vocalization, that he recognizes his parents or siblings. By contrast, around the age of six months most infants become extremely selective in their social responsiveness, objecting strenuously to the departure of the parent or to the appearance of a stranger. Several distinctive behaviors are normally taken as indicators of the existence or strength of attachment, including smiling, separation anxiety, and stranger fear. Considerable caution must be exercised in drawing conclusions about the relative onset or strength of attachment in blind and sighted infants on the basis of such indicator behaviors, since it cannot be assumed that the behaviors are equivalent indicators.

Smiling

Smiling has been of concern to those interested in early social development for two reasons. First, the child's smiling is an important elicitor of social contact from other people, and second, smiling may be taken as an indicator of the infant's participation in a social relationship. Sighted infants begin to smile toward the end of the first month of life. An effective stimulus for early smiling is the human voice. Evidence of discrimination between voices may be seen in the fourth week, when the infant may show a selective response to the mother's voice (Wolff, 1963). In general, though, smiling in sighted infants occurs fairly indiscriminately up to about six months of age. That is, the infant will smile at any face or any voice, in spite of the fact that he can clearly discriminate important people much earlier than six months. Gradually the smile becomes more selective, and during the second half of the first year there is a marked decrease in the occurrence of smiling to people other than the objects of attachment. Since this progression toward more selectivity accompanies other indices of the infant's growing attachment to the parent and his selectivity in social responses, the smile is taken by some as an indicator of the strength of the developing attachment bond.

In an early study of the development of facial responses in children from seven weeks to 13 years, Thompson (1941) reported that, compared to a group of age-matched sighted children, blind children showed a decrease in the amount of facial expression in the smile after four or five years of age. Thompson discussed the decrease in terms of the visually mediated imitation that is needed to maintain smiling. Reports of the early similarity of smiling are frequent (Freedman, 1964; Gesell, Ilg, & Bullis, 1949; Koehler, 1954, cited in Freedman, 1964; Parmalee, 1955). Apparently auditory, tactile, and kinesthetic stimulation serve as effective elicitors of the smile for the blind infant. However, several of these writers report that the developmental course of smiling of blind infants diverges from that of sighted infants at an early age. Freedman (1964), for example, found that in the second quarter of the first year, the smiles of blind infants were not entirely normal but consisted of a series of reflexive movements. It seems reasonable to argue that it is in this period that visual stimulation and feedback begin to play a significant role for the sighted child. Fraiberg (1970) discussed some of the differences in environmental stimulation for the blind and sighted infant. She noted that

> At two to two and a half months, where the visual stimulus of the human face evokes an automatic smile with a high degree of regularity, there is no equivalence in the blind baby's experience. The blind baby's smiling becomes more frequent from the second month on, and the pattern of selective smiling for the familiar voice or sound becomes increasingly demonstrated in favor of the mother, but even the mother's voice *will not regularly* elicit the smile (p. 115).

Despite the irregularity of smiling in the young blind infant, Fraiberg also noted that smiling in blind infants is more selective for the parents' voices during the three- to six-month period than it is for sighted infants. Fraiberg argued convincingly that the smile may therefore not be taken as an equivalent indicator of social attachment in blind and sighted infants. Rather, "we found that responsive vocalizations offered more differentiating criteria for valuation of the mother than the smile itself" (p. 117). Thus the smile would seem to be a dangerous index on which to compare blind and sighted infants as to the existence or strength of social attachment.

The issue does not end there, however, since the infant's smile probably does serve as an important elicitor of social attention from others. The parent of a blind infant, not knowing that smiling occurs less frequently than in sighted infants, may interpret the relative lack of smiling as an indication that the child is unresponsive or that he, the parent, is inadequate. It would seem that the real smiling question is thus not how to get the blind infant to smile more, but rather how to ensure that the parents of blind infants regard the smiling phenomenon in the proper perspective. This is not to argue that blind children should not be encouraged to smile—smiling undoubtedly serves a useful function in facilitating interpersonal relations. However, simply producing an increase in the frequency of smiling, which may easily be done by operant conditioning, will not necessarily produce a closer social bond.

Separation anxiety and fear of strangers

Another behavior that has been taken as an indicator of attachment in sighted children is separation anxiety (Schaffer & Emerson, 1964). Separation anxiety is simply the protest that the infant shows when the object of attachment, usually the parent, leaves the infant. To be taken as an indicator of attachment, separation anxiety must occur selectively—that is, the infant must show more distress when the attachment object leaves him than he does when a stranger leaves him. The protest may be expressed in several ways, although motor disquiet and crying have been used most frequently as indices. During the second year, typically, overtly expressed separation anxiety subsides. Cognitive factors play a role both in the developmental onset of separation anxiety and in the subsequent diminution of the anxiety. In order for the onset of selective separation anxiety to occur, the infant must have a concept of the parent as a consistent and identifiable person. Later, a lessening of separation anxiety may occur because of the child's ability to evoke and maintain an image of the attachment figure even in the absence of the person.

The evidence is that there is no delay in the blind infant's ability to distinguish his parent from other people on the basis of voice. In fact, Fraiberg (1972) reported that the selective response to voice stimuli occurs earlier in blind infants than in sighted. However, among the 10 blind children that Fraiberg studied, there were no incidents of separation anxiety during the first year. Separation anxiety did typically occur in the second and third years. This pattern definitely suggests a developmental lag. In discussing this result, Fraiberg pointed out that while vision may provide a source of continuous information to the sighted infant about the existence of the parent, this source is absent for blind children. The parent may be physically close to the infant, but if he does not generate effective sensory information, he is effectively out of the child's perceptual field. The sensory evidence for the presence of the parent is by its nature discontinuous even when the presence is actually continuous. The significance of this difference in the infant's perception of the parent's continuity and presence is not clear. It may be, for instance, that the absence of the continuous information source retards the development of the blind infant's expectation that the parent is present. The blind infant is continually experiencing effective separations, some due to physical separation but many due to the sensory separation that is a result of the absence of a continuous information source. Thus the blind infant might be more habituated to the parent's presence. There is not nearly enough evidence available to allow the resolution of this issue, however.

With respect to the eventual decrease in separation anxiety, there is even less evidence. As mentioned above, it has been argued that the child's increasing capacity to evoke and maintain an image of the parent is instrumental in the reduction of the anxiety. Fraiberg (1972) noted that "In the case of the blind child, the capacity for evocative memory is markedly delayed by sighted child standards" (p. 358). While this suggestion may be reasonable, there is very little evidence against which to test it, and the issue cannot at this time be resolved. There have apparently been no studies of the comparative frequency or intensity of episodes of separation anxiety in blind and sighted infants.

Another phenomenon that has been taken as an indicator of attachment is fear of strangers. This phenomenon is often found in sighted children at about the same time that other indices such as separation anxiety appear. There has not been much treatment of fear of strangers in the blind-infant literature. The dynamics that might produce differences between sighted and blind infants may be similar to those for separation anxiety—that is, the blind infant does not have vision available as a source of continuous information about the identities of people around him. As already noted, blind infants discriminate between parent and other at least as early as sighted infants do on the basis of sound alone. Fraiberg (1970) noted that an attentive quieting occurs regularly in the blind infant in response to a stranger's voice during the second half of the first year. This quieting was not interpreted as fear of strangers, however. True fear of strangers, as evidenced by negative reactions such as squirming or crying, was found to occur in the seven-to-15 month range for nine of the 10 children in Fraiberg's sample; this is roughly the same age as for sighted infants. Fraiberg (1975) appropriately urges caution in making such comparisons, noting that the situations in which stranger fear are found are not necessarily comparable. For several reasons, then, the fear-of-strangers index may not be one on which valid comparisons of attachment strength should be made.

Separation

There is some literature on the effects of separation on both child and separated parent. Separation may occur for a variety of reasons. These include conditions specific to blindness (for instance retinoblastoma often requires periods of hospitalization of the child) as well as conditions that can also occur for sighted children. The issue of separation may be an especially important one for the blind child, since to the extent that his emotional attachments are more tenuous because of the lack of vision, they may be more susceptible to the disruption that may accompany separation. In the case of hospitalization of the child, the experience of separation from the parents is accompanied by exposure to a new and strange set of experiences, ones that may be more threatening to the blind child than they would be to the sighted child who is able to obtain more information about them.

Several interesting case reports deal with the reactions of blind children to the separations caused by various conditions. Colonna (1968) described in detail the case of a retinoblastoma victim who was hospitalized for surgery several times during the period from 14 months to five years, in addition to frequent brief periods of hospitalization for radiation treatment. The situation was still further complicated by the birth of a sister when the subject was just over three. The subject showed various psychiatric difficulties, characterized generally by the fear of being rejected or discarded. Perhaps the most significant aspect of the case as described by Colonna was the extent to which the mother's reactions to the developing situation exacerbated the child's problem. The mother became depressed at the child's visual problems, and she changed her response from her previous warmth and acceptance of a "normal" child to a relative rejection of a "damaged" child who had, at 14 months, lost one eye by operation. Discussing the general problem of parental reaction to the child's blindness, Colonna noted

> We have by now come to expect that the mothers of blind children experience profound and often prolonged periods of depression. During this abnormal state the capacity to perceive and respond to the child's needs may be markedly impaired. Unless the mother is given help at the right time, the small child who, like Richard, loses his sight some time after birth suffers not only from this loss: while he finds himself in a bewildering new world of darkness, he simultaneously suffers the loss of the mother and her help just when he needs it the most. . . . Unfortunately, in some of the blind children we observed, the mothers' withdrawal meant that the verbal communication decreased markedly and the child also suffered from lack of auditory contact. When the mother is depressed, as Richard's mother was, her voice can become flat and affectless (pp. 394-5).

The parent's response to the disability may be critical. The child is faced with enough difficulty even given the best of emotional interaction with others around him. It becomes a most insidious progression when negative parental response to the discovery of the visual problem is followed by hospitalization or other separation, since these factors may add to the child's perception of rejection. The spiral may then continue when the parent, perhaps already feeling guilty, perceives the child's response to the rejection.

Fraiberg (1968) described the case of a 17-month-old child which illustrates that even a short separation, and one not accompanied by the trauma of an operation, may lead to pronounced behavioral problems in the child. In this case, the mother was gone for only three days, but shortly after she returned, the child's hitherto normal development showed regression in several areas. He rejected his food, engaged in screaming fits lasting for hours, and at times showed an apparent craving for physical contact with the mother similar to the phenomenon of affect hunger described by other writers. In another case described in the same paper, the mother was not physically separated from the child, but was, because of a severe depression, in effect absent for periods of time. Before the onset of the maternal depression, the child's developmental progress was quite adequate, but when the mother began to fail to control her withdrawal and depression when the child was 13 months old, he showed an abrupt change in developmental progress, losing his social responsiveness and cognitive progress and showing increased rocking behavior.

Separation may occur for various reasons, many of them unavoidable. Children will have to be hospitalized, parents will have to leave the home for periods of time, and emotional withdrawal by the parent may occur for various reasons. These situations have potentially serious consequences for the social development of the child. In fact, as Fraiberg (1972) pointed out, separation may have more serious implications for the blind child than would be the case for the sighted child, since "(1) We have a child whose own adaptive capacity to sustain loss is diminished by blindness. (2) We have a mother who must deal with a developmental crisis in her blind child's experience without anything in her own experience which can help her understand the extraordinary significance of loss to a blind child" (p. 359). To these points it may be added that the parent's problem may be intensified by his own reaction to the child. It would seem that the greatest hope for success in these situations lies in effective counseling of the parent, and of the child where possible. If the parent must leave the home, he should deal with the separation in such a way as to minimize the likelihood that the child will interpret his leaving as a personal rejection of the child. If the child must be separated by hospitalization, he must be prepared for the new experience as well as for any period of separation from the parents, and the actual separation should be reduced to a minimum. Again, it is crucial to ensure that the separation is not interpreted as rejection. It is particularly distressing to read case reports in which the parent was so depressed or otherwise affected by the hospitalization situation that he did not visit the child in the hospital. It should be incumbent upon the medical profession to ensure that proper preparation along emotional dimensions occurs in situations involving hospitalizations.

Fraiberg's Educational Program

Since extensive reference has been made to the work of Fraiberg and her associates, it may be appropriate at this point to provide a brief picture of the educational program out of which the published reports have emerged, as well as a short summary of some of the major premises on which the program is based. Fraiberg's work is presented in a series of articles spanning many years, and is summarized in her excellent book, *Insights from the Blind* (1977). Fraiberg often explicitly notes that difficulties in perceptual and motor development are closely tied up with problems of ego formation. While one may not want to embrace the theoretical foundations of psychoanalytic approaches to behavior, the psychoanalytic orientation of Fraiberg's work does not make it in any way less interesting to, or important for, the more behaviorally oriented reader. The case reports are some of the best descriptions available of congenitally blind children. Furthermore, the educational program is not obviously heavily grounded in the psychoanalytic tradition and should not repel the behaviorist. Fraiberg herself noted (1968, p. 270) that "We do not provide psychotherapy for our families. We consider ourselves consultants to the families on problems of rearing a blind infant and young child and our work can be described as 'educational'." The orientation of Fraiberg and her associates to the problems of ego development is healthy in that this group is not inclined, even when talking about what is apparently purely perceptual, cognitive, or motor behavior, to restrict consideration to a narrow view of development. There is evidence from a variety of sources that the child's perceptual and motor behaviors are closely related to his emotional condition. Exploratory behavior, for example, is heavily restricted if the child does not feel secure. Probably one of the most important contributions of the Fraiberg approach is that the child's abilities are not dissected into areas that are not in fact separate but that are too often kept separate, apparently primarily for the simplicity that compartmentalization affords the researcher.

A quote may serve to better exemplify the closeness of the relationship between perceptual and personality domains:

> We must assume from the evidence presented by large numbers of healthy and educable blind children that other sensory modalities can substitute for vision in the process of ego formation. There remain the questions: how are these substitutions made, and how does ego formation take place in the absence of vision? All theorizing concerning the process of ego formation is predicated upon the utilization of vision. It occurred to us that developmental studies of infants should help delineate the role of vision in ego formation and the vulnerable points in this early development which may lead to adaptive failures and ego deviations (Fraiberg & Freedman, 1964, p. 114).

Thus the goal of the research and educational program is to search for appropriate structuring of experiences that will allow the optimal development of the remaining perceptual modalities.

Fraiberg preceded the establishment of her educational program by several years of observation of blind infants. Some characteristics of the developmental perceptual-motor pattern of the congenitally blind child are a prolonged and excessive use of the mouth for exploration, to the detriment of the use of the hands ("the hand appears to have no autonomy of its own"); failure to engage in mutual exploration of the two hands and failure to maintain the hands in a midline posture; excessive stereotypic behavior, such as body rocking, head banging, and arm waving; very late or absent creeping; and delayed walking.

Not surprisingly, a major goal of the educational program is the establishment and enhancement of emotional ties between the child and his parents. As already noted, this component seems critical, since it can be argued that even the most ideal perceptual stimulation may fail to have a beneficial effect if the infant is not secure enough to maintain extensive contact with it. Parents are encouraged to be aware of the extent of their natural tendency to protect the child from potentially dangerous encounters with the world (Fraiberg, 1975). The danger of parental overprotectiveness has been cited often, and it is easy to see how overprotectiveness and oversolicitousness by the parent may have serious retarding effects on the child's perceptual and motor development.

As noted earlier, Fraiberg has reported a lag in manual exploration, a lag which she attributes largely to a prolonging of oral exploration. This viewpoint is shared by some others, for example Burlingham (1979). Fraiberg has argued that one reason for the prolonged oral exploration is that the infant needs to maintain the constancy of objects and people, and that the hand is a developmentally later vehicle for this purpose than is the mouth. Many people have argued that the blind infant has greater difficulty in establishing an effective body image, and it may well be that it is therefore a more difficult cognitive feat for the blind child than the sighted to acquire object constancy mediated by the hand. According to Fraiberg, the development of the object concept is a critical one for the blind infant, since it is only upon attainment of the object concept that he can feel secure enough to put something down or let go of a person in order to explore the rest of the environment. Thus training toward establishment of object constancy is an important feature of the educational program. In the case of Peter (Fraiberg & Freedman, 1964) such techniques were utilized as teaching him to find valued objects (such as the cookie jar), and making pots and pans available for banging and manipulating. Peter was shown that he could put something down and find it again, and that it would still be the same object if it were found in another place. After a year of slow progress, he was demonstrating search patterns characteristic of sighted children. Fraiberg stresses the importance of a parent or other adult as a "unifier of perceptual experiences" to aid in the development of the object concept.

A closely related aspect of manual behavior is the cooperative function of the two hands. Fraiberg has noted a lack of intermanual play and of the bimanual handling of objects. Part of the program involves encouraging the child to place both hands on his bottle and other objects, and to play games such as pattycake which involve repeated contact between the two hands. Toys which require manipulation by the two hands together are considered especially important.

Fraiberg and others have pointed out that the blind infant shows adequate gross motor development throughout much of the first year, but that he typically does not begin to crawl at the appropriate time even though he gives evidence of being physically ready. Fraiberg (1968) and Wills (1970) have both argued that a critical event in making the sighted child crawl at the appropriate time is the reaching out of the hand for a visually experienced object. This reaching does not occur for the blind child, and reaching to an auditory stimulus does not occur until late in the first year for blind or sighted children. Fraiberg and Freedman (1964) cited the case of a blind infant whose developmental accomplishments were at or ahead of the norms for sighted children until the last half of the first year, when she showed the same impasse in beginning to crawl that Fraiberg has reported for other infants. The relatively advanced infant overcame the impasse within a couple of months, and further locomotor developments quickly followed the development of crawling. Fraiberg and Freedman described the child's home environment as extremely positive and the child's other capabilities as outstanding. Yet the locomotor lag still occurred. It may be that the lag is unavoidable even given the best of circumstances, but Hart (1983) suggests an alternative view, noting that many blind babies, particularly those prematurely born, resist being placed in the prone position. This resistance can be countered, thus leading the infant to develop the upper-body strength necessary for reaching and crawling.

Another important aspect of the Fraiberg program is designed to facilitate the development of concepts of external spatial relations, and to provide a coordination of external spatial relations with the child's concept of his hands and body as soon as he can sit unsupported. The infant is seated at a table surface that surrounds him on three sides. The child develops a familiarity with this restricted "space," in that he can explore it and find his toys in various places on it. Somewhat later, the use of a playpen is encouraged, and again the notion is that a relatively restricted space is provided that the infant can come to know well and feel secure in.

Fraiberg's program presents an interesting and difficult dilemma that parallels, in some respects, the frequent disagreements between researchers and practitioners. As Fraiberg herself has pointed out, the developmental progress of the infants in her study should not be taken as normative data, since the infants for whom she reports data are privileged in that they have the benefit of the educational program. Furthermore, the educational program has been modified over time, so that its effect on development is likely to be different for different infants. The dilemma is clear, and it is one that is by no means restricted to the area of visual impairment. Normative data are needed, if for no other reason than to serve as a basis for the evaluation of intervention programs. On the other hand, there is a substantial ethical commitment to providing the best experiences possible for any target population, whether it be blind children or some other group.

2
Perceptual and Motor Development

The importance of sensory and perceptual abilities for the blind hardly needs to be documented—totally blind individuals must rely on their other senses to obtain all the information about the world that they need, and partially sighted individuals need to make greater use of nonvisual information than sighted people. The role of perception in other areas of behavior is vast. This involvement is perhaps most obvious in locomotion, where the functions that nonvisual information must serve are reasonably clear. Perception is also critical in learning, and in cognitive and language development. Perception is important for socialization and personality development—a child must be able to perceive information about the wishes of other people in order to become socialized. Because of the pervasive involvement of perception in other areas of development, I will treat it first.

Because of the importance of perception, it is especially important to know how well blind children develop various sensory and perceptual abilities, and even more important, what variables affect the development of these abilities. Most of the research designed to evaluate sensory and perceptual abilities has not involved children younger than five years of age. There is some material on infants, but it is much less comprehensive, and typically less rigorous from an evaluative point of view, than the work with school-age children. The infancy work was described in Chapter 1. This chapter concerns the postinfancy work.

Almost no research is available on the age range between infancy and five or six years. There is thus a significant gap in our knowledge about young blind children. There are two primary reasons for this. First, school-age children are available as "captive" populations, relatively more accessible to the researcher than preschoolers. Some researchers have made the intensive effort required to conduct research with young infants, because of the extreme importance of understanding development in infancy. The range between infancy and school age, though, has apparently not been considered so critical. Second, the research methods available for school-age children are often not appropriate for younger children. These methods often use verbal instructions which the younger child may not be able to follow, and the methods may demand motor responses which younger children are less able to do. Researchers who work with infants have developed an entirely different set of techniques, but appropriate research methods have not been extensively developed for the intermediate age ranges.

Tactile Discrimination

Cutaneous sensitivity

Axelrod (1959) studied light-touch and two-point thresholds in early blind (before 18 months) and sighted subjects and in a small number of later blind (after two years) children. Subjects ranged from nine to about 20 years of age. Light-touch threshold was measured by applying light hairs to the fingertips. There was no overall difference between the early blind and the sighted groups, but Axelrod found a significant interaction between group and sex: the sighted girls were more sensitive than the blind girls, while the sighted boys were less sensitive than the blind boys. Since there were only 12 later blind subjects, no statistical treatment was presented for that group. In his test of fingertip two-point threshold, Axelrod found no striking differences between early blind and sighted subjects, although there was a tendency for the blind to have lower thresholds on the right index finger.

Thus, in general, Axelrod's results did not show overall differences between early blind and sighted subjects. Although statistical treatment was not provided, there appeared to be no consistent difference in peformance between the late blind group and either of the other groups. A wide range of ages was included in each group, but no analyses of possible age trends were reported. Interestingly, Axelrod found no differences between the index fingers of the preferred and nonpreferred hands in either light-touch or two-point threshold.

Renshaw, Wherry, and Newling (1930) assessed the ability of eight-to-14-year-old congenitally blind children and adults to point to a touched area of the forearm or back of the hand. The results were compared with those from a previous study on sighted children and adults (Renshaw, 1930). Blind adults were better than sighted adults at cutaneous localization, but blind children were worse than sighted children. The blind subjects showed an age-related improvement. Significant improvements were made with practice by all groups.

Jones (1972) followed much the same procedure as Renshaw with larger groups of subjects, including some younger children. Jones' blind group ranged from five to 12 years of age. They had at most light perception (LP), and all but two were blind from birth. Sighted subjects were age-matched to the blind. Each subject performed both the cutaneous localization task and a kinesthetic task which will be discussed later. Comparison of the total groups of blind and sighted children showed a significant superiority of the blind in cutaneous localization, although analysis at each age level showed a significant advantage for the blind only at 11 years. A general improvement with age occurred both for blind and sighted groups. Jones' results for children thus contradict those of Renshaw, who found that the sighted performed better. Since Jones studied the age range much more thoroughly with more subjects, his results are probably more reliable. Any advantage of the blind, however, is slight.

Rosenstein (1957) studied another variant of tactual perception, the perception of rhythmic patterns on the skin. Unfortunately, no information about the visual characteristics of the blind subjects was presented, although they attended a school for the blind and were apparently within a normal range of intelligence. The age range was 11 to 13. The subject placed his forefinger on a vibrator on which pairs of rhythmic stimuli were successively presented. The task was to judge whether the members of a pair were the same or different. The blind children were consistently better than their age-matched sighted controls.

There has not been as much study of the discrimination of texture as one might expect, given the importance of this skill for the blind child. Nolan (1960) and Nolan and Morris (1960) used varied abrasive paper stimuli to study the texture-discrimination abilities of blind children from five to 14 years of age. Both studies found that improvement in performance occurs during the early grades but levels off by third grade. Results reported by Gliner (1966) indicated that texture-discrimination performance in sighted children follows a similar developmental course. Stellwagen and Culbert (1963) studied blind and sighted adolescents (15 and older) and adults and found no difference between blind and sighted groups in their ability to discriminate 10 textures. However, no information was provided about possible age trends in either group, and since the blind subjects ranged from 15 to 39 years it is possible that an age-by-sight interaction may have been masked. On the basis of age trends in other tests of tactual discrimination, though, it seems likely that any substantial improvements would have occurred at ages younger than 15.

Form discrimination

There has been more work in tactual form discrimination than in cutaneous sensitivity. Information about age trends in form discrimination is available from a series of studies using the Tactile-Kinesthetic Form-Discrimination Test (TKT). The test involves same-different judgments for pairs of geometric forms embossed on plastic sheets. Schwartz (1972) used the TKT with blind and sighted children in kindergarten through fourth grade. The blind subjects, all blind from birth, were drawn from residential and integrated school settings. The sighted controls were about a year younger than the blind children, although school grade was equated. Schwartz's hypothesis, that the blind children would show better discrimination, received only mixed support. In one analysis, in which the entire group of blind children was compared with sighted children, the blind children were significantly better than the sighted. Neither blind subgroup was significantly better than the sighted group, although the differences tended to favor the blind. On the whole, the Schwartz data did not strongly support the notion that blind children have better tactile discrimination.

Crandell, Hammill, Witkowski, and Barkovich (1968) presented TKT results from residential school blind children ranging in age from 10 to 21 years, mean age 16. The subjects retained no useful vision and had been blind from birth or within the first four years. TKT performance was found to correlate strongly with IQ, as measured by verbal WISC or WAIS, but less strongly with grade level. Unfortunately no analysis of the possible effect of age at blindness was reported. In a similar study, Hammill and Crandell (1969) used the TKT to study the relationships between tactual form discrimination and several other variables. Subjects ranged in age from six to 11 years and included both totally blind and partially sighted children, some braille readers and some print readers. Age of onset was not analyzed, although some of the totally blind group had lost vision as late as five years of age. Performance on the TKT was not significantly related to chronological age (CA), but it was related to mental age (MA). A difference was found in favor of the braille readers over the print readers, but no difference was found among three groups divided on the basis of visual acuity.

Weiner (1963) described an interesting study of the simple and complex tactual abilities of good and poor braille readers. All subjects had become blind by 18 months of age, and all were from residential schools. The poor readers read at least a grade below their actual grade placement (which ranged from second to sixth, mean CA 11.2), while the good readers read at or above their actual grade placement (mean CA 10.2). Unfortunately, matching on school grade produced a significant difference in IQ favoring the good reachers. Six tests were given, of which three have relevance to this section: a simple matching test, which required the child to find a match for a stimulus card from among a set of similar cards; a complex sorting test, which required the child to sort nine blocks into sets on the basis of various characteristics such as shape, texture, edging, and thickness; and a complex figure-background perception test, which required the child to explore a card and find a design which was different from the other designs on the card. On all three tasks, the good readers performed significantly better than the poor readers. Correlational analyses failed to produce a pattern of relationships with IQ or other subject characteristics, a finding which partially mitigated the mean difference in IQ between the two groups. Weiner discussed the results in the context of a greater neural sensitivity in the finger tips of some children, a sensitivity which allowed them to become better braille readers. The question of causality is complex, however. It seems just as likely that the children who become better braille readers are those who spend more time practicing it, and that they develop better tactual abilities as a result of this practice. The question of the "educability" of tactual functions, as well as of many other abilities, is an important one that has received too little attention. It is important to know about the possible effects of practice on discriminative functions, and how practice might interact with naturally occuring differences in sensitivity. Furuta, Homma, and Muranaka (1977) reported a study in which 4½-year-olds were provided with Optacon training in the discrimination of katakana symbols. Some improvement occurred, but performance was not impressive. The results suggest that Optacon training at this age is not likely to produce important benefits.

Pick and Pick (1966) used a task somewhat similar to the TKT in a study of sighted (age six to 13, plus adults), and partially sighted and totally blind subjects age seven to 17. The visually impaired children were braille readers who had been blind since early infancy. The task required simultaneous exploration of a pair of the Gibson, Gibson, Pick, and Osser (1962) letterlike forms and judgment of whether the forms were the same or different. The stimuli were made of raised metal lines on a metal background and were designed by imposing various transformations (such as perspective, line to curve) on a set of standard forms. Because of the small numbers of subjects in the two visually impaired groups, statistical comparisons were not made with the sighted group. However, comparison of the graphs suggests that there were no striking differences between groups for any of the transformations. If anything, the visually impaired groups may have had an advantage for some stimuli. Statistical analysis did show a general improvement with age for the sighted group, but there was no such trend for either visually impaired sample. The visually impaired subjects were grouped for the purposes of these comparisons into seven-11, 12-14, and 15-17 year ranges, while the sighted subjects were grouped by single years. Substantial improvement occurred for several transformations in the younger sighted groups, and it seems likely that the more inclusive age grouping of the visually impaired subjects may have masked corresponding trends, particularly within the youngest group. This suggestion found some corroboration from a study by Morris and Nolan (1961), who did *not* find age-related improvement above grade four. The task was similar to that of Pick and Pick in that it involved making judgments of same–different for pairs of simultaneously presented stimuli.

The form discrimination task is changed, of course, when a memory requirement is introduced. In some relatively simple form discrimination situations, memory is implicitly involved. An example is the study by Simpkins (1979c), in which the subject felt a standard tactual stimulus, then chose a match to the standard from among a set of four alternatives. Memory, however brief, is involved, since the standard must be remembered in order to test the comparisons against it.

Other researchers have varied memory variables systematically in order to investigate the influences on memory for tactual material. Kool and Rana (1980) compared sighted children, age 9 to 11 years, with children who had been totally blind from birth or up to a year. The stimuli were pairs of three-dimensional nonsense shapes. The standard was first presented, then the comparison shape was presented after either a 5- or 30-second unfilled delay. The subject judged whether the comparison was the same as the standard or different. Both errors and latency of response were evaluated. There were no systematic differences between groups in the frequency of errors. The blind were slower to respond than the sighted, and across both groups the 5-second delay produced faster responding than the longer delay. In another condition, the subject was required to count backward during the delay. This verbal distractor did not interfere with performance, suggesting that the memory was not mediated by verbal coding. In a second experiment with 13- to 16-year olds, the verbal distractor was compared with a tactual distractor during the delay periods, which ranged from 0 to 30 seconds. The tactual distractor consisted of handling another nonsense form: this activity would be expected to interfere with memory of the stimulus shape if that memory was specifically tactual. The tactual distractor interfered with performance, but more so for the blind than for the sighted subjects. The results indicate that the memory code for blind subjects was indeed tactual; the lesser interference with the performance of the (blindfolded) sighted subjects suggests that they had some capability for visual encoding of the tactual forms, a conclusion that has been reached in other research as well.

Millar, in a series of papers, has produced the most systematic attack on the problem of tactual memory in blind children, using for the most part braille letters as stimuli. In an early paper in the series, Millar (1975c) noted that previous research had established that phonological features of tactually presented letters are encoded in memory: the argument is based on the fact that recall is more adversely affected by phonologically similar items than dissimilar items. Analogously, she reasoned, if tactual features are encoded in memory, then there should be corresponding interference patterns depending on the tactual similarity or dissimilarity of the items in the recall set. The subjects were children with at most light perception who had been blind from birth or within the first 18 months, and ranging in age from six to 10. There was indeed more interference within sets of tactually similar than dissimilar items, thus demonstrating that tactual features (as well as phonological ones) were encoded in memory. In a subsequent study, Millar (1977a) used braille letters of two sizes, presenting pairs of letters simultaneously and asking for rapid judgments of whether the members of the pair were the same letter or different letters. Thus the subject had to generalize across the size difference. Performance was faster when the letters were the same size than when the size differed, indicating that the tactual size characteristic was part of the tactual encoding process. The children in this study were early blind and nine to 11 years of age, with at most minimal light perception.

Millar (1975a) used an interference task with four to ten-year-olds to study the similarity of encoding of verbal and tactual features. As the size of the to-be-remembered set increased, the interference functions for verbal and tactual material differed, supporting the conclusion that the verbal and tactual material must be encoded by different processes.

Millar (1978a) further corroborated the basic difference between processes for memory of verbal and tactual material, using a method involving the grouping of items to be recalled. It is known that the grouping of items within a serial string of verbal material facilitates memory of that material. If tactual memory operates as verbal memory does, a similar grouping effect should be found for tactual material. The subjects were seven to 11-year-old children who had been blind from 20 months of age or less, with at most minimal light perception. The stimulus lists with verbal association were composed of braille letters, while the nonassociative lists were nonsense patterns produced by a brailling stylus. The results supported the hypothesis of a differential memory process, since grouping facilitated recall of the material with verbal association (the braille letters) but interfered with the recall of nonsense shapes.

With respect to her work on the processing of the tactual material of braille stimuli, Millar (1978b) posed the issue as follows: In learning braille, the child is faced with the task of learning associations between tactual stimuli and the letter names. What, though, is the nature of the effective tactual stimulus to which the association is made? Millar concluded that the tendency, particularly for younger children, is to regard the dots forming a given braille letter not as a unified form, but rather as a set of related dots. Presumably exercises designed to induce the child to process the dot pattern as a form rather than as a set of dots would simplify the associative learning process, by virtue of simplifying the tactual stimulus into an integrated shape rather than a set of complex interrelationships of dots. It is an interesting question whether this tendency of blind children to interpret a dot pattern as a set of separate dots rather than as an integrated form is related to the tendency in younger sighted children to have difficulty interpreting a set of visual dots as representing a visual form. It would not be surprising to find an underlying developmental process expressed in both visual and tactual perception, and such a process would set natural limits on the usefulness of dot patterns (such as braille) for the education of blind children, or at least define an important area for the exploration of perceptual training with young blind children.

Studies by Hermelin and O'Connor (1971) and by Mommers (1980) serve to illustrate the complexity of the tactual perception involved in braille reading. Hermelin and O'Connor supposed that, because letter configurations are spatially distributed, they would be better processed by the right hemisphere of the brain, which would mean that right-handed subjects should read braille better with the left hand than the right! Their results, from blind children age eight to 10, supported this hypothesis. Mommers (1980) sought to replicate the finding with totally blind right-handed children ranging from seven to 12 years of age. Both word lists and braille numerals were used as test stimuli. The pattern of results was not straightforward: although there was a tendency for performance to be better with the left hand, the variability was considerable and statistically significant results were not obtained. In any case, the relationships between brain function and the task demands of processing braille stimuli are not likely to be simple: the verbal nature of the material should favor the left hemisphere, at least for more mature right-handed readers, while the spatial patterning of the dot patterns might well favor the right hemisphere. In any case, the issue is an interesting and potentially important one if, as seems evident, the braille task is one that makes demands on both hemispheres and therefore may be a more involved task than the visual reading of print by sighted readers.

Fox (1965) reported a study which, if not entirely convincing, represents an interesting approach to tactile discrimination. Ten congenitally blind fifth and sixth graders, with at most light perception, were tested on a set of tactile discrimination items including both shape and texture. Then olfactory stimulation (peppermint spray) was introduced into the testing room. After 10 minutes, the subjects were retested on the tactile forms. Test-retest comparisons indicated a significant improvement on the shape items, no improvement on the texture items, and a combined improvement that was significant. The design of the study was not reported clearly, but there was apparently a confounding between grade level and order of test conditions. Further, there was unfortunately no test-retest control group that did *not* receive the olfactory stimulation. Because of these procedural difficulties, it is probably unwise to interpret the findings seriously.

Size and length discrimination

Size discrimination is an ability that is related to form discrimination and has received some direct attention. There are various approaches to the problem, including some involving motor reproduction of sizes and lengths.

Berla' and Murr (1975) conducted a psychophysical study of the discriminability of line width, in an attempt to generate performance data on which to base the design of maps and other tactual educational materials. The subjects were all blind braille readers, and they were divided into grade groups of four to six, seven to nine, and 10 to 12, with mean ages for the groups respectively of 12, 16, and 18.5 years. There were no differences between males and females or between age groupings. The threshold functions did not in general conform to Weber's Law. Variations from wider lines (up to 0.5 in.) were relatively more discriminable than variations from narrower lines. The fact that sensitivity improved (both increases in accuracy and decreases in variability were found) across the sets of test trials suggests that attempts to train line width discrimination might prove rewarding.

Duran and Tufenkjian (1970) conducted a study whose goal was to investigate the haptic discrimination of length. The children were, for the most part, blind before two years of age, and had, at best, LP. Their age was from five to 14 years, and the IQ range was from 70 to 135. A method of constant stimuli was used, in which the subject had to judge which of a pair of steel rods was longer. Difference thresholds for the discrimination of length were determined for a series of rods. Thresholds were not correlated with IQ or age, and there was no sex difference. An interesting finding was the variety of methods used by the children for the judgment of length. These included juxtaposition, palm span, reference to some body part, time required to slide the finger along the rod, and pitch differences between rods when they were tapped against the table. The authors emphasized the need to consider individual differences in the spontaneous use of such different strategies, and they discussed the possibility of using various training techniques to induce better length discrimination. They also pointed out that variations in performance IQ scores may depend not so much on intelligence as on the ability to perform very simple tasks such as discrimination of relative size.

The data of Pick and Pick (1966) suggest that perspective and size transformations were the most difficult for sighted, partially sighted, and totally blind groups, and that the line-to-curve transformation was also relatively difficult. Both size and curvature variables have received other experimental attention. Hunter (1964) studied children totally blind from birth, age 12 to 18, and sighted controls, in an investigation of the ability to transpose a curved extent to a flat surface. The subject explored the circumference of a cylinder and then attempted to reproduce the distance along a meter stick. Hunter did not provide mean errors or estimates of variability, but he stated that the congenitally blind children were significantly worse at this type of performance than the sighted children. In a related study, Jones (1972) studied the ability of blind and sighted children (five to 12 years, as described earlier) to reproduce a hand movement. The subject moved his hand along a track to a preset stop, then attempted to replicate the extent of the movement with the stop removed. When the ages were collapsed, the blind children (mostly blind from birth) were significantly better than the sighted. Analysis of more homogeneous age groups showed significant advantages by the blind children between 8 and 11 years but not at age 12. A graph of Jones' result suggests that the blind group improved at an earlier age, reaching asymptote at about eight or nine years, and that the sighted subjects were still improving at the upper age limit studied. Thus it seems likely that the difference between blind and sighted children is not a difference in potential performance, but rather a developmental lag by sighted children.

The apparent discrepancy between the results of Hunter and those of Jones bears comment. The Jones task was a simpler one, requiring simple reproduction of extent rather than the more complex transposition of a two-dimensional spatial experience into a unidimensional one. Warren, Anooshian, and Bollinger (1973), in their discussion of various spatial tasks, suggested that relatively simple spatial tasks are not as strongly affected by visualization ability as relatively complex ones. The absence of visualization may thus have depressed the performance of Hunter's blind subjects, while inability to visualize would not have adversely affected Jones' blind subjects on their relatively simple task. Another possibility is that the apparent discrepancy in results is related to the differences in ages of the two samples (Jones' oldest subjects were 12, while Hunter's youngest were 12). In any case, the potential importance of length-estimation abilities in mobility-map reading make it important to have more research in this area. Close attention should be given to possible age effects and to individual differences in strategies.

Hanninen (1970) studied the effect of texture on the length estimation of blind and sighted children. The 29 blind subjects ranged in age from nine to 16 and were all clearly blind (at less than six months). The maximum vision was perception of hand movement at 18 inches. In the initial testing phase the children were given a series of strips with varying degrees of abrasiveness and asked to make judgments of relative length. Hanninen's hypothesis that coarse textures would be underestimated and fine textures overestimated was not supported for either the blind or the sighted children. Comparison of the groups in terms of correctness of response was not possible, since the procedure involved a forced choice with stimuli that were actually equal in length. Following the initial test, a training phase was conducted in which half of each group received a procedure designed to facilitate their length judgments, and the other half received a procedure designed to interfere (procedures based on a study by Corsini & Pick, 1967). After the training, the testing with equal lengths was repeated. The two training procedures had the predicted effect for the sighted children. The subgroup that received the interference condition made more errors in reaching a criterion, but there was no such difference for the blind group. Unfortunately, no direct comparisons of blind and sighted groups were available in the report, except a brief discussion suggesting that the effect of the training was to produce in the sighted group a trend contrary to the hypothesis regarding the effect of texture on estimation of length, but to decrease any interfering effect of texture on length estimation in the blind group. In a follow-up study, Hanninen (1976) found only inconsistent relationships between texture preference and discrimination of textured lengths for subjects ranging from 11 to 20 years of age.

Block (1972) compared early blind children with sighted children on tasks involving size discrimination, weight discrimination, and the size-weight illusion. The blind subjects had all lost vision by the age of six and the amount of useful vision ranged widely, with vision as good as 20/100 in two cases. The age range was from eight to 14 years. The method of constant stimuli was used for size discrimination, with the rectangular stimuli varying only in width. The blind children tended to overestimate size consistently more than sighted children, and the tendency to overestimate increased with age. Sato and Anayama (1973), on the other hand, found that first-to-sixth-grade totally blind children performed better than sighted children on tests of size and length discrimination.

Berla' (1972) studied the effects of physical size and complexity on the ability of first- and second-grade blind children to discriminate forms. The subjects were braille readers enrolled in schools for the blind. Presumably they were severely blind, although this information is not provided in the report, nor is information about the age at onset of blindness. The subjects were required to make same-different judgments about pairs of stimuli, which were raised line, irregular geometric figures. The stimuli varied in size (one, two and four inches square) and complexity. Both increasing complexity and increasing size led to increases in the time needed for response. Neither variable had an effect on the accuracy of response. There was no difference between first and second graders on either time to explore or correct responses. In a related study, Morris and Nolan (1963) varied the size of tactually presented forms to determine the optimal size range for tactual educational materials for blind children. The subjects were drawn from fourth through 12th grades and had LP at most. A two-inch standard pattern was presented along with seven alternatives, one of which was the same pattern as the standard. All seven alternatives on any given trial were the same size, and the size varied from 0.5 to two inches on a side. Generally, the eighth to 12th graders performed better than the fourth to seventh graders. There was an apparent break in the response series, where response alternatives smaller than 0.75 were selected less accurately than those larger than one inch. It is not clear from the study whether this size effect is a result of absolute size or of the relationship between stimulus size and response size. The former possibility would have stronger implications for map design.

Weight discrimination

There has been very little work done on weight discrimination. Block (1972) compared the ability of blind and sighted children to make weight judgments. The method of constant stimuli was used, where the subject lifted two weights simultaneously and judged which was heavier. The blind children were significantly better at this task than the sighted children, and there was no significant change over the eight- to 14-year age range. Sato and Anayama (1973), however, found no difference between blind and sighted children in grades one to six.

If two objects are equivalent in weight but different in size, the smaller of the two tends to be judged as heavier. The phenomenon is known as the size-weight illusion. Pick and Pick (1967) found a developmental increase in the magnitude of this illusion when sighted children were blindfolded and had only haptic information available for size and weight judgments. Menaker (1966) studied the size-weight illusion in 100 congenitally blind children (most had visual loss before six months), aged six to 17, and in a group of sighted controls. The magnitude of the illusion increased significantly with age for both blind and sighted groups. At each age level through age 11, though, the blind children tended to show less illusion than the sighted. In fact, the magnitude of the illusion for any given blind group corresponded roughly to the magnitude of the sighted group about four years younger. Menaker discussed this developmental lag in the integration of size and weight in terms of the relatively restricted learning opportunities of the blind child in the home, and she suggested that, except in unusual circumstances, the learning environment of the blind child is inadequate until he begins school.

In the same study in which she investigated size and weight discriminations, Block (1972) assessed susceptibility to the size-weight illusion in blind and sighted children. The age range was from eight to 14 years, and the visual characteristics of the blind subjects were quite heterogeneous. Comparison of the entire groups of blind and sighted subjects, without regard to age, revealed a significantly weaker illusion in the blind group, thus supporting one aspect of Menaker's results (1966). There was no support for the developmental lag reported by Menaker, however. Comparison of the data from the two studies shows that even the sighted children performed differently: Menaker's subjects showed a generally stronger illusion than Block's, and Block's subjects showed a decreasing illusion after a peak reached at age nine. Block's blind subjects also showed a weaker illusion than Menaker's, with a marked divergence beginning at age 12, where Menaker's group showed a far greater magnitude of illusion. Block did not discuss extensively the differences between her results and those of Menaker, aside from pointing out that there may have been some important differences in ages, samples, or procedures. The procedural factor seems heavily implicated, since there were substantial differences in the performance of the sighted subjects in the two studies. In any case, the comparative study of illusions in blind and sighted children is of questionable importance. Illusions in general are poorly understood in sighted children, and so the comparison of blind with sighted children cannot be expected to provide results that are unambiguously interpretable, even if differences between studies did not occur.

Summary

An overall view of the tactile discrimination research suggests that there are no striking differences between blind and sighted children. When differences do emerge, they are typically, although not strongly, in favor of the blind children. Examples are cutaneous localization (Jones, 1972), form discrimination (Schwartz, 1972), length matching (Jones, 1972), and weight discrimination (Block, 1972). Davidson (1976) concluded that such differences are probably due more to differences in strategies of attention than to basic differences in sensory acuity. Block (1972) also found blind children somewhat worse than sighted children on a test of size discrimination. Several studies have not made blind-sighted comparisons but have evaluated relationships between discrimination performance and variables such as CA and IQ within groups of blind children. There has unfortunately been very little research designed to assess the effects of variables such as age at onset of blindness and degree of residual vision.

Form Identification

The studies on form perception that have been discussed to this point were concerned primarily with form *discrimination.* There is also a substantial body of literature on the *identification* of tactually perceived forms. Comparisons have been made in these studies between blind and sighted groups, and among blind groups with varying characteristics.

Within the work that provides comparisons of blind and sighted children, some studies report equality of performance while others report better performance for sighted children. Among the former group are studies by Ewart and Carp (1962), Gottesman (1971), and Eaves and Klonoff (1970). Ewart and Carp used a task in which the subject was given a block, told to feel it and remember the shape, and then was given four comparison blocks successively, from which he was to pick the one identical to the stimulus block. The blind subjects were predominantly blind from birth, had at most LP, and ranged in age from eight to 16 years, mean age 12. Analysis of variance indicated that the blind as a group were not significantly different from the sighted. Unfortunately, the distribution of IQ scores in the blind group was higher than that in the sighted group, and the interpretation of the results is correspondingly clouded.

Gottesman's (1971) study was similar to that of Ewart and Carp in that the subject was given a stimulus block and was then asked to choose a match from a set of four alternatives. Subjects ranged in age from two to eight years (Ewart and Carp's youngest were eight). The blind were blind from birth and had at most LP. There were no significant differences between the blind and the sighted groups. Both blind and sighted children apparently improved with age, although not enough data appeared in the report to allow a firm conclusion.

Eaves and Klonoff (1970) studied the performance of blind and sighted children on the Tactual Performance Test (TPT), which is a modifiction of the Seguin Formboard. The blind children were congenitally blind, age six to 16, about half with "guiding vision" and the other half with no vision or LP. Sighted controls were matched for age and sex. For the TPT, no overall differences were found between blind and sighted groups, although there was an indication that the totally blind children were somewhat better than those with guiding vision or normal vision when the dominant hand was used for performance. This superiority was complicated by the finding that the totally blind subjects scored significantly higher on both the WISC verbal and the Hayes-Binet Intelligence Scale for the Blind. Eaves and Klonoff suggested that the superiority of the totally blind subgroup may be a situational result attributable to the fact that the sighted and partially sighted subjects were restricted from exercising their normal degree of dependence on vision. This suggestion receives support from the fact that both groups with some vision improved more across the testing session than did the totally blind group. The dominant versus non dominant hand differences were unfortunately confounded with order of performance. That is, the poor performance of both sighted and partial vision groups with the dominant hand may have been a result of the fact that the dominant hand trials were always performed first and therefore did not receive the benefit of practice.

Among the studies which have found superior performance by sighted children, Worchel's (1951) report has received wide attention. In this study, he compared blind and sighted children on two tactual form tests (and a locomotor spatial relations test, which will be discussed later). The subjects ranged from eight to 21 years, average age 15. The blind children were all totally blind but varied in age at onset of blindness. In the first experiment, the subject was presented with a cutout block and was asked to make various responses to it. The response measure that seemed to involve the least confounding of other abilities was verbal description, and on this measure the sighted subjects gave more responses that were rated as "excellent" than the blind and fewer that were rated as "fair" or "poor." In a second task, Worchel had subjects feel the two parts of a form, one part with each hand, then choose one form from a set of four that corresponded to the combination of the two separate forms. The sighted were significantly better at this task than the blind. Drever (1955) reported a replication of Worchel's block combination task with teenage children (range 12-19, mean 15). Drever's blind group was quite similar to that of Worchel, and his results provided corroboration of Worchel's finding of a significant superiority of sighted children.

One of the tasks conducted by Witkin, Birnbaum, Lomonaco, Lehr, and Herman (1968) is related to the tactual identification of form. The tactile embedded-figures test involved presenting a complex raised-line figure for the subject to explore, then presenting a simple figure, then presenting the complex figure again and asking the subject to find the simple figure in the complex one. The blind subjects ranged in age from 12 to 19 and were totally blind from birth. They were significantly slower at finding the simple figure than were the sighted controls performing blindfolded.

Ayres (1966) compared the ability of blind and sighted adolescents, age range 11 to 18, to identify familiar objects from tactual information. The blind subjects had LP at most and were congenitally or early blind. The sighted subjects were significantly better than the blind at identifying the objects. In contrast, studying younger (4-7 years) children, Simpkins (1979a,b) found no differences between sighted, partially sighted and blind groups in tactual identification of familiar household objects. The overall performance level of about 87° correct suggests that a ceiling effect may have masked any possible differences between the groups.

The common feature of the tasks on which blindfolded sighted subjects perform better than the blind is that most of these tasks seem to involve a more complex use of spatial-relations abilities. This is certainly true of the Witkin embedded-figures task, and of the block-combination task used by Worchel in which the subject had to imagine what the combination of two forms would be. In contrast, the form-matching task used by Ewart and Carp and by Gottesman requires the retention of a form in memory, but not the mental manipulation of the form. The formboard test similarly requires the matching of a form to a correspondingly shaped hole, but not a complex mental manipulation of the form.

Marmor and Zaback (1976) demonstrated that mental rotation may be a factor in such tasks for adults. They compared early and later blind with sighted adults, ages 17 to 40. The task involved the presentation of one form in an upright orientation, with a subsequent form presented in various degrees of rotation from the upright, in multiples of 30 degrees. The subject had to judge whether the second form was the same as or different from the first. The subjects who became blind before six months of age were slower and less accurate than the later blind or the blindfolded sighted subjects. All three groups showed a linear increase in (reaction time) RT as a function of amount of rotation of the comparison stimulus, suggesting that rotation was indeed the basis of performance. However, the better performance by the later blind and sighted subjects was hypothesized to result from their ability to use visual imagery mediation for the task, whereas the early blind subjects could use no such mediation strategy.

Contrasting results were found by Carpenter and Eisenberg (1978) with 15-to 18-year-olds. The stimuli in this study were capital letters (B and F). On each trial, a letter was presented in either normal or mirror image form, and either upright or rotated to a multiple of 60 degrees. The subject had to judge as quickly as possible whether the letter was normal or a mirror image. Presumably such a task should benefit from the ability to use visual image rotation, of which the later blind but not the early blind should be capable. The subjects had all been visually impaired from birth, but some had had very limited amounts of residual vision, while the remainder had had none. There was no difference in RT between these subgroups. If the task involved mental rotation, as was suggested by the RT functions, then at least the totally blind subjects must have had some means of performing the task without the benefit of visual imagery. In follow-up experiments, a group of sighted subjects performed the task both visually and haptically. Their visual performance was better than the haptic performance of the blind, but their haptic performance was worse. It should be noted that the blind subjects in this sudy were as a rule haptically skilled, generally being braille readers and having had some experience with the Optacon. In any case, the results leave open the possibility that the early blind can perform such tasks relatively well on the basis of other than mental rotation of visual images.

That the congenitally blind can perform spatial tasks involving mental rotation is not at issue. Cleaves and Royal (1979) provided yet another demonstration, using a task that involved learning a finger maze to criterion, then responding to various points in the maze under mental transformation requirements such as left–right and up–down reversals. A group of congenitally blind young adults performed better than chance on such tasks, but worse than later blind subjects or sighted subjects performing without vision. The age at onset of blindness within the later blind group was a significant predictor of performance, as was the length of time since becoming blind. Interestingly, an index of "proportion of life spent blind" (calculated by dividing the number of years spent blind by the subject's age) was a very good negative predictor of performance in this group.

Stephens, Simpkins, and Wexler (1976) used a task called Rotation of Squares to compare the mental rotation abilities of six- to 18-year-old blind and sighted children. Two squares are mounted on a common axis, and while one stays fixed, the other can be rotated into different relationships to the fixed square. The subject's task is to imagine where one corner of the rotated square will be in relation to its original location, and select the correct alternative from a set of choices. The results showed the same kind of developmental lag that Stephens has reported in other work (Chap. 3), with the blind performing at levels characteristic of sighted children as much as eight years younger. However, it should be noted that the sighted subjects apparently performed with vision available while the blind had to perform the task tactually, selecting the correct alternative from a set of raised-line drawings. The comparison does not seem a particularly appropriate one.

Millar (1976) reported a study that is similar in concept to the foregoing studies involving mental rotation. The subjects were six- to 11-year-olds, with sighted subjects matched to the blind on the basis of age, sex, and digit span. The blind subjects had for the most part become blind very early in life and had at most light perception. In one task (Exp.1), a headed matchstick was glued onto a cardboard square, and the subject's task was to feel it, then select from an array of choices what the orientation of the stick would be to an observer at a location different from his own. Both sighted and blind older subjects performed better on this task than younger ones, but there was no overall difference between the blind and the sighted groups. The oldest (10-11 years) group of blind subjects was composed of half early blind children and half who had become blind between the ages of two and six years. Comparison of the performance of these two subgroups showed a definite superiority of the later blind over the early blind, a result which corresponds to many other findings (cf. Warren et al., 1973).

In a second experiment using the same subjects, Millar used two tasks which further imposed a recall requirement. In a *rotation* task, the subject felt a slot in a square board, with the slot vertical to his own location. He then felt the square board and was asked to draw the orientation of the slot as the board was rotated to different orientations on the table, without recontacting the slot. In a *perspective* task, the subject felt the slot initially, then moved around the table and had to draw, from a variety of locations, what the orientation of the slot would be if viewed from the new locations. The perspective task was more difficult than the rotation task, older subjects performed better than younger subjects, and the sighted blindfolded subjects performed better than the blind. Interestingly, the blind were comparable to the sighted when orthogonal (right angle) directions were involved, but were not as good with the oblique directions, particularly those which involved the longest movements. Millar reasoned that the blind relied on memory of movement sequence in performing the task, whereas the sighted were making use of a spatial representation. This conclusion was further strengthened by results reported by Millar (1975d), in which blind children were worse at backward recall of the elements of a spatial display, whereas backward and forward recall were equivalent for blindfolded sighted subjects.

These various results suggest that, while both blind and sighted children can perform tasks that appear to require mental rotation, the performance of the blind and sighted may be based on different strategies for dealing with information. If, as Millar (1975d, 1977b) hypothesizes, the primary strategy available to the blind involves coding movement sequences, then it may be possible to achieve better performance in such situations by giving extended practice in the movements and their sequence.

Berla' (1974) studied the ability of school-age blind children to reorient a figure to match a previously perceived orientation. The subjects were braille readers, enrolled in grades 2, 4, 6, and 8 in schools for the blind. Details of visual condition were not reported. At each grade level, the children could reorient shapes at a better than chance rate, and the accuracy of performance improved significantly with grade level. However, even at the eighth-grade level, errors averaged 30 degrees. Thus, while all the children clearly had the concept of orientation in space, they were not very good at using the concept, even in the eighth grade. Interestingly, Berla' noted that differences in performance over grade seemed to be related to the adequacy of choosing and relocating a distinctive feature of the shape. The younger children did not explore the shapes so carefully and seemed to choose a feature more impulsively.

Along similar lines, Berla' and Murr (1974) found that different children spontaneously used different strategies for exploring a tactual graphic map: those who made a vertical scan using the two hands together were more effective than those who used various horizontal scanning strategies. Children in the early grades benefitted from training in the vertical scan strategy, whereas older children did not improve. Children who scanned tactual shapes on such a map with organized movements were better at discriminating those shapes, particularly if they searched for particular distinctive features of the various shapes (Berla', Butterfield, & Murr, 1976). In another study, Berla' and Butterfield (1977) reported again that regular scanning and attention to distinctive features facilitated good map performance, and that training in these strategies was effective. Finally, Berla' (1981) had blind children search a nine-item test puzzle tactually, try to remember the location of the parts, and then replace the parts in their correct locations on a new board. Three groups averaged 11, 15, and 19 years of age. Training in a vertical scanning strategy was given to half of each group. There were no obvious effects on vertical location errors, but for horizontal errors the youngest group was aided by the training, whereas the middle group was not affected, and the oldest group's performance was decreased by the training. The age pattern of results was thus reminiscent of that reported by Berla' and Murr (1974).

Berla's analysis of shape orientation in terms of distinctive features is reminiscent of Gibson's formulation (1969), and it would seem valuable to pursue research designed to evaluate the distinctive features used tactually by the blind, especially in view of the growing use of tactual maps for mobility. In this same connection, Solntseva (1966) suggested that the difficulties that the blind child experiences in the "formation of (tactual) images of the external environment" are due to delay of the differentiation process, that is, of the ability to differentiate distinctive features of tactual experience.

As was pointed out in connection with the study by Eaves and Klonoff, there is some question about the appropriateness of using blindfolded sighted subjects as a control group against which to assess the abilities of blind subjects. The case of the blindfolded sighted subject is not as simple as it may appear. First, many writers have suggested that sighted subjects have some type of visual imagery available to them even when blindfolded, and so it is not simply the case that blindfolding produces a test of strictly nonvisual abilities. Second, the blindfolded sighted subject is at the disadvantage of having just lost his sight and of not having had a chance to practice using sources of information that he might typically ignore. In most studies, little practice is apparently allowed, and the performance of the blindfolded subject may represent not a reliable ability level but rather an arbitrary point taken from an improving practice curve. This second factor tends to produce results showing the blindfolded sighted subject to be worse than he might be with even a few minutes more practice. The visual imagery factor, by contrast, probably leads to an overestimation of the blindfolded sighted subject's tactual abilities. These two factors undoubtedly work against one another in many cases, but their relative effects on performance are unknown. It seems likely that performance might be especially facilitated by visualization on tasks involving complex spatial relations, and it is in fact those tasks on which the blindfolded sighted subjects have been found superior to the blind. In any case, the comparison is not as clear-cut as it appears, and caution should be duly exercised in the interpretation of results from such studies (Warren, 1978).

A more satisfying group of studies includes those that allow comparisons of the performance of blind subjects who differ in such characteristics as the age at onset of blindness, the degree of remaining useful vision, and indices such as CA and IQ. Among the studies that provide information about the effects of age at onset of blindness (duration of vision before onset) are those by Sylvester (1913), F. Merry (1932), and Worchel (1951). Sylvester compared the formboard performance of groups of children who were blind from birth, blind before the age of three, and blind after the age of three. Group mean ages ranged from 13 to 15. Although no statistics were reported, the results for both average time-per-trial and average number of errors indicated that the performance of the congenitally blind was worse than that of the early blind, and the later blind performed substantially better than the early blind. Sylvester concluded that the early visual experience provided visual imagery that led to more effective performance than the necessarily purely tactual performance of the congenitally blind.

F. Merry (1932) conducted an investigation of the ability of blind subjects, who ranged in age from six to 24 and had no useful vision, to recognize two-dimensional tactual representations of common objects and geometrical designs. There was a wide range of IQ and age at onset of blindness, although the median age at onset was within the first year. The geometric designs proved to be somewhat easier to recognize, since no subject failed to identify any of these figures correctly, while about 16 percent of the subjects failed to recognize any of the representations of common objects. Merry did not find a significant relationship between the age at onset of blindness and performance on either type of picture. The fact that the median age at onset was within the first year suggests the possibility that there may not have been enough variability in the age at onset to allow a correlation to emerge.

As noted earlier, Worchel (1951) used two tests of tactual form perception. In the test which required recognition, description, or matching of a stimulus form, most comparisons showed the adventitiously blinded children (age at onset ranging from one to 11 years, median six) to perform significantly better than the congenitally blind. Similarly, on the test that required the subject to judge the effect of combining two component forms, the adventitiously blinded group showed significantly better performance.

Thus the weight of the evidence on the age-at-onset factor would seem to be in favor of better performance by the later blind. This type of result has typically been discussed in terms of a residual visual imagery ability of the later blind. An extensive analysis of the effects of early vision on spatial relations performance has been made by Warren et al. (1973).

Studies that have evaluated the effects of residual vision on form perception include those by R. Merry (1930), Eaves and Klonoff (1970), and Pick, Klein, and Pick (1966). R. Merry's study was similar to the aforementioned study by F. Merry, although only representations of common objects were used. The purpose of the study was to ascertain how useful such representations might be in educational settings. The subjects ranged in age from six to 14 years, and residual vision ranged from none to 20/200. Fifteen of the 50 subjects did not recognize any of the 10 pictures used. Eleven of these 15 were among the 22 totally blind subjects, although the overall difference between the LP-or-less group and the partially sighted group was not significant.

An extensive discussion of the Eaves and Klonoff study has already been made, and as noted, there was some superiority of the children with LP or less over those with "guiding vision" (better than LP) when the dominant hand was used. As noted, however, this superiority must be evaluated in the light of the fact that the group with less vision showed higher scores on the IQ tests. In any case, the effects of residual vision on form perception are not clear and deserve further attention. One potentially important issue that has not received discussion is the question of whether training in tactual form perception for children with some remaining vision might make effective use of the vision, or whether encouraging these children to use the residual vision might actually interfere with the development of better tactual abilities.

Pick, Klein, and Pick (1966) reported an interesting variation on the tactual form identification paradigm, in which they had subjects identify which of two opposite orientations of a figure was right side up. Since the forms were nonsense designs, there was in fact no correct response. The consistency of judgments among subjects within each group was assessed. Blind children were drawn from school populations, had been blind since birth or infancy, and ranged in age from six to 21 years. They were divided into partially sighted (legally blind) and totally blind groups. The partially sighted subjects were braille readers. The sighted children ranged in age from four to nine years. Sighted subjects made both visual and tactual judgments of the stimuli, while the blind groups both made only tactual judgments. There was consistency in the visual judgments of the sighted group across the whole age range, but the tactual judgments of the sighted group did not show consistency. The tactual judgments of the totally blind group showed a similar lack of consistency. Interestingly, there was some consistency in the tactual judgments of the partially sighted group, and the pattern of judgments was quite similar to the pattern of visual judgments for the sighted subjects. It is unfortunate that there were not sufficient numbers of partially sighted or blind subjects to allow analysis by age group. Such an analysis would be particularly interesting in the case of the partially sighted, since the role of partial vision in providing structure for the tactual mode might be expected to change over age. The question of the lack of consistency in the tactual judgments of the sighted group also deserves mention. It seems reasonable to hypothesize that the greater dependence of the partially sighted group on information gained via touch makes them more likely to create an organization of their tactual experience. The totally blind are no less dependent on touch, certainly, but their relative lack of consistency suggests that vision plays an important role in providing tactual structure.

Intelligence has received some attention as a possible contributing factor to form perception. R. Merry (1930) reported no relationship between IQ and performance, but in a later study F. Merry (1932) reported "some correlation" between IQ and performance on the recognition of geometric forms. Eaves and Klonoff (1970) found a positive correlation between IQ and formboard performance for totally blind subjects, but the correlation was not significant for the group of blind subjects with "guiding vision." Ewart and Carp (1962) divided both blind and sighted groups into high- and low-IQ subgroups. The interaction between visual condition and IQ was significant and indicated that the high-IQ blind subgroup was significantly better at form matching than any of the other subgroups. The low-IQ blind subgroup did not differ from either of the sighted subgroups. Thus the IQ factor was related to performance in the blind group but not in the sighted group. The similarity of this pattern to that found by Eaves and Klonoff should be noted, although in that study a lack of relationship was found in a partially sighted group rather than a fully sighted group. Warren et al. (1973) reviewed studies in which the relationships between IQ and various types of spatial behavior were evaluated. Warren et al. (1973, p. 158) suggested that it is not surprising

> to find that especially in tasks involving learning (such as the maze tasks), IQ correlates with performance. The suggestion that the relation may be stronger for the blind, and that it may extend to nonlearning tasks, deserves some attention. One possibility, for example, is that tasks involving a visual frame of reference may be relatively easy for the sighted and may thus not be differentiated by IQ. The same task may be relatively more difficult for the blind because of the lack of a visual frame of reference, and the blind may depend more on verbal or other cognitive interventions for successful performance.

A final factor which has been studied as bearing on the form perception tasks is CA. R. Merry (1930) and F. Merry (1932) found no relationship between recognition performance and CA, although the range in the groups was substantial (six to 14, six to 24). In his test of tactual form recognition and matching, Gottesman (1971) did find some improvement over the age range of two to eight years, although the group of two- to four-year-olds performed surprisingly well.

Review of the literature revealed only two longer-term training studies that were concerned specifically with tactual object identification. F. Merry (1933) reported a training procedure designed to help blind children aged five to 14 in their ability to recognize two-dimensional representations of geometric figures and common objects. None of the children had useful vision. The younger group, ranging in age from five to nine years, ranged somewhat below average in IQ, while the older group, age 10 to 14, were slightly above average. Training consisted of thrice-weekly short sessions in which the child was shown the representation, was asked to pick a figure out of a set, and was asked to construct the figure using upholsterer's tacks. For the pictures of common objects, functional uses were explained and the child was encouraged to explore the figure and answer simple questions about it. For the group of older children, the training was made somewhat more demanding. Both groups showed significant improvement, with the least improvement apparently occurring in the younger group for the common objects. Merry concluded that training efforts in teaching the discrimination of two-dimensional form might be effective, but that energy expended in attempting to teach the discrimination of two-dimensional representation of real objects would be less rewarding.

Garry and Ascarelli (1960) administered a training program to many blind children, ranging in age from five to 15. The training program was geared to various aspects of performance, including posture and movement, structuring extended space, perception of objects, and language. Considerable detail about the training procedures was included in the report, but unfortunately much less detail appeared in the evaluation of the effects of the training. A control group was tested in addition to the training group, but the groups differed substantially in important characteristics, thus making strict comparisons unwise. The control group was 1.7 years older in CA and 2.5 years older in MA than the experimental group, and perhaps more importantly, the pretest scores of the control group were much higher than those of the experimental group. In fact, even though the experimental group showed a dramatic improvement from pre- to posttest, their spatial relations posttest performance was still substantially lower than even the pretest performance of the control group. The control group did not show a significant change from pre- to posttest. A further weakness of the study is the failure to subdivide the test scores more fully. For example, although several distinct aspects of spatial relations and object perception training were discussed, the only test results provided were from a spatial relations performance test which apparently included both object perception and spatial relations. Thus although there is little firm conclusion to be drawn from the study, it is an important example of the need for adequate evaluation of the effects of training programs. The thought and effort that went into the training program were not wholly wasted, but the study is of little use in identifying the best possible training procedures. One simply cannot ascertain whether the dramatic increase in the spatial relations scores of the experimental group was a function of passing time or in fact due to the training procedure. Furthermore, it is quite likely that some aspects of spatial relations or object identification training were better than others, but it is impossible to ascertain which is which because of the lack of detail in the reported results of the evaluations. Certainly it is important to conduct training programs, but the results of these programs must be evaluated adequately if the work is to contribute to progress in the field.

Audition and the Other Senses

Considering the importance of auditory information for the blind child, it is surprising that there is not more literature available. Furthermore, some of the existing research does not inspire confidence. A study by Hayes (1933) is cited often and deserves historical mention. Hayes reported that Sargent, working with an audiometer, tested the thresholds over a wide frequency range for blind boys and girls, whose ages and visual characteristics were not specified. The blind children showed systematic deficits when compared to a group of sighted college-age women. (Although the college group is sometimes referred to as a "control" by other writers reviewing Hayes' paper, it can in no sense be regarded as such, and Hayes himself did not refer to it as a control group.)

Hare, Hammill, and Crandell (1970) studied auditory discrimination in detail, comparing blind and sighted children ranging in age from six to 10 years. The sound discrimination test of Irwin and Jensen (1963) was used. This test requires the subject to make same-different judgments about two successively presented words spoken by the tester. The members of the test pairs differ in only one phoneme. Comparison of sighted and blind children showed no different in phoneme discrimination. The total sample of 85 blind children was also divided into three groups on the basis of visual acuity. There was no evidence of a significant relationship between degree of residual vision and auditory discrimination. Hare et al. (1970) determined that performance on the sound discrimination test was significantly related to both CA and MA in both the blind group and the sighted group. This study is an excellent source of information on sound discrimination in blind vs. sighted children. The results show convincingly that there are no basic differences in discrimination, and that degree of residual vision does not play a part. Not unexpectedly, there was an improvement in discrimination with age. The lack of basic differences in auditory abilities was further documented by Stankov and Spilsbury (1980), who used a wider variety of auditory tests than had previous researchers. Although some differences were found on selective tasks, the weight of the results supports the "no difference" conclusion.

Lane and Curran (1963) presented a provocative study of the auditory generalization gradients of three severely retarded children, blind since birth. Button-press responses were conditioned to two tones, and generalization gradients for tones surrounding the conditioned tones were established. The shapes of the gradients for these subjects were not drastically different from those that had been obtained with college students in a previous study. One can presume that generalization gradients for blind children without additional handicaps would be similar to those of sighted children, although there are no data available to document the presumption. The question is not purely of academic interest—nobody would argue with the contention that auditory discrimination is vitally important to blind children. Generalization between auditory stimuli is a topic closely related to discrimination, and it would make a great deal of sense to study both discrimination and generalization closely in blind children to determine what limits there may be on their ability to discriminate the parameters of the various sounds in the environment.

Results reported by Witkin, Oltman, Chase, and Friedman (1971) bear on the question of the blind child's ability to pick auditory patterns out of an auditory background. The subjects had been totally blind from birth from various causes, and they ranged in age from 12 to 19. A group of sighted subjects was matched to the blind. Both groups were within the normal to high-normal IQ range. The auditory embedded-figures test was included in a battery of five tests which will be discussed in more detail in Chapter 3. The auditory test involved the ability to recognize whether a short three-to-five-note tune occurred in a longer tune. The congenitally blind subjects were significantly better than the sighted at this task. Although the test may be viewed as a form of abstraction test, it should be noted that the blind performed much worse than the sighted on a tactile embedded-figures test. It is thus not possible to conclude that the blind were better at abstraction in general. In fact, Witkin et al. (1971) accounted for the results by suggesting that the blind children had developed better auditory attentive abilities.

In another study bearing on auditory abilities, Gibbs and Rice (1974) examined the profiles of groups of visually impaired and sighted children on the Illinois Test of Psycholinguistic Abilities (ITPA). The visually impaired children all had better than light perception, and they were matched by a group of sighted children on the basis of age, verbal IQ, sex, and ethnic group. The age range was 6.5 to 10 years. As expected, the visually impaired group showed worse performance than the sighted group on the visual scales, but there was no difference between the subgroups of visually impaired subjects divided on the basis of severity of handicap. The highest subscale score for the visually impaired group was auditory memory. It should also be noted, though, that the sighted group also showed quite a high score on auditory memory and was apparently not significantly lower than the visually impaired group on that scale. Stankov and Spilsbury (1980), on the other hand, did find 10–15-year-old blind children to be better than their sighted counterparts on a test of letter span with auditory presentation.

There has been surprisingly little work on the effectiveness of auditory localization in blind children. Hayes (1935) reported that Sargent conducted a study using blind subjects ranging in age from 10 to 35 years, median age 16. Localization performance showed an overall pattern of superiority of the blind, which was discussed in the context of the greater experiential demands on the blind for auditory localization skills. Two problems with Hayes' conclusion should be noted. First, statistics were not reported, and although the data needed to conduct analyses are not presented in the report, the within-group variability at the various target positions suggests that such tests would not show significant differences. Second, the response that was required involved the use of a spatial-representational numbering system similar to the numbers on a clock. It is not possible to conclude that any differences that may have been present in the data were attributable to auditory localization rather than to the ability to use the response system adequately. It is, therefore, not possible to make any firm conclusions about the relative auditory localization abilities of blind and sighted subjects from the study as reported.

Worchel, Mauney, and Andrew (1950) reported what seems to be the only study of the obstacle sense in children. The age range was eight to 23 years, mean age 14.8. The subjects were all totally blind and had become blind at ages ranging from birth to 11 years. The subjects were tested out of doors on their ability to detect, avoid collisions with, and approach as closely as possible a masonite board about four by five feet. Substantial individual differences were found, although 27 of the 34 subjects were judged, on the basis of the combined criteria, to have the obstacle sense. Unfortunately, no information was provided about the covariation of the accuracy of the obstacle sense with such significant variables as age or age at onset of blindness. However, the conclusion that the obstacle sense is present before adulthood seems quite reasonable.

Speigelman (1976) reported a study in which he compared the auditory localization performance of early and later blind and sighted children. Mean ages for the groups ranged from 13.6 to 15.2. The early blind group were all RLF children, while 12 of the 18 later blind were retinoblastoma victims. The late blind and sighted groups had mean IQ scores significantly higher than the RLF group, whose mean was 100. The task involved presenting an auditory target (1 sec, varying frequency, 50 db) at one of 12 locations surrounding the subject. Results from both fixed-head and free-head conditions showed no difference between the sighted and RLF groups, while the later blind group was significantly superior. Spiegelman discussed the results in the terms of a visual framework underlying auditory localization that is built up in the early years. Such a framework would allow better localization of auditory stimuli in the later blind. But sighted subjects should also have such a framework available, and therefore, their poor performance was perplexing. A possible reason for such performance was discussed earlier—the blindfolded, sighted subject is one who has just lost the use of an information system on which he has come to depend heavily. Spiegelman provided a related suggestion, that the sighted subjects were not as used to having to pay attention to auditory cues as the blind were.

Although Rice (1970) studied adults in his work on echolocation, the work should be mentioned here because of the difference between his results and those of Spiegelman. Rice's early blind subjects (visual loss before six months) showed better echolocation performance than those who became blind after the age of three. Similar results were found by Juurmaa and Jarvilehto (1965), who reported that the adequacy of obstacle perception is negatively correlated with age at blinding in adults. Rice (1976) discussed several possible reasons for the apparent discrepancies between his and Spiegelman's results. The auditory localization tasks were not identical, but there seems to be no task-related reason to expect a difference, and both sets of results were quite strong. Rice pointed out that early blind people may show a distinct bimodal distribution in mobility and perceptual skills, and that the criteria for being accepted as a subject in his research would tend to select the more mobile type of person. Also, Rice's subjects were adults while Spiegelman studied children, a difference creating variation in length of blind experience. This factor may be important in relatively simple spatial behaviors (Warren et al., 1973). Still another possibility is that with development, the congenitally blind become better at auditory localization at a faster rate than the other groups. Gomulicki (1961) found sighted five-year-olds to be significantly better than congenitally blind children, but by age 16 the groups performed at an equivalent level.

In any case, there is clearly a need for comprehensive and careful work on auditory localization abilities of blind children. Particular attention should be paid to subject characteristics such as length of blind experience and age at onset of blindness. Effort should also be directed to evaluating the effectiveness of possible methods for training auditory localization.

Simpkins (1971) reported the results of a training program for the identification of sounds. Children from kindergarten through third grade were included in the study. An auditory test was administered to a sample before, and to another sample after, the six-week training program. The test included predominantly language-related terms, although there were a few "environmental sounds" such as a woman walking in the hallway. The details of the training program were not specified, although there were apparently various activities suggested by teachers and culled from the literature. The specific content of the training program was varied to fit each child's particular needs. Comparison of posttest and pretest performance indicated a clear improvement in the ability to identify environmental sounds, but the improvement in language sounds was not statistically significant. It is difficult to assess the precise meaning of this pattern of results, since it is not clear from the report whether the training program may have included work with some of the specific items in either the language or the environmental sound test. Presumably the test items would not have been intentionally avoided during the training, and it may be that the concreteness of the environmental sounds, as well as their smaller number, helped to produce the greater improvement. It is unfortunate that the statistical analyses did not allow assessment of age-related results, since substantial differences might be expected across the age range involved in the study. However, this point does not detract from the promise implicit in the results of the training study, that the identification of environmental sounds which are critical in the orientation of the blind child may be improved by training intervention.

Pitman (1965) provided a brief review of the previous work that had been done on the musical abilities of blind and sighted children. Pitman concluded that there is little evidence that blind children have better musical abilities, although there are some reports of selected areas of superiority of the blind. For example, Fladeland (1930) reported superior musical appreciation in blind children. In his own research, Pitman used the Wing Test of Musical Intelligence with groups of blind and sighted children. The blind subjects ranged in age from eight to 11, but no specification of visual characteristics was given except that the group was "fairly representative." The overall test score for the blind groups was somewhat greater than that of the sighted groups, although the pattern of results was mixed. Specifically, the blind were better on subscores representing the estimation of the number of notes in a chord and detecting the direction of change of one note on the second playing of a chord. The sighted were somewhat more consistent at expressing a preference for a certain phrasing when a tune was played twice. Another interesting finding was that there was significantly more variability within the blind group than the sighted, suggesting that "any musical potential possessed by a blind child is more likely to be developed than in the case of an equally gifted sighted child" (p. 77). Simply for perspective, it should be noted that some other authors (e.g., Elonen & Zwarensteyn, 1964) have suggested that a very outstanding musical (or other) ability may mean that less than adequate attention has been paid to the development of the child's other abilities.

There apparently has been no systematic research comparing the vestibular senses of blind and sighted children. Leonard (1969) reported a study on balancing abilities of adolescents; this study will be discussed later in this chapter. There are a number of tasks that have been used with blind children in which vestibular functioning may play a part, but vestibular function has not been analyzed separately. For example, in a locomotor task requiring the subject to reproduce a given extent of turn, vestibular sensitivity may be involved. Kohler (1966) discussed some interesting preliminary work on electrical stimulation of the vestibular system that may have implications for the trained avoidance of veer.

Research on the smell and taste discrimination of blind children has apparently not been reported.

Given the importance of auditory sources as substitutes for visual, particularly in the acquisition of textual material, interest in the possibilities for accelerated presentation of auditory textual material to the blind is natural. Some research has been reported, although not as much as might be expected given the importance of the issue. Programs to provide blind persons with records and tape recordings (e.g., Talking Books) are well known. The rate of presentation of such material is about 175 wpm, or about twice the speed of very efficient braille reading. This speed, which is restricted by the speaking rate of the narrator, apparently does not tap the potential comprehension rate of listeners. Playing the recording at a faster speed than its recorded speed increases word rate, but the increased speed is accompanied by changes in pitch and voice quality that are unpleasant to most listeners. An alternative procedure is speech compression. Speech is tape recorded, and very short, randomly selected segments are then excised from the recording. The potential usefulness of compressed speech depends on the comprehensibility of the material so delivered. Foulke, Amster, Nolan, and Bixler (1962) tested blind sixth- to eighth-grade braille readers, who had no previous experience with compressed speech, at 175, 225, 275, and 325 wpm. Comprehension for the 175 and 225 wpm rates did not differ from that for braille, but comprehension began to drop off at 275 wpm for some material. (The braille reading rates for these subjects ranged from 57 to 70 wpm.) Gore (1969) compared the comprehension and one-week recall of material presented at 175 wpm (the normal recording rate) with that for 270 wpm accelerated and 270 wpm compressed speech. Comprehension and recall did not differ for normal and compressed speech, but the accelerated speech produced worse performance on both measures.

Myers (1978) used speech compression rates of 180, 220, 262, and 302 wpm, comparing the performance of braille and large-print readers at the high school level. A learning efficiency index was used, representing the amount of time (spent in relistening to the recordings) needed to reach 100-percent correct comprehension scores. An immediate test was followed by a test for recall conducted 24 hours later. The two faster rates of speech showed higher learning efficiency scores than the two slower rates: that is, the material was initially learned to a 100 percent criterion more quickly with the faster presentation rates. The 24-hour recall test produced no differences in comprehension as a function of presentation rate: thus the initial efficiencies produced by the faster presentation rates did not erode over time. There was not a significant relationship between IQ and either initial learning efficiency or 24-hour recall.

On a related topic, Rhyne (1982) reported a study of practice effects with four 11- to 13-year-old braille readers on comprehension of synthetic speech as presented by the Kurzweil Reading Machine. Each child listened to four recordings per day over 10 days, and periodic comprehension tests were administered. The results showed increasing comprehension scores with practice.

Much research remains to be done with the emerging electronic devices for the presentation of auditory textual material, and the positive outcomes of preliminary research over the past decade or two should serve as valuable incentives for the conduct of such work.

Residual Vision

During the past few years there has been increased attention to the desirability and feasibility of enhancing the use of any residual vision among visually impaired children. Although it is not a new attitude, it contrasts with the stance which has been expressed in past times, that visually impaired children should be kept from attempting to use any remaining visual capacity.

The term "visual efficiency" refers to the effectiveness with which any remaining visual function is actually used. The thrust of Barraga's (1964) approach has been (a) to assess the upper limits of the child's visual function, and then (b) to provide training and experience so as to maximize the use of that remaining function. The intent, thus, is not to increase the child's visual acuity (which is set by physiological factors in any case), but to increase the efficiency of visual functioning within any physiological limits.

In her early work, Barraga (1964) administered a two-month training program to a group of six- to 13-year-old children whose vision ranged from not less than object perception to not greater than 6/200 in either eye. All were visually impaired since birth and none had additional handicaps. The daily lessons were designed "to evoke maximum proficiency in attention to communication and interpretation of visual observations" (p. 85). As expected, pre- to post-training acuity measures did not show a significant improvement, but the scores of the training group on the Visual Discrimination Test (designed by Barraga) showed a highly significant improvement. The strong implication of the work is that visual attention can be trained in children with some residual vision. That is, with appropriate training strategies, low vision children can be made to utilize their available visual capabilities to a greater degree than they might spontaneously.

The Visual Discrimination Test (Barraga, 1964) was subsequently modified and published as the Visual Efficiency Scale (Barraga, 1970). Harley, Spollen, and Long (1973) assessed the reliability and construct validity of the scale for a group of sighted children ranging in age from four to 6.5, and Harley and Spollen (1973) made a similar study of the scale on a group of low vision (maximum acuity 6/200) children ranging in age from six to 14 years. The results were similar: reliability was reasonable (0.78 and 0.86 for the two studies, respectively), and the construct validity was good, although about a third of the items were not discriminatory.

Subsequently, a Diagnostic Assessment Procedure (DAP) has been developed, based on the Visual Efficiency Scale: development of and rationale for the DAP is described in a series of articles by Barraga and her colleagues (Barraga, Collins, & Hollis, 1977; Barraga & Collins, 1979; Collins & Barraga, 1980). The DAP is the diagnostic part of the larger Program to Develop Efficiency in Visual Functioning, and a great deal of dissemination and training work has been done with professionals in the field using the program.

Berla', Rankin, and Willis (1980) conducted a psychometric evaluation of DAP, using a sample of 112 legally blind persons ranging in age from five to 20. The sample was selected so as to be roughly representative of the population of visually impaired children, except that of course totally blind individuals were excluded from the study sample. The DAP was evaluated with respect to its content validity, its reliability, and the hierarchical structure of the eight categories on the test. Berla' et al. concluded that the content validity of the DAP is very good, noting that it was developed on the basis of an exhaustive review of the literature and with the advice of many professional consultants with extensive experience in the field of visual impairment. Reliability was assessed both from internal consistency measures and from test-retest correlations, and was extremely high on both types of measures (the test-retest correlation, for example, was .96, with a two-to-three-week interval between tests). There was considerable evidence for hierarchical ordering of the categories of the test, although factor analysis showed a single factor that subsumed fully 91 percent of the variance. That the hierarchy of categories was not a rigid one was further demonstrated by the ability of children to perform items at one level even though they had not been fully successful at earlier levels. All in all, Berla' et al. (1980) concluded that the DAP is a very useful and important diagnostic instrument.

The emphasis on the effective use of any visual function for visually impaired children is a welcome and important development in the area in the past two decades. As Barraga (1976) and others have noted, it is only a relatively small proportion of the legally blind population that is totally blind, and the role of residual vision for the education, in particular, of visually impaired children deserves concentrated attention. The implications of residual vision and visual efficiency go well beyond the purely educational, though. In virtually every area of development, it may be documented that the child with some residual visual function is at least *potentially* at an advantage over the totally blind child. Realizing the potential, though, requires concentrated attention on the effective role that vision can play in development in all areas, from perceptual-motor to personality. Effective exploitation of this area is clearly one of the tasks of the next decade for researchers, teachers, and other professionals in the visual impairment area, not to mention parents!

The reader is referred to Barraga (1976) for a full discussion of partial vision.

Spatial Relations

There has been a great deal of speculation about the nature of the spatial world of the blind—in fact, there is more speculation than useful research. It is not my intent to review the speculation, but by way of introduction to the spatial relations section, it may be useful to mention some of the more important issues involved.

Implicitly, the spatial relations issue with the blind centers around the question of the role that vision plays in the conceptualization and use of space by sighted people, and of the comparative nature of space when vision is absent. If vision does play an important role in spatial relations for the sighted person, then to what extent can the remaining modalities substitute for, or get along without, vision in the blind?

Révész (1950) provided some perspective on the complexity of this issue by noting that various theorists have interpreted the visual restoration phenomena (people regaining vision upon operative repair of the eye) in completely opposite ways:

> The fact that many people born blind were unable, after being operated on, to recognize well-known objects visually or distinguish forms or make correct statements on differences in size and distance led a number of research workers to the conclusion that spatiality is but secondarily transferred to the visual impressions. It is characteristic of the empirical basis of this theory that on the same grounds other authors were induced to put forward the diametrically opposite view. They interpreted the findings in a different way and denied the spatial character of the tactile

> impressions and assumed that the spatiality, especially the three-dimensionality of our spatial perceptions, entered our tactile impressions only through our visual perceptions (p. 10).

Révész suggested a third alternative, that there are normally

> two sensory spaces independent of one another: an autonomous haptic sensory space and an autonomous optic space. The lack of orientation in the visual space experienced by blind persons following operations, their failure to recognize objects, forms, and distances, was explained by assuming that following removal of the cataract a new world of space is opened up to the blind, a world of space which they first have to conquer, just as in infancy they had gradually conquered the tactile space (p. 11).

Of course, Révész was referring to people blind from birth, and consideration of the effects of a period of early vision followed by blindness introduces still more complexity into the issue. Critchley (1952) emphasized the role that a period of early vision may play in establishment of visual imagery. He argued that the spatial world of the blind is effectively smaller than that of the sighted person, since vision conveys information about distance and height. On the other hand, tactual space may be more elaborate in the blind since touch is an effective source of information about the solid properties of small objects. An extensive review of the role of early vision in spatial relations and spatial behavior was provided by Warren, Anooshian, and Bollinger (1973), and certain issues about the duration of early vision were further discussed by Warren (1974). It suffices here to say that much of the evidence supports that notion that a period of early vision may provide an integrative basis for spatial relations that endures even after vision is lost, providing the later blind person with substantial advantage over the person blind from birth.

The issue of the existence of an auditory space has also received some attention. A useful discussion of the questions involved is provided by von Fieandt (1966), who concluded that "it appears reasonable to assume that all discernable sounds are referred to the visual-tactual system of coordinates" (p. 282). Rogow (1975), expressing a somewhat different viewpoint, argues that the spatial orientation of the blind must be understood in terms of the tactile and auditory properties of space, not its visual representation, and that neither the tactile nor the auditory sense becomes spatially dominant for the blind person to the same degree that vision does for the blind.

The spatial relations literature is difficult to organize, since several apparently quite different types of performance have been studied extensively under the name spatial relations. Studies of the maze-learning abilities of blind and sighted subjects have a long history. Carr (1921) cited data of Koch from three blind subjects tested in a stylus maze. One subject who had some residual vision performed similarly to sighted subjects, while two who had been totally blind from birth were much worse than the sighted both in number of errors and in time to acquisition. Knotts and Miles (1929) studied subjects ranging in age from 10 to 22. Two maze types were used, a stylus maze and a raised-finger maze. Since the blind group was extremely heterogeneous with respect to age of onset and extent of blindness, three subgroups were formed for the purpose of analysis: no detail vision later than the fourth year, blindness as a result of accident or illness after the fifth year, and partially blind since birth. The first two groups are of special interest as representing early and late blindness. Although the numbers of subjects precluded meaningful statistical analysis, the performance was clearly better by the later blind. On the finger maze, which Knotts and Miles argued is a better test for the blind than a stylus maze, only one of the nine later blind subjects performed worse than the mean or median of the early blind groups.

Knotts and Miles did not analyze for the effect of length of blindness on maze performance, but the data allow retrospective assessment of this effect. Three performance measures were reported: trials to criterion, number of errors, and time. For the stylus maze, length of blindness did not correlate significantly with any of the three measures. For the finger maze, however, all three measures were significantly correlated with length of blindness in a direction suggesting that the longer the subject had been blind, the worse was his performance.

Merry and Merry (1934) attempted to assess the suitability of the Knotts and Miles maze as a supplementary test of intelligence for blind children. The children ranged in age from eight to 16 and were totally blind. Most had been blind before the age of five, and more than half were blind within the first year. IQ ranged from 81 to 146, but the method of assessment was not specified. Measures were taken of trials to criterion, errors, total time, and the average time per trial. The first three measures were correlated about 0.50 with both CA and MA. The correlations with MA were consistently a few points higher than those with CA, although the authors' implication that the MA correlations were significantly higher is probably unwarranted. Interestingly, and in contrast to the results of several other studies, the correlation between the performance measures and the age at blinding was close to zero.

Berg and Worchel (1956) studied children who ranged somewhat younger (seven to 21 years) than those of Knotts and Miles. The blind sample included 17 congenitally blind children, who tended to be the younger subjects, and 11 subjects who became blind at ages ranging from one to 12. Normal and deaf groups were also studied. Two types of maze were used, a right-angle maze and an X-maze, which was a series of end-to-end diamonds where the subject had to learn which side of each of a series of diamonds was not blocked. The X-maze was thought to require a verbal solution (remembering a series of right or left decisions), while the right-angle maze was thought to require a visual or motor solution. For the right-angle maze, the blind and sighted groups did not differ significantly on either trials to criterion or error measures, although the means for the sighted group indicated somewhat better performance. For the X-maze, the sighted were significantly better than the blind on both error and trials to criterion measures. Within the blind group, comparison of congenitals (five of the youngest children were excluded in order to equate CA) with later blind subjects showed a significant superiority of the later blind group on only the X-maze. Unfortunately, no results were reported about any possible relationship between age and maze performance for any of the groups. Berg and Worchel concluded that the visualization that is available to sighted subjects aided their performance. It is not clear why visualization should have aided only in the X-maze. In fact, it seems reasonable to expect that the groups would not differ in performance on a maze whose solution is amenable to verbal mediation. If the right-angle maze has a visual component, the sighted should show better performance.

Gomulicki (1961) studied congenitally blind and sighted children over the five- to 16-year age range. Both tactual and ambulatory mazes were used, and Gomulicki was concerned not only with the comparative performance levels of the blind and sighted children, but also with the possibility of positive transfer from learning one type of maze to learning the other type. Both groups performed better on the tactual maze as a result of prior experience on the ambulatory maze, but neither group showed the reverse transfer. The younger sighted subjects performed better than the blind on both types of maze, but by age 15, the performance of the blind was equivalent to that of the sighted subjects. The equivalence of the older congenitally blind and sighted groups is in contrast to the results of numerous other studies, and the reason for the discrepancy is not evident. It may be that the congenitally blind were truly improving with age relative to the sighted, but it is also a possibility that the older sighted subjects were relatively more disadvantged by the blindfolding procedure than the younger sighted subjects, and thus the older sighted subjects were not performing near their optimal level.

Simply for the sake of completeness, a study by Bottrill (1968) may be mentioned in this section. The maze was a U-maze, apparently similar to the right-angle mazes used by Berg and Worchel and others. No differences were found between blind and sighted groups. The results are open to question, however, since the blind group included one subgroup of mean age 12.6 and another subgroup of mean age 34.1, while the sighted group was homogeneous with respect to CA, mean age 20.7.

An overview of the relationship between blindness factors and maze learning performance indicates that where age at onset of blindness effects are found, they are in favor of the later blind subjects. Warren et al. (1973) discussed these effects in terms of a residual visual frame of reference that may be available to subjects who experienced a period of early vision. Effects of the length of blind experience have not typically been reported in these studies, with the exception of the work by Knotts and Miles (1929). Subjects who had been blind for long periods of time performed worse on the finger maze, but not on the stylus maze, than subjects who had been blind for shorter periods.

Warren et al. (1973) suggested that where both duration of early vision and duration of blind experience factors are involved, the effect of duration of early vision is stronger and supersedes any advantage that might otherwise be enjoyed by subjects who have been blind longer and therefore have had more blind experience.

Several block arrangement and pattern reconstruction tasks have been used with blind children to assess spatial relations abilities. Drever (1955) used a pegboard task in which he guided the subject's fingers over three or four pegs that were arranged to form a pattern, and then asked the subject to reconstruct the pattern with the board rotated. Drever's blind subjects had LP or less, included both "early" (defined as blind by the age of four) and later blind, (and ranged in age from 12 to 20. The blind group as a whole was better than the sighted group on the pattern reconstruction task. Subdivision of the blind group, however, showed that the early blind were not different from the sighted, while the later blind were much better. No significant relation was found between test performance and CA or IQ. A second task used by Drever was designed to evaluate the dimensions of tactual experience that were most salient to the blind and sighted subjects. Small groups of peg patterns were designed to vary in number and shape, as well as in other attributes such as symmetry. A set of three patterns was presented tactually, and the subject was asked to judge which two were alike, and what the basis for judgment was. The blind subjects reported judgments on the basis of shape significantly more often, and judgments on the basis of counting pegs less often, than the sighted subjects. There was no difference attributable to age at onset of blindness. In a subsequent experiment, the details of which were not reported, a group of sighted subjects performed a similar task using visual stimuli. They used shape more than number. The overall pattern of results was thus interesting: the tactual performance of the blind was more similar to the visual performance of the sighted than was the tactual performance of the sighted. These results are somewhat reminiscent of the study by Pick et al. (1966), in which the tactual orientation judgments of sighted subjects did not show consistency, while the tactual judgments of a group of partially sighted children showed a consistency similar to that of the sighted subjects' visual judgments.

Hunter (1964) used a task that was similar to Drever's first task. Subjects were sighted and totally congenitally blind ranging in age from 12 to 18 years. The task involved having the subject explore tactually the positioning of a set of eight objects on a display, then reproduce the same pattern on another display. No data or statistical tests appeared in the text, but Hunter concluded that the blind were not as good as the sighted on this task, in that the blind took more time and were less certain about the adequacy of their performance. Whether they made more errors is not reported. The conclusions of Hunter thus appear to contradict those of Drever, who found that the early blind group performed as well as the sighted. The discrepancy may be attributable to the very late cutoff for "early blindness" in Drever's sample. That is, the performance of Drever's early blind group may have been elevated by the inclusion of subjects who had had three or four years of visual experience. If the results for the subjects blind from birth had been assessed, they might have been worse than those of the sighted subjects, and the results would be congruent with those of Hunter. This example may be used to illustrate the need for analyzing visual characteristics in as much detail as is possible. For example, age at onset of blindness should be treated as a continuous variable whenever possible. If there is a range of age-of-onset, the subjects should not simply be dichotomized into groups. Rather, correlations of task performance with age at onset should be conducted. In the absence of adequately detailed treatment, one can only speculate about the apparent discrepancies between two studies such as those of Drever and Hunter.

Simpkins and Siegel (1979) reported a study that is nicely illustrative of some of the differences between visually impaired and sighted children in their ability to handle spatial relations concepts. The subjects were 30 6- to 11-year-olds with LP or less. The experimental materials were a rectangular and a circular board, with two barns that could be used as reference markers for the construction of a fence, using eight fenceposts. The task was simply to build a fence in a straight line, between the two barns. The barns were either set at the corners of the rectangular board, or set such that a fence connecting them would parallel a side of the board. With the circular board, the barns were placed such that the correct fence would be horizontal, vertical, or diagonal with respect to the child's location. In such tasks, sighted children show a regular developmental progression from reliance on an egocentric frame of reference to the ability to use appropriate external frames such as the edges of the board. Sighted children also tend to show difficulty dealing with diagonals even after they perform the rectilinear task well (Larendau & Pinard, 1970). Although Simpkins and Siegel (1979) found a general age progression with their visually impaired sample, age was not a good predictor of a child's performance. The strategies used did not generally suggest that the child was using an external frame of reference, although sometimes a child would trace a line with his finger between the two barns before beginning construction of the fence. More often the construction indicated awareness of relationships between neighboring posts, but not an overall concept. Interestingly, in contrast to sighted children, the blind did not have greater difficulty with the oblique directions. Simpkins and Siegel concluded that "the developmental stages for the blind subjects did not parallel those produced by the sighted sample [of Larendau & Pinard]" (p. 238). The developmental progression in this area is worthy of additional study, although as Millar (1981a, 1982) points out, the issue is far more complicated than simply a progression from internal to external frames of reference.

Although performance tests of IQ will be discussed more fully in Chapter 4, several studies should be mentioned here that have compared the performance of blind and sighted children on these tasks. Wattron (1956) designed a block test to be used as an indicator of performance IQ. Three sides of wood blocks were finished with various textures easily discriminable by touch: one was smooth, one somewhat knurled, and one heavily knurled. Various designs were to be created using the textures in a way parallel to the use of color in the Kohs Block Design Test used with sighted children. Wattron compared the performance of totally blind children with a group of sighted controls, aged seven to 17. The blind children were blind from birth or before the age of three. Although the results were marginally in favor of the blind, there were no significant differences between blind and sighted. There was, however, some tendency for the younger blind children to perform more poorly than the younger sighted children, while the older blind performed somewhat better than the older sighted. Both blind and sighted groups presumably showed improvement with CA, although the data were not reported. For the blind group, correlations between two measures of block test performance and MA as assessed by the Interim Hayes-Binet were highly significant.

In a study cited earlier, Witkin et al. (1968) compared congenitally blind children with a sighted sample aged 12 to 19 years on a variety of tasks. The tactile block design task was similar to that used by Wattron, in that the subject had to recreate a design by the placement of a set of blocks differing in texture. Although the results suggested the superiority of the sighted group, the difference was not significant. Following the suggestion in the discussion of the Hunter and Drever studies, later blind subjects might be expected to perform better than the congenitally blind, and perhaps also better than sighted controls.

Bitterman and Worchel (1953) compared blind with sighted adolescents (age range nine to 24 years) on judgments of horizontal and vertical. The blind subjects were students at a school for the blind and were all totally blind since birth. Two variations of the task were used. In one, the subject stood up and adjusted a rod to horizontal or vertical, and in the other, he was tilted 42° from the vertical and again made the horizontal and vertical settings. There were no significant differences between blind and sighted in either condition. In another analysis using a combination of both right-tilt and left-tilt settings, the blind were found to perform significantly better than the sighted subjects. The authors attributed the deficit by the sighted as evidence of their being at a greater disadvantage in having vision excluded, rather than as a true superiority of the blind. Presumably, then, the sighted subjects would improve with practice to a level equal to that of the blind. No analysis of the relationship of performance to age was reported.

Using a somewhat different approach to the perception of the upright, Gipsman (1979) compared blind and partially sighted with blindfolded sighted children in the ability to adjust themselves to an upright position in a stabilimeter chair. There were modest improvements with age over the eight- to 14-year range, but there were no notable differences as a function of visual status.

Crossmodal Functions

As O'Connor and Hermelin (1971) pointed out, the term crossmodal is used generally to refer to several situations, including ones where the subject experiences an event in one modality and then tries to identify a corresponding event in another modality, and where he learns a principle using information obtained via one modality and then attempts to apply the principle to a problem in another modality. Although there has been a great deal of research done with sighted children on their ability to perform tasks requiring various crossmodal comparisons, there has been little such work done with blind children. Much of the crossmodal work with sighted children has involved vision and another modality, and so it is not surprising that there is less work with the blind. In view of the possibility that vision serves an integrative function with respect to the other modalities (Warren, 1974), however, it is important to ask whether, for example, the relationship between proprioception-kinesthesis and audition is the same for blind children as it is for sighted children.

Warren and Pick (1970) examined the resolution of a spatial conflict created by the presentation of discrepant auditory and proprioceptive information. The subject placed his finger on a small speaker which emitted a clicking sound. The source of the sound was displaced laterally by means of "pseudophones." The subject was asked to point with his other hand to where he felt his finger to be, or to where he heard the sound to be. The age trends for groups of sighted second and sixth graders and adults were compared with the age trends for three groups of blind children. The blind subjects represented a continuous age range but were divided in three groups, with mean ages of 8.3, 13.6, and 17.8, for purposes of comparison with the sighted groups. For the sighted subjects, the ability to ignore discrepant proprioceptive information in responding to auditory information improved significantly with age. At the same time, the ability to ignore discrepant auditory information showed a tendency to lessen with age. That is, auditory information became more important with age, both in being less biased by proprioception and in exerting more influence on proprioception. For the blind sample, there were no significant age trends. A further analysis included only those subjects who had been blind from birth. The subjects with LP or better showed an age trend similar to that of the sighted subjects, while the totally blind group showed no age trend at all. The results were discussed in the context of the possibility that the existence of even a small visual capability may provide an organizational framework within which information from the other "spatial modalities" may be interpreted. However, the specific way in which such an organizational function might operate was not discussed in detail.

McKinney (1964) conducted a study which bears further on the possibility that blindfolded sighted children interpret tactual information within a visual frame of reference while congenitally blind children do not. The subjects ranged in age from four to eight years. One of the subject's fingers was touched, and the hand was then either left alone, turned over 180°, or turned 180° and then turned back to its original position. When asked to identify the finger that had been touched, the sighted subjects made the most errors in the second condition, while the errors of the blind subjects increased steadily with the numbers of turns of the hand. McKinney interpreted the pattern of results to indicate that the sighted subjects had a "visual schema" of the hand that was effective in mediating performance whenever the hand was in its original stimulated position. The blind subjects, with no such visual representation, became progressively worse with increasing intervening movements of the hand.

Hermelin and O'Connor have reported several experiments designed to examine the encoding of spatial and temporal information by blind and sighted children. Their work is summarized in O'Connor and Hermelin (1978). In an experiment on spatial coding (Hermelin & O'Connor, 1971), they studied a group of blind and two groups of sighted subjects, one that performed with vision and one that was blindfolded. The age range was from six to 14, and the blind subjects were all congenitally blind or had become blind within the first year. Four of the 10 blind subjects had some LP. During a training session, the subject learned four words, one corresponding to each of his fingers in a spatial location. The situation was designed to be ambiguous, in that the subject was not instructed whether the word was to be associated with the finger or with the spatial location. The testing session was designed to evaluate which association had in fact been made. The blindfolded sighted children and the blind children made finger responses about 75 percent of the time. The unblindfolded sighted children, however, made about 60 percent responses to external spatial location. In discussing the location responses made by the blind children, Hermelin and O'Connor implied that, in contrast to the group picture, some of the congenitally blind children had made primarily location responses. They suggested that response to spatial location is not dependent on the ability to visualize. Rather, "It is conceivable that spatial representations were constructed on the basis of kinesthetic and motor cues, such as distance from the body and amount and direction of movements required" (p. 131).

The notion that blind children tend to use body cues as referents for spatial tasks received further support from Hermelin and O'Connor (1975). Ten- to 15-year-old children who had been blind from birth or the first few months were compared with sighted children of comparable age, performing blindfolded, on tasks involving the reproduction of spatial movements and the end-locations of those movements. Three kinds of task were used: reproduction, in which the child simply had to reproduce a vertical hand movement from a set starting point to a set end point; location, in which the child had to replicate the end point of a movement starting from a different distance; and distance, in which the child had to repeat a movement of a given distance from a different starting point. The blind and blindfolded sighted children were equivalent in their ability to perform the reproduction and locations tasks: note that in both of these tasks the end point of the replication movement was at the same location in space as in the original movement, and therefore the movement could be correctly done simply by coding a single point in space with respect to the body—no processing of the more complex distance information was required. In the distance tasks, though, the sighted performed better as the distance increased. Here, there are no spatially invariant locations and thus it is not possible to perform the task based on a simple kinesthetically mediated location. The deteriorating performance of the blind when spatial relativity was involved suggests that a visual basis is important for this type of task.

The question of the blind child's use of external spatial referents was further studied by Millar (1979). The subjects included both congenitally totally blind children and children who had some early visual experience or who had some residual, though low level, visual capability. The age range was from five to 15 years. In a first experiment, the child was presented with two boards, both square in one task and both diamond-shaped (therefore without orthogonal axes) in another, and was asked to transfer a set of objects from their locations on one board to the corresponding location (corner) on the other board. Millar hypothesized that when vertical movements were involved, they could be self- (i.e., body-) referenced movements, whereas horizontal movements would have to be externally referenced, and that therefore the vertical would be equally well done by both subgroups of subjects but the horizontal would be better done by those with some visual history. Further, the subgroup with some visual history should perform better with the square board backgrounds because of their orthogonality than with the diamonds, whereas for those without visual experience the shape of the board should make no difference. These hypotheses were generally born out by the results: external reference was important for those with visual experience, and self-reference was used by those with no visual history. Blindfolded sighted subjects in another experiment corroborated these conclusions. In another experiment with the blind children, the attempt was made to enhance the use of the background board cues by introducing a raised vertical line on the board. This had no effect for the subjects with no visual history, but it tended to enhance the background referent for those with visual experience. Millar concluded that the subjects with and without visual experience were using entirely different approaches to the tasks—it was not a matter of the congenitally and totally blind subjects showing a developmental lag, but rather a matter of their entire failure to realize that external cues were available or potentially valuable in performing the task.

In a related study, Millar (1981b) separated the issue of movement reference from self-reference, demonstrating that these are different modes of processing spatial information. The blind subjects had at most LP and ranged in age from six to 14. The task made use of a rotatable display, such that particular response characteristics could be inferred as resulting from primarily coding of movement sequences as opposed to the location of self-reference. The blind subjects, regardless of age, used primarily a self-referent approach.

Millar concludes that this approach is perfectly reasonable for them: "Blind children thus have little reason to believe that external relations can serve as useful references. By contrast, coding relative to the body provides consistent feedback in many blind tasks" (p. 263).

This theme is developed in a more theoretical vein by Millar (1981a, 1982). She argued persuasively that there is nothing inherently different in the information processing capabilities of the blind and the sighted, but rather that *preferred strategies* develop as a result of the typical ways that subjects gain their primary spatial information. "If blindness leads subjects to neglect external cues, they will learn less, and know less about directional connections between external cues. This, in turn, strengthens the preference for strategies derived from the remaining modalities" (Millar, 1982, p. 119). The strategies actually chosen for spatial (and presumably other) information processing tasks are not necessarily the most optimal ones: a visualization strategy may not be optimal for a given task, but the sighted child may use it nonetheless, because of the effectiveness of visualization in many of his prior experiences. Similarly, the blind child may have external spatial referential strategies available, but tend not to use them because the *primary* source of spatial information—touch—tends to elicit internally referenced strategies. The implications of this formulation for practice seem clear: In order to make available to the child the widest range of effective strategies of spatial information processing, he or she must be brought to dissociate strategies from modes of experience and their natural constraints. Tactual experience, for example, must be structured in such a way as to lend itself easily to external reference systems, so that those systems become flexibly available to the child, along with the internal ones.

In a study quite similar in rationale to that of Hermelin and O'Connor (1971), O'Connor and Hermelin (1972a) studied the perception of temporal and spatial auditory stimuli. They presented sequences of three spoken digits via an array of three spatially separated speakers. The digit orders were designed in such a way that when asked for the "middle" digit, the subject would have to choose between the digit that had occurred at the spatially middle speaker and the digit that had occurred in the temporal middle of the sequence. The average age of the 10 blind subjects was about 13 years. Presumably they were totally blind, although details of visual condition were not reported. The performance of the blind and sighted groups did not differ—both showed strong choice of the temporally middle digit rather than the spatially middle one. Another group of sighted children was tested on a similar task involving visual, rather than auditory signals. With sequences of visually presented digits, the subjects showed an overwhelming choice of the spatially middle digit.

O'Connor and Hermelin concluded that for sighted children, there is a close relation between the nature of the stimulus material and the manner of response. The auditory modality is more suited to temporally presented material, while the visual modality is more appropriate for spatially presented information. The input modality "triggers" either a temporal or a spatial organization of the stimulus material. This formulation carries the implication that totally blind children are at a disadvantage in dealing with spatial information because the spatial mode of organization cannot be triggered appropriately. Such a simple conclusion may not be warranted, however. Some of the congenitally blind children in the Hermelin and O'Connor (1971) study apparently did encode location into a spatial framework. It may be that the manner of coding information is determined both by stimulus type and by subject characteristics that may be modifiable. Freides (1974) has provided an extensive and insightful discussion of the concept of modality-appropriateness and its implications for various perceptual handicaps.

Battacchi, Franza, and Pani (1981) reported an interesting variation on the spatial/temporal correspondence paradigm, using as subjects eight- to 10-year-old sighted, blindfolded sighted, partially sighted, and congenitally totally blind children. Six loudspeakers were arranged in a semicircle around the subject, separated by at least 25 degrees and therefore highly spatially discriminable. On any given trial, a sequence of six names was presented, one through each speaker, at a rate of one per second. In the congruent condition the sequence started at one end and proceeded regularly to the other end of the set of speakers, while in the incongruent condition the names occurred in a randomly distributed order over the speakers. After the presentation, the child was asked for the names that had come from two of the speakers (the two were chosen at random by the experimenter). The partially and totally blind groups, as well as the blindfolded sighted group, performed essentially at chance on both congruent and incongruent tasks, while the sighted group performing with vision performed better, and did the congruent task better than the incongruent. With a less stringent criterion for success, the blindfolded sighted subjects performed better than the visually impaired groups. Thus the spatial order that was present in the congruent task proved to be an advantage to the sighted subjects in improving performance over the difficult incongruent task. For the blind, though, the regular spatial order did not provide an advantage: apparently, the external spatial structure provided by the regularity of presentation was not a sufficiently salient characteristic of the situation. Replication of the conditions with sighted and blind groups of young adults showed no difference between these groups, with both performing the congruent task better than the incongruent. Battacchi et al. (1981) concluded that with age (and experience) the blind young adults had developed better strategies for the retention of temporally and spatially distributed information.

In a related study, O'Connor and Hermelin (1972b) assessed the strategies of blind and sighted children in solving three-term series problems. The children were seven to nine years old. Two types of sentences were constructed, each expressing a relationship among three items. In one type, the sequential order of presentation of the items corresponded to their logical relationship, and in the other the sequential and logical orders did not correspond. The subject was asked two types of question, one dealing with the logically middle member of the triad and the other dealing with one of the two extreme members. There was not an overall difference between blind and sighted groups. There was some indication, however, that the blind subjects tended more than the sighted to report the sequentially middle item when it was incorrect, that is, in the series where the sequential and logical orders were not congruent. O'Connor and Hermelin suggested that the sighted children may have had a spatial code available for solution of the problems where it was appropriate, while the spatial code was less available to the blind who relied on a temporal code even when it was inappropriate. Their conclusion is thus reminiscent of that drawn by Millar (1979).

Two lines of attack on these questions should be actively pursued. First, training procedures should be designed to attempt to elicit spatial coding. One such procedure might be directed to selective attention. Evaluation of such procedures should not be limited to the training task itself, but should include tests of the extent of transfer to other tasks involving spatial performance. Second, an attempt should be made to identify those early experience variables that may produce differences in the spontaneous use of spatial information in blind children. There may have been identifiable differences in the experience of those children who did use spatial coding in the Hermelin and O'Connor (1971) study and those who did not. The retrospective search for experiential factors will be a difficult one. In fact, adequate ways of describing the ongoing perceptual environment are not available. The ever-increasing evidence that experience and environment interact to shape fuure abilities makes such an undertaking a potentially valuable one.

O'Connor and Hermelin (1971) compared crossmodal transfer performance of blind and sighted children, as well as deaf children. The study was designed, in part, to bear on the hypothesis that crossmodal performance depends on verbal mediation. The blind children ranged in age from 6.8 to 8.3. None had better vision than 3/60, but other details of visual status were not specified. They were matched by a control group of sighted children of corresponding CA, as well as a group of "subnormals" whose MA corresponded to the CA of the normal sighted controls and whose CA ranged from eight to 12 years. The children had to learn a discrimination between tactual stimuli of long and short durations. The discrimination was then tested at other positions in the same dimension, on other dimensions within the same (tactual) modality, and in another modality (auditory, for the blind children). The blind group learned the initial discrimination with fewer errors than the other groups, although the subnormal sighted group also had fewer errors than the normal sighted group. The blind, however, were worse on the intermodal transfer task, despite the fact that nine of the 10 blind subjects verbalized the solution to the initial discrimination task. The relatively poor intermodal transfer performance of the blind group was discussed in the context of the need for visual experience concurrently with experience in other modalities in order for effective intermodality organization to occur.

Millar (1975d) reported an interesting study designed to explore the types of spatial coding used by early blind (before 20 months) and sighted children. The subject traced a stylus through a simple five-sided path, and he encountered a block at a specific point in the path. The block was then removed and the path was completed. The subject then had to retrace the path, starting either at the original starting point (forward condition) or at the end point (backward condition), and he had to stop at the point where the block had been in the original path. The distance from the correct blockpoint was scored. Blind and sighted children did not differ markedly in the forward condition, but in the backward condition, the performance of the blind was worse than in the forward condition, while that of the sighted was better. Millar concluded that the coding of spatial information was different for the two groups. Specifically, she argued that the blind "relied on haptic memory which decays with time or is interfered with by subsequent movements rather than on verbal coding and rehearsal," while the sighted used "visual representations" (p. 456). Performance improved for both blind and sighted subjects across the six- to 12-year age range, but the relative performance of the blind and sighted children did not change with age.

The "visual organization" hypothesis, advanced by Warren et al. (1973) and others, seems to provide a reasonable framework for the interpretation of much of the intermodality space-perception research. Jones (1975) suggested an alternative hypothesis, that it is motor activity, not vision, that provides the integrating bridge between the other senses. The typical disadvantage of the congenitally blind child as compared to the later blind or sighted child is a result of the curtailed motor activity of the congenitally blind infant and child. The lower level of motor activity is, of course, in large part a result of the lack of vision, but Jones argues that the direct cause of poor spatial behavior is lack of motor activity, not lack of vision. Research should be designed to resolve this theoretical issue, but it will not be an easy question. Spatial behavior will have to be assessed as a function of degree of motor activity, with severity and onset of visual impairment held constant. For both theoretical and practical reasons, then, careful research should be conducted on the role of various kinds of early perceptual and motor experience in determining the adequacy of later spatial behavior and the kinds of information processing strategies used by subjects with differing visual characteristics.

Motor and Locomotor Abilities

There have been numerous studies of the motor and locomotor abilities of blind children aged five and older. Buell (1950) noted various areas of motor performance related to physical education where blind schoolchildren do not meet sighted norms. He attributed these lags to the child's failure to engage in sufficient physical activity before entering school. In turn, the limited physical activity was attributed to the parental overprotection that often accompanies visual impairment. Buell advised that "insofar as motor performance is concerned, parental neglect is to be preferred to overprotection" (p. 71). Jankowski and Evans (1981) corroborated the Buell findings with a sample of 20 blind children, age span four to 18 years, from a progressively run school for the visually impaired. Despite the excellent physical facilities of the school and the requirement of two 30-minute periods of physical education activity per week, the vast majority of the subjects were overweight, had low grip strength, low oxygen uptake, and generally showed an "increasingly sedentary lifestyle." The authors suggested that a daily program of vigorous exercise would bring the physical fitness of these children into normal limits within a period of about eight months. Royster (1964) suggested several ways to encourage more extensive physical activity by the young blind child, among them providing a puppy (suggested by Cutsforth, 1951) or another child as a playmate. Royster also advised the involvement of an orientation and mobility specialist with the child in the preschool period to encourage integration of spatial relations and mobility skills.

Duehl (1979) provided an eight-week program of creative dance training to four congenitally and totally blind children, age eight to 10, and administered the Cratty and Sams (1968) test of movement and body control both before and after the program. The activities in the program involved having the subjects creatively enact various concepts by body movements. The posttest showed substantial improvements in many areas of motor performance and control, and the research suggests that some of the motor awkwardness and developmental delay reported by researchers may be avoided or overcome by such programs.

In discussing orientation and mobility in the preschool blind child, Eichorn and Vigaroso (1967) stressed the need to provide extensive explanations of nonvisual perceptual experiences. "The imaginative parent will foresee not only the tactile, but the many auditory and olfactory aspects of the household which will need clarification, and the child's quest for greater knowledge and orientation should be nurtured" (p. 49). Such ideas were by no means new in the 1960s: Totman (1935), for example, stressed the need to begin in infancy to emphasize auditory and tactual experience, particularly by the appropriate selection of toys.

A somewhat different view of motor lags was given by Burlingham (1965). She argued that the motor passivity that is seen in many blind children is due not to an absence of motivation for movement, but rather to strong inhibitions of normal tendencies for movement. The child is simply protecting himself by not moving around, and under conditions where he is sure that the environment is safe, he will engage in normal motor activity. Although Burlingham's view seems different from that of the other writers cited, her position does share, at least implicitly, a concern for the role that the parents may play in encouraging the child's contact with the environment.

Adequacy in areas of motor performance is of great importance for the development of effective mobility, both in the informal sense of the term and in the context of formal mobility training programs. Warren and Kocon (1974) provided an extensive review of the broad range of factors related to mobility success, and the interested reader is referred to them for a more complete treatment of the literature. A complete treatment of all aspects of orientation and mobility is found in an excellent work edited by Welsh and Blasch (1980).

In spite of several pleas, such as that of Graham (1965), for ways of assessing locomotor abilities and readiness for formal mobility training, there has been relatively little useful work along these lines. A notable exception is the work of Lord (1969), whose project was designed "to define or identify the behavioral components in orientation and mobility which are relevant for young blind children and . . . to develop scales for the measurements relating the implied performances" (p. 77). Through a process of selecting a large pool of motor performance tasks, having professionals rate the developmental course and significance of the tasks, and testing the resulting sequence on a population of blind children, Lord produced a refined set of measurable abilities that are important in orientation and mobility. To the extent that these abilities are vital to orientation and mobility, Lord's scales should be useful for the diagnostic goal of selecting those candidates that are best prepared, in terms of having certain basic skills, for formal orientation and mobility training. At the same time, the use of such scales may allow the identification of specific areas of weakness in other candidates, who can be given special attention in a remedial training program.

There have been numerous research projects designed to study the various types of locomotor ability that are thought to be involved in general mobility success. It is clear that, since mobility occurs in space, it is not useful to study such abilities without considering how they are related to spatial relations concepts, and much of the research on motor abilities could be viewed as another approach to spatial relations. Cratty has produced a great deal of research, and some training procedures based on research, on various locomotor skills. Cratty (1967) studied the veering tendency in an open-field situation in which the subject was simply asked to walk in a straight line. Subjects varied widely in visual characteristics, age, and mobility history. There was apparently no significant difference between those subjects who had participated in formal mobility training programs and those who had not. Interestingly, however, subjects who reported traveling with a guide dog were markedly worse in straight-line locomotion than were those who traveled either with a cane or with a sighted guide. Subjects who had been blind from birth veered less than than the adventitiously blinded. However, an interaction of onset-of-blindness with age occurred where the older adventitiously blinded subjects veered more than the younger subjects who were blind from birth. The length-of-blind-experience factor was also important, in that subjects who had been blind for less than 10 years veered more than those who had been blind for more than 20 years. Finally, a group of sighted subjects who were matched with the blind on various characteristics showed more veer than the blind.

In the same study, Cratty evaluated the blind subjects' sensitivity to the incline and decline of paths. A larger percentage (92 percent) of persons who reported using dog guides for travel were able to perceive a slight gradient than persons who used the cane (63 percent) or who used sighted guides (42 percent). This pattern of results provides an interesting contrast to the veering results from the same group of subjects, where travellers who used dog guides were much worse than those who used cane or sighted guides. With this exception, however, the pattern of results for sensitivity to incline was similar to the pattern for veering.

Cratty, Peterson, Harris, and Schoner (1968) reported the performance of congenitally blind and adventitiously blinded children on various locomotor spatial tasks, one of which involved walking through curved pathways with varying radii of curvature. In this task, the later blind subjects were "usually correct" in their responses, while the congenitally blind made errors over half the time. Cratty et al. suggested that a well-developed concept of laterality is prerequisite for this task, and that laterality was less well developed in the congenitally blind children. Warren et al. (1973), however, discussed these results in the context of the possible residual effect of early vision on the spatial performance itself. It seems likely that early vision affects performance both directly and indirectly through its effect on laterality.

Cratty has also studied the ability of blind children to execute various angle turns, but discussion of this research will be deferred to a later section on training studies. Worchel (1951) used a task in which the subject was led over two sides of a large right triangle and was then asked to return to the starting point via the hypotenuse. In a variation of the task, the subject was led along the hypotenuse and was asked to return to the starting point via the two other legs of a right triangle. The blind and sighted subjects ranged in age from eight to 21 years, averaging about 14.5. Although the blind were all totally blind, the age of onset ranged from birth to 11 years. On both variations of the triangle test, the sighted group performed significantly better than the blind group. The relation between performance and CA was not significant, and there was no significant relation between performance and age at blinding.

Leonard (1969) assessed static and mobile balancing in teenaged children who varied widely in residual vision. The mobile balancing test required the subject to walk along a narrow beam, using whatever residual vision might be available. The relation between the balancing scores was complex: while poor static balance predicted poor mobile balance, good mobile balance did not necessarily accompany good static balance. Residual vision was also related to mobile balance. Subjects with very little residual vision performed poorly on mobile balancing, but those with a large degree of residual vision did not necessarily perform well. Gipsman's (1980, 1981) results from a training study of stabilimeter balance performance were mixed on the issues of age and sight as determinants of performance; training was, however, effective in producing improved performance a month later.

Leonard and Newman have been engaged in interesting work, primarily with blind adults, on the use of tactual maps in moving through unfamiliar environments. They report briefly the results of an extension of some of this work to 14–15 year olds (1967). Most of the children, who were congenitally and very early blind, were reasonably successful in using the maps, although their time scores were substantially higher than those informally reported for partially sighted subjects.

Some attention has been given to the role of posture in mobility. The relationship between posture and mobility in the blind seems straightforward enough: while the sighted person has vision available to mediate his perception of the vertical, the blind person must rely on proprioceptive and vestibular cues to maintain a stable correspondence between body and environment. To the extent that the blind person has postural difficulties, his perception of the vertical (and of other spatial directions when they depend on the vertical) may be inadequate. Poor posture effectively removes the stable correspondence between body and environment, and thus should make mobility more difficult.

Turner and Siegel (1969) stressed the necessity of good posture and balance for effective mobility. They provided an evaluation form for the assessment of physical characteristics and abilities, gait, and concepts of body image and orientation, in addition to the ability to execute turns. Physical therapy procedures were described that are geared to correction of the individual's pattern of difficulty, whether it is primarily based on faulty foot placement, posture, or balance. Siegel and Murphy (1970) provided a much more detailed analysis of the role that posture plays in orientation and mobility, as well as specification of training procedures for correcting postural difficulties. Their sample consisted of 45 students, ranging in age from 17 to 58, who showed both postural defects and mobility deficiencies. After the diagnostic phase, both mobility and medical (postural) treatment phases were initiated and continued for 12 weeks. About two-thirds of the students showed mobility improvement. More important, there was a strong correlation between improvement in posture and improvement in mobility. No relationships were found between age, sex, or IQ and either postural or mobility improvement. Although it is undeniably risky to conclude a causal relationship from correlational research, the elimination of age, sex, and IQ as relevant variables in the mobility improvements lends strength to the argument that correction of postural difficulties leads to more effective mobility.

Cratty does not concur with the position that good posture is especially important for mobility. In his work on the veering tendency and the perception of inclines (Cratty, 1967), he found that physical characteristics such as head torsion, leg length, and hand and leg dominance did not contribute to prediction of veer. He thus argued that training in postural factors may prove to be less successful than training in "perceptual organization (i.e., what a person thinks is a straight pathway)" (p. 34).

Body image

Cratty also places emphasis on the role of a good body image in successful orientation to and mobility in the environment, and much of his research and training emphasis is on assessment and improvement of the body image of blind children. The "term body image" is used in at least three ways, and in combinations of the three, and it is necessary to provide some perspective on the uses of the term. Hapeman (1967) used the term to refer to a child's knowledge of the parts of his body and of the relationships among those parts (the fingers are connected to the hand). A second use of the term is represented by Siegel and Murphy (1970), who defined body image as the mental "picture" one has of one's body in space. This use differs from that of Hapeman in that it refers to external space, not just to the body. Other investigators have used the concept to refer to both these levels. For example, Garry and Ascarelli (1960) wrote about "awareness of body position—which is awareness of the spatial relationships of parts of the body to its axes, and of the body as a whole to other bodies" (p. 9). Mills (1970) defined body image "as a knowledge of body parts, how the parts relate to each other, how the parts may be utilized both individually and collectively for purposeful activity, and how the parts relate to the child's spatial environment" (p. 81). A third level of meaning is characteristic of the psychoanalytic literature, and it has to do with the differentiation of the ego from the external world. This use is similar to the second use, but it carries a somewhat stronger implication of a developmental process. To quote Cohen (1966), "to achieve objectivity requires confirmation of all the senses that the self is an individual, separate, and to some degree, independent of others. Since vision is the sense which inherently presents the outside world as exernal, it is instrumental in the natural development of ego differentiation" (p. 152). Cohen's reference to the role of vision in producing ego differentiation is echoed by many writers. Witkin et al. (1968) discussed the role of vision in producing an articulation not only of external space, but also of the body concept. To the extent that the lack of vision interferes with the normal development of body image (referring, now, to all three levels of definition), the blind child may be at a disadvantage in mobility.

Although many writers have discussed the importance of body image for adequate mobility, few have provided a way of assessing body image concepts objectively. In the Witkin et al (1968) study cited above, the child was given a ball of clay and was asked to make a person. The creations were rated according to a five-point scale. (The clay-modeling procedure has, like the Goodenough Draw-A-Man Test, been criticized for involving the child's artistic ability to a great extent, and it may, therefore, not be an ideal test of body image.) Mills (1970) listed a series of questions designed to evaluate body image, but did not indicate how the child's responses were interpreted as an indicator of body image. Cratty and Sams (1968), on the other hand, presented a body image survey form that requires the child to perform a large number of activities, from simple pointing to parts of the child's own body to describing movements made by the interviewer. The survey form seems to be the best of the few assessment procedures available, and it has had test-retest reliability checks performed. It should be pointed out that, without agreement on definitions and use of terms, and without objective means of evaluating concepts such as body image, progress in the study of body image development will be very slow.

Several investigators have reported attempts to produce better body image through training. Siegel's postural training program stands out in this area, as does Cratty's work. Turner and Siegel (1969) described the use of a life-size mannequin for training and implied some success in its use, although no objective evaluation of improvement of body image was reported. Siegel and Murphy (1970) again discussed the use of the mannequin. Walker (1970, 1971, cited by Walker, 1973) presented a structured set of lessons in body image training to groups of kindergarten (1971) and early elementary grade (1970) blind children. The body image test developed by Cratty and Sams (1968) was used for evaluation. The results for the kindergarten children indicated that the program "was effective in improving the body image of kindergarten-age blind children. Furthermore, the program produced greater gains when used with children without useful vision, whose general intellectual levels were below average" (Walker, 1973, p 224).

Cratty and Sams (1968) presented perhaps the best justification for body image training, arguing that a well developed body image forms a basis from which the child can learn to structure external space. Cratty puts special emphasis on the appropriate development of laterality. The laterality notion appears in his discussion of the veering tendency (Cratty, 1967), as well as in specific sections in his body image evaluation form (Cratty & Sams, 1968). Cratty and Sams argued that, for any given type of disability, body image training should be geared to the specific abilities at the individual's disposal. In particular, "the blind must rely upon kinesthetic, tactual, and auditory information when forming concepts about themselves and their environments" (p. 37). Furthermore, they pointed out that it is important to encourage the child to *think* as part of this training: it is through the building of "cognitive bridges" that body image can become an effective basis for the development of good spatial relations abilities.

Cratty and Sams identified four (temporally overlapping) phases of body image development, identified as (1) body planes, parts, and movements (two to five years), (2) left-right discrimination (five to seven years), (3) complex judgments of the body and of body-object relationships (six to eight years), and (4) another person's reference system. The age ranges referred to are normative figures for blind children "of normal intelligence," indicating again the authors' regard for cognitive factors in body image acquisition. Cratty and Sams described a number of exercises designed to produce adequate progress through these stages, and the reader is referred to the published paper for the details. Some general aspects of the program are as follows. First, it appropriately has a multimodal aspect, stressing auditory, motor, tactual, and kinesthetic aspects as well as verbal mediation, and stressing the importance of providing simultaneous multimodal experience to the child. Second, as fits a set of developmental stages, it stresses experiences that are appropriate to the age (or developmental level) of the child. Third, it emphasizes the necessity of providing a variety of activities to produce adequate generalization of concepts. Finally, it stresses the importance of a gradual externalization of body image concepts on which to build a concept of external space using the body image as a basis.

Cratty and Sams emphasized the importance of the child's very early experience in producing a sound body image. The regard for early experience also appears, not surprisingly, in the psychoanalytically oriented treatments of body image. Wills (1970) serves as a good example. Like the Fraiberg group, Wills has studied the development of reaching for objects and of locomotion in blind infants and has found significant developmental lags. The lags are discussed as being attributable to the lack of vision as an external verifier of the existence and identity of objects. Without vision, the integration of tactual and auditory experience is more difficult, and a major source of stimulus for the child to reach outward and contact the external world is absent. In psychoanalytic terms, this situation is described as a lag in ego-differentiation, or in the realization that there is an important distinction between self and world. The difference in vocabulary should not be allowed to obscure the fact that Wills is talking about the same set of events as is Cratty. The effects of the absence of early vision are reasonably clear—what remains is the vital search for effective means of providing substitute experiences that can provide, even in the absence of vision, for the effective development of body image, and for the effective construction of concepts of external space from a well-developed body image. The trend in the literature on the blind toward recognizing the importance of early experience is a healthy and needed one. Significant progress in this area, though, will have to await more adequate ways of assessing the body image, and the willingness of investigators with ideas about early intervention to make a rigorous assessment of the effectiveness of their techniques.

Training studies

There have been more training studies in the area of locomotor functions than in the areas of perceptual performance that were reviewed earlier. Interestingly, though, there have been surprisingly few formal evaluations reported of mobility training programs. An inclusive review of this material was provided by Warren and Kocon (1974). A notable recent example is the work of Harley, Wood, and Merbler (1975, 1980), who developed and field tested a set of instructional materials for an orientation and mobility program for multiply handicapped blind children. The evaluation of the program was done by use of the Revised Peabody Mobility Scale (described in the same article), which assesses the child in motor development, sensory skills, concept development, and mobility skills. The instructional program addressed these same areas, and was evaluated on a sample of children ranging in age from four to 14, with at most light perception and one additional handicapping condition. The Maxfield–Buchholz social maturity scores of the children ranged from between 1½ and 6 years, so all were low-function children. The training program was divided into two eight-week phases, the first concentrating on sensory and motor components and the second on concept development and mobility areas. Compared with control groups of comparable children, the children who received the training program showed significant gains on the Revised Peabody Mobility Scale. Harley and Merbler (1980) reported a corresponding evaluation of their program for multiply impaired low vision children, with similarly positive results. The approach to the evaluation of orientation and mobility programs represented in the Harley work is worthy of note: the work is carefully and appropriately designed and conducted, and should serve as a model for other investigators.

Mills and Adamshick (1969) reported a broad-range training study directed specifically to the question of whether formal mobility training would be effective after a program of sensory training. The goals of the training program dealt with such things as body image, auditory identification and localization, comprehension of mobility terms, and tactile-kinesthetic development. After receiving the training program, which was described in some detail in the article, a group of high school students participated in a five-week orientation and mobility program. Their progress in the program was compared with that of a comparable group of students who did not receive the sensory training. The mobility instructors rated their trainees on orientation and mobility subskills. The sensory training group was able to be instructed on more skills than the control group, and the training group was markedly superior in overall proficiency rating.

Mills and Adamshick provided a list of uncontrollable variables, not related to the sensory training itself, which may have contributed to the group differences. These variables are primarily related to the motivation and attitude of the students. To the extent that motivation and attitude differed as a result of the sensory training program, of course, these factors may be considered a legitimate, although nonsensory, aspect of the training program. Whatever the reasons, it is clear that the sensory training group responded better to formal orientation and mobility training. It would be beneficial to pursue this type of training study further, evaluating in particular the source of the improvement in individual children. It may be that attitude was the only improved factor for some children, and it may be possible to produce adequate changes for these children more effectively in other ways than sensory pretraining. The training itself may have been the important factor, but again, it may be possible to diagnose more precisely the exact needs of the individual, so that sensory training specific to those needs can be provided.

Several studies further illustrate the training approach. Garry and Ascarelli (1960) included a section on "structuring extended space" in their training program for topographical and spatial orientation. A wide range of training experience was provided, directed to perception of surfaces, of objects and their relations to each other, and of the child's own relation to objects. A control group did not receive the training. On the spatial relations test (which included a variety of types of performance) the pre- to posttest improvement of the training group was highly significant, while the control group showed virtually no improvement. It should be noted that the control group performed much better on the pretest than did the training group (42.7 vs. 16.5), and that, despite the significant improvement of the training group, the control group still performed better on the posttest (46.7 vs. 31.1). The confounding of pretest performance with group assignment is an unfortunate weakness in the design of the research. However, it does seem unlikely that the entire pattern of results can be attributed to this point; it would have been possible for the control group to improve substantially from its pretest performance before reaching the ceiling on the test (which was 60). In studies such as this, where there is clearly some pretest difference between groups and substantial variability within groups, it is of particular importance to try to identify, in a post hoc analysis, characteristics of individual subjects that are related to their performance. Extension of training studies such as that of Garry and Ascarelli to include specific evaluation of mobility skills as they may be influenced by the spatial relations training would be of particular benefit to the mobility literature.

In the report of training techniques by Turner and Siegel (1969), orientation training was included, but unfortunately no objective evaluation of the effectiveness of the training was presented. The training procedures specific to orientation included practice in making turns of 90, 180, and 360 degrees, and in using cues such as the air currents produced by a fan. Trainees also crawled through tunnels designed to draw their attention to turns and the orientation of body to environment. Although these training methods seem intuitively reasonable, and although the authors concluded that "this activity has proved useful not only to the student's learning program, but also to alert the therapist to specific concepts which the students lack or find difficult" (p. 1368), it would be of great value to others working in the field to have more objective evaluations available.

Cratty's (1969) report of a training study illustrates this added evaluative step. Blind children, age seven to 14 years, were pre- and posttested on a position relocation task that involved being led along two legs of a right triangle and then being required to return to the starting point along the hypotenuse of the triangle. A control group received no training during the eight-week period before posttesting, while the training group participated in an eight-week program involving straight-line walking and executing various turns (90, 180, 360 degrees). Feedback on the veering task was given tactually by having the child trace a piece of wire bent to the shape of the path he had actually traversed on that trial. For the turning trials, the subject was corrected by the trainer on each trial. The improvement in walking a straight line was about 24 percent over the course of the eight-week session, while the turn performance also "evidenced improvement which was significant" (p. 171). Pre- and posttests of triangular relocation were also administered, and although no direct training on this task was given, "the children evidenced a significantly improved ability" (p. 171) on this task as well. It should be noted that the improvement, although significant, still left the children far from perfect performance: the hypotenuse of the triangle measured 22 feet, and the improvement was from an initial mean error of 25 feet to a posttest mean error of 19 feet. Other aspects of mobility, orientation, and spatial relations were also reported to show improvement in the trained group, although formal measures were not reported.

While this type of training procedure seems to hold great promise for the preparation of blind children for formal mobility training, the usefulness of the research as reported is diminished by the failure to report any results for the nontrained control group. The control group may also have improved significantly. If so, at least part of the improvement of the training group would have to be attributed to the pretest exposure or to the other variables not related to the training itself. The price of an eight-week training program is a small one to pay if it prepares children better for formal orientation and mobility training. At the same time, it does represent a substantial investment, and it is important to determine just how much of the improvement is attributable to the training program itself.

Morris (1974) described a specially designed play environment for blind children that was designed to encourage the development of the use of perceptual cues as well as of spatial concepts and effective mobility. The play environment consisted of a series of circular play courts arranged to allow mobility from one to another, guided by various perceptual cues including tactual, textural, temperature, and auditory cues. Some tactual maps were also provided to facilitate the child's orientation to the areas. Morris evaluated the play environment by asking for the reactions of a group of mobility and other professional specialists. The responses were in general positive, although concern was expressed with the use of maps and with the general notion of providing a special play environment for the blind child. A more valid test of the effectiveness of such an environment would be accomplished by the study of a group of blind children who were exposed to it for an extended series of sessions. Although the concept of a "special" environment may be criticized, the crux of its success should be measured by its effect on blind children. Such an evaluation should clearly be conducted.

Two studies serve as examples of training in the use of spatial relations language. The study by Garry and Ascarelli (1960), described earlier, included a training section on language. Several aspects of training were given, dealing with distance, direction, relative location, and geographic directions. No separate evaluation was made of spatial relations vocabulary, but as noted earlier, significant gains were made in spatial performance tests. Hill (1970, 1971), reported a study in which seven- to nine-year-olds were given a three-month training session on the use of various spatial relations terms. The training consisted of using each word in each of a series of progressively more advanced contexts. Comparison of the pretest and posttest performance on functional use of the words showed that a significant improvement occurred for the training group. A control group that did not receive the training showed only minimal improvement.

It may be useful, in providing an overall perspective on the question of motor and locomotor abilities in the blind child, to quote extensively from the discussion of Warren and Kocon (1974, pp. 213-215):

> How realistic is it to think that we can provide the child with the experiences that will adequately prepare him for mobility? Much of the material reviewed in this paper indicates that this goal is not an unreasonable one. Although there are definite gaps in the available knowledge, it is clearly possible to identify factors that are associated with mobility success. These factors range widely from perceptual through cognitive and language abilities to personality and social environmental characteristics. Furthermore, and quite importantly, it is certain that we can in many of these areas exercise the influence that is needed to produce the relevant characteristics. We can provide the blind child with the stimulating sensory environment that he needs to develop his nonvisual senses to their optimum. We can provide him with a speech environment that is conducive to his acquisition of a language that is useful in mediating his representation of the physical world as well as his social relationships with other people. We can certainly influence his attitudes toward his blindness.
>
> It is noteworthy that virtually all of these types of mobility-related factors undergo significant development in infancy or very early childhood. This is true for perceptual functioning, for the bases of cognitive growth, for language acquisition, for attitudes, and for modes of social interaction. It may well be that at least for the congenitally or early blind child, broad limits are set on his eventual mobility success in the first five years of life, long before formal mobility training begins.
>
> Clearly much research needs to be done on the factors that prepare the blind child poorly or well for mobility. We simply do not know enough to be able to specify the details of how to deal with the blind child, although we can, as noted at various points in this review, provide at

least a broad outline for such treatment. The psychoanalytically oriented writers have long recognized the importance of early experience for all children, and their concern with the early experience of the blind child has provided important information and hypotheses. For example, both Burlingham (1961) and Fraiberg (1968) have noted that some aspects of the development of blind and sighted infants are virtually identical for at least six months, and only diverge after that time. The divergence that occurs seems particularly significant for mobility—there is adequate external stimulation for the sighted child to crawl and reach outward into the environment, while the blind child may, at the normal time of the onset of locomotion, fail to be stimulated to the experience that is vital in establishing an effective differentiation between self and externality. With well designed and executed and carefully evaluated research, we may be able to discover ways to enhance the blind infant's experience at the appropriate times so that his visual handicap is a less significant aspect of his life. Our being able to do that research will depend to a large degree on adequate definitions of the problems needing research, however. Here, again, the careful and thorough observations of the psychoanalytically oriented writers serve as a useful model. For instance, Fraiberg concludes that the blind infant begins to regress at the onset of locomotor behavior because auditory and tactile information do not adequately define objects in the external world. This formulation should be treated as a hypothesis, not as final truth. As a hypothesis, it gives us hints about what we might try, and when we might try it, in order to bring the blind child successfully past this critical stage. It is not sufficient to accept Fraiberg's formulation as final: we must follow its implications and evaluate the results of our interventions. Although they are perhaps less well defined than this particular example, there are other suggestions in the literature for similarly critical times in the blind child's development, and these should also generate interventions and evaluations.

On the basis of the material reviewed in this paper, it is certainly reasonable to be optimistic about our chances to influence the blind child to become able to "travel safely, comfortably, gracefully, and independently." The success of this venture will depend on our conduct of relevant research, on the development of applications from that research, on the evaluation of those applications, and on the continuing interplay among research, applications, and evaluation.

Spatial Cognition

Research on both blind and sighted human subjects has been increasingly focused in the past several years in an area referred to as "spatial cognition." In the sighted literature, this emphasis has reflected the growing realization of the extent to which cognitive processes play a vital role in functions that have traditionally been regarded as "perceptual." The issue at hand is the extent to which spatial behavior occurs on the basis of real-time information coming in through the perceptual channels, as opposed to being influenced by, or critically dependent upon, cognitive or "thought" processes—those which draw upon stored knowledge, strategies, reasoning, and the like. Of course it is not a new concept that an apparently perceptual or perceptual-motor task, such as walking to the grocery store, can involve stored information. Tolman's rats, after all, were hypothesized to use some kind of stored spatial representation of their maze in order to negotiate it via an alternative route when the learned route was blocked.

But recently, and in some measure in reaction to Gibson's (1979) accounts of perceptual-motor behavior as being dynamically stimulus-controlled with a minimum of cognitive influence, numerous researchers have reconcentrated their efforts on the interplay between the immediate perceptual array and the stored information in such perceptual-motor activities, and particularly on the role of cognitive strategies and predispositions in influencing the subject's selection and use of aspects of the stimulus array to guide functional perceptual-motor activities. This orientation has had its expression in research with the blind, and relatively novel research paradigms have emerged that have good promise for furthering our knowledge about the spatial abilities and behavior of the blind. While these paradigms clearly hold promise, their use has been limited, and optimal research progress will depend on developing a broad context for this work.

The term "spatial cognition" does not encompass all of what is traditionally known as spatial relations. A reasonable working definition is that "spatial cognition is getting to know a life-sized space." "Getting to know" implies a process that involves learning and takes place over time. "Life-sized" requires the activity to take place in "real" space rather than the constrained artificiality of the experimental table-top. Thus excluded, for example, are the learning of finger mazes (these are not life-sized), the walking of straight lines or hypothetical triangles (these are not getting to know the space, but rather involve performing some inner-directed pattern in a vacant space which imposes no constraints), and walking a balance beam (the space imposes constraints, but there is no "getting-to-know" process). In general, the paradigm involves exposing the subject to an environment about which something must be learned, and examining the nature of the subject's learning. This apparently simple paradigm has many important variations. The subject's exposure to the environment may be systematic or unsystematic, and it may be spontaneous or directed by the experimenter. The manner of delivery of the information may be tactual, locomotor, or even verbal. The characteristics of the environment may of course vary. The space may be large or small, it may be familiar or unfamiliar, it may contain landmarks or not, and so on. Further, there is the question of the use of a model as a way to deliver information about an environment. The subject may be given repeated trials, may be asked to attend particularly to specific features or landmarks, and so on. The nature of the performance requested of the subject can also vary in important ways. The subject may be asked to point to locations in the space, to describe them verbally, or to move to requested locations. The task can be varied to require different mental manipulations. Individual differences variables such as age, visual history, and intellectual characteristics may be assessed.

A coordinated body of knowledge in this area, which we may have available in a few years, should provide us with thorough information about the nature of the visually impaired person's learning about, and ability to get around in, a new environment. Although there have been some valuable first steps reported, there remains much important research to be done.

The studies reviewed in this section are not limited to those that concern children, because there are studies with adults that not only help to illustrate important variables but that contain information about the dependence of aspects of spatial cognition on such developmental variables as early visual history.

A major distinction may be drawn between two types of studies, those which assess the subject's knowledge of environments which are assumed to be totally familiar, and those which evaluate the subject's ability to learn about a new environment. There has been less work in the former category and it will be reviewed first.

Assessing familiar environments

McReynolds and Worchel (1954) studied the ability of various blind children to use geographical directions. The sample was divided into two age groups, above and below 15 years (ranges not specified), total vs. partial blindness groups, congenital vs. accidental groups, and high- and low-IQ groups (divided at 105). The tests involved pointing to places on the school campus, in the city, to other cities, and to compass directions. The subject was also asked questions designed to tap his ability to deal with directions between other cities. No main effects were found for any of the four grouping variables. However, it seems possible that the response measure may have masked some differences. In the pointing tasks, the circle in which the subject stood and against which his pointing was evaluated was divided into 20-degree segments. A finer response division might have led to positive results on some variables. For example, within the totally blind group, comparison of high-IQ with low-IQ subgroups reveals a consistent pattern of superiority by the high-IQ subjects across the six task categories: in fact, there is not a single instance where the low-IQ group performed better. Yet no main effect of IQ appeared, and no interaction of IQ with degree of blindness was reported. Some evidence of correlation between CA and test performance does appear in the data. This result is not surprising, since most of the tests were designed to tap specific experience rather than general ability. There was also a trend, although not statistically significant, for later blind subjects to perform better on some of the tests.

Casey (1978) assessed the map-making ability of adolescent students who had been at a residential school for at least a year, and who as a result presumably were familiar with the spatial layout of the school grounds. Ten congenitally blind students were in grades 10 through 12, age range 17 to 20. Ten partially sighted students were from the same grades, age range 16 to 21, and were tested blindfolded. Each subject was asked to construct a map of the school buildings and grounds using a modeling kit consisting of 22 wooden buildings, labeled in print and braille, and adhesive strips to represent roadways and paths. These items, as many as the subject wished to use, were placed on a board, and the result was photographed and evaluated by two judges as to organizational accuracy. The number of correct elements was relatively underplayed in the scoring. The partially sighted scored higher in organizational accuracy and included more elements than the totally and congenitally blind. The totally blind tended to cluster groups of items together rather than using a larger organization. However, there were some totally blind subjects who did relatively well, and these tended to be those who received relatively high ratings of independent travel ability.

Although the Casey results make intuitive sense, they may nevertheless be questioned on methodological grounds. Casey made the critical assumption that the map-making ability of totally blind and partially sighted subjects is equivalent. If their ability is equivalent, then the maps may be evaluated and conclusions drawn about the quality of their conceptualizations of the spatial layout. However, the assumption *is* a questionable one, and one may wonder whether the differences that were found were in fact due to the differential abilities of the two groups to construct maps, rather than (as was assumed) to conceptualize a familiar space.

A methodological advance over the map-construction technique was reported by Lockman, Rieser, and Pick (1981). Their subjects were 10 adventitiously blinded adults, LP or less, who had had vision for at least 12 years. The multidimensional scaling technique involved naming three landmarks from a well-known environment, and asking the subject which two of the three were farthest apart and which two were closest together. From the collection of a subject's responses to a number of such triads, a map was generated by computer to represent the subject's spatial conception of the environment. Another program was then used to rotate the map and expand or contract it to show how accurately it fitted a Euclidean map of the space.

The evidence suggests that the technique is a useful one. An element of criterion validity is provided by the fact that there was a relationship between the subject's map quality and that subject's evaluated ability to travel within the space. The technique apparently does not depend on the subject's own map-making ability, since it asks only for simple judgments of relative distance, rather than absolute position or even relative position of elements within the space. Further, although Lockman et al. (1981) did not use it with children, the method would seem to be potentially useful with children as well as adults because of its simplicity.

A variation on the Lockman et al. (1981) methodology was explored by Rieser, Lockman, and Pick (1980) with adult subjects, but again there are potential extensions to children. The environment in question was a familiar one: the goal was to ascertain whether specific visual experience with this environment, as only the sighted would have, or general visual experience, as the adventitiously blinded would also have had, was important in allowing the subject to make accurate distance estimates. Each subject was first asked to make a distance estimate between two locations in the familiar environment. Then the subject was asked to make a Euclidean distance estimate and a functional distance estimate. Euclidean estimates ask for "as the crow flies" knowledge, whereas functional estimates of distance refer to the "walking distance" between two points. In general, the visually impaired subjects were very good at estimating both functional and Euclidean distances in the familiar space. However, the Euclidean task was done best by the sighted, then the later blind, and worst by the congenitally blind. The pattern of results suggested that both specific and general experience are important in representing space. The congenitally blind showed particular difficulty in shifting from the functional to the Euclidean basis of judgment.

Aside from these studies, there has been little work with the spatial cognition of familiar space. We move now to research on the acquisition of knowledge about novel or unfamiliar space.

Learning novel environments

The study reported by Fletcher (1980, 1981a,b) serves as a good introduction to this area. Fletcher's subjects ranged in age from seven to 18. The blind subjects had visual acuity of LP or less and onset of blindness at age three or earlier; the sighted subjects were matched for age and rated intellectual ability. The procedure involved exploration of a life-sized or a model room containing items of furniture. Each wall of the room had a permanent distinguishing feature such as a door, and during exposure care was taken to draw the subject's attention to this feature in relation to the items of furniture that were placed near that wall. Two kinds of exploration were used. *Guided exploration* involved the experimenter's leading the subject around the room in counterclockwise direction. *Free exploration* was completely self-guided by the subject, in whatever fashion desired. The questions asked were of two types, "route questions" and "map questions." *Route questions* asked for relationships among items according to the subject's sequence of exploration, whereas *map questions* required the subject to depend on a synthesis of the relative relationships among the several items (such as asking for the location of an item across the room from a given item). Up to five trials were conducted with each subject in each condition, but the condition was terminated early if the subject answered all questions correctly on two successive trials.

Fletcher (1980) reported results of the type of question (route vs. map), age (7 to 10, 11 to 14, 15 to 18 groups), and sighted status. The age variable did not have a significant effect. The sighted subjects, who performed blindfolded, were generally better than the blind. There was also an interaction of question type and visual status: the blind subjects did better on the route questions than they did on the map questions, whereas there was no such difference for the sighted. Note that the route questions asked for information within the sequential order to which the subject had been exposed to it—a simple memory approach should be sufficient to answer such questions, whereas the map questions were designed to require the subject to have placed the information within a spatial framework. These map questions were more difficult for the blind. In a subsequent article on the same research, Fletcher (1981a) reported the variables of environment size and mode of exploration for the blind group. There was not an effect of room size—the subjects performed as well with model rooms as they did with the life-size room. The spontaneous exploration strategies used by subjects were classified as unsystematic, clockwise, counterclockwise, or as involving systematic checking of diagonals and opposites. There was not an impressive relationship of performance to exploration strategy, although there was some indication that regularity in exploration is advantageous, as would be expected.

In a final article on the research, Fletcher (1981b) examined the relationship of the performance results of the blind sample to various individual differences characteristics. In general, performance on route questions (on which the blind subjects did better than they did on the map questions) was not predictable from such individual differences factors. For the map questions, however, teacher-rated intelligence was a significant predictor, as was the availability of some functional vision during the first three years. RLF children generally performed worse than those of other etiologies. Together, these three factors accounted for 70 percent of the variance in the map questions. For the route questions, only the early visual history factor was significant; those who had had some functional vision during the first three years performed better than those who had not.

Rieser, Guth, and Hill (1982) reported a study similar to that of Fletcher, although the subjects were adults. The study was similar in that the subject's task was to learn the layout of an unfamiliar room containing several items such as tables and chairs. The subject was initially led in turn to each of the objects in regular order, then was asked to use a pointer to point to each object, then was led to each object again. After this exposure, two tasks were conducted. In the *Locomotion* Task, the subject was taken from the starting point to one of the other locations and was asked to point to each of the other objects from that new station point. In the *Imagination* Task, the subject was asked to imagine that he was at one of the other station points, and to point at each of the other objects from that imagined place. The first task, then, engaged the locomotor system as a way of getting the subject "placed" in his mental representation of the space. In the imagination task, this locomotor reference was not available, and the subject had to rely on a more abstract strategy.

Three groups were tested, sighted (performing under blindfold), early blind (at birth for the most part, although one as late as 2½ years), and later blind (after 8 years of age, and blind for at least 5 years). All three groups reported the imagination task to be extremely difficult, and in fact they performed it slowly and with considerable error in pointing. The locomotion task was easier for the later blind and sighted groups, who performed it more quickly and more accurately than they had the imagination task. For the early blind, though, the locomotor task was nearly as difficult as the imagination task, and they reported that they had tended to use computational rather than perceptual strategies, in contrast to the other groups. The early blind, then, were not aided by the locomotor mediation of traveling to the station point, and had to rely on the more difficult cognitive, or computational, strategy.

Rosencranz and Suslick (1976) used an interesting variation on the manner of the subject's exposure to the environment, which was again in this case a room in which objects could be arranged to create a novel array. In this case there were a door and seven objects in a rectilinear grid, so that the spatial array of the objects could be related to the spatial layout of the room as a containing structure. The subjects were late adolescents and adults, four early blind (although as late as age six according to the criteria used) and three later blind. Interestingly, the exposure to the room was given not by map or by travel within the room, but by verbal description. The arrangement of objects in the array was described verbally in a linear, sequential manner, until the subject had it memorized perfectly. Four conditions of exposure were created by the use of two variables in a 2 x 2 matrix. One variable was whether the array was described with reference to a hypothetical route through the room (e.g., encounter the table, then turn left and move to the chair, etc.) as opposed to describing the set of relationships between pairs of items (the table is to the right of the chair and behind the wastebasket, etc.). The other variable had to do with whether the array was described with reference to the borders of the room and the location of the door, or independently of this frame of reference. Each of the four conditions was used with each subject in varying order, with the arrangement changed from one condition to another.

The method has the advantages, it should be noted, of ensuring that the subject has thoroughly learned the information that is presented about the array, and that his learning can be assessed by a (verbal) means that is independent of that to be used in the experimental test itself. The experimental test consisted of asking a series of questions about relationships among the objects, such as "what is in the front left corner?" and "what is to the right of the chair?" The questions of particular interest were those involving synthesis. Successful response required that the subject had placed the verbal information into a framework of spatial relations that was independent of the order of the information as it was verbally presented. On these synthesis questions, the subjects with previous visual experience performed much better than those without significant early visual experience. Further, the vocabulary test from the Stanford–Binet IQ test was given, and those subjects with relatively high scores performed better than those with lower scores. Thus two factors, visual experience and IQ (vocabulary) score, accounted for much of the variance in the results on the synthesis questions: those subjects with early vision and higher IQ performed best.

Another variation on the manner of presenting spatial information to the subject was reported by Herman, Herman, and Chatman (1983). In this study, exposure was given by means of a map, and then testing was done in a full-scale environment. The array involved a layout of four objects arranged in a diamond pattern. In the exposure phase, one object (a box) was designated as the "home" item, and the subject was shown by use of a tabletop model the distance and direction relationship of each of the other three objects to the box, until the array was well learned. This learning was accomplished relatively quickly, generally within 10 minutes. Then the subject was taken to a gymnasium and was shown life-sized versions of the four objects, which were then placed in the same array on the gym floor. The subject started at one station point and walked to the supposed locations of each of the other objects. This procedure was repeated using each object as a station point. The 12 subjects were totally blind by the age of 11 months, ranged in age from 12 to 24 years, and showed roughly normal IQ distribution.

It was thought that the box might serve as the most effective station point from which to find the locations of the other objects, but this did not prove to be the case. Nor did any of several other reasonable ways of arranging the data produce any significant effects. More basically, though, one must question whether the performance of the subjects was much better than might be expected by chance, and thus whether any learning occurred with the model that could be effectively transferred to the larger-scale environment. In general, attempts to learn large-scale environments from maps have proved to be less than fully successful. For example, Siegel, Herman, Allen, and Kirasic (1979) found very little positive transfer for sighted children from learning of a small-scale model to a large-scale environment. Schmitt (1978) examined performance of visually impaired and sighted adolescents on a locomotor route for which they had previously learned a tactual map route. There was some positive transfer from the tactual route to the locomotor route for the sighted subjects, but not for the blind. The magnitude of the error scores in the study by Herman et al. (1983) bear out the supposition that significant transfer did not occur: The correct distances in the larger environment were on the order of 10 to 20 feet, and the average deviation scores ranged around 8 feet! Performance was not very good, and the study may simply provide evidence that learning about larger scale environments from maps is not generally effective.

Landau, Gleitman, and Spelke (1981) report the only study with very young children that is relevant to this section. Their single subject was a 2.7-year-old RLF girl. The study was similar to those of Fletcher (1980, 1981a, 1981b) and Rieser, Guth, and Hill (1982) in that the experimental setting was an unfamiliar room in which objects could be arranged to create a distinctive spatial array. In this case the room contained four landmarks (table, basket, pillows, and the child's mother) arranged in a diamond pattern. In the exposure phase, she began at her mother's location and was walked to each of the other landmarks and back twice. Then she was placed at each of the landmarks in turn, and was asked to walk to each of the other items. Her performance was videotaped and was scored as to whether she moved to the correct 40-degree segment of the room containing the requested object. She was successful in eight of 12 trials. Her performance was apparently based on the relationships among the objects, since she subsequently performed five successful trials out of eight with the array of objects rotated 90 degrees within the room, but retaining the relationships within the array. This condition supposedly ruled out the use of acoustic cues from the walls as well as any other dependence on the larger structure within which the array was presented. (A group of five sighted 3-year-olds under blindfold performed similarly, averaging 8.2 correct trials of 12. Blindfolded sighted adults averaged 11 out of 12.)

Impressive though the performance of the blind child seems to have been, there are grounds on which to urge caution in using the findings to conclude that congenitally blind youngsters are very good at this sort of task. First, her reported success does not square well with the general findings that the congenitally blind perform very poorly on tasks of spatial relations (cf. Warren et al., 1973, for review). Second, she was but a single subject, and given the first point it seems particularly dangerous to generalize in this instance from the single case. She may indeed have performed very well, but be atypical. Third, however, the criterion for judgment of a "success" seems exceptionally liberal: in a room of the dimensions used, the child could have missed the target by half to three-quarters of a meter and have the trial counted a success. Fourth, diagrams of the routes that she actually traversed show considerable curvature rather than straight-line locomotion. This suggests that, despite the experimenters' attempts to prevent it, she was using updating information to approach the target, rather than a route based on Euclidean projection.

Thus while the Landau et al. (1981) study is of interest, it should probably not be taken as solid evidence that congenitally blind preschoolers are generally excellent at locomotor spatial relations performances.

Dodds, Howarth, and Carter (1982) also exposed children to a novel environment and studied their acquisition, but in this case a *route* was to be learned, rather than the spatial layout as in the case of Fletcher's work. The subjects were of normal intelligence, 11½ years of age, some congenitally blind and others adventitiously blinded, with no remaining vision. All had had at least one year of formal mobility training and could travel independently with the long cane. As if playing a game, the subject was started from a "home" location and was shown the route to "his friend's house." After the initial exposure to the route, which was about two city blocks square, the child drew a map using a raised-line kit. Then after each of four successive trials, a map was drawn, and at various route locations the child made pointer responses to other locations on the route. After this route was learned, the child was shown a new route to "his friend's house," this route consisting of a mirror image of the original route configuration. Pointing responses were again required to locations on the original route. Thus an inferential spatial performance was required, in that the child had to point to a known location from a new station point.

Most of the children had little or no difficulty with this type of task. In general, with the pointing responses the later blind subjects were better than the congenitally blind, and the former improved more quickly than the latter as well. On the second part of the task, in which the child was required to point to locations on the initial route from locations on the second route, the later blind performed much better—they were better able to combine information from two routes to perform a novel response.

Each child's performance was judged as falling into one of three categories: rigidly self-referent, less rigidly self-referent, and externally referent. The congenitally blind subjects tended strongly to the use of rigidly self-referent responses, while the later blind did not. One congenitally blind subject, though, performed rather well and with external reference; this suggests that congenital lack of vision can be overcome in performing this sort of task. It is notable that the other congenitally blind subjects were able to travel the route successfully, even after only one exposure trial, and yet could not effectively integrate spatial information from the two versions of the route.

Herman, Chatman, and Roth (1983) report a study of similar conception, although with subjects ranging in age from 12 to 24 years. Twelve subjects who were blind by 11 months of age were tested, as were groups of sighted subjects performing both with vision and under blindfold. The sighted groups performed better than the blind, but the IQ ranges were substantially different, and despite the authors' claim that this should make no difference, the difference invalidates any comparison between the groups. Nonetheless, the results from the blind are of interest. An artificial "hallway" with several turns was constructed within a large room. The subject was initially walked through the hallway by the experimenter, who pointed out several identifiable items placed at various locations. Then the subject was returned to each of the object locations, in random order, and was asked to use a pointer to indicate the direction of each of the other objects. Better performance was found for "closer" objects, that is those that were fewer turns away from the station point. No difference was found as a function of whether the object to be pointed to had been encountered before or after the current station point in the initial exposure walk. Subsequently, two subjects with substantial early visual experience and two partially sighted subjects were tested. These four subjects performed significantly better than the congenitally blind.

Hollyfield and Foulke (1983) also tested learned performance on a novel route. Their subjects were adults, ranging above 20 years in age. Two sighted groups were used, one performing with vision and the other blindfolded. A group of early blind (less than one year) was used, as was a later blind group with at least 12 years of sighted experience. The route was of a larger scale than the previous studies, covering five city blocks and about half a mile in length. The initial exposure was an experimenter-guided trip over the route. Then five trials followed, during each of which the subject tape-recorded verbal comments, and after each of which the subject used a modeling kit to make a map of the route. On the fifth such trial, the subject was stopped at a midway point in the route, and was informed that there was a roadblock and that he would have to find an alternative route to his destination.

The verbal reports were of little use. The remainder of the results are of mean walking speed (rather than errors). The sighted performing with vision were much better than any of the other groups. The early blind and later blind groups were comparable, though the early blind group seemed to perform marginally better throughout. The blindfolded sighted subjects were very poor to begin with, but improved to approximate the later blind by the fourth trial. Both blind groups showed a significant effect of practice. The detour task interfered greatly with performance in all nonvisual groups.

Perspective

Since it is a relatively new body of research literature that has been reviewed in this section, it may be helpful to discuss some untested assumptions and uncharted areas in the field. Foremost among the untested assumptions is the issue of maps and models. Those studies in which maps or models have been used either as a means of exposing the subject to the environment or of assessing the nature of the subject's understanding of the environment need to be questioned in their basic assumptions. Take first the issue of exposing the subject to the environment via a map or model, as was done by Herman, and Chatman (1983). The performance results in the larger-scale environment were poor. One must question whether the subjects had learned effective information about the spatial layout from the model in the first place. This issue was not addressed: there was no independent demonstration of the adequacy of the initial learning. The matter is an important one. So, too, is the matter of whether subjects can effectively construct maps or models as a means of demonstrating their knowledge about spatial relationships in an array. Casey (1978), Hollyfield and Foulke (1983), and Dodds et al. (1982) each asked the subject to make a map, in the first case of a familiar environment and in the latter cases of a novel environment. In no case was there independent verification of the subject's mapmaking abilities. Thus one is left to wonder whether the results reflect perception and understanding of the environment, or ability to construct a map. To be sure, the pattern of results is a logical one in much of this work. For example, Dodds et al. (1982) found the later blind to be better at the task than the early blind. But this pattern of difference may just as logically be expected in mapmaking abilities as in spatial cognition, and in any case if a set of results has to be validated by pointing out that it is consonant with the existing body of knowledge, then it does little to add to that body of knowledge!

An important variable that should receive some summary comment is just this issue of the nature of the response. A criticism of map- or modelmaking has been noted above. The relative advantages and disadvantages of the other response methods should receive study, though. Pointing to locations, travel to locations, and verbal descriptions of layouts have all been used in the literature reviewed. Each presumably has its strong points in relation to a specific research question that may be at issue, but in every case the selection of a response method should be carefully considered.

The method of exposure to the spatial array should also be carefully considered. Exposure by means of a map or model may be seriously questioned. Other methods also have their advantages and weak points. A locomotor exposure, in which the subject is led around or is asked to guide himself around the space, seems reasonable, but preexisting differences in locomotor abilities may influence how well the subject actually receives the information. If the subject is guided by the experimenter, then it may be that the subject will pay inadequate attention to the route, as happens when one rides in a car rather than driving it himself. If the subject guides himself around the space, then is the less confident traveler able to devote as much attention to the spatial information to be learned as the more confident one? The use of verbal delivery of information, as exemplified by Rosencranz and Suslick (1976) would seem to be a valuable technique, but the method may have its own as yet unidentified difficulties.

The use of familiar environments, of course, allows this difficulty to be circumvented: since the environment is familiar, there is no need to expose the subject to it anew. This assumption should not be accepted without question, however. The fact that a subject has been exposed to an environment repeatedly over a long period of time does not necessarily guarantee that he has good spatial knowledge of it. The answer lies in an assessment of his spatial knowledge, done independently of the other goals of the study. In any case, the study of *only* familiar environments would curtail this research area unnecessarily, since the study of the acquisition of knowledge of and ability to negotiate *new* environments is a key issue.

Still another variable is the nature of the environment to be learned. A distinction must be made between the learning of routes and the learning of spatial arrangements. In the former case, concentration may be solely on the acquisition of a linear route—a sequence of turns and segments—but it can include the question of overall spatial construction as well, by asking for the negotiation of alternatives to a known route (e.g., Hollyfield & Foulke, 1983). In the study of spatial arrangements, the emphasis is typically more clearly on the internal organization among the elements than on a sequence of the landmarks and the actions linking them. However, an important variable in this work has to do with whether or not an external frame around the arrangement of elements is used, as by Rosencranz and Suslick (1976). Presumably a different sort of knowledge is gained when a frame of reference is available than when just the internal arrangement among elements is to be learned.

Aside from the issues identified above as needing more attention, there is considerable need for study of individual differences in subsequent work in the spatial cognition area. One important area of individual differences is visual characteristics and visual history. Generally the work available to date follows the previous literature on spatial perception, in showing that those who have had sight for some period before becoming blind are at an advantage, and that those with some remaining visual capability also are at an advantage, compared to the totally blind. Attention should continue to be given to these variables, however, and particularly to the role of partial vision and to the means for optimizing the use of any remaining vision that may be available.

Another important dimension of individual differences has to do with the role of intellectual functioning in spatial cognition tasks. The results that are available to date are logical, such as the finding by Rosencranz and Suslick (1976) that Stanford-Binet Vocabulary performance was positively correlated to spatial performance. Intelligence has not been given much attention in the recent literature, and it should not be ignored.

Finally, the issue of development itself needs considerably more attention. Recent research has not generally been concerned with the development of spatial cognitive abilities. Fletcher (1980, 1981a,b), to be sure, included a range of ages in her study, but the age range at which important developmental progression should be expected is the early school years, and most studies have not examined children this young. It may be expected that, as the child's ability to assume a more external than egocentric frame of reference develops, important changes in spatial cognitive abilities will show up in the research paradigms used in recent work. Attempts to study developmental *process* should prove rewarding.

Summary

The new work captured under the rubric of spatial cognition is a potentially promising body of research. Yet there is much still to be learned. It is important that this research area not fall into the trap that the previous decades' research on spatial relations did—that is, the trap of self-containment and lack of adequate cross-reference to other areas of research. The considerable body of older research on maze learning, form combination, and the like is interesting in itself, but it is self-limiting and leaves much to be desired in its ability to guide those who work with the visually impaired population. This provincialism should be avoided in the spatial cognition area. By definition, the area does bring together spatial perception and cognition, and this is a promising start. The research needs to be placed in an even broader context to fulfill its considerable potential, however. As an example, it seems likely that there is a significant affective dimension that must influence the behavior of visually impaired children in their locomotor activities and their willingness to engage new environments in effective ways.

At the same time, the search for the wider context should not be allowed to substitute for the need to conduct the research in a careful way, to define and explore the significant variables (such as the method of exposure to the environment) thoroughly. A delicate balance will be necessary for this research area, which is one of the most exciting ones in recent decades, to fulfill its considerable promise.

Sensory Aids

For decades the hope has existed that it might be possible, through the development of appropriate technological applications, to provide an effective substitute for vision for the blind person. A lesser hope, but perhaps a more realistic one, has been that effective supplements to the other senses might be developed, not so much to replace vision as to assist the other senses in some of the functions that vision might ordinarily perform. Certainly the grander hope has not materialized—there is no technological substitute for vision. On the lesser scale, though, a variety of devices have been developed that provide the blind or visually impaired person with some of the information that the dysfunctional visual sense cannot. Although devices have been developed to serve a variety of functions, there are two areas in which most of the effort has been made: these are the perception of printed material as a substitute for visual reading, and the perception of spatial information, primarily as an aid to orientation and mobility in the physical environment. Notable in the former category are the Optacon, a device that delivers vibrotactile stimulation to the fingertip corresponding to the shape of the letters (or other material) that are scanned by a bank of miniature photoelectric cells; and the

Kurzweil Reading Machine, a device that provides an oral rendition of printed material scanned by sensors. There has been relatively little research on the effectiveness of these devices for visually impaired children. The concentration in this section will be on the latter category, the devices that are related to the processing of information about the physical spatial environment.

Primary among such devices are the Lasercane, the Russell Pathsounder, and the Sonicguide™. Most of the work with these devices has been with adults, although in the past few years a body of literature has gradually developed that is devoted to the use of such devices, particularly the Sonicguide™, with blind children and infants. Humphrey and Humphrey (in press) provide a very useful overview of this research.

Several theoretical or speculative accounts of the role that aids might play with infants and children have been offered without documentation. For the most part these are positive in tone. For example, Baird (1977) saw the Sonicguide™ as more potentially helpful than either the Lasercane or the Pathsounder, and agreed that it should be most useful with children before the onset of formal mobility training, particularly in support of the training of the conceptual bases of environmental perception. Vopata (1978) similarly offered guidance for the use of the Sonicguide™ with premobility and early mobility children, listing various activities for which the aid might prove useful. Again the emphasis was on early use. The emphasis of Strelow and Boys (1979) was more on the description of the Sonicguide™ and its basic operation. Although the article was not intended as a guide to the use of the aid, Strelow and Boys outlined the potential research usefulness of the device with visually impaired children. On the more cautious side, Warren (1977), in response to the report by Bower (1977a) of the use of the Sonicguide™ with human infants, urged that such use with blind infants be undertaken only with extreme caution, since it was (and remains) unknown what the effects of such use might be on development in other areas, such as selective auditory attention. More recently, Ferrell (1983) argued that caution must be exercised in using the Sonicguide™ with infants, citing evidence that suggested that the development of intermodality coordination may be delayed as a result.

Aside from these arguments, there have been a number of case studies reported in the recent literature. Newcomer (1977) discussed the use of the Sonicguide™ in the school setting with four children of various ages from kindergarten to senior high school, addressing the question of the value of the device to the children and in particular the question what they could do with it that they could not have done without it. Newcomer identified several notable advantages, but cited several disadvantages as well, including the need for adaptation of the device to individual children at different ages. His conclusion was guardedly positive with respect to the utility of the device in the educational setting.

Strelow, Kay, and Kay (1978) reported two cases, one a developmentally delayed 2½-year-old and the other a bright 6-year-old. The former subject had good physical development but serious motor and language delays and social development problems, showing very much the typical autistic syndrome. Work with the Sonicguide™ was begun at a rudimentary level and showed some success at simple tasks. Intensive work produced general progress in locomotor skills over a six-month period, during which time the child became able to stand up, take several steps, and eventually follow his mother or the experimenter around for several minutes at a time. Daily use of the device aided his further locomotor development considerably, and he showed increased responsiveness to people and sounds. No doubt the larger rehabilitation program played a significant part in his development; nevertheless, it seemed evident that the aid played a vital role, particularly in his gaining the ability to make effective use of spatial information. The second case was that of a 6-year-old girl, verbally precocious but without independent locomotion. Intensive use of the Sonicguide™ in a highly individualized program produced regular advances in independent mobility, and it was clear that the aid was instrumental to her progress.

With younger children, it is less clear that the Sonicguide™ is uniformly beneficial. Ferrell (1980) reported results from four children ranging in age from 6 to 26 months at the beginning of work. Her results showed mixed success with the Sonicguide™. All of Ferrell's subjects had been premature and were blind due to RLF. The oldest child, who was locomotor at the outset, seemed to interpret the aid signal readily and to make use of the Sonicguide™ in mobility. The youngest showed aid-mediated reaching to objects within two months of training. The two middle children, aged 10 and 14 months, showed much slower progress. Interestingly, stereotypic behavior was observed to decrease during periods when the Sonicguide™ was operating.

Strelow (1983) reported four cases, the older two of which (24 and 26 months at onset of intervention) are of interest here. The 24-month-old presented serious problems to the intervention program—many competing behaviors seemed to combine to defeat the possible effectiveness of the program, and his case would have to be termed a failure from the point of view of the use of the Sonicguide™. The oldest subject, 26 months at the outset of aid use, showed more progress, although her program was unfortunately interrupted at several points. Both these 2-year-olds showed less than satisfactory progress, apparently because of the existence of established behavior that worked to decrease their appropriate responsiveness to the aid signals.

Strelow (1983) had more success with his two younger subjects, aged 10 and 21 months at the outset of the study. The youngest was developmentally normal but congenitally blind. For the first three months he showed little tendency to reach toward a toy presented to the sensor, in part because of competing behavior. During a period following his 13th month, intensive work with the Sonicguide™ produced definite evidence of reaching to objects on the basis of the aid's sound. More extended study of this child was unfortunately not possible. The 21-month-old, despite motor problems stemming from meningitis, learned in just one session to reach for an object presented to the sensor, and subsequently learned, through an extended period of training, to guide a significant amount of her mobility via the Sonicguide™.

It is clear from both Strelow's (1983) and Ferrell's (1980) studies that use of the Sonicguide™ does not yield entire success with these children: in Ferrell's words, "The Sonicguide is certainly not the panacea that has been suggested" (p. 216). On the other hand, both studies found considerable success with some children. It is not clear what the factors are that produce more or less success, except that the existence and maintenance of significant kinds of competing behavior (i.e., such as are incompatible with those related to effective aid use) is a negative factor.

Bower (1977a) reported the use of a Sonicguide™ with a 7-month-old visually impaired infant. His concern was initially to test the perceptual developmental hypothesis that the sensory modalities in human infants are initially undifferentiated, and only later become differentiated and then reintegrated. If there is an initial nondifferentiation of the senses, then the blind infant should be very capable of using the auditory information delivered by the Sonicguide™ to denote spatial location—the use would in fact be easier than that by older infants whose sensory modalities have become differentiated. Bower reported that the infant made appropriate reaching or defensive reactions to the presentation of an object to the sensor after very few trials. In fact, Bower reported one response in particular (an appropriate "placing" or reaching response to a pair of batons) which Kay, the creator of the Sonicguide™, argued could not be mediated by the form of the aid which Bower had used. Instead of perceiving two batons, the infant should perceive a single object midway between the two and, if anything, reach to that location (Kay & Strelow, 1977). Bower's rejoinder (Bower, 1976b) on this point was not particularly convincing, and Ferrell (1980) suggested that residual vision may have been involved in the successful performance on a task which should not have been possible to perform with the Sonicguide™ alone.

Nevertheless, the notion that very young infants may find it easier to use the information of the Sonicguide™ than older infants or children is a provocative one not only from the point of view of practical application in this field but also from the theoretical standpoint of the initial undifferentiatedness of the sensory modalities. The theoretical issue will go unresolved for some time simply because of the inherent difficulties in conducting the necessary research. However, there is other information bearing on the applied issue. Aitken and Bower (1982a) described a program of both short-term and long-term use of the Sonicguide™ with visually impaired infants. The eight congenitally blind subjects ranged from 4 to 20 months of age at the beginning of the project. The short-term subjects had total exposure ranging up to seven hours. No hard data were offered, but it was noted that tracking, reaching, and other appropriate responses to approaching objects occurred with some regularity. Interestingly, the younger infants were reported to show the appropriate responses with less experience than the older infants. Transfer of responses to new situations was also reported, in support of the argument that what was involved was spontaneous perceptually based behavior, rather than learned behavior. On the other hand, Humphrey, Harris, Muir, and Dodwell (in press) reported finding virtually no selective responsiveness to presentation of the signal of the Canterbury child's aid (essentially the Sonicguide™) by a 6-month-old infant.

Three infants, initially aged six, eight, and 13 months, were studied by Aitken and Bower over a longer term with frequent Sonicguide™ sessions given by the parents. The results were mixed. The youngest subject was reported to show appropriate reaching, grasping, and placing responses on approximately the same timetable as sighted infants. The two older subjects were less successful, the older of them (begun at 13 months) showing no apparent benefit from the Sonicguide™ at all.

In another report, Aitken and Bower (1982b) reported the same study again, with the addition of three subjects to the short-term sample, one begun at eight months and the others at 20 and 25 months. In brief, the results were positive with the youngest subject and rather negative with the two older subjects.

Kay and Kay (1983) furnished an initial report of a further adaptation of the Sonicguide™, called the Trinaural Sensor. In essence, this device adds a central foveal field of greater resolution to the binaural field contained in the Sonicguide™, the function of which should be to increase central resolution and therefore make spatial tasks requiring finer discrimination more feasible. Kay and Kay reported very briefly an apparently successful pilot program with school-age children in a school setting.

A number of important questions remain unanswered by this work to date. One is the question of the most appropriate approach to exposure. Most of the projects (e.g., Ferrell, 1980; Strelow, 1983) have used the Sonicguide™ within a larger context of an intervention program. Bower (1977a; Aitken & Bower, 1982a,b), on the other hand, argues that at least younger infants (for whom verbal instruction would be less appropriate anyway) can spontaneously acquire the meaningfulness of the aid's signals. A second question is related to age. With older children (roughly age four and up), the Sonicguide™ seems to have a uniformly positive effect. With very young infants, such as some of those reported by Aitken and Bower (1982a,b), it may be that more spontaneous acquisition may occur, although the evidence offered is unconvincing. In between these two age ranges (roughly a year to three years) there is mixed success (cf. Strelow, 1983; Ferrell, 1980), and success may depend largely on the ability of the program to circumvent the interfering effect of competing behaviors and already developed inappropriate spatial and mobility behaviors. A third question is the degree to which any positive effect is attributable to the aid itself and the specific signals that it presents, as opposed to the larger context of the intervention program. A fourth and critically important question has to do with the suitability of intensive intervention of this sort with infants and young children. One suspects that some of the unsuccessful attempts have failed because the experience of the child with the sensor has been too limited: if more intensive experience had been provided, perhaps more progress would have been found. But it is imperative for prospective researchers in this area to consider the impact, on the child's overall development, of devoting a large proportion of the child's energy to learning the use of the aid. A particular concern, especially with younger infants, is the possible negative impact in areas such as the development of selective auditory attention and intermodality coordination. The researcher has a vital moral obligation to consider such possibilities.

No doubt the research of the next few years will provide many of the answers to these questions. At this point it seems safe to conclude that neither the Sonicguide™ nor any alternative device will successfully serve as a *substitute* for vision. Rather, it is likely that such devices, carefully used, will serve as effective *supplements* to the sensory information that visually impaired children gain through their other sensory modalities.

In any case, significant progress in the field will depend on the ability to leap beyond existing conceptualizations of aids. Emerging technologies will certainly allow such leaps. It is imperative that technology be guided effectively, though. We need to understand, better than we now do, the nature of functional spatial knowledge and its acquisition. What are the key elements of the construction of the child's knowledge both of spatial structure in general and of specific spatial layouts? What information is important, and what is not? How is the information constructed into a cognitive representation of space? How can sensory aids be designed to provide the necessary information while not overloading the user with unnecessary information? And we need to know how learning proceeds best and most naturally, so that programs of training in the use of sensory aids can be structured to mirror most optimally the natural course of learning.

Summary

There are various reasons why broad generalizations cannot easily be drawn from the preceding review of perceptual and motor abilities in blind children. There appears to be no rule that fits all the results. Blind children have been found to be better in some areas of performance, while sighted children have been found to be better in others. In still other areas, no differences have been found. One reason for this variance in results, aside from true differences in abilities, is the somewhat abnormal situation that sighted subjects experience when they are blindfolded and asked to perform a task. Normally they would have vision available in performing tasks involving tactual or auditory information. Since the ways that vision helps or interacts with the other senses are not very well understood, it is difficult to know just how much and in which specific situations the preclusion of vision is detrimental to the performance of the sighted. It must be concluded that in many studies the comparison of blindfolded sighted with blind subjects may not lead to clearly interpretable results.

Another difficulty in generalizing is the heterogeneity of the blind population. There are at least five dimensions on which blind children may vary that may affect their performance on perceptual and motor tasks. The five are chronological age, mental age (or IQ), age at onset of handicap, severity of impairment, and cause of blindness. There is very little information about the differences in skills in various etiological groups, except for some obvious points such as the fact that children with visual impairment due to rubella often have auditory difficulties as well. There is somewhat more information, although still relatively little, on the effects of the severity of the visual handicap. Most studies on perceptual abilities have used children who are either totally blind or have at most LP. Some interesting exceptions exist. For example, Pick et al. (1966) included a partial-vision group in their study on tactual orientation judgments. This study serves as an example of the generalization that when partially sighted subjects are studied, they typically show different patterns of results from either fully sighted or totally blind groups. This point, along with the fact that partially sighted but legally blind individuals make up a fair proportion of the population of visually impaired children, argues for a considerable investment of research attention to this group.

The age-at-onset factor has received much more attention, and the fact that there are some distinct differences between early and late blind subjects makes the results of many studies which do not consider this variable open to question. Warren et al. (1973) concluded from a review of the spatial performance literature that age of onset plays a greater part in tasks that are relatively complex. Thus, for example, later blind subjects have typically been found to perform better than early blind on maze-learning tasks. Such superiority is often attributed to some kind of visualization by the later blind, although it is not known just how such visualization operates or what its limits are.

Mental age and IQ have received a fair amount of attention in the perception literature. In tests of nonvisual discriminative abilities, MA has typically not been found to play an important role in determining performance. In various integrative perceptual abilities, however, MA has been found to be involved. In fact, one of the two major categories of IQ tests for the blind involves spatial relations. Hammill's group, in particular, has studied performance on the Tactile-Kinesthetic Test as an indicator of MA. Warren et al. (1973) discussed two general ways in which MA may be involved in spatial behavior. One is the spatial relations abilities that are tapped by the TKT and block-design tests. The other involves verbal IQ. In several studies of maze learning where differences have been found, higher IQ has been related to better performance. It should also be noted that, where results for sighted controls are reported, the IQ-performance relations are typically absent or weaker than in the blind. Verbal mediation of maze-learning performance has also been reported, and it is not unreasonable to expect that verbal mediation would be more effective in subjects with higher verbal MA, thus producing the relationship between verbal MA and performance.

Finally, chronological age itself has been found to bear a significant relation to various types of perceptual performance, ranging from simple discriminative skills (such as texture or shape) to complex behavior. The CA results have been noted in the body of this chapter. It remains to be emphasized that not nearly as much attention has been paid to CA as should be. Results from subjects spanning a wide age range are often averaged, and no correlation of CA with the dependent measure is presented. This lack is especially unfortunate when it becomes obvious that, in some areas, asymptotic performance is reached by some particular age. Training directed toward such performance would presumably be maximally effective before the asymptotic age. To design effective experiential programs, age information is critical.

3
Cognitive Development

Many writers have discussed the possibility that cognitive abilities develop more slowly or in a different way in blind children than in sighted children. Lowenfeld (1948), for example, pointed out that blindness imposes three general restrictions, all of which may have effects on cognitive development: range and variety of experiences, ability to get about, and control of environment and self in relation to environment. The totally blind child must, of course, build up concepts of the world on the basis of other than visual information, while visual information is extremely useful in building concepts for the sighted child. Hearing is of more limited value than vision, and touch is inappropriate for the experience of distant, very large, very small, fragile, or dangerous objects. Color cannot be directly experienced at all. These various limitations make the total experience of the blind child more restricted, and as Lowenfeld noted, they decrease the range of available learning experiences. Foulke (1962) made similar points, noting in general that the nature of the concepts an individual acquires depends on his range of experiences, and therefore it may be expected that the concepts of the blind child are in some ways more restricted than those of the sighted child. In addition to the tactual limitations noted by Lowenfeld, Foulke pointed out that touch does not serve to mediate two-dimensional representations of three-dimensional objects. Foulke also noted that the blind are more dependent on secondhand experience, that is, on what can be conveyed by verbally transmitted information from other people. The blind child's dependence on verbally transmitted information also places him in a position of greater dependence on effective verbal communication, and thus verbal facility may be more important to the cognitive development of the blind than the sighted. Foulke noted, finally, that the sensory restrictions of the blind child may tend to make him more self-oriented, with possible consequences for personality characteristics. That is, he may become "egocentric and. . . interested primarily in sensations connected with his own body" (p. 5).

Similar potential problems with cognitive development are discussed in the psychoanalytic literature. Wills (1965) provided several examples. The blind child may have more anxiety about the use of fantasy and about the distinction between fantasy and reality. He has more difficulty in gathering and collating varied experiences about situations or events, leading to slower establishment of adequate concepts. Echoing a similar point made by Foulke (1962), Wills noted that blind children may prolong the tendency to understand objects by relating or comparing them with their own bodies, rather than with external objects or events. Finally, Wills noted a greater tendency toward animism in blind children than sighted—that is, the blind child is more likely to attribute feelings and other human characteristics to inanimate objects.

The discussions of Lowenfeld, Foulke, Wills, and others (e.g., Hampshire, 1977; Santin & Simmons, 1977; Swallow, 1976) are useful in delineating areas of possible cognitive developmental differences between blind and sighted children. The substantial body of research on these areas in the postinfancy period will be reviewed in this chapter. Chapter 1 contains relevant material for the infancy period.

Understanding the World

Considerable attention has been directed toward the sighted child's understanding of properties of the world and of objects. Piaget has been a primary catalyst for this research with his extensive evaluation of the developmental course of the understanding of object constancy, classification, and the various conservations. Although this area has been much less completely studied in blind children than sighted, there is a body of literature available. Wolff (1966) outlined some of the relevant questions. Is the cognitive development of the blind slower than that of sighted children? To what extent can any developmental lags be attributed to blindness itself? Are there effects of blindness on the child's distinction between self and nonself? What substitute channels of information does the blind child use in place of vision?

Classification

Classification is one of the abilities most basic to cognitive processes. How do children come to be able to note similarities among objects, what dimensions are most salient, what are the relationships between the ability to classify (disregard differences and concentrate on similarities) and the ability to distinguish (attend to key differences)? Foulke (1964) described the initial construction of a classification test which uses a series of blocks that vary on seven dimensions. The dimensions include audition (bell vs. no bell), vision (black vs. white), and several tactual dimensions. The child can be asked to group the blocks spontaneously in different ways, and his flexibility in switching rules, as well as his sensitivity to information from several modalities, may be assessed. Although performance norms were not reported, Foulke noted that the typical procedures that blind children followed at various ages were similar to the procedures that sighted children follow, such as spontaneous switching of grouping characteristics and perseveration.

Hatwell (1966, French ed.; 1984, English ed.) reported an extensive series of studies with blind and sighted children, among them experiments on classification. Her subjects ranged from five to 10 years of age. The blind subjects had light perception or less and were of a normal range of intelligence (verbal IQ of 80 or greater). The congenitally blind were diagnosed at birth or within the first year of life, whereas the adventitiously blinded had had vision until after the age of four years.

In one experiment on classification, the subject was presented with four pieces of wood, three of which shared features in common but the fourth of which differed on a key feature such as shape, texture, size, or direction of an indicator line. In a game situation, the child was required to select the one object that was different from the others in order to receive a candy reward. Congenitally blind and adventitiously blinded subjects were tested, as were sighted subjects performing tactually or with vision. The sighted subjects with vision were distinctly better than the other groups (that is, they performed successfully at younger ages); the sighted subjects performing tactually were better than the congenitally blind. The smaller group of adventitiously blinded subjects, compared with an age-matched subset of the congenitally blind, did significantly better than the congenitally blind.

In a second experiment, Hatwell used as stimulus materials eight pieces of wood of various shapes (cubes, flat squares, spheres, flat discs) and sizes, asking the subject to sort them into two boxes on the basis of a similarity, then to resort them on the basis of another similarity, and so on. There was roughly a two-year lag shown by the congenitally blind compared with the sighted subjects, regardless of whether the sighted performed tactually or with vision. The adventitiously blind were superior to the congenitally blind.

Higgins (1973) conducted a study designed to test several questions, among them whether congenitally blind children show a developmental lag in classification skills compared with sighted children, and whether there would be patterns of "developmental asynchrony" among the blind, with some selected types of classification showing a lag. Specifically, Higgins hypothesized that blind children would be less able than sighted children to classify when abstract content was involved than when concrete content was involved. The blind children ranged from five to 11 years, had at most LP, and had been blind from within the first year of life. The children from seven to nine years of age were studied more intensively than the others, and these children (19 in all) were matched with a group of sighted control subjects. The blind children all had IQ of 75 or higher (verbal WISC), and the mean IQ for the seven-to-nine-year group was 99.5, not significantly different from that of the sighted control group. The three tests, Modified Kofsky Battery (MKB), Tactual Test of Class Multiplication, and Verbal Test of Class Inclusion (VCI), tapped a variety of classification skills. Higgins found no overall difference between blind and sighted children on the MKB. Performance on the VCI, however, did show some asynchrony within the blind group. Specifically, the blind subjects scored significantly worse on concepts involving abstract content than on the concrete content concepts. There was not a corresponding difference between concrete and abstract for the sighted subjects. Higgins' work allows several conclusions. First, there was no evidence for a general developmental lag of the congenitally blind children. Further, the general principle derived from Piagetian theory that preoperational skills are mastered before operational abilities emerge was supported in a corresponding manner for the blind and the sighted children. There was no evidence that different general principles of cognitive growth are involved in blind and sighted children. Finally, Higgins concluded that the asynchrony of the blind children with respect to abstract categorization did not represent a generalized deficit, but rather "reflected a child's previous activity with the elements about which he had to reason. The likelihood of a correct response was significantly greater if the child had performed perceptual or motor actions in relation to the elements specified in the class inclusion questions" (p. 33).

Higgins' discussion of the implications of his findings for educational questions is especially instructive. He noted that his findings support the notion that the congenitally blind child does not show deficits in the general intellectual processes involved with classification, but that he "may be handicapped in exercising these capabilities because he cannot obtain the prerequisite data from his surroundings. It may be the case, therefore, that the problem facing the educator is not so much how to compensate for a deficiency in the blind child's classificatory structuring but how to help him derive maximum benefit from his available senses so that the information flow is sufficient to support the thought of which the child is capable" (p. 37).

In another study designed to pursue Hatwell's findings (1966, French ed.; 1984, English ed.), Friedman and Pasnak (1973a) studied classification and seriation skills in groups of blind (age six to 14) and sighted (six-, eight- and 11-year-old) children. The 21 blind children were from grades one through six of a residential school. About half were congenitally blind, and 12 had LP or less. The study was directed to Hatwell's finding that blind children were several years delayed on manipulatory tests of classification, while they were a year or so advanced on verbal tests. Friedman and Pasnak used both verbal and manipulatory tests of classification and seriation. The sighted and partially sighted subjects were blindfolded during the manipulatory versions of the tests. The patterns of results for classification and seriation tasks were quite similar. The sighted subjects showed a significant improvement over the age range, but the trend of the blind, although it suggested improvement over age, was not significant. Comparisons of the eight-year-old blind and sighted groups did not produce significant differences, while comparison of the 11-year-old groups showed a significant superiority of the sighted children.

The increasing divergence between blind and sighted subjects with age was somewhat stronger for the verbal versions of the tasks, although the differences between verbal and manipulatory tasks were not impressive. Although it is not possible to make a conclusive argument from the data as presented, it seems likely that at least part of the increasing divergence between blind and sighted subjects over age was due to sampling differences. The sixth grade sighted children were apparently clustered closely around age 11, while the sixth grade blind children apparently ranged up to 14 years of age. The fact that some of the blind sixth graders were much older than the normal age for sixth grade suggests that these subjects were more heterogeneous in school-related abilities than the sighted subjects, and specifically that the blind sample may have included subjects with lower ability ranges than the corresponding sighted sample. Despite the admitted shortcomings of IQ tests, it would be useful in studies such as this one to have IQ characteristics reported. In any case, Friedman and Pasnak concluded that tests of classification and seriation may depend too heavily on perceptual factors to serve as effective indices of cognitive abilities.

Hatwell (1966, French ed.; 1984, English ed.) also studied seriation, the ability to order a series of elements according to some criterion such as size. Tasks involving size, length, and weight were administered. In the seriation of length and size, the congenitally blind lagged from one to three years behind the sighted performing with vision, who in turn did not differ from the sighted performing tactually without vision. There was no difference between the congenitally and adventitiously blind, although Hatwell noted that a ceiling effect was probably operating for these subjects to the eight to ten year old range. On seriation of weight, the congenitally blind showed only a slight delay compared to the sighted. There was no difference between congenitally and adventitiously blind.

Hall (1981b, 1983) studied children over the age range seven to 17 who had been visually impaired (less than form perception) since within the first year of life. Subjects were given three tasks, a concrete task, a verbal task with high imagery words, and a verbal task with low imagery words. Various questions were asked that were designed to tap classification strategies, and specifically whether grouping would be done on the basis of perceptible (sensory), functional, or nominal attributes. It was expected that the children would show more perceptible attributes in the early years, with functional and nominal groupings occurring with more frequency with increasing age.

In addition, the formation of equivalence groupings was expected to vary with the degree of concreteness and imagery level of the task. With the concrete task, subjects tended to concentrate heavily on perceptible attributes, with no effects of age. Hall suggested, based on this result, that the use of concrete tasks may not promote cognitive growth and higher level thinking skills, a conclusion with significant implications for instructional strategies. Further contrary to logical expectation, the perceptible grouping strategies were commonly used by all ages, regardless of the degree of imagery required in the task.

Several studies are available that have attempted to improve classification abilities in blind children by training. Adkins (1965) reported the outcome of a one-session training procedure that was administered to children from age six to 16. Three groups were tested, one totally blind, one ranging from LP to large-print readers, and one sighted. About three-quarters of the blind subjects had been blind from birth (many were RLF), and all had become blind by the age of three. A pre- and posttraining classification test involved the sorting of 16 blocks which varied on four dimensions, size, shape, texture, and weight. The training procedure, adapted from a report by Hanfmann and Kasanin (1937), involved assigning a verbal label to a designated correct block, and then the judgment, accompanied by feedback, of whether each of a series of comparison blocks also had that label. There were no significant differences between the groups on verbal or performance measures on the pretest, although the performance of the sighted group was somewhat worse. The training produced a significant improvement in the sighted group but not in the blind groups. The final performance level, however, was not different for the three groups. It is tempting to accept Adkins' suggestion that the significant improvement from pre- to posttest for the sighted group was attributable to an artifactually low pretest score, produced by their "sudden blindness" (all subjects performed blindfolded). Thus Adkins' results should probably not be taken as evidence that classification is more trainable in sighted than in blind children. In fact, it may be argued that Adkins' approach did not allow a valid assessment of the training question for blind or sighted children, since the training procedures were not intensive. The entire session, including pretesting, training, and posttesting, took only 45 minutes.

A much more intensive approach to the training question was used by Friedman and Pasnak (1973b), who studied the feasibility of accelerating classification skills in blind children. The subjects were two groups of early blind children (most from birth, two years at the latest), ranging in age from six to 12 years. Etiology and severity of handicap were heterogeneous. Eight pairs of subjects were matched on various characteristics, and one member of each pair received the training while the control member received an enrichment program that was not specifically directed toward classification skills. The classification training program used a learning set, or generalization approach. Various types of classification tasks were used, including verbal and tactual discovery of class problems, and form, orientation, texture, and size classification problems. Each child's progress through the program was self-paced. Each training session took 30 minutes, and the number of sessions ranged from three to 26, covering from two to 13 weeks. Pre- and posttests were administered using classification problems that were not used in the training program. The classification training group showed a significant improvement from pre- to posttest while the control group did not. Furthermore, the mean posttest performance for the classification training group was not different from the performance of a group of sighted subjects of similar ages. Friedman and Pasnak carefully noted that, in contrast to many training studies with sighted children, their study did not attempt to train a cognitive skill at an earlier age than it would normally occur in sighted children. "Rather, children who were chronologically mature were aided in acquiring a concept that they had failed to master because of a sensory handicap" (p. 337).

Lebron-Rodriguez and Pasnak (1977) reported a similar training study in which the effects of training in classification and seriation were compared with those of seriation-only training and with a no-training control group of visually impaired children, ranging from total congenital blindness to 20/500 and from six to 11 years of age. In addition to pre- and posttests of seriation and classification, the verbal WISC and the Slosson Intelligence Test (SIT) were used for assessment. Classification training included tactile problems as well as verbal analogs to them, and covered form, size, texture, and orientation. The seriation training problems were similar and similarly included verbal analogs. Classification and seriation tests involved similar, though not identical, problems. After pretest and resulting division of the subjects into groups, one group was given a series of training sessions on seriation, and then upon reaching mastery of the problems, on classification. The no-training control group was tutored for an equivalent amount of time on various school subjects. The seriation-only group received the seriation training, and then individual tutoring. The training extended over a substantial period of time: seriation training ranged from five to 58 sessions, while classification training averaged 12 sessions per subject. The control group showed negligible gains on both seriation and classification tests. The seriation-plus-classification group showed substantial gains on both tests, while the seriation-only group gained significantly only on the seriation test. On both the verbal WISC and the SIT, the seriation-plus-classification group showed significantly more improvement than the control group, while the seriation-only group was intermediate. The gains on the verbal WISC were impressive — the average gain was 14 points for the classification-plus-seriation group and eight points for the seriation-only group.

Thus the preliminary answers to Wolff's (1966) questions for classification skills are, first, that there are selective developmental lags among blind children; second, that the lags apparently can be attributed to specific aspects of the lack of visual experience; and third, that there are training techniques that may be used effectively to bring blind children to the level normally demonstrated by sighted children. All these answers are oversimplified, though, and there is a great deal of research yet to be done before more detailed conclusions may be reached. First, more information is needed about the specific abilities that show lags. Higgins' work is a good model for such work. Second, although it is tempting to be satisfied with statements that deficits can be traced to areas of inadequate experience, not very much is known about just how specific cognitive abilities are dependent on specific types of experience. Before optimally effective training programs can be designed, detailed information of this sort is needed. In their training study, Friedman and Pasnak found a significant effect of the training procedures for the group as a whole, but they found some children did not respond well to the training program. Such differences are also found among sighted children, of course, but it would seem especially critical to study individual differences in blind children, and to ascertain which training methods might be optimally effective for children with different characteristics and different experiential histories. Third, it is not well understood just how serious the selective lags in classification skills may be for other areas of cognitive performance which depend on classification. Higgins' discussion of educational implications is a good step in this direction, but his treatment was designed to ask questions rather than answer them. Finally, it is an important question, to which we shall return, whether the concept of developmental lag, as Wolff (1966) posed it, is an appropriate way of viewing cognitive differences between blind and sighted children.

The relative deficits in abstract reasoning noted by Higgins (1973) have also been found by other researchers. For example, Tillman (1967b) reported a factor-analytic study of the responses of blind and sighted children, ranging in age from six to 13, on the WISC verbal scales. Most of the blind children had been blind from birth, and children with large-print capability or better were excluded. On the Similarities scale, two factors emerged for the sighted group. The factors represented relatively concrete and relatively more abstract items. For the blind group, only one factor was identified, and it was similar to the concrete factor for the sighted subjects. The difference in factor structure must be taken with caution, though, since the mean IQ of the sighted group was significantly higher than that of the blind group. No correlations between abstractness and IQ were reported for the sighted group, and it seems quite possible that a group of sighted subjects matched to the blind for IQ might also have shown a single, less abstract factor. Alternatively, a blind group matched to the higher IQ of the sighted group might have produced both factors. In a similar study, Zweibelson and Barg (1967) evaluated the abstractness of the responses of blind and sighted children on the Similarities and Vocabulary scales of the WISC. The blind children were 11 to 13 years old, were primarily blind from birth, and were all either totally blind or had LP at most. The blind subjects and their sighted controls varied over a wide IQ range. There were significantly more concrete and functional scores obtained by the blind group and more abstract scores obtained by the sighted. As was the case in the Tillman study, a question occurs about the relationship between abstractness and IQ. Specifically, it would be instructive to know if there was a greater tendency toward abstract scores among the higher-IQ blind children, and whether the relationship between abstractness and IQ was similar for blind and sighted subjects.

A report by Schwartz (1972) stands in contrast to the abstractness results of Zweibelson and Barg (1967) and Tillman (1967b). Schwartz compared congenitally blind with sighted children from the lower grades on an "Abstraction Test," among other tests, and found no differences between the groups. Again, the meaning of this result is clouded by the existence of significant differences on two variables that may be related to abstract reasoning. The blind children ranged in age from 6.5 to 10.5 years, while the sighted children ranged about a year younger, and the mean IQ (SIT) of the sighted group was significantly higher than that of the blind group. The nature of the relationships between these variables and abstract reasoning is not well understood, and thus the ways that the group differences on these variables might have affected the abstract-reasoning scores are not clear.

Hammill and Powell (1967) provided some evidence about the relationships between abstract reasoning and IQ and CA in blind children. The aurally administered Abstraction Test was one developed and used by Irwin and Hammill (1964) with cerebral palsied and by Hammill and Irwin (1966) with mentally retarded children. The blind children studied by Hammill and Powell were five to 10 years old, of normal intelligence (test not specified), and had varying degrees of residual vision. Scores on the Abstraction Test significantly discriminated the high and low extremes of both CA and IQ, indicating that, at least for this test of abstract reasoning, abstraction ability is positively related to both variables.

It is noteworthy that in the studies on classification reported in this section the youngest children used were five years. Yet classification is a fundamental cognitive ability that begins to develop much earlier than five years old, and methods should be devised to study the issue with younger children. An example of such an approach is reported by Gerhardt (1982), who studied a blind infant between the ages of 14 and 18 months. The subject was developmentally relatively normal, having been born full term with no additional handicaps, and having warm and supportive parents. Her motor development was delayed compared to sighted infants but was reasonable compared to blind norms: she sat at 5 months, walked at 16, and reached for objects on tactual cues at 8 months and on auditory cues at 11. She was examined at 14, 16, and 18 months of age. In each session, a free-play technique was used, in which the experimenter sat on the floor with the child and handed her various sets of objects to play with. The objects different from one another in size, shape, noisemaking characteristics, and so on, with some objects the same as one another and others differing. The manner of her handling and grouping the objects was observed. It was hypothesized that she would, like sighted infants, progress developmentally from grouping dissimilar objects to grouping on the basis of their various physical similarities. This progression was observed over the four-month span; however, the subject grouped dissimilar objects at 14 months and progressed to similarity-based classification by 18 months, whereas sighted infants show similarity grouping at 12 months.

It is obviously risky to draw firm conclusions from only one subject, but the Gerhardt study is important in its demonstration of a possible methodology for the study of classification in infants. The issue is an important one.

It is clear that more research must be done before the relationships between abstract reasoning abilities and other variables such as age and IQ are understood. Studies that evaluate simple relationships will not provide adequate answers. There may be complex interactions between visual characteristics and these other variables, and only research that takes the complexity into account will allow significant progress in this area.

Conservation

Much of the better known work of Piaget has involved the various "conservations." Conservation of a property refers in general to the ability to retain correct judgment of the property even in the face of perceptual transformations. For example, conservation of substance or mass is usually evaluated by showing the child two equal balls of clay, having him judge them as being of equal substance, then changing the shape of one of them without removing any substance and again asking for a judgment of comparative substance. If the child replies that the two are still of equal substance, although now differing in shape, he is said to have conserved the property of substance, while if he responds incorrectly, he is labeled a nonconserver. There is an extensive literature on the development of various conservations in sighted children. The orderly progression in the development of these cognitive abilities is, to oversimplify, typically explained by citing the child's need to maintain a state of equilibrium between his cognitive structures (schemas) and his perceptual information about the world. That is, his improving perceptual and cognitive skills necessitate periodic revisions in his cognitive representations of the world. Given the importance that is attributed to perceptual experience in Piaget's theory of cognitive development, it is reasonable to ask whether blind children might attain the various conservations in different ways or in different time sequences than sighted children.

In almost all the work to date, the technique with blind children has been simply to modify what is usually a purely visual or visual-tactual task to create a purely tactual task, to make it suitable for the blind. The validity of this approach can be severely questioned, as will be discussed presently.

Hatwell's (1966, French ed.; 1984, English ed.) work was the first large scale investigation of the development of the conservations in blind children. She reported a general lag of several years in the acquisition of various conservation abilities, with conservation of substance showing a three-year lag (at 10 years vs. seven) and conservation of weight a four-year lag (12 years vs. eight). More recently, several investigators have studied conservation abilities in detail, with special concentration on conservation of volume, weight, and substance (mass).

Research on conservation of substance has been reported by Miller (1969), Tobin (1972), Gottesman (1973), Foster (1977), and Davidson, Dunn, Wiles-Kettenmann, and Appelle (1981). Miller's subjects were 26 blind children with heterogeneous characteristics, including 17 totally blind ("no usable vision") and nine "partially sighted" children, who performed under blindfold. The children ranged in age from six to 10, and all but one were blind from birth. The technique involved deforming one of a pair of clay objects in various ways and asking the subjects for judgments of equality. Only four of the children showed evidence of conservation of substance; all four were in the partially sighted group. Although the ages of these four children were not reported, conservation of substance was reported to correlate significantly with both CA and IQ. Tobin (1972) studied the conservation of substance in blind and partially sighted children, age range five to 16, using a technique similar to that used by Miller. Results from a study by Elkind (1961) were included for comparison purposes. Comparison of the results of Tobin's blind subjects with the sighted samples of Elkind strongly suggests a developmental lag of a year or two for the blind. The 90-percent level of conservation performance was reached at 11 years by the blind. Tobin's subjects were classified into three vision groups: counting fingers, movement perception, and LP or less. Unfortunately, the two more severely handicapped groups did not contain enough subjects at any age level to allow reliable assessments of possible developmental differences between groups, and Tobin concluded that he "was unable to show any differences attributable to degree of vision" (p. 197). However, comparison of the results of the least handicapped blind group, where there were adequate numbers of subjects, with Elkind's results for sighted subjects suggests that a substantial developmental lag occurred even for the group that was able to count fingers. Unfortunately, it was not reported whether the partially sighted subjects were allowed the use of their limited vision during the experiment.

Gottesman (1973) reported the results of a study quite similar to those of Miller and Tobin. Three groups of subjects were tested: sighted, blindfolded sighted, and blind (LP or less). Within each group, the subjects were divided into age levels of four to five, six to seven, and eight to 11 years. The sighted group had full use of vision throughout the tasks involving conservation of substance, weight, and volume, while the blindfolded and blind groups used only touch. The order of difficulty of the tasks was the same in the three groups, with substance easiest, followed in order by weight and volume. This order is the same as is typically reported for sighted children. For the conservation of substance task, the most marked difference between blind and both sighted groups appeared in the six-to-seven-year-old group, where about half the sighted subjects conserved in contrast to only one of the 15 blind subjects. In the youngest group very few subjects showed conservation, while in the oldest group nearly all did. Thus there was a definite developmental lag by the blind children, but the blind had apparently almost caught up with the sighted by the eight-to-11 age range. The sighted group performing without vision did about as well as the group with vision. Davidson et al. (1981) also found a developmental lag of about four years in the attainment of conservation of mass, comparing blind children with sighted subjects using vision. A sighted group performing under blindfold was intermediate.

Results from a study by Cromer (1973) show an apparent contradiction to the developmental lag evidence found by Gottesman and others. Cromer made several criticisms of the methodological approach taken by Hatwell (1966). For example, the blind sample was drawn partly from rural areas while the sighted sample was drawn from an urban environment, and the blind children had apparently had two years less school experience than the sighted children of equivalent age. (As Hatwell [1984] has subsequently explained, there was no perfect way to match blind and sighted groups under the circumstances.) Cromer's blind and sighted groups were more straightforwardly matched. Two groups of sighted children were matched on CA and sex to a group of 12 congenitally blind children of normal intelligence, age range 5.6 to 9.5 years. One group of sighted children had vision available during the tasks, while the other group performed blindfolded. Thus the experimental design was quite similar to that of Gottesman (1973), although there were far fewer children than in Gottesman's work. Responses on the conservation of mass problems were classified as nonconservation, partial conservation, or conservation. Statistical comparisons produced no significant difference between any pair of groups, and thus the results appear to contradict those of Gottesman and others. A closer analysis of the pattern of responses suggests, however, that the contradiction in more apparent than real. Gottesman tested 15 subjects in each of the three age groups, four to five, six to seven, and eight to 11 years. For the conservation of mass task, Gottesman found a difference between blind and sighted groups in the six-to-seven-year group but not in the eight-to-11-year group. If only the subjects who were less than eight years of age in Cromer's study are considered, twice as many conservation responses occurred for the sighted group as for the blind group, with the blindfolded group intermediate. Of the seven blind subjects below eight years, only the two oldest showed consistent conservation responses, while four of the corresponding sighted children were consistent conservers. Furthermore, as Cromer noted, there were no subjects in the age range between 6.9 and 7.8 years, and it is just that age range which might be especially sensitive to blind–sighted differences. Thus, the results of Cromer do not contradict those of Gottesman. In fact, although the numbers of subjects in Cromer's groups were not large, his results were similar to those of Gottesman in important ways, including the finding that there was apparently no difference between the older blind and sighted subjects.

Cromer included an interesting type of analysis that has gradually come to be used in the blindness literature as well as the sighted: The children were questioned about the reasons for their responses. The major differences that emerged were between conservers and nonconservers, rather than between blind and sighted children. The blind conservers gave reasons that were not different from those of the sighted conservers, and the (faulty) reasons of the blind and sighted nonconservers were similar. Thus there is evidence that the cognitive processes involved in conservation are similar for blind and sighted children.

Miller (1969) used a conservation of weight task in the study discussed earlier. The results as reported are extremely difficult to interpret, but apparently two of the four partially sighted subjects who had shown conservation of substance also showed conservation of weight. Conservation of weight did not show a significant correlation with CA over the six-to-10-year range, but the correlation with IQ was highly significant. Partial conservation credit was given for some responses, but no data were presented for the frequency of various responses. Swanson (Swanson, 1979; Swanson, Minifie, & Minifie, 1979) evaluated partially sighted children over a wider age range, from six to 15 years. With the greater age range, an effect of CA did emerge. The partially sighted group, presumably performing with blindfold, performed roughly like a blindfolded sighted group, and worse than a sighted group tested with vision.

Gottesman (1973), as noted earlier, also studied conservation of weight. At the youngest age level (four to five years), few blind or sighted subjects showed conservation, while at the upper age level (eight to 11 years), most subjects in both groups conserved. In the intermediate age group (six to seven years), a definite lag was found for the blind group. Brekke, Williams, and Tait (1974) administered a weight conservation task to sighted and visually impaired children, age six to 14. The latter included children from both residential and integrated schools. All were legally blind, but about half were large print readers. It is not reported whether they were tested with residual vision occluded. The developmental course of weight conservation was not significantly different for the nonresidential visually impaired and the sighted group, but the residential school children showed a significant lag in acquisition. There was some evidence that the large print readers were earlier conservers than the braille readers (who presumably had greater visual loss), but the effect of this variable was not as great as that of school environment, with the residential school children generally performing less well.

Conservation of solid volume is a relatively late development in sighted children, and it is similarly late in the visually impaired. Results were reported by Miller (1969), Gottesman (1973), and Swanson (1979; Swanson et al., 1979). As noted earlier, Miller's results are difficult to interpret. The number of subjects showing conservation was not reported, but it must have been small, since only two subjects of the sample of 26 showed conservation of weight, and volume was reported to be more difficult than weight. Some partial credit must have been given for volume conservation, since, although the correlation of volume conservation with CA was not significant, that with IQ was reported as highly significant. Gottesman's results are much more clearly reported, and they reflect the difficulty of the volume conservation task for both blind and sighted children. In fact, almost negligible numbers of subjects in both the sighted and the blind groups showed conservation, and it is clear that the task was not a sensitive one for the age range studied (four to 11). Swanson et al. (1979) also found volume to be a more difficult conservation task than substance or weight for partially sighted subjects, who showed negligible success even in the age group 12–15 years.

Canning (1957) reported a study on the conservation of liquid volume. She studied 45 blind children, age 3.5 to 10 years, from schools for the blind. The sample included both totally and "educationally" blind (the latter designation was not further defined). The procedure involved having the subject pour water from one of two filled larger glasses into two equal and smaller glasses, and then making a judgment about the equality of water in the smaller glasses and the remaining larger glass. According to Piaget, conservation of liquid volume by sighted children occurs in the 6.5-to-eight-year range. Canning's results indicated a general lag, with some children not demonstrating conservation even at 10 years. There were, however, some children who conserved as early as 5.5 years. There was an apparent difference between the totally and educationally blind groups. There were older nonconservers in the totally blind group, and about half the conservers in the educationally blind group were younger than the youngest conserver in the totally blind group.

Conservation of number, or discontinuous quantity, refers to the ability to maintain the judgment of equality of two groups of items even when the one-to-one physical correspondence between pairs of items is disturbed. For example, two rows of items, with equal numbers in each row, are lined up with a member of one row opposite a member of the other row, and the child judges the rows as having the same number of items. Then one row is expanded or contracted in length, and the child is queried about the equality of numbers of items in the two rows. Conservation is said to occur if the rows continue to be judged as having equal numbers of items. Cromer (1973) used an interesting variation on this scheme, in which ping-pong balls were placed in wire cylinders of different dimensions and the subjects were asked for judgments of relative number. A group of six-to-10-year-old congenitally blind children with at most LP peformed virtually the same as sighted children tested with blindfold, and both groups performed somewhat worse than sighted children using vision. The differences between groups were not dramatic, though, and six of the seven blind children over the age of seven showed perfect conservation responses. Simpkins (1974) reported the results from children aged six to 10 on two number conservation tests. The congenitally blind children with at most LP performed somewhat worse than sighted children performing with vision, although the differences were not as dramatic as those found for some other conservation tasks. Stephens and Simpkins (1974) found only minimal differences on a term-to-term task between their age-groups of blind and sighted children. Similarly, Adi and Pulos (1977–78) tested children from age six to 12 and found no significant differences between the distributions of conservers and nonconservers for sighted and congenitally, totally blind groups. Thus the weight of the available evidence on number conservation supports the conclusion that the visually impaired child is not at a marked disadvantage compared with the sighted child of the same age.

Stephens and Simpkins (1974) studied a wide range of conservation abilities in blind and sighted children. The age range was from six to 18 years, and the blind children had at most LP, and had been blind by the age of four. The IQ range was restricted to from 90 to 110 for both blind and sighted samples. Ten conservation tasks were given, covering substance, volume, weight, length, and liquid. Several tests of classification, symbolic imagery, and formal operations were also administered. The blind performed tactile versions of the tasks, while the sighted performed the traditional visual version, apparently. Severe deficits were found for the blind children in many tasks: the lags were typically greater than those reported by other investigators. The subjects were divided into age groups of six to 10, 10 to 14, and 14 to 18 years. For the sighted groups, there were substantial differences in performance between the six-10 and 10-14-year groups, reflecting the changes in cognitive abilities during the middle childhood period. For the blind groups, the differences were not marked between the six-10 and the 10-14 groups. Differences did emerge between the six-10 and the 14-18-year groups. Thus the evidence suggested that the blind children were progressing at a much slower developmental pace than the sighted children. Comparison of blind with sighted groups supports this conclusion: there were few differences in level of performance between the six-10-year sighted group and the 14-18-year blind group.

The question naturally arises: Can the developmental lags reported for visually impaired children on Piagetian cognitive tasks be avoided by the provision of appropriate experience, or remediated once they have occurred, so that the visually impaired child is brought on to sighted norms? The avoidance question has not been addressed with Piagetian tasks, although various early intervention programs are reported to have advantageous effects in the area of cognitive development. The remediation issue has been squarely addressed in studies by Stephens and Grube (1982) and Lopata and Pasnak (1976). For their training group, Stephens and Grube used 13 of the subjects from an earlier project (Stephens & Simpkins, 1974), including five 6-10-year-olds, four 10-14-year-olds, and four 14-18-year-olds. These subjects were matched by a group of blind control subjects and by a group of sighted subjects. The control groups did not receive the training program. Each group received a pretest and, after about 18 months, a posttest. These included various conservation and classification tasks. During the 17-month intervention period, the training-group subjects received an extensive individualized training program which averaged about 95 hours per child. The teachers who administered the training were coached in the use of a "discovery process" method.

Generally, the blind training groups advanced to the level of the sighted control groups, although there were still some differences, particularly in the tests of spatial and mental imagery. No significant differences were found on ten conservation measures or six classification measures. The formal operations measures also tended to show no differences between the blind training group and the sighted control group. The blind training group, compared with the blind control group, showed general superiority, except in tests in the spatial relations and mental imagery areas. Stephens and Grube noted the various school subjects, such as mathematics and science, that should benefit from advancement in these various cognitive skills (conservation, classification, spatial relations, formal operations), but they did not evaluate the issue of external validity.

Lopata and Pasnak (1976) reported a training study that was equal to that of Stephens and Grube (1982) in breadth, if not so intensive and over such a lengthy period. The subjects were legally blind eight-to-13-year-olds (thus a subset of the Stephens and Grube range) and ranged more widely in intelligence, with Slossen scores of from 62 to 131 at the beginning of the study. Twenty-eight children were given a pretest involving weight and substance conservation tasks, then were divided into two groups for training and control conditions. The groups were thus matched on the basis of visual characteristics, age, IQ, and cognitive pretest. The pretest, as well as the posttest, was constructed from a culling of the literature to create a battery of weight and substance tasks. The training sessions were built around a learning set approach and included training on measurement to a standard, seriation, classification, and substance conservation. The exercises did not duplicate the tasks used in the pretest, but were similar to them. Each subject was given one hour per week of training for as long as it took to progress through the training protocol: the average was 10.2 hours. The matching subject in the control group was given an equivalent amount of exposure to the experimenter, but not with materials related to the training. At the end of the training segment for the experimental child, both that child and the matched control child received the posttest and the IQ test. Responses were evaluated on a four-point scale, ranging from zero for an incorrect response to 3 for an abstract, conceptual response. The trained group showed significantly improved substance and weight conservation, as well as increased IQ. The control group did not improve significantly on any of these tests.

The results were straightforward: training on Piaget-type cognitive skills improved performance on those skills. The Lopata and Pasnak results are significant in another important respect, however, in that improvement also occurred on the IQ test. The training on conservation tasks apparently generalized to a cognitive test which is not designed specifically to evaluate those tasks. This result lends an important element of external validity to the evaluation by the Piagetian tasks, and suggests that there is a more generalized cognitive effect. Training studies should be based on just this premise—Lopata and Pasnak recognized the importance of demonstrating this generality empirically, as should other researchers.

The evidence from many studies supports the conclusion that blind children show a slower course of cognitive development as represented by conservation of weight, substance, and volume. Several questions remain, however. First, why do lags occur? Two possibilities are evident. One is that lags in the development of operations such as the conservations may be a result of carryover lags from the sensorimotor period. The other possibility is that the blind child's experience during the operations period is restricted in significant ways that hamper the development of operational thought. It is difficult to distinguish clearly between these two possibilities, and it seems likely that both operate to some extent. Piaget and Inhelder (1969) provided one perspective: "The sensory disturbance peculiar to those born blind has from the outset hampered the development of sensory-motor schemes and slowed down general coordination ... action learning is still necessary before these children develop the capacity for operations on a level with that of the normal child" pp. 88–89). Unfortunately there are few direct data on the progress of the blind infant through the sensorimotor substages, but Stephens (1972) noted a number of areas where the restricted experience of the blind infant might well have retarding effects, and it is reasonable to expect sensorimotor delays to carry over into the preoperational and operational periods. In addition, though, it seems quite likely that the continued restrictedness of the school-age blind child's experience produces a continued depressing effect on the acquisition of conservation abilities. Evidence in support of this factor comes from studies such as that of Brekke, Williams, and Tait (1974), where blind children from family environments did not differ from sighted children in weight conservation, but residential school blind children showed a significant developmental lag.

Gottesman (1976) suggested a somewhat different perspective on the observed lags in conservation abilities: "These delays, however, can be explained not on the basis of the effects of total blindness per se, but on the younger child's reliance on less sophisticated sensory discrimination abilities" (p. 94). Gottesman based his argument on his earlier finding (Gottesman, 1971) that congenitally blind children were worse than sighted children at identifying and matching geometric forms. Although his is probably a reasonable formulation, a clarification of terminology should be provided. As discussed at length in Chapter 2, there do not seem to be notable deficits in the sensory *discrimination* abilities of blind children of school age. However, there are distinct differences between blind and sighted children in the ability to *identify* objects tactually and to perform other tasks that require the use of stored information. Thus although there are not marked differences in sensory discrimination abilities, the differences that exist between blind and sighted children in the ability to use meaningful characteristics of objects might well restrict the development of conservation abilities, as Gottesman (1976) suggested. Gottesman went on to argue that older blind children are able to perform conservation tasks because of their "increased reliance on integrative processes of cognitive functioning, rather than a reliance on the less sophisticated sensory discrimination abilities" (p. 99).

Although most of the research in conservation supports the conclusion that there are developmental lags by blind children, there is less agreement about the duration of the lags. Gottesman (1973) found that the proportions of blind children showing successful conservation performance were smaller than those for sighted children during the early elementary years, but that most blind children in the eight-to-11-year group had attained conservation of weight and substance. Stephens and Simpkins (1974), however, found that even 14-to-18-year-old blind children did not show evidence of mature conservation abilities. Older subjects were not studied, and thus it is not clear whether they might eventually have shown adequate performance.

The reasons for these apparent conflicts in results are not clear, although the issues are important ones. Several factors may have contributed to the discrepancies between the Gottesman and the Stephens and Simpkins work. First, over half of Gottesman's (1973) blind sample were taken from public school settings, while only 20 of Stephens and Simpkins' (1974) 75 blind subjects were from public schools. Thus Gottesman's sample may have represented a more cognitively capable population. A more critical factor may have been the scoring criteria used in the two studies. Gottesman dichotomized responses into conservation and nonconservation responses, while Stephens and Simpkins used a more finely graduated nine-point scale designed to reflect the type of reasoning used by the child in producing his conservation response. Simpkins (personal communication) noted that if dichotomous scoring had been used, the results would have more closely paralleled those of Gottesman. It may be that the two studies are not as discrepant as they seem, if sampling and scoring differences are taken into account.

Another variable that deserves much fuller examination as bearing on possible differences between blind and sighted children, and among blind children, is the manner of tactual exposure to the stimuli. Davidson et al. (1981) examined this variable in their study of conservation of mass in sighted children from five to 12 years of age and blind children from 10 to 17 years. Half the sighted group was tested with blindfold and the other half with vision available. The sighted subjects using vision showed conservation at an average age of 8.9 years, compared to 10.1 years for the sighted with blindfold and 13.5 years for the blind group. Thus the blind conserved successfully at a higher age than the sighted performing under blindfold. Of particular interest, however, are the results bearing on the use of tactual search strategies. The tactual activities were classified from videotaped recordings as involving global search, detailed search, palmar search, kinesthetic measurement, weighing, and passive touching. An index of the maturity of search was created such that, for example, simultaneous exploration of both stimuli (thought to be a more effective strategy than successive comparisons) was rated as more mature. Interestingly, despite the lower mean conservation age of the blindfolded sighted group, their exploration maturity index was lower than that of the blind group. However, within the blind group itself, conservers showed more mature search strategies than nonconservers. The close examination of perceptual strategies used in conservation tasks should contribute to our understanding of cognitive processes.

An analysis of the development of cognitive skills that is quite similar to the Piaget-inspired work was provided by Boldt (1969), who posited a series of three levels to characterize the scientific (logical) thinking of the developing child. In Level I, there is "a naive subjective relation to the phenomena which are understood from the meaning received from their immediate experiential importance for the subject." The similarity of this level to the sensorimotor stage of Piaget is clear. In Level II, "a certain change of objectivity of the phenomena is now recognizable, but . . . still bound very strongly to the subjective experience." In Level III, there is "real scientific thinking. In a truly casual sense, the phenomena are accepted in total scientific objectivity" (p. 6). In summary of a study of 103 blind and partially sighted children, age seven to 17, Boldt reported that the same processes of scientific thinking were found for both blind and partially sighted children, but that "blind children at the age of 10 are retarded by two years, on the average. This retardation will be largely made up by the 15th year" (p. 6). Boldt found the lag to be greater for congenitally blind children than for adventitiously blinded children. Thus Boldt found blind children to progress through stages of cognitive development similar to those of partially sighted children, but at a delayed rate that is quite reminiscent of the delays in cognitive skills as measured by performance on Piagetian tasks.

Substantial additional research will have to be conducted before the acquisition of cognitive abilities in blind children is understood. In particular, this research should take note of the experiential histories of the children. Attention to experience is demanded by the role that experience plays in the Piagetian theoretical framework, and several results in the literature suggest that a careful regard for the experiential history of the subjects would be rewarding. For example, Brekke, Williams, and Tait (1974) found no differences in conservation of weight between sighted children and blind children from a family environment, but did find significant differences between these groups and a group of residential school blind children. Gottesman (1976), in a supplementary analysis of the data from his earlier study (1973), also found a significant difference between the subgroups of blind subjects from residential school and home environments, with the residential school subjects performing worse. Besides the issue of tactual search strategies, discussed above, another variable that should receive careful attention in studies of conservation and other cognitive abilities is intelligence. It may well be that performance on conservation tests will prove to be a better predictor of learning aptitude, as discussed by Newland, than IQ tests are. In any case, IQ tests do provide an indication, albeit not well understood, of some aspects of cognitive abilities, and it is important to analyze the IQ characteristics of the samples on which other cognitive work is done. In particular, it would be worthwhile to know whether the lags in aquisition of conservation and other cognitive abilities are different for high, medium, and low IQ samples of blind children.

Perspective on Cognitive Development Research

The general conclusion that one reaches, based on the considerable body of research using Piaget-type tests of cognitive development with the blind, is that blind children lag significantly behind sighted children in their development of classification and conservation skills. I wish to propose that this conclusion is at best premature, that it is based on a generally faulty research rationale, and that the issue in any case is an irrelevant one.

Let us examine the reasoning that leads to the general conclusion of developmental lag. In much of the work in which comparisons of blind and sighted children are made, the task that the sighted children perform is the traditional task that makes heavy use of vision, and the task that the blind children perform is the closest tactual analog of the sighted subjects' task. Sometimes an additional group of sighted children performs the same task that the blind children do, using only touch and performing without benefit of vision. I submit that the comparisons among such tasks are generally not meaningful.

Touch for the blind child does not serve the same function that sight does for the sighted child. Touch may provide information about the same or similar events in the environment (such as spatial relations) that vision does, but touch differs in major ways from vision, particularly in its successive manner of delivering information and in its far less detailed discrimination of the spatial field. Assume for the moment that the child *does* have a given cognitive ability, such as the conservation of mass. Can this ability be demonstrated via touch by the blind child equivalently to its demonstration via vision by the sighted child? It cannot. The experimenter who makes the easy comparison is, in essence, comparing potatoes and turnips.

Nor does comparing the tactual performance of a blind child with the tactual performance of a blindfolded sighted child help the issue much. The comparison rests on the assumption that touch serves the same role in the perceptual ecology of the blindfolded sighted child that it does for the blind child. This is certainly not a valid assumption. Many of the tasks for which the blind child relies on touch are mediated by vision in the sighted child, and removing the vision of the sighted child by means of a blindfold does not suddenly allow touch to serve the same role that it serves for the blind child. The question is not which is better or worse; the two situations are simply different.

The studies that include a sighted group performing with vision and a sighted group performing with blindfold are instructive, although not on the issue to which they are typically directed. Some of these studies (e.g., Cromer, 1973; Gottesman, 1973) find little or no difference between these groups. All well and good, but this result does not prove the functional equivalence of touch and vision—the counterexamples that find differences (e.g., Swanson, et al., 1979; Davidson, et al., 1981) in fact *disprove* the functional equivalence of touch and vision for such tasks. Does the poorer performance of a sighted child when he is wearing a blindfold than when he performs with vision mean that he is at a lesser stage of cognitive development when wearing a blindfold? Certainly not—the acquisition of a cognitive stage is a far more robust phenomenon than this. The logic of experimentation makes a single valid demonstration of a difference a far more meaningful piece of evidence than many demonstrations of nondifference. This may be an uncomfortable thought, but it has stood the test of time since Descartes.

The tactual version of a test of conservation for the blindfolded sighted child undoubtedly measures something of interest to the developmental psychologist, as does the same tactual test applied to the blind child. But the leap in reasoning that calls for these to be taken as the equivalent of one another, or for either to be taken as the equivalent of the visual version of the test for the sighted child, is simply not justified.

Presumably tests of conservation and other cognitive abilities are justifiable because they serve as indices of functional cognitive behaviors. This is an easy assumption, which many researchers apparently make but rarely examine. Warren (1978; also cf. Chapter 9) discussed this issue in the context of what he called vertical integration of research design. The concept of vertical integration refers, in part, to the relationship between an indicator test that is used in a research study and the ability of which the test is assumed to be an indicator. The issue is validity, and perhaps the best example is intelligence—does a test that results in a number that we call the "IQ" validly evaluate the ability (or set of abilities) that we mean by the concept "intelligence"? We do not know whether it does or not unless we examine the validity of the test. Similarly, does a test of conservation of liquid volume, for example, adequately evaluate the underlying cognitive ability? Unfortunately, most of the research with Piaget-type cognitive indices simply begs this important question. It is a rare study that addresses the relationship between performance on a conservation test and real-life cognitively based behavior. The lack, in Warren's (1978) terminology, is one of vertical integration.

If comparative studies of the performance of blind and sighted children on tactual and visual versions of conservation tests were to address the issue of vertical integration, and if they were to find that the visual test for the sighted child and the tactual test for the blind child represent the same functional ability to address real-world problems, then the comparisons would be justified. Without this additional step, the studies are of little value and may, in fact, lead to unwarranted conclusions.

Consider the following logic for an example. Based on comparisons of the performance of sighted subjects (performing with vision) and blind subjects (performing with touch), one reaches the conclusion that the cognitive development of the blind child lags behind that of the sighted. Naturally one wishes to remediate this "deficiency" in the blind, so one designs a training program intended to bring the tactual performance of the blind to equality with the visual performance of the sighted subject. The program apparently succeeds —the blind, performing tactually, now reach milestones of cognitive development at the same ages as the sighted, performing with vision. Success, clearly. But the issue is not that easy. First, the initial comparisons that led to identification of the need to "remediate" the developmental progress of the blind are faulty for the reasons offered above. There is no basis for the assumption that the initial tests evaluated comparable abilities. At best, it may be that the children's time was wasted. Worse, though, it may be that the time that was spent on the training program would have been far more productively spent by the blind child in other activities for which he was developmentally ready. And the cognitive "gains" may be superficial ones, abilities to perform tactual versions of cognitive tests but not to handle the real-world demands of which the tests are assumed to be an index.

Of course, all the easy assumptions that researchers in this area tend to make may be valid. But we do not know. It is incumbent on those researchers to look beyond the easy assumptions and verify or reject them. It is equally incumbent on their sources of research funding to *require* them to do so. An obvious requirement should be to demonstrate that gains based on training interventions result in advances in those abilities of which the tests are assumed to be representative. This is, again, the issue of validity, and researchers in this area should be no more immune to it than those in any other area of psychology or education.

There is far more research needed here, not only in the area of comparative cognitive development but in other areas in which developmental progress is compared. We need, though, not just "more of the same." We need a different research paradigm, one that is based on an examination of critical assumptions and that in particular addresses the notion of vertical integration of research and the validity issues that this notion entails.

I do not believe that comparative research involving sighted subjects will be of much value in this quest. The issue concerns the blind. The goal should be to ascertain the set of experiential conditions that will optimize the process of cognitive development for the blind, taking into account both the developmental rate and the solidity of the conceptual progress that is accomplished.

Imagery

In 1913, Fernald reported a study of imagery in two university students, one blind from birth and the other partially sighted. Fernald reported that the partially sighted person used visual imagery abundantly, while the totally blind person never used visual imagery. Both apparently relied effectively on tactual imagery. Using a formboard task, Sylvester (1913) found that the teenaged blind subjects who had lost vision after the age of three performed better than a group who had lost vision after birth but before age three. A group that was blind from birth had the worst performance. From these results, Sylvester concluded that "those who have had visual experience retain their visual imagery" (p. 210). He concluded further that tactual imagery was not sufficiently well developed in the congenitally blind to compensate for the lack of visual imagery.

These early conclusions about imagery have been followed by a great deal of subsequent concern with imagery in the blindness literature, but there has been relatively little direct research on imagery. Imagery is a difficult concept to define adequately and therefore to study. Two basic approaches have been used, and each has its disadvantages. The study by Fernald is an example of one approach, where the subject can be asked to describe his imagery orally or in writing. The description technique is completely confounded with the issue of language usage. It is almost impossible to attribute reported differences in imagery to real differences in imagery rather than to differences in the use of language to describe images. In the other approach, of which the study by Sylvester is an example, the subject is given a task that is thought a priori to require some kind of imagery for its solution. In such performance tasks, it is usually risky to conclude that a difference in imagery is the only possible cause of differences in performance results for various groups.

However difficult imagery is to define and study, there are several interesting and important questions to be answered, particularly in the area of development. Research on imagery can provide information not only about the nature of phenomenal experience, but also about the nature and development of intermediary abilities (such as the ability to imagine an intended route of travel) that may be important in facilitating various types of performance (such as locomotion).

Schlaegel (1953) reported an extensive study that was similar in intent to that of Fernald (1913). The subject heard words or phrases and responded by writing down whether his initial image was "see, hear, muscle, touch, temp., smell, or taste." The blind group, mean age 16 years, was heterogeneous with respect to age at onset and severity of blindness. No differences in distribution of response were found between the blind group as a whole and the sighted group. However, significant differences emerged from an analysis of the blind subjects when they were divided into subgroups on the basis of amount of residual vision. These groups were heterogeneous with respect to age of onset. For the group with LP or less, the dominant mode of imagery reports was the auditory, 36.4 percent, as compared to 27.9 percent visual images. An intermediate visually impaired group consisted of subjects whose vision ranged from some movement detection to counting fingers at five feet. This group showed an imagery distribution that was primarily visual, 42.4 percent, with 29.8 percent auditory images, and that was virtually identical to that of the sighted control group which gave 41.7 percent visual and 30.8 percent auditory reports. The third group included subjects with vision better than 5/200. This group reported substantially more visual images, 58.6 percent, and somewhat fewer auditory images, 25.8 percent, than the other groups. A further division of the blind groups on the basis of age of onset was particularly suggestive about the role of early vision in imagery type. In the lowest vision group, the subjects with onset at younger than five years reported almost no visual imagery at all, while those with later onset showed about 57 percent visual imagery, more than the sighted control group. A similar difference, although less marked, appeared for the intermediate group. For the visually impaired group with most vision, the division by age of onset did not produce a difference. It is also interesting that many of the images reported as visual by the total blind group were, upon closer examination, found to be primarily verbal descriptions or images which the subject had reported as visual simply as a figure of speech. In discussing the unexpectedly high percentage of visual images reported by the intermediate and least visually impaired groups, Schlaegel pointed out that these partially sighted subjects may have somehow sensed pressure to respond in visual terms. Thus, the visual percentage for these groups may be artifactually high, although it is difficult to judge the magnitude of this possible effect. In any case, Schlaegel's study of modes of imagery supported the basic conclusions of Fernald, that subjects with some residual vision give reports of visual images. An important additional result of Schlaegel's study was that the age of onset of blindness was also an important determinant of the type of imagery report.

Hall (1981a) provided a thorough and thoughtful account of the areas of thought and behavior in which imagery may be involved. Her conclusion forms a useful context for this section. The different experiences of visually impaired and sighted children produce a different sort of imagery in the two, and to the extent that various cognitive operations depend on imagery, they may be expected to differ between the visually impaired and the sighted—differ, presumably, qualitatively as well as quantitatively. Hall's approach is also important in outlining how imagery may be of *functional* importance in mediating various kinds of behavior, and may play a different role for the visually impaired child than for the sighted.

Imagery and spatial behavior

Reports of imagery occur in several of the studies on maze learning and other types of spatial performance, described in Chapter 2. In the study by Knotts and Miles (1929), the subjects, age 10 to 21 years, were asked to report how they had learned the stylus and finger mazes. The responses were classified as verbal, verbal–motor, motor, or visual. Knotts and Miles did not adequately report their response classification criteria, although responses were apparently counted as verbal if they made reference to counting, while motor responses were those for which subjects said that they remembered by the "feel." The major differences between blind and sighted subjects were a greater incidence of verbal responses for the blind (51 percent, vs. 38 percent for the sighted), greater incidence of motor responses for the blind (28 percent, vs. 18 percent for the sighted), but a greater incidence of verbal–motor responses for the sighted (36 percent, vs. 18 percent for the blind). Visual responses were rare but were more common for the sighted group. It is interesting that subjects who reported using a verbal method were better at learning the maze, although unfortunately the incidence of imagery types was not broken down by age. Duncan (1934) made a similar analysis of the introspective reports of her 13- to 25-year-old subjects about their approaches to maze problems. Responses were classified as verbal, visual, kinesthetic, or verbal–visual. The only notable difference in the distributions of blind and sighted subjects occurred in the verbal category, where the sighted group showed a somewhat greater frequency (54 percent vs. 44 percent). The blind group gave a substantial percentage of visual responses (23 percent). Unfortunately, Duncan did not provide a tabulation of responses by age, degree of blindness or age of onset categories. From the results of Schlaegel (1953), it is reasonable to assume that the visual responses occurred primarily in those blind subjects who had either residual vision or who had considerable visual experience before becoming blind. Note that Duncan's conclusion about the efficacy of the verbal approach is similar to that of Knotts and Miles (1929): maze performance was better for those subjects who reported verbal approaches.

Worchel (1951) compared blind and sighted subjects, age eight to 21, on two form identification tasks and a locomotor spatial relations task. He obtained introspective reports from the subjects about how they solved the tasks, and although distributions of response types were not reported, several interesting points appear in the discussion. In all tasks, the congenitally blind were more uncertain about the nature of any imagery they had used. In the task where identification and verbal description of a form were required, the congenitals' descriptions tended to be in tactual terms, referring often to the "feel" of the shape. The adventitiously blinded, however, tended to refer to "mental pictures," and Worchel interpreted these reports as indicating a visual imagery resulting from early vision. Sighted subjects tended even more strongly to visual imagery, that is, visual interpretation of the tactual experience. In a task where the subject was to feel two shapes and report what their combined shape would be, the reports were more vague but tended to support the conclusions from the first task. In the task where the subject was led over part of a triangle and was to complete the figure, some sighted and blind subjects made use of time estimates. Such an approach would presumably depend on verbalization, although not of a complex nature. The sighted subjects also reported visualization, but this tendency was not marked among the adventitiously blinded, even for those subjects who had reported visualization in the first two tasks.

Worchel's results support the notion that the sighted, and to a lesser extent the adventitiously blinded, tend to make use of visualization in performing these tasks. It is interesting to note that on the triangle task, where the tendency of the adventitiously blinded to report visualization was not strong, performance within the blind group did not relate significantly to age of onset of blindness, or to the congenital–adventitious distinction. On both form tasks, though, the adventitiously blinded reported more visualization, and they also performed the task better than the congenitally blind.

Thus there is some agreement in these studies that more visual imagery occurs in subjects who either had substantial early vision before becoming blind or who have some useful residual vision. Several reservations should be expressed, however. First, it is not at all clear that the differences that are found represent true differences in imagery rather than artifactual differences in the use of a visually oriented vocabulary. Second, it is not possible to ascertain from reports of the relative incidence of imagery types exactly how it is that a "visual" spatial image serves to facilitate performance in a spatial task. Progress on this question will have to await better methods of describing images and of ensuring that vocabulary differences do not cloud the issue. Third, there is virtually no developmental information to be gained from the studies cited. The studies are developmental only in the sense that they included children of various ages in the sample. Information about any relationship between imagery types and age is totally lacking.

Even if these difficulties were overcome, the question of the function of visual and other imagery is complex. The study of Worchel (1951) in particular suggests that different spatial tasks may evoke different types or degrees of imagery within the same subjects. Even more important in assessing the real effectiveness of visualization is the question of whether any reliance on visual imagery by the adventitiously blinded is really advantageous. It may be, for example, that in certain situations a reliance on residual visualization may tend to prevent the later blind child from developing modes of mediation that may in the long run be more effective for him.

Because of their relation to the spatial imagery question, several studies on spatial concepts may be mentioned here before consideration of other types of imagery. Hill and Blasch (1980) provide an excellent review of the various tests that have been designed to assess spatial concepts. Swallow and Poulsen (1973) used Piagetian techniques with a group of low vision girls to investigate the applicability of Piaget's findings about the developmental acquisition of spatial relations concepts for low vision subjects. The subjects were large-print readers, ranging in age from 12 to 18, with visual acuity ranging from 20/70 to 20/400. A series of tests was used, including tasks of topological, projective, and Euclidean space. The group showed a substantial lag compared with expectations based on Piaget's formulations for sighted children. Swallow and Poulsen stated that "the visually-limited subjects were not able to achieve total decentralization of thought, thereby not allowing their spatial concepts to develop independent of perception and action" (p. 143). In general, the responses placed the subjects in the concrete operations stage of cognitive development, a stage that according to Piaget normally ends around the age of 12.

Hartlage (1968, 1969) reported evidence that congenitally blind children show deficits in spatial concepts, but not in nonspatial concepts. He tested blind children from grades two, three, five, seven, and 12, as well as matched sighted controls. An example of a spatial item is "Mary is in front of Bill. Bill is in front of John. What is Mary's relationship to John?" A corresponding nonspatial item substituted "smarter than" for "in front of." Averaged across grade level, the blind subjects were worse than the sighted on the spatial concepts, while the groups did not differ on the nonspatial concepts. From the graphically presented results, it is apparent that most of the difference on the spatial concepts occurred at the second and third grade levels, while at the fifth, seventh, and 12th grade levels, the blind and sighted were not obviously different. It was not reported whether the blind children participated in formal mobility training in the later grades. Some improvement in the use of spatial concepts might be expected as a result of such training. In a subsequent study, Hartlage (1976) tested groups of blind and sighted children at each grade level from two to 12. The blind children were selected from schools for the blind, but their degree of impairment and age at onset were not specified. There was no difference between sighted and blind groups on the nonspatial concepts, but the blind children performed worse than the sighted children on the spatial concepts across the entire grade range. The spatial concept performance of the blind children was also uniformly worse than their own nonspatial concept performance. Nevertheless, it should be noted that the spatial concept performance of the blind children did improve with grade level: inspection of the graphically presented results suggests that the grade-12 blind group performed at a level like that of the grade-eight sighted children. The general shape of the grade curves suggests a developmental lag by the blind children, rather than a complete inability to use spatial concepts. This suggestion receives support from a report by Tufenkjian (1971), who studied congenitally blind and sighted adults. She compared their ability to create spatial relationships ("in front of" and "behind") as directed by verbal instructions, and to respond verbally to the use of spatial words in sentences. The congenitally blind group did not differ markedly from the sighted group in the adequacy of their spatial concepts. About one-third of the blind subjects, but no sighted subjects, gave evidence of ascribing their own front–back system to an object rather than using the object's own front–back relationship. Tufenkjian argued that this usage was different, rather than wrong: the usage was consistent, and demonstrated "a different mode of experiencing some aspect of their world" (p. 41). Developmental work designed to bridge the work of Hartlage and Tufenkjian would be useful, particularly if it were addressed to questions of the development and significance of individual differences.

The lack of more comprehensive information about the adequacy of spatial concepts is unfortunate, since, as Hapeman (1967) pointed out, concepts of space may be critically important bases for the development of effective mobility in space. Hapeman suggested that, although formal mobility training does not typically begin until the early teens, the spatial concepts critical to mobility are those that emerge in sighted children between the ages of three and six. Hill (1970, 1971) reported the results of a study designed to assess the effectiveness of a training approach for spatial concepts. Congenitally blind subjects, aged seven to nine and varying in intelligence and degree of residual vision, were divided into a control and a training group. All children were pre- and posttested on an extensive test of the use of positional terminology. This test, presented fully by Hill (1971), required response to verbally presented items in three categories: relationship of body parts ("touch the center of your face"), relationship of body to external objects ("place the chair over your head"), and relationships among external objects ("put the cup in the center of the desk"). After the pretest, the training group received training sessions several times a week for three months. The training included sections on verbalization, identification, manipulation, and recognition of changing relationships. The training group showed a significant improvement from pretest to posttest, while the control group showed minor, nonsignificant gains. Although Hill discussed several possible contributors to improved performance aside from the training itself (such as the contact with the training instructor), the conclusion seems justified that the training program was effective in producing improvement in the use of spatial concepts. Unfortunately, no information was reported about the relationships between concept improvement and age or degree of residual vision.

Hill and Hill (1980) reported a refined version of the test, called the Hill Performance Test of Selected Positional Concepts. The test was used with a national sample to generate norms, and evaluations of validity and reliability were very favorable. The use of the test in research on spatial conceptual issues should provide useful information. Miller's (1982) use of the test in relation to judged mobility competence did not yield the expected correlations. This was probably due to the reported unreliability of Miller's homemade mobility evaluation scale, however.

An interesting approach to the study of blind and sighted children's knowledge about the characteristics of their environments was reported by Kephart,

Kephart, and Schwarz (1974). The blind and sighted children were five, six, and seven years old. The blind subjects had LP at most and were drawn from residential populations. The Kephart Scale was used for both blind and sighted children. In addition to a section on body image, the Kephart Scale taps the child's knowledge about various aspects of his environment, including the exterior and interior structure of the house, house furnishings, the neighborhood, the streets, and the town. On virtually all measures, the blind children showed less correct and complete knowledge about these aspects of the environment than the sighted children at each of the age levels. Kephart et al. (1974) discussed the results in terms of the restricted experience of the blind children, and they suggested the advantages of certain methods of enhancing the blind child's experiential content. Webster (1976) described a concept training program for first- and second-grade blind children. The emphasis of the program was on active participation by the child in a wide variety of activities, from learning about parts of the body to experience with automobiles to actual travel in the environment. Although formal evaluation of the program was not conducted, Webster noted that "through trial and experience, the instructors feel that now the program has finally reached the level where it is preparing young first and second grade blind children for future orientation and mobility training in the best possible manner" (p. 197). The importance of such programs cannot be too heavily emphasized.

Paivio and Okovita (1971) used a paired associate learning paradigm to study auditory and visual imagery in sighted and congenitally blind children, age 14 to 20. All subjects were above average in IQ, and the blind subjects were drawn from a school for the blind. They were presumably severely visually impaired, although this characteristic was not specified. In the first experiment, the sighted subjects were better than the blind at learning word pairs that were high in visual imagery but low in auditory imagery, while the groups were equal at learning pairs that were high in both visual and auditory imagery. In this latter condition, the blind were presumably able to rely on auditory imagery to make the words more meaningful. In a second experiment, however, some doubt was cast on these results. Sighted and blind subjects performed about equally on a condition that involved words high in visual imagery but low in auditory imagery. The basis for the contradiction in results is not clear. One possibility lies in subject selection. In the first experiment, the blind and sighted groups were equated for CA, while in the second, the groups were equated for grade (eight–12), with the result that the blind subjects ranged in CA from 15 to 20, mean 17.1, while the sighted ranged from 13 to 17, mean 14.8. Further, nine of the 14 blind subjects in the second experiment had participated in the first. These factors may have led to a spuriously high performance by the blind group in the second experiment.

A related study was reported by Craig (1973), who compared the serial learning ability of sighted subjects with blind (70 percent congenital, heterogeneous with respect to residual vision, although all were in braille classes).

Words for the serial lists were chosen for high or low imagery. The type of imagery was not as carefully specified with respect to modality as in the Paivio and Okovita experiments. The sighted subjects were better at learning both high and low imagery lists, although the interaction between vision group and imagery was significant and indicated that the advantage of the sighted subjects was greater for the high imagery lists than for the low. Unfortunately, a serious problem occurred in subject selection. The blind subjects ranged in CA from 14.8 to 21.2, mean 17.6, while the sighted group (all college students) ranged from 17.8 to 33.7 years, mean 20.9. The overall disadvantage of the blind group may have been due in part to the inclusion of subjects who were almost three years younger than the youngest sighted subjects, although there may have been relatively few young blind subjects.

Although the procedural problems with both the Paivio and Okovita and the Craig studies preclude firm conclusions about the relative usefulness of word imagery in blind and sighted subjects, both studies suggest that sighted subjects are better able than blind subjects to make use of imagery characteristics of words in some situations. When imagery modality is taken into account, as in the work by Paivio and Okovita, it becomes evident, not surprisingly, that it is primarily the visual imagery characteristics of words that produce the difference. In fact, in their first experiment, there was no difference between blind and sighted when the words were high in both visual and auditory imagery, suggesting that the blind subjects were quite able to use the auditory imagery aspects of words. In their second experiment, an additional condition was used in which the words were of high auditory but low visual imagery. In this condition the blind performed much better than the sighted, again suggesting that the blind make better use of auditory imagery (though again, it should be noted that the blind group was somewhat older, and that some had participated in the first experiment).

Carefully designed research on imagery could be quite useful. Word imagery clearly is effective for the blind. It would be interesting to know how the effectiveness of word imagery is related to IQ, and whether the relationship between word imagery and IQ is the same for blind as for sighted subjects. The question of whether specific experiential factors are important in imagery use is especially interesting.

Kenmore (1966) studied the paired associate learning abilities of blind and sighted third- and sixth-graders, matched for IQ, sex, and CA. The blind groups were heterogeneous, including a range of residual vision (totally blind to 2/200), with a small number of children with additional handicaps. The speed of paired associate learning was assessed in various conditions involving verbally and tactually presented material of varying familiarity. In a procedural variation on most research comparing blind and sighted subjects, Kenmore allowed the sighted subjects to use vision as well as hearing, while the blind were restricted to touch and hearing. The rationale for this procedure was that it is useful to know about the relative associative learning abilities of blind and sighted subjects under the optimal set of circumstances available for each group. Kenmore hypothesized that there would be, for the most part, no differences between blind and sighted subjects, but that the older blind might show a better ability when the stimuli were verbally presented and were relatively unfamiliar. Her reasoning was that the school experience of the blind children was largely verbally structured, and that, because of the lack of direct experience of the blind children with the objects that they learn about, the blind might be relatively better at learning the unfamiliar material. The results generally confirmed the hypothesis. In particular, the sixth-grade blind subjects were superior on the verbally presented unfamiliar words. An additional hypothesis suggested that, because of the heavy emphasis on verbal learning for blind school children, tactual experience might be relatively neglected and lead to worse learning of tactually presented material by the older blind children. This hypothesis was also supported.

A study by Martin and Herndon (1971) is also related to the topic of paired associate learning in blind children. The age range was 11 to 17, and the degree and onset of blindness were unspecified. The purpose of the study was to investigate the nature of verbal strategies in remembering associated pairs of words by blind subjects. Specifically, would the strategies be similar to those used by college students (reported by Martin, Boersma, & Cox, 1965)? These included repetition, single letter memory, multiple letter, word formation, superordinate, and syntactic strategies. Over half the responses of a group of blind children who did not have strategies suggested to them by the experimenter could not be classified into the strategy categories, compared to about 15-percent unclassifiable responses by sighted subjects. (The sighted group was presumably the college student sample, so there was a difference in mean age of at least five years.) Another group of blind children received instructions about possible strategies to use in the learning task, with an apparent emphasis on the syntactic strategies. The subjects who received strategy hints performed significantly better in the association task than did the control subjects. It was concluded that paired-associate performance may be aided by the provision of appropriate strategies for learning. Furthermore, it was found that, within the control group, those subjects who used more classifiable strategies performed significantly better on the learning task itself. Although it is clear from this study that the use of higher level strategies was facilitative of learning, no comparisons of blind and sighted children are appropriate.

Imagery in dreams

Several reports of the dream imagery of blind children have appeared in the literature, but there is some disagreement within this literature and the evidence is not good. Deutsch (1928) provided some dream reports from blind children, as well as some of the content of her own dreams. She concluded that the belief that dreams are absent or incomplete in blind children is mistaken, although, as later writers have pointed out, she did not provide any comparative evidence about the frequency or richness of dreaming in the blind children whose dreams she reported. By contrast, Blank (1958) stated that the dreams of the blind are more reality-oriented, more closely tied to the day's residue, and thus less imaginative.

Singer and Streiner (1966) investigated the imaginative content of the dreams of blind and sighted children by means of an interview approach. The blind children were selected from a school for the blind, and they ranged in age from eight to 12 and in IQ (Hayes–Binet) from 73 to 123, mean 90. All had become blind before the age of five, and none had functional vision. The sighted subjects were matched with the blind on IQ, sex, and socioeconomic status. Ratings of imaginativeness were based on evidence of flexibility of space–time relations, variety of character, and originality of content. The imaginative content of the dreams of the sighted children was significantly higher than that of the blind children, and Singer and Streiner thus supported the position taken by Blank (1958). Kirtley and Cannistraci (1974) criticized the Singer and Streiner results on several grounds, and presented evidence which they argued contradicted the previous conclusions about the depressing effect of blindness on dream imagery. The Kirtley and Cannistraci study is itself not immune to methodological criticism, though, and it cannot be taken as contradictory to the Singer and Streiner conclusions, because only two of the (adult) subjects had become blind before the age of five, while all of Singer and Streiner's subjects had become blind before five. Deutsch reported that her six cases all experienced visual imagery in their dreams. All six had had some early vision, ranging from one-and-a-half to nearly five years. Other writers have argued that a longer period of early vision is necessary for the existence of visual dream imagery. Jastrow (1900, cited by Blank, 1958) suggested that five to seven years of early vision are necessary, and Blank supported that figure. One problem in trying to answer this question is that verbal report is, of necessity, involved in assessing dreams and their content. Blind children may tend to use visual language in describing their dreams, even when there may have been no visual imagery. This methodological problem is one that was discussed earlier, and there appears to be no ready solution to it.

Creativity

There has been a great deal of interest in recent years in constructing tests of creativity for sighted children. Some researchers have used these tests to compare the creativity of blind and sighted children. Blackhurst, Marks, and Tisdall (1969) studied the relationship between divergent thinking and mobility in 10- to 12-year-old blind children from residential and day school settings. The children were primarily congenitally blind. It was hypothesized that highly mobile blind children are more willing to engage in risk-taking behavior, and should therefore show more evidence of divergent thinking. Teacher ratings of mobility success were compared with the results on 16 subtests taken from various tests of creativity, including word fluency, product improvement, unusual uses, ideational fluency, and recognizing problems. In general, the hypothesis was not supported, although there was a weak pattern of positive correlations fro the day-school group. In a subsequent paper, Tisdall, Blackhurst, and Marks (1971) compared the divergent thinking results from the same group of blind children with those from a comparable group of sighted children. It was concluded that blind and sighted children do not differ substantially in their tendency to divergent thinking. The blind children tended to exhibit more verbal fluency than the sighted, whereas visual familiarity with the environment apparently gave the sighted children an advantage on a small number of tasks. However, any interpretation of the data is clouded by the fact that the sighted subjects were significantly higher in mental age than the blind subjects. Although the authors cited evidence of low correlations between creativity and IQ, some research contradicts this position (Wallace & Kogan, 1965).

Halpin (1972) used the Torrance Tests of Creative Abilities to compare 81 sighted children with 61 blind residential school children and 20 blind day school children on verbal fluency, verbal flexibility, and verbal originality. The six- to 12-year-old blind children were all functionally blind, and were matched on age, sex, and race (but not IQ) with sighted children, whose data were drawn from archival files. There were no significant differences between the residential and the day school groups. Both blind groups scored significantly higher on all three scales than the sighted group, indicating that blind children are more creative. Halpin suggested that blind children are superior in these abilities because they are more dependent on verbal communication, are forced by their handicap to be more flexible and imaginative in dealing with the environment, and are not as pressured to conform to behavioral norms as their sighted counterparts. However, Halpin's conclusions are weakened by the lack of IQ information in the same way as those of Tisdall et al. (1971). The same criticism applies to two related reports (Halpin, Halpin, & Tillman, 1973; Halpin, Halpin, & Torrance, 1973) on the creative abilities of blind children.

Johnson (1979, 1980) compared the "creative imagery" of 10- to 21-year-old subjects, visually impaired since birth or a year of age, with that of sighted subjects of comparable age and IQ. The test, called Onomatopoeia and Images, scores responses as to type, degree of creative imagery, and complexity. The visually impaired scored somewhat higher than the sighted on complexity of imagery. The absence of any age-related trends (despite the 10- to 21-year-age range) or of IQ-related effects (despite the 45- to-142 range) make one suspect the reliability and validity of the test. In fact, the scoring of the test seems not to control for *inappropriate* responses, as tests of creativity are normally expected to do.

McAndrew (1948a,b) investigated the relative rigidity of blind and sighted children (a deaf group was also included in the study). Rigidity was treated within a Lewinian framework, was defined as a lack of variability and adaptability, and as such was regarded as the opposite of creativity. Twenty-five blind children and 25 sighted children, matched on age (10 to 15 years) and intelligence, were tested in situations involving satiation (relative persistence in performing a dull task), level of aspiration, and restructuring by classification. The results on the satiation test, and to a lesser extent on the restructuring test, indicated a greater rigidity on the part of the blind children. McAndrew interpreted the results as supporting his hypothesis that the blind are more isolated from the environment and thus develop a more rigid personality structure.

There has been surprisingly little study of the relative creativity of blind and sighted children as expressed in artistic ability and creations. Although the blind are popularly regarded as being musically creative, there is little firm evidence for this position. Pitman (1965) reviewed the literature and concluded that the blind are not substantially different from the sighted in musical ability. Pitman used the Wing Test of Musical Intelligence to compare the musical ability of 90 blind children, ages eight to 11, with a sighted group of approximately similar age and socioeconomic status. The overall scores of the blind children were higher than those of the sighted, and Pitman noted that the blind excelled on those subtests in which aural perception was of particular importance. He argued that any greater musical ability on the part of blind children represents not a greater potential, but simply a fuller development of the potential which is probably equivalent for blind and sighted children.

There has been little comparative study of the sculptural creations of blind and sighted children. The work of Révész (1950) is the most detailed available, but the developmental aspects of the work are not strong. Révész took the position that all aesthetic insight, and thus all artistic creation, depends on vision, and therefore anyone born blind could not possibly develop more than a rudimentary aesthetic sense. Révész's approach clearly emerges from a sighted framework, though, and his conclusions are based on the responses of sighted judges to the creations of blind persons. There is apparently no work which has taken the approach that the creativity and artistic expression of blind artists should be evaluated from the point of view of other blind people, and it therefore seems risky to attribute a lesser degree of artistic creativity to the blind.

Lowenfeld and Brittain (1964) were much more concerned with the importance of sculpture as a subjective creative expression of the blind child than with its adherence to the aesthetic "standards" of the sighted. Lowenfeld and Brittain divided all people, blind and sighted, into two creative types, the visual and the haptic. The visual type starts with a total impression of external reality and arrives at details through analysis, while the haptic type synthesizes the details into a whole guided by his own internal feelings. The terms visual and haptic thus refer to a type of mental organization rather than to perceptual capabilities. Lowenfeld and Brittain maintained that, although there are differences between the blind and the sighted in their means of expression, the creative process is equivalent for both groups.

Witkin, Birnbaum, Lomonaco, Lehr, and Herman (1968) studied, among other things, the ability to clay-model the human figure by congenitally totally blind and blindfolded sighted children, age range 12.6 to 18.8 years. The figures created by the blind children were rated less accurate than those of the sighted children. Witkin et al. suggested that these results are indicative of a less well-developed body image among blind children. Kinsbourne and Lempert (1980) used a similar procedure, although with a different goal. Their congenitally blind subjects with LP or less were 7.9 to 13.6 years of age. Sighted controls were matched for age, sex, and IQ, and performed alternately under blindfold and with vision. Each subject was asked to model the human figure using plasticine clay. The Goodenough–Harris drawing test was used as the basis for development of a scoring procedure, yielding judgments in three primary categories: body proportion, presence of body parts, and appropriate placement of body parts. There were no significant differences at all on either of the last two measures, although in each case the mean scores suggested that the sighted with vision were best, followed by the same group without vision, followed in turn by the blind. On the index of body proportion, the sighted scored equally whether blindfolded or not, and the blind were significantly worse. Kinsbourne and Lempert concluded that blind children do form a "nonverbal representation of the human body. But that image is imperfect and systematically distorted" (p. 37).

Neither the Witkin et al. (1968) nor the Kinsbourne and Lempert (1980) study adequately distinguishes between the possibilities that the blind child (a) may not have an adequate internal representation of the human form, or (b) may have an adequate internal representation but may simply not be able to model it in acceptable form. A study by Millar (1975b) addresses this question, although through the use of drawings rather than modeling. Millar's subjects were 30 six- to 10.5-year-old early blind children with at most LP, and 30 sighted children matched for age, sex, and digit span, who performed with and without blindfold. Each subject was simply asked to make a drawing of the human figure, and to name each body part as it was drawn. After making the drawing, the subject was asked to indicate the position of the floor on the picture and its relation to the human form. The Sewell Raised Line Drawing Kit was used: the child draws on a plastic sheet with a ball-point pen, which produces a raised line. Millar's goal, briefly, was to ascertain whether any performance differences between blind and sighted subjects were due to basic inability by the former to conceptualize the human figure adequately, or to inadequate understanding of "translation rules," the rules that govern the representation of the real world by drawings (such as the use of a flat line at the bottom of a drawing to denote a floor). Scoring was based on the general body scheme, the appropriate connection of body parts, details such as fingers and toes, and the alignment of the body with the floor.

The measure of the general body scheme showed the six- and eight-year-old blind children worse than their blindfolded sighted peers. The ten-year-old groups showed no such difference, although the blind group still used somewhat less detail in their drawings. However, there was a dramatic difference between the blind and blindfolded sighted children in the relationship of the body figure to the floor, with the latter making relatively few errors but the former making errors of more than 45 degrees in over half the drawings. The blind subjects, in Millar's terminology, simply were not aware of the "translation rules," by which people represent such things as floors and walls in drawings. Millar makes the point that sighted artists took centuries to come to common agreement on the manner of representation of spatial relationships in pictures, and that it is therefore unreasonable to expect that the blind child would be able to accomplish this without specific instruction in just a few years. Thus Millar concludes that the blind child has the basic abilities for pictorial representation at a relatively early age, and that he can acquire an understanding of the conventions, the translation rules, with experience.

Kennedy (1980, 1982, 1983; Kennedy & Dormander, 1981) is just as positive as Millar about the picture-making capabilities of the blind, but his is rather a nativistic view, contrasted with the empiricist view of Millar (1975b). Much of Kennedy's work has been with adults, although some has been with children, and has been directed to the issue of the nature of pictorial representation. The blind, particularly those without any history of visual experience, offer potentially important evidence, since if they were to show similarities in depiction to the sighted, some sort of universal principles must be operating, rather than a strictly learned ability. This, indeed, is Kennedy's basic conclusion. Some of the lines of observation that lead him to that conclusion are the following. One important question is whether the blind can tactually recognize raised-line depictions of objects. Kennedy's (1980) answer is an emphatic yes: although the early blind subjects were initially not as good as the later blind, with minor hints about the identity of objects they performed relatively well. Another question concerns the blind subjects' own drawings, which were made with a stylus that produced raised-line arrays. Although some of the pictures shown by Kennedy (1980) are scarcely recognizable, most are recognizable and differ from pictures that sighted subjects would produce only in the precision of attachment points, such as of table legs to the tabletop. Many of the configurations are easily recognizable. Kennedy (1983) further argued that the pictures of the blind can show perspective, evidently without direct visual experience of it. Supporting the argument that perspective is meaningful even to the blind child, Kennedy (1982) reported that five- to 15-year-old blind children, when pointing simultaneously to the two corners of a room from a location close to the corners, point their arms at a wider angle than when they are farther from the wall, a difference that parallels the change in visual angle as one moves away from a wall. Further, both adults and children find acceptable ways of depicting movement, as for example making the spokes of a moving wheel curved.

Kennedy and Dormander (1981) asked blind children and adults to depict such events and states as the wind, a shout, and pain. They found that the blind, much as the sighted, spontaneously use such metaphoric representations as wavy lines to represent the wind. The comments made by the subjects typically demonstrated that they realized that such representations should not be taken literally, but metaphorically.

That the drawings of the blind suffer from their creators' lack of vision is not in question: virtually all available drawings by the blind are, understandably, less well configured and proportioned than those of the sighted. It is clear that many blind children, as well as adults, understand what it means to represent a scene pictorially. Whether this ability is innate or learned is unclear, since there is evidence on both sides of the issue. It is worth noting, in any case, that this area is open to much interpretation. With any set of drawings by the blind, one can see elements of configuration and of detail that are impressively mature. On the other hand, one can also see many aspects that are immature. In part, one can find what one is looking for, since there is little agreement on any objective method for evaluating drawings. There is much interesting work to be done in this area.

Play

Play is generally considered to be a major outlet for and expression of creativity in childhood. Play may therefore be a useful indicator of differences in creativity and imagination between blind and sighted children. There has been very little empirical research done to compare the play patterns of blind and sighted children. Most of the information on the play of blind children comes from observational reports and case histories. Many of these reports indicate that blind children exhibit far less creativity and imagination in their play than their sighted peers (Burlingham 1965, 1967; Rothschild 1960; Sandler 1963; Sandler & Wells 1965; Tait 1972c,d; Wills 1968). The play of the blind differs not only qualitatively but also quantitatively from that of sighted children: the blind child appears to be less interested in play. According to Rothschild, "the blind child may not be accustomed to express and to involve himself in play. Play, in many instances, may be a far less frequently pursued endeavor and considerably less important in the blind child's life than in the life of the child with full vision" (p. 330). Many blind children show little interest in toys or other inanimate objects. They tend to motor inactivity and to be abnormally content to be left alone. Tait (1972d) even suggested that "the blind child must actually be taught to engage actively, creatively and independently in spontaneous play activities" (p. 368). If constantly encouraged and supported by adults, blind children can be stimulated to play at age-adequate levels; however, Wills (1968) noted that as soon as the adult stimulation is withdrawn, they quickly regress into simple, primitive activities. Much of the play that they do engage in is repetitive. They practice well-learned activities such as opening and closing doors, or they relive certain experiences over and over through role playing.

Wills (1968) suggested two possible reasons for the development of these aberrant play patterns. First, people are cathected more heavily by the blind child, resulting in disinterest in objects such as toys. People offer more stimulation to the blind child than objects do. Second, Wills suggested that the excessive anxiety to which blind children are prone "narrows the field of the blind child's play" (p. 218). Some blind children become extremely withdrawn because of their fears. Wills cited the example of a young boy who was afraid of a teddy bear because he could not decide if it was alive or not. Personification of inanimate objects, which is so important in fantasy play, was thus lacking in his play because of the anxiety it provoked. Others have noted a greater incidence of animism in the blind, though.

On the other hand, several authors have reported that the play of blind children does not differ substantially from that of seeing children, and some claim that the blind are even more prone to fantasy. Avery (1968) stated: "The intriguing aspect of play therapy with a blind child is the original fashion in which play materials can be used" (p. 42). She did not clarify, however, whether the originality of the blind children she studied was spontaneously present or a result of the play therapy. Morrissey (1950) reported that blind children, because of their loneliness, indulge in more fantasies than do the sighted, but he stressed that this is not necessarily a sign that the blind are mentally abnormal. Deutsch (1940) also reported on the fantasy of the blind. He observed blind children playing with various wooden blocks and noted their reactions to and fantasies over the loss of one or more blocks. According to Deutsch, the blind children showed "a striking readiness to give up reality and escape into fantasy" (p. 140).

The above observations were made by people experienced at working with blind children. There are few research data against which to compare their conclusions. In their experiment mentioned earlier, Singer and Streiner (1966) tested the imaginative content of the fantasy play of blind and sighted children. The blind children scored significantly lower than the sighted controls on "Imaginativeness of Play" and "Imaginativeness of Spontaneous Fantasy." The play of the blind children was described as less imaginative, less flexible, and more concrete. Only in the significantly greater use of imaginary companions did the blind show any greater predilection for fantasy. Such fantasy playmates occur fairly frequently in younger seeing children, but in blind children they persist to a later age. These fantasy companions are "generally of a clearly wishful or compensatory character" (p. 480) in that they are generally sighted companions who can do things that the blind child cannot. Morrissey (1950) also commented on the use of fantasy by blind children to construct a world in which they have admiring and appreciative friends.

Cowan (1972) assessed sex-role typing in blind children by measuring their choices of play activity. The 21 blind subjects ranged from second to eighth grade in public school, and the sighted controls were chosen from the same classrooms as the blind children. The children were asked to indicate whether they liked, disliked, or were unfamiliar with 68 games and activities that can be played by both blind and sighted children. It was hypothesized that there would be differences in the choices of games between the blind boys and the sighted boys and between the blind girls and the sighted girls; however, no significant differences were found. These results have little to say about the imaginative content of the games, but they do suggest that the choice of play activity is like that of sighted children. Cowan noted that the blind children seemed less familiar with the games, suggesting that their world of play was more limited that the data revealed. It was also emphasized that the blind children attended public school, and thus were more likely to develop the play interests of sighted children than if they had been segregated in schools or institutions for the blind.

Tait (1972a) compared the play of blind and sighted children, and the results of her study apparently contradict those of Singer and Streiner. The 29 blind subjects ranged in age from four to nine years. The play situation was unstructured, in that the child was free to play with several common objects. The 15-minute sessions were tape recorded, and an observer in the room kept notes. Play behavior was scored for three categories: dramatic play, which involved assigning roles to the play objects, the observer, or the subject himself; manipulative play, in which the subject handled the objects but assigned no roles to them; and "other" play. Nine of the blind children engaged in manipulative play, whereas only one sighted child did. More importantly, however, there was no difference between the blind and the sighted children in the time spent in dramatic play, thus suggesting an equal amount of creativity and imagination. These findings seem to disagree with those of Singer and Streiner, and, in fact, with comments made elsewhere by Tait. However, Tait's study recorded only whether dramatic play was present or not; she did not make a qualitative assessment of the content of the play behavior. In view of the previous comment that blind children frequently engage in repetitive, nonimaginative role playing (Sandler & Wills, 1965), it is possible that the dramatic play of the blind differed qualitatively if not quantitatively from that of the sighted. This possibility received some support in a related paper by Tait (1972b) from the same experiment. In the play session, the sighted children assigned 20 roles to one of the play objects and 15 roles to another, whereas the blind children assigned only seven roles to each object. The results suggest a more limited imagination in the play of the blind children.

The appreciation of humor is another sort of play which also bears on the issue of cognitive development in children—the comprehension of verbal humor such as riddles and jokes may be a useful index of their cognitive development. Tait and Ward (1982) studied 51 visually impaired and 51 sighted children on comprehension of verbal humor. The samples ranged in age from seven to 15 years, and in IQ from about 70 to 140. Each child was given a series of jokes, each printed on a card, and was asked to label them as jokes or nonjokes. Age, IQ, and visual status were examined as predictors of appropriate jokeness judgments in a multivariate analysis. Age and IQ accounted for significant portions of the variance, while visual status did not. Reading of the sample items suggests that the distinctions between jokes and nonjokes may have been rather obvious, and one is led to wonder whether the same results would have occurred with more subtle distinctions.

Rogow (1981) reached a similar conclusion about the comparative appreciation of riddles by blind and sighted children, aged seven to eight years. The samples were not as equivalent as would be desired—several of the eight-year-old blind children turned out to be "riddle collectors," and the blind sample was generally more heterogeneous. Each child was given a set of 20 riddles, and the answers were scored with respect to how the incongruity of the riddle was addressed. The blind children scored somewhat higher on the language-based riddles, and the groups were equivalent on the concept-based riddles. Appropriately, given the nonequivalence of the samples, Rogow did not draw conclusions based on the slight superiority of the blind children. Nonetheless, the seeming equivalence of the blind and sighted children has implications for overall conclusions about relative cognitive development. Much of the research discussed earlier, which makes use of Piaget-type tasks, shows the blind lagging developmentally behind the sighted.

The appreciation of verbal humor is clearly a cognitively-based matter, though dissimilar from the tests of classification and conservation, and the results on humor suggest that it is important to look at other indices of cognitive skills beyond the Piagetian tasks.

Cognitive Style

Witkin and his colleagues have reported a series of studies designed to investigate individual differences in certain cognitive characteristics, aside from IQ, which are collectively called cognitive style. A dimension of particular interest has been the global-articulated dimension. "Experience is articulated, rather than global, if the person is able to experience parts of a field as discrete from background when the field is structured and to impose structure on a field, and therefore experience it as organized, when the field has relatively little inherent structure. Articulation thus has two aspects—analysis and structuring" (Witkin et al., 1968, p. 768). In developmental studies of sighted children the Witkin group has generally found a progression from global to articulated cognitive style; that is, with increasing age children become more able to differentiate structure within a field and more able to impose structure when little exists. The dimension has to do with cognitive organization. Witkin et al. hypothesized that congenitally blind children would show individual consistencies of cognitive style, but that they would be relatively more global in their cognitive functioning than sighted children of comparable age, since vision should play a major role in the developing articulation of the perceptual field. Vision should play a role in articulation not only in visual perception itself, but as an aid to visualization and therefore articulation of experience gained through other modalities. The blind subjects were all blind from birth (20 of 25 due to RLF) and were totally blind. The age range was 12.6 to 18.8, mean age 14.5. A sighted control group was matched on CA and school grade. The IQ scores (verbal WISC, WAIS, or Wechsler–Bellevue) ranged from 92 to 153 for the blind, mean 115. IQ for the sighted group was comparable. Each group contained half boys and half girls.

A series of cognitive tests was administered to all subjects. There were two tests of Analytic Ability in Perception (a tactile and an auditory embedded-figures test), and two tests of Analytic Ability in Problem Solving (tactile block design and tactile matchsticks test). In addition, a test of body concept was administered. There was strong evidence for consistency of results across the various analytic tests. With the exception of the auditory embedded-figures test, the correlations among the tests were significant. Comparison of the blind group with the sighted control group showed some support for the hypothesis that the blind would show less articulation. In the tactile embedded-figures test, which involved finding a simple figure within a larger, more complex figure, the blind were much worse than the sighted. The performance of the blind was also significantly worse on the test of body image, which involved making a clay model of a person. The blind performed significantly better on the auditory embedded-figures test, and the difference was attributed to the blind child's having developed a better ability for concentrated attention to auditory information. On the tests of Analytic Ability in Problem Solving, which did not involve differentiation of a complex field, the blind performed somewhat more globally than the sighted, although the differences were not statistically significant. Thus, although there was some support for the notion that sighted children show more articulated cognitive styles, the pattern of results was complex and does not allow strong generalization.

Cognitive functioning clearly cannot be treated as a single entity when comparing blind with sighted children. Depending on the particular demands of the task, and presumably on the experiential histories of the children, performance may vary widely. It is especially noteworthy that, although there were differences in the embedded-figures tasks (one favoring the blind, the other favoring the sighted), there were no significant differences between groups on the problem solving tasks. There was substantial variation between individuals in the blind group: "Some individual blind subjects, in fact, show highly developed articulation in their cognitive functioning and, from the suggestive findings for the clay-models test, in body concept as well" (p. 779). The authors suggested that, for some blind children, blindness may serve as an impetus for the development of differentiation, although the dynamics of such an influence were not specified. It is interesting that articulation among the blind was not significantly related to the measures of verbal IQ that were taken. This result was parallel to the evidence for sighted children. It should be pointed out, however, that the blind sample included subjects in the normal to superior IQ range, and the possibility still exists that articulation may be related to verbal IQ in the lower IQ range. Further, measures of performance IQ were not taken from the blind subjects. Since the problem solving tasks were somewhat similar to the tasks used in tests of performance IQ, it may well be that relationships between articulation and performance IQ would be found in the blind. In fact, Witkin's group has reported such relationships in sighted groups.

At least two studies have been conducted in partial replication of the Witkin work. Suinn (1967) studied the relationship of articulation, measured by the Ohwaki-Kohs Tactile Block Design Test, to performance on subscales of the WAIS. The subjects were totally blind adults, 46 congenitally blind and 62 adventitiously blinded (age at onset not reported). The results for both groups were supportive of Witkin's findings, in that articulation scores were not significantly correlated with the verbal comprehension subtests. Suinn also tested a corollary of Witkin's hypothesis that the development of an articulated cognitive style depends on early vision. This hypothesis was not supported, in that the patterns of results for the congenitally blind and adventitiously blinded groups were not markedly different. Two points necessitate caution in rejecting the hypothesis about the importance of early vision, however. One is that the age at onset of blindness was not reported in Suinn's study. Presumably there was a range of onset. It would be interesting to know whether those subjects who had enjoyed a longer period of early vision showed more articulation than those adventitiously blind subjects who became blinded relatively early. Second, Suinn's subjects were adults, mean age 33.4 years. It may be that cognitive style tendency changes gradually with increasing duration of blindness. That is, early vision may be effective in producing relative articulation, but the articulation may gradually erode. Further research, with careful attention to both duration of early vision and duration of blindness variables, should provide a more definitive answer to the question of the role of early vision in producing an articulated cognitive style.

Huckabee and Ferrell (1971) provided additional evidence about the role of residual vision in performance on the Tactile Embedded-Figures tests used by Witkin et al. (1968). The blind subjects were adolescents (ages unspecified), while the sighted controls were college students and, presumably, somewhat older than the blind. Six subjects were totally blind, while the remaining 12 were legally blind with some residual vision. Age at onset was not specified. As predicted from Witkin's hypothesis about the importance of vision in the development of an articulated cognitive style, the sighted group performed best on the embedded-figures task, while the partially sighted group was worse than the sighted group but significantly better than the totally blind group.

Cognitive style in the blind deserves more thorough study. The importance of considering cognitive style in educational approaches has received increasing attention. On the basis of the research currently available, however, the determinants of cognitive style in the blind are not all clear. As noted earlier, there have been individual differences reported in the totally congenitally blind (Witkin et al., 1968), and it would seem important to determine the factors involved in producing the differences. Degree of residual vision is clearly implicated (Huckabee & Ferrell, 1971), and the evidence is not clearly against the contribution of early vision. It seems clear that experiential factors, as discussed by Witkin (1965, cf. Suinn, 1967), are important, and adequate research will require concomitant attention to early visual history and residual vision characteristics.

4
Intelligence and IQ Tests

Intelligence Tests for the Blind

There are several excellent reviews of the history of intelligence testing of blind children: Dauterman, Shapiro, and Suinn (1967), Davis, (1970), Goldman (1970), Tobin (1978), Vanderkolk (1977). Scholl and Schnur (1976) comprehensively reviewed the various tests and cited examples of their uses, and Coveny (1976) discussed current research needs in the context of a valuable historical review. This section will not repeat what is comprehensively covered in these reviews, but rather will summarize some of the more important points about the evaluation of verbal and performance aspects of intelligence in the blind.

Verbal tests

The most commonly used tests of verbal IQ are the various versions of the Binet tests (Interim Hayes–Binet and more recently the Perkins–Binet) and the verbal scales of the WISC. Hayes selected the verbal content from forms L and M of the Stanford–Binet test (Goldman, 1970), and the resulting Hayes–Binet test (Hayes, 1929, 1930) was extensively used. A later version of the test, the Interim Hayes–Binet, was based on a later revision of the Stanford test (Hayes, 1942). It has been standardized for blind children and is considered to be reliable for children as young as six years (Hepfinger, 1962). The Perkins–Binet is also receiving validation. The scales of the WISC that have typically been used with blind children are the Information, Comprehension, Arithmetic, Similarities, Vocabulary, and Digit Span scales. Parker (1969) noted that the usefulness of these scales for blind children suffers from the absence of standardization of the scales on blind samples.

Several studies contain reports of various evaluations of the Binet and WISC tests. The examples discussed here do not constitute an exhaustive review but may serve as a sampler of this field of research. Gilbert and Rubin

(1965) administered both Hayes–Binet and WISC tests to 30 blind residential school children between six and 14 years of age. The WISC was given first in most cases, followed by the Hayes–Binet within an 18-month period. The mean performance of the group on the WISC was 3.1 points higher than on the Hayes–Binet, but the difference was not significant. The correlation between the two sets of scores was 0.90. Gilbert and Rubin pointed out, as did Hepfinger (1962), that the Hayes–Binet is a lengthy test to administer, with the attendant possibility of loss of attention and unreliability of results. Gilbert and Rubin conducted a second administration of the WISC for 20 of the children after intervals ranging from 2.4 to 3.9 years. The correlation between the two sets of scores was 0.91, and although the mean IQ for the second administration was about six points higher, the difference was not significant.

Hopkins and McGuire (1967) conducted a similar study in which the test–retest reliability of the Hayes–Binet was assessed with a mean interval of 4.1 years. The 30 subjects were all congenitally and totally blind (all RLF), and they were drawn from public school classes. They averaged 8.4 years of age at the first Hayes–Binet test and 12.5 years at the retest. The mean IQ for the first test was 105.8, that for the second was 118.5, and the correlation between the two administrations of the Hayes–Binet was 0.71. Changes between the original and the follow-up tests ranged from five to 53 points. The same authors (Hopkins & McGuire, 1966) reported a comparison of scores on the verbal WISC with those Hayes–Binet scores from the follow-up test, reported above. The mean IQ on the WISC was 110.0, significantly lower than the mean IQ for the Hayes–Binet that was given at about the same time. Interestingly, the second administration of the Hayes–Binet correlated more strongly with the WISC (0.86) than it did with the original administration of the Hayes–Binet. This result is not surprising in view of the four-year interval between administrations of the Hayes–Binet. These results, like those from many others studies of IQ scores, should be received with caution because the relatively small sample was distributed over a substantial age range. Komisar and MacDonnell (1955) evaluated test–retest data for 89 children (ages not reported) enrolled in a school for the blind. The ages of the children were not reported. Time between tests ranged from one year to more than four years. The WISC, Wechsler–Bellevue Intelligence Scale, and Interim Hayes–Binet tests were used. The correlation between the two administrations was 0.80, and 61 of the 89 cases showed a gain in IQ. The mean gain of 6.3 points was significant. There was a significantly greater improvement among children with initially lower IQ.

Jordan and Felty (1968) conducted an archival study of records at a residential school for the blind. They were able to test hypotheses about the relationship between IQ and several variables that might have an effect on IQ in blind children. The age range was six to 18 years, and the sample included a variety of etiological and residual vision characteristics. Intelligence scores were taken from the Interim Hayes–Binet and from the verbal scales of the Wechsler–

Bellevue 1 and the WAIS. Results indicated that IQ was not significantly related to age at onset of blindness, degree of blindness, or etiological category.

A test that has not received as much attention as the Hayes-Binet or the WISC is the Slosson Intelligence Test (Slosson, 1963). Hammill, Crandell, and Colarusso (1970) administered the SIT to 32 children, characteristics unspecified, who ranged in age from 6.3 to 9.9 years, with a mean of 8.3 years. Split-half consistency within the SIT was high (0.91), while test-retest reliability over a three-month interval was 0.96. Correlation of the SIT scores with IQ scores obtained from school records (WISC and Hayes-Binet) was 0.83. The Williams Intelligence Test (Williams, 1956) is primarily verbal, and was developed using material from both the Stanford-Binet and the WISC scales. Standardization was conducted using relatively large samples of totally blind and partially sighted children, but a single set of norms was developed on the basis of the results of the combined groups.

A modification of previous Binet-type tests has been made by Davis and is called the Perkins-Binet (Davis, 1970, 1980). Extensive norms have been developed for the five-to-15 age range for both partially sighted (Form U) and blind (Form N) children. The test consists primarily of items from the 1960 and 1937 revisions of the Stanford-Binet, although some items were taken from the Williams and the Hayes-Binet tests. About one-fourth of the items are nonverbal. Coveny (1972) reported a study designed to assess both the reliability of the Perkins-Binet (in its prepublication version) and its correlation with the WISC verbal scales. Thirty braille readers were tested with Form N and 25 print readers with Form U. The children, ranging in age from eight to 16 years, were drawn from a residential school for the blind. Each subject performed on the appropriate form of the Perkins-Binet and on the six verbal WISC scales. Split-half reliability was assessed for the Perkins-Binet. The coefficients for both forms were impressively high, 0.96 for Form N and 0.94 for Form U. Correlation of the WISC with Form N was 0.86, and of the WISC with Form U was 0.74. Although both correlation coefficients were highly significant, Coveny pointed out that the tests are not interchangeable, since the standard deviations of both Perkins-Binet forms were substantially greater than those of the WISC. Similarly, Teare and Thompson (1982) examined the relationship of the published form of the Perkins-Binet to the Wechsler scales. Their subjects were 14 children without useful vision and 14 who though legally blind did have some usable vision. The sample averaged 13 years of age. Form N of the Perkins-Binet was administered to the former and Form U to the latter subgroup, and the verbal portion of either the WAIS or the WISC-R was also given. Correlations between the Perkins-Binet and the Wechsler scores were extremely high, ranging upward from .93. Teare and Thompson, as had Coveny (1972), found higher variabilities for the Perkins-Binet tests, and therefore reiterated Coveny's caution against using the tests interchangeably.

On the basis of Coveny's and Teare and Thompson's results from relatively small groups of children, it may be concluded that the Perkins-Binet holds promise not only because of its norms for blind children but also because of its internal reliability and its inclusion of nonverbal material. Although the correlations with WISC scores are impressive, the critical test of external validity of the Perkins–Binet will be accomplished only over a period of years as data are collected on the ability of the test to predict success in academic and other functional situations.

Goldman (1970) summarized some of the problems inherent in relying on strictly verbal tests of intelligence for blind children. One problem is that "verbal measurements might be less truly representative for blind than for seeing persons" (p. 78). Another problem concerns the issue of verbalisms, or use of words without adequate experiential referents. A related point is that, because of their relatively restricted range of experience, blind children's verbal abilities may not adequately reflect their overall abililties. Dauterman, Shapiro, and Suinn (1967) have noted that the verbal abilities of the blind may be relatively overdeveloped: "Blind persons who are exposed to educational experiences in the Western culture, whether in school or elsewhere, frequently perform well on verbal tests, while having less than average ability to cope with vocational and other activities of daily living" (p. 8). This issue is apparently not resolved, but the fact that there is contradiction in the literature about the value of verbal tests for the blind is sufficient reason to view their results with caution. Still another difficulty is that, while the verbal WISC is reasonably reliable and somewhat shorter than the Hayes–Binet, it does contain items inappropriate for blind children, such as, "What should you do if you see a train approaching a broken track?"

Performance tests

Performance IQ testing of blind children has enjoyed a shorter history than has verbal IQ testing. In an extension of previous work with maze tests (Duncan, 1934; Knotts & Miles, 1929; Koch & Ufkess, 1926), Merry and Merry (1934) studied the usefulness of finger-maze performance of blind children as a supplementary test of intelligence. Over half the 30 subjects, who ranged in age from eight to 16 years, were blind at birth or within the first year, and 83 percent were blind before the age of five. Correlations of various measures of maze performance with MA (method of assessment not reported, although presumably a variation of the Binet was used) ranged from 0.21 to 0.61. Thus, although there was a substantial relation between maze performance and MA, the maze test did show considerable variation that was not accounted for by the MA measure. Bauman (1947) developed the Non-Language Learning Test for use with the blind, although the test may not be used with blind children below 10 years of age (Goldman, 1970). The Haptic Intelligence Scale, developed by Shurrager and Shurrager (1964), is similarly inappropriate for children.

Wattron (1956) investigated the possibility of using a tactual adaptation of the Kohs Blocks Test with blind children. Instead of the colors used for visual patterns, Wattron used texture differences embossed on wood blocks. Twenty children, all having at most LP, ranged in age from seven to 17. All were blind within the first three years. In addition to the Hayes–Binet, each subject was given the block design performance test. Correlation between the block test and the Hayes–Binet was 0.84. It should be noted that the sample was of above average intelligence as measured by the Hayes–Binet: while the CA range was from 7 to 17, the MA range was from 10.2 to 22.1.

Although there has apparently not been continued work with the Wattron variation of the Kohs Block Test, another variation has been developed and has received more attention. Ohwaki and his colleagues developed an adaptation of the Kohs Blocks, called the Ohwaki–Kohs Tactile Block Design Intelligence Test for the Blind, in which cloth texture differences were substituted for the color differences. Interesting reports of the development of the test are available (Ohwaki, Tanno, Ohwaki, Hariu, Hayasaka, & Miyake, 1960; Oi, Koyanagi, & Maehigashi, 1956). The former paper contains a description of the norming procedures that have been conducted for the test. Although children ranging in age from 6 to 21 were studied, the authors did not consider the numbers of subjects to be sufficient for norming below the age of eight or above 20. Results were obtained for 253 subjects between the ages of eight and 20. The distribution of IQ scores from a somewhat larger sample ($n = 276$) was bimodal, with an overall mean of 84.6 and standard deviation of 27.3, but with a distinct peak at about 70 and a lesser peak at about 120. Ohwaki et al. noted that the size of the sample was not large considering the range of ages included, and that it is not possible to conclude that the performance IQ of blind children is in fact bimodally distributed. It is unfortunate that distributions of IQ scores were not provided for finer age categories. Test–retest reliability was assessed with an interval of two months in two separate samples (combined $n = 79$). The average reliability was 0.82. Substantial improvements (of 17 and 12 IQ points for the two samples) occurred from the first to the second administration of the test. Validity of the test was assessed by conducting correlations between test results and performance in various school subjects, and the coefficients ranged from 0.24 (social studies) to 0.55 (arithmetic).

Although Ohwaki et al. concluded from their assessment of the test that "this tactual intelligence test may be adequate as an intelligence test," there are substantial weaknesses in the norming that they reported. This conclusion was also reached by Rankin (1967), who noted fallacies in the test manual as well as various weaknesses in the norming procedures, and advised that the test should not be used without substantial additional study of its characteristics.

Rich and Anderson (1965) reported an investigation of a tactual form of the Raven Progressive Matrices Test. Anderson (1961) had used a similar test with the adult blind and had found significant positive correlations with WAIS verbal scores. The Tactual Progressive Matrices Test (TPM), used by Rich and Anderson, consisted of 36 items, each consisting of a raised design and each having a section missing. The subject's task was to explore the design tactually and choose the correct completion section from a set of six choices. The sample included 115 blind children, age range six to 15 years, who were drawn from schools for the blind and public schools. No subject could distinguish patterns visually, and all but eight had been blind from birth. For the children in the six-to-eight age range, split-half reliability was only 0.44, while for the nine-to-11 and 12-to-15 age groups, split-half reliability coefficients were respectively 0.94 and 0.96. Thus, the test is clearly of limited value below the age of nine. The correlation of the TPM score with CA was 0.50, while the correlation of the TPM score with the WISC verbal scale was 0.31. Correlations between the TPM scores and the WISC subtests ranged from 0.24 to 0.43. Thus, while the correlations were significant at the 0.01 level, the TPM score shared relatively little of the variability in WISC scores. The relatively low correlations between the TPM test and the WISC verbal (as compared with the 0.80 to 0.90 correlations between the Hayes–Binet and the WISC verbal reported in other studies) does not necessarily mean that the TPM test is not a useful measure of some aspects of intelligence, since it is certain that there are some aspects of intelligence that are not well represented by the verbal tests. Rich and Anderson drew correlations between the TPM scores and other measures of performance, including grade-point average, academic ability rating by the teacher, and braille reading ability judged by the teacher. Grade-point average and academic rating showed some correlations with the TPM scores (correlations were in the 0.20s through age 11, and about 0.60 in the 12-to-15 age group). Correlation of TPM score with braille rating was not significant. Thus, it must be concluded that the TPM test is not a good predictor of these aspects of performance, especially at the lower age range. Observations of the qualitative approach of the subjects to the matrices task seem relevant here—most children younger than nine did not approach the task in an appropriate way, and while older children of normal intelligence did approach the task appropriately, the lower-IQ older children did not do so, and they could therefore not be said to have been adequately tested by the TPM test. As Rich and Anderson correctly noted, their results "reflect the need for continued research before the tactual test can be used on a clinical basis" (p. 918).

The Boehm Test of Basic Concepts (BTBC) (Boehm, 1971) was developed to evaluate the sighted child's mastery of concepts commonly tapped by instructional materials. The BTBC makes heavy use of pictorial material. Caton (1977) reported the development and evaluation of a tactile version of the test for visually impaired children, called the Tactile Test of Basic Concepts (TTBC). Instead of pictures, the TTBC uses raised-line adaptations (typically of geometric figures) that are in general simplifications of the corresponding BTBC pictures. Evaluation of the TTBC involved 75 children, 25 in each of kindergarten and first and second grades, all of whom had sufficient loss of vision to require the eventual use of braille as a reading medium. Those who had any light perception at all were tested under blindfold. Two goals were set: First, characteristics of the test such as relative item difficulty and reliability were evaluated and compared with the sighted version, and second, the relationships were assessed between TTBC performance and various status variables such as grade placement, age, sex, and the like. Age, grade placement, and amount of school experience showed significant correlations with performance. Several results from the item analysis are worth mention. Items requiring self-reference (such as the concepts "behind" and "next to") were generally easier than relational concepts (such as "middle" and "half"). As does the BTBC, the TTBC showed progressively better performance with increasing grade level, indicating that the blind children were acquiring the concepts tapped by the test. However, while the blind kindergarten children performed at least as well as the sighted, the first and second grade blind children did not do as well as their sighted counterparts. The easy conclusion that the blind show a progressive conceptual lag compared with the sighted should be heavily qualified by the point that the relative difficulties of the visual and tactile forms of the items may not be equivalent. Even so, it should also be noted that Caton's comparison showed the visually impaired children not to lag nearly as far behind sighted children as the weight of research with Piagetian-based cognitive tasks would suggest. The bulk of the evidence, presented in Chapter 3, for cognitive lag is indeed based on Piaget-type tasks, and it is worth emphasizing that the cognitive-assessment approach represented by the TTBC does not solidly corroborate the conclusion of cognitive lag. Still, Caton's findings did show a slight lag in first and second graders that was not present among kindergarteners, and indeed it would be surprising if there were developmental equivalence, given the extent to which developing concepts such as those assessed by the test are dependent on an experiential base, in which the majority of visually impaired children are undoubtedly restricted compared with their sighted age-mates

In 1952, Newland began work on the Blind Learning Aptitude Test (BLAT). It is appropriate, before giving a brief description of the test, to provide some perspective on Newland's approach to the issue of testing of blind children. It is not by chance that the term "intelligence" does not appear in the title of the test. Newland (1964, 1979) considers the term "intelligence" to be too ambiguous and to obscure the differentiability of adaptiveness in learning situations. He points out that, while subscale scores are often available, Hayes–Binet and WISC scores are typically given as unitary scores. That this procedure may be misrepresentative can be seen from the results of studies that assess subscale performance (for instance, the work of Tillman, to be discussed in the next section). A more critical concern of Newland is the extent to which performance on the WISC and Hayes–Binet tests depends on specific information. It is widely recognized that most intelligence tests are not culture free, and this fact may be particularly serious in the case of the blind whose experience with some areas of cultural content is very sparse. Newland makes a differentiation between *product* ("which reflects mainly achievement") and *process* ("which reflects mainly the psychological operations fundamental to learning"), and notes that both the Hayes–Binet and WISC tests evaluate primarly product. The BLAT is designed to evaluate process.

The BLAT consists of a series of embossed form problems. Although there is verbal interaction with the child, the verbal requirements of the test are minimal. Three categories of problems are designed to tap the child's abilities to: (1) discover differences among items, (2) identify commonalities among items, and (3) extrapolate the relationship among a series of items. The test has been extensively normed on children ranging in age from six to 16, although it is considered most meaningful in the six-to-12 range.

Several general points seem appropriate in summary. First, tests of verbal IQ have been more thoroughly developed and may be used with more confidence with blind children than tests of performance IQ. However, the existence of items on the WISC verbal test that are wholly inappropriate for blind children must be noted, and their inclusion in the test when it is used with the blind detracts from the usefulness of the test. Some of the more recent tests have succeeded in minimizing this problem. Second, there has not been sufficiently sustained attention to the problem of the testing of performance IQ in blind children. Such tests, with the exception of the BLAT, are of limited value at this time. Progress in this area will require extensive validity testing. Since the purpose of performance tests of IQ is to tap components of intelligence that are not adequately represented by verbal tests, it will not be sufficient to assess validity by reference to correlations of performance tests with verbal tests. If performance tests are to become useful, their ability to predict defined areas of competence must be assessed. Third, the verbal IQ tests do not seem to be appropriate for young blind children. Although the Hayes–Binet has been standardized for children as young as four, several writers (Hepfinger, 1962, for instance) point out that the length of the test may interfere with its reliability at the younger ages. Parker (1969) suggested that the Wechsler Pre-School and Primary Scale of Intelligence (WPPSI) may prove useful with younger blind children, but noted that little data are available on its adequacy. Several studies have been made of the usefulness of social maturity scales, such as the Vineland Social Maturity Scale and the Maxfield–Buchholz Scale of Social Competence, for assessing aspects of competence in young blind children. Gillman and Goddard (1974), for example, found some evidence that social quotient (SQ) before age six was positively correlated with IQ after age six. Since tests of social maturity are more clearly related to the area of social development, they will be discussed more fully in Chapter 6.

Comparison of Blind and Sighted Children

The question of the comparative intelligence of blind and sighted children is one that is fraught with difficulties. The major problem is that it is virtually impossible to administer a common test to the two groups to provide information that is equally meaningful for both. Tests for sighted children rely heavily on vision, both in content and in administration of the tests. Much of the material is thus inappropriate for the blind in its regular form. Until recently, the bulk of the IQ testing with blind children has been conducted using that material from normal tests that may be administered to the blind. Typically this procedure necessitates exclusion of the performance scales of IQ tests. Comparison of blind and sighted children on the verbal scales, even excluding items that require visual experience for solution, does not constitute a satisfactory comparison of intelligence, though, since verbal intelligence is normally considered only one facet of intelligence. In the past decade or so there has been an increased interest in developing measures of the performance aspects of intelligence that may be administered to the blind. The Ohwaki modification of the Kohs Block Design Test is perhaps the best example. The Kohs Blocks are color-keyed blocks with which various designs are created by the subject. In the Ohwaki modification, the color distinctions are represented by surfaces of varying textures, so that the subject may perform the test haptically. Although it is possible to administer this type of test to blindfolded sighted children, comparison of the results with those of blind children are probably invalid. Sighted children do not typically perform haptic tasks without vision, and they would be at a disadvantage that would probably depress their performance.

In short, it is extremely difficult, if not impossible, to make direct comparisons of blind and sighted children on identical instruments if those instruments adequately cover the range of abilities considered to be part of the overall notion of intelligence. Further, the question of the general equivalence of intelligence of blind and sighted children is probably of little importance.

Despite the problems in making comparisons between blind and sighted children, it is an interesting question whether the IQ tests that are used with the blind evaluate them in a way comparable to the evaluation of sighted children. Tillman and his colleagues have conducted a series of informative analyses of the WISC. Tillman (1967a) administered the verbal WISC to a sample of 55 blind boys and 55 blind girls. Age range was from seven to 13, mean 9.9 years. Children who could read large print were excluded. All blind subjects were drawn from residential schools. Most of the children were blind at birth or within the first year, and more than half were RLF children. A comparison group of sighted children was matched closely for age and was also given the WISC. The mean IQ for the blind group was 92, range 55 to 133, while for the sighted group the mean was 96.5, range 58 to 130. The difference in means was significant. Subscale analysis showed an interesting pattern of results. The sighted children were significantly superior to the blind only on the Comprehension and Similarities scales, while there were no differences on Information, Arithmetic, or Vocabulary. Results for the Digit Span scale were not available for some of the sighted children. Several additional facts should be noted. First, the reliability (Kuder–Richardson) of the scales was somewhat lower for the blind than for the sighted group. In fact, it was on those scales where the blind were significantly worse that the reliability was lowest for the blind group (0.71, 0.76). Second, there were items in some scales that showed a higher success rate for the blind than for the sighted. Some items, however, seem to be totally inappropriate for the blind, and this may be one reason for the lower reliability in the blind. Third, some writers have noted that the blind tend to score better than sighted children on the Digit Span scale, for which there were no comparability results in the Tillman study. Tillman noted, in fact, that for the blind sample, where Digit Span results were available, the overall IQ score was increased by the Digit Span scale by an amount approximately equivalent to its depression by the relatively low performance on the Comprehension and Similarities scales. Tillman concluded that an appropriate test for blind children may be one where the total score is prorated from performance on only the Information, Arithmetic, and Vocabulary scales.

In a subsequent paper, Tillman (1976b) presented the results of factor analyses of the IQ results for the same groups of subjects. For the Information scale, the factor structure was comparable for blind and sighted children. Two factors emerged, one represented by items "the answers to which the average ten-year-old could pick up in the course of maturation" (p. 107), and the other characterized by items that required more specific, educationally related information. The factor loadings were somewhat weaker for the blind. A similar two-factor structure appeared for the Comprehension scale for both blind and sighted children, although there were again somewhat fewer and weaker loadings for the blind group. By contrast, the Arithmetic scale produced factors that were equally strong for the blind and sighted groups. On the Similarities scale, two factors appeared, differing in the degree of conceptualization required. One factor involved concrete and functional reasoning, while the other required "a higher abstraction." Comparison of blind and sighted groups indicated an overall lower level of conceptual functioning for the blind group. On the Vocabulary scale, the structure for the sighted children showed a word-definition factor and a word-richness factor. For the blind, there was a single factor that was similar to the word-definition factor of the sighted group. Tillman noted the relation of this difference between blind and sighted to the concern, discussed in Chapter 5, that the vocabulary of the blind is not based on as articulated a set of direct experiences as that of the sighted children. The interesting differences in factor structure found by Tillman should, as he noted, be regarded within the context of the small but significant difference in overall IQ between the samples.

Tillman and Osborne (1969) reported the results of a subsequent study in which the overall IQ (based on all six verbal scales of the WISC) was equated for blind and sighted groups. Further, single year age levels were isolated in the seven-to-11 age range to ascertain whether any scale differences between blind and sighted samples might change over age. Analysis of variance showed a significant interaction between group (blind vs. sighted) and scale. The interaction was produced by the superior performance by the sighted children on the Similarities scale and the superior performance by the blind on the Digit Span scale. There was no evidence that this pattern changed with age.

Taken together, these three studies reinforce the notion that it is doubtful that blind and sighted children can be compared directly on a single summary measure of IQ. This point was further corroborated in a study by Tillman and Bashaw (1968) in which discriminate function analysis was used to assess whether blind and sighted subjects could reliably be distinguished on the basis of their WISC subscale performance. The samples were comparable to those used in the earlier Tillman studies. The sighted sample performed significantly better on the Similarities scale, while the blind performed significantly better on the Digit Span and Information scales. Discriminate function prediction allowed a success rate of about 75 percent. That is, the pattern of performance by an individual subject was informative enough to predict correctly in 75 percent of the cases whether the subject was in the blind or the sighted sample.

Smits and Mommers (1976) reported a similar study with seven- to 13-year-old children in the Netherlands. Groups of blind and sighted children, matched on age, sex, and verbal IQ, were given the six WISC verbal scales, and various analyses were performed to ascertain the comparability of the scale structure for the two groups. The Comprehension scale showed worse performance and the Digit Span scale better performance by the blind group, a result supporting previous findings. Smits and Mommers noted that most of the blind-sighted differences on these scales were produced by a small number of items. For the most part, the comparative profiles of blind and sighted children corroborated the results from previous work, although, in contrast to Hopkins and McGuire (1966) and Tillman (1967a), Smits and Mommers found a stronger pattern of subscale intercorrelation for the blind. Smits and Mommers also found a general advantage in a totally blind subgroup over a partially sighted subgroup, but they attributed the difference to sampling artifact.

Generally, then, the research that has compared blind with sighted performance patterns on tests such as the WISC supports the notion that the profiles for the groups differ substantially. The variation is not random, though; factors such as better auditory attention by the blind and selective exposure to specific content areas may account for most of the differences.

Several points of perspective may be in order on the issue of intelligence testing. Intelligence has to do with the ability of the individual to adapt to, or get along in, his environment. Certainly the environments of blind and sighted children are different. As Goldman (1970) pointed out, the blind child is forced to rely much more heavily on tactual information about his environment than the sighted child. Thus the adaptive needs of the children are different, and the issue of whether the adaptation is equally adequate cannot be answered simply by administering a common test. Any common test, whether it is designed primarily for blind or sighted children, is likely to underrepresent the primary adaptive modes of one group or the other. As Bateman (1965) pointed out, it is often the goal of the examiner to assess the ability of the blind child to function in the environment of the sighted. While this point is well taken, it should not be used as support for the notion that the blind child should have his IQ score interpreted with respect to norms for sighted children. The need for separate norming for blind samples has to do with the validity of the test, not with the type of environment that has to be met. The use of sighted test norms will not allow adequate prediction of the blind child's success if that child's tested IQ is not a valid estimate of his potential.

The adequate treatment of this issue is equally important for blind and sighted children. A test should not be used for prediction in situations where it has not been demonstrated to have good predictive validity. Further, the fact that predictive validity for a particular IQ test for sighted children's success in a situation such as schoolwork has been established is not sufficient grounds on which to base use of the test for the prediction of blind children's success in that situation. Thus adequate norming has to be done for IQ scales for blind children. If a test is designed to be used to predict success for blind children in a particular set of situations, then the predictive validity of the test has to be established for blind children for those situations. Coveny (1976) has pointed out the scarcity of predictive studies with blind children. It would seem critical to exercise extreme caution in using test results to establish a predicted "highest level of attainment" for a blind child, given the present level of uncertainty about what IQ is and how it might best be tested in the blind child. Foreclosure of opportunity is a questionable use for any test on ethical grounds, and particularly so in the case of blind children whose potential is prone to be underestimated by any measure. The danger is particularly severe in an educational system that has historically been characterized by an excessive tendency to compartmentalization.

Retinoblastoma: A Special Case?

Blindness due to retinoblastoma is especially interesting in the context of IQ because there have been reports that many retinoblastoma victims are retarded, on the one hand, and of superior intelligence on the other. At least two studies have found samples of retinoblastoma children to be markedly superior in IQ to samples of nonretinoblastoma blind. Thurrell and Josephson (1966) reported an archival study of 15 retinoblastoma children, whose ages were not reported. They had been enrolled at a school for the blind, and all were totally blind. A group of blind children, some of whom had LP, was used for comparison. Each retinoblastoma subject was matched with a nonretinoblastoma comparison partner. Age was matched within two years. Hayes–Binet scores were available for the large majority of the children. Mean IQ for the retinoblastoma group was 120, while that of the comparison group was 99. The difference was highly significant, and it was especially striking in view of the fact that subjects with known brain damage were eliminated from the comparison group, but not from the retinoblastoma group (apparently one or two of the low-scoring retinoblastoma subjects did have some brain damage). In discussing the results, Thurrell and Josephson pointed out that, while most of the retinoblastoma subjects had become blind between the ages of two and four, the controls were primarily congenitally blind. Although the argument that two to four years of early vision does not confer effective "retention of visual memory" is probably ill-founded and, certainly oversimplified, the mean IQ of 120 for the retinoblastoma group is impressively high when compared to the mean of 99 for the other sample. Although the issue was not discussed extensively in the paper, the authors mentioned the possibility of a genetic linkage of retinoblastoma and intelligence, as well as the possibility that the therapeutic irradiation of the eyes of the retinoblastoma subjects affected the results.

M. Williams (1968) provided similar evidence of the IQ superiority of retinoblastoma children. Fifty retinoblastoma subjects were drawn from a wide range of schools for the blind in England and Wales. Their age range was from five to 16 years. Children with additional handicaps were eliminated from the sample. A comparison group of 74 nonretinoblastoma subjects was drawn from the schools. A range of etiologies was included in this sample, and children with additional handicaps were again excluded. Sixty sighted children were selected to serve as an additional comparison group. All subjects were administered the Williams Intelligence Test Scale, which is a primarily verbal, Binet-type test, standardized on blind and partially sighted children. The mean IQ of the retinoblastoma group was 119.7, significantly higher than the means for the nonretinoblastoma blind group (102.8) and the sighted comparison group (102.7). None of the retinoblastoma children had a below average IQ. This result was in contrast to those of Thurrell and Josephson (1966), whose sample included scores of 65, 81, and 94.

Taktikos (1964) presented statistics which are at least superficially contrary to those reported by Williams. Of a sample of 300 retinoblastoma patients, he found 9 who were retarded (the definition of retardation was not given). This incidence of retardation was about 10 times the rate in the overall population (England). Taktikos discussed the possibility that "these manifestations. . . represent neuro-ophthalmological variants of a wide, genetically determined syndrome" (p. 497). The possibility that retinoblastoma may be genetically linked with some general intelligence factor was also mentioned by M. Williams (1968) and Thurrell and Josephson (1966), although these authors discussed the genetic possibility in connection with high rather than low IQ scores. All these authors pointed out that, while some retinoblastoma is sporadic (nonfamilial), a substantial proportion of cases can be identified as having familial precursors. The issue of the heritability of intelligence is extremely complex, and well beyond the scope of this review. It can reasonably be stated, though, that the level of intellectual functioning of a given individual is determined jointly by hereditary and environmental factors. However, the possibility that retinoblastoma is genetically linked to a general intelligence factor seems unlikely in the light of the apparent complexity of any genetic contribution to intelligence. If indeed there is a genetic linkage, it seems more reasonable to expect retinoblastoma subjects to have certain characteristic patterns of intellectual functioning. A study that bears on this possibility was reported by Witkin et al. (1971), who assessed the performance of a group of retinoblastoma subjects on a battery of tests designed to evaluate cognitive patterning. The 28 subjects ranged in age from 11 to 24, with a mean age of 16 years. All were totally blind with no LP, and enucleation had occurred at ages ranging from within the first two years to as late as 15. Results for comparison groups of congenitally blind (nonretinoblastoma) and sighted subjects were also reported. For the retinoblastoma group, the mean verbal IQ (WISC or WAIS) was 122.3, while the mean for the congenitally blind group was 114.8. Mean IQ for the sighted group was not reported. The battery of tests was described in Chapter 3. Three dimensions of cognitive functioning were evaluated. On the verbal-comprehension dimension, there were no significant differences between any pair of groups. On the attention-concentration dimension, there was no difference between the two blind groups, and both were superior to the sighted group. This result was attributed to the superior ability of the blind to sustain auditory attention. For the global-articulation dimension, the retinoblastoma group was significantly superior to both the other groups. A uniform pattern of results was found for most of the tactile tasks involved in this dimension, including tactile matchsticks, tactile embedded figures, and tactile block design. On the clay-modeling task the retinoblastoma group was better than the other blind group, but not significantly different from the sighted group.

The Witkin et al. results are important in that they showed specific areas of performance in which the retinoblastoma subjects were superior. Thus it may not be as useful to state that verbal IQ is superior among retinoblastoma subjects as to say that there are specific areas of cognitive-perceptual performance in which the retinoblastoma group is superior. In particular, tactile discrimination was superior in the retinoblastoma group, and the differences in the global-articulated dimension may be attributable to this difference. It also seems possible that the differences between the retinoblastoma group and the other blind group were due to the early vision enjoyed by the retinoblastoma subjects, although the authors pointed out that perceptual disembedding performance was superior even in those retinoblastoma subjects who lost their sight during the first year of life. They also noted that little is known about the possible effect of very early and limited visual experience on such performance. In this regard, Warren (1974) has suggested that the period from three to six months of age may be especially critical, since it is then that significant visual control of manual behavior emerges in the infant with sight. Another interesting possibility was suggested by Witkin et al. to account for the group differences: "The possibility must also be considered that parents, aware of the impending loss of sight, may treat their children in ways that foster the development of articulation" (p. 45). It would seem important to ascertain just what the critical aspects of such parental treatment may be, since some of these aspects may be adaptable for use with infants without vision.

A theme that runs through the available literature on retinoblastoma is the hereditary factor. As noted earlier, the suggestion is that high intelligence tends to occur in retinoblastoma cases because of the genetic association of an intelligence potential with a potential for retinoblastoma. In an attempt to evaluate the genetic and environmental contributions to the superior intelligence of retinoblastoma groups, Levitt, Rosenbaum, Willerman, and Levitt (1972) studied a group of 44 retinoblastoma subjects, along with a control group composed of siblings of the subjects. The 44 retinoblastoma subjects included 16 with unilateral blindness, 19 with bilateral retinoblastoma who were blind in both eyes, and nine with bilateral retinoblastoma but with sight remaining in one eye due to radiation or chemotherapy. The subjects ranged in age from 2.3 to 23 years. Estimates of verbal IQ were made by use of the WAIS and WISC tests in many cases, while the Stanford–Binet was used for the younger sighted children and the Williams Test for the younger blind children. Various analyses were performed. The overall comparison of retinoblastoma subjects with the sighted control group did not show a significant difference. However, the bilaterally blind group did show a significant superiority (10 IQ points) over their sighted controls. In contrast, the bilateral retinoblastoma subjects who had some vision were significantly worse (18 IQ points) than their sighted controls. Analysis of subscales provided interesting information about the pattern of superiority of the bilaterally blind. They scored significantly better on the Information, Arithmetic, and Digit Span scales, but not on the Comprehension, Similarities, and Vocabulary scales.

The results of Levitt et al. (1972) show that the pattern of IQ comparisons between retinoblastoma subjects and their sighted controls is not a simple one. It is apparently not the existence of the disease itself, since the bilateral retinoblastoma subjects with vision were significantly lower than sighted controls, but its combination with the condition of bilateral blindness that is associated with higher IQ. If the retinoblastoma of the bilateral subjects who had remaining vision had not been arrested, these subjects would have belonged in the bilateral blind group. The fact that there was a striking IQ difference between the bilateral blind and the bilateral residual vision subgroups thus argues against a simple relationship between IQ potential and retinoblastoma potential. Clearly some set of environmental factors is implicated. These results make it plausible to suggest that the apparent contradictions in the previous literature are attributable to differences in sampling of subjects. It is clearly unwise to discuss retinoblastoma as a category without distinguishing between bilaterally blind and partially sighted subgroups. It is similarly inadequate to speak of an overall IQ factor without attention to subscales. The issue certainly deserves more detailed attention. It is especially important to ascertain whether components of superior performance may be traced to differences in early experience.

RLF: A Special Case?

Hayes (1952) reported some early data on the comparative IQ distributions of RLF and non-RLF blind children. His data showed no evidence of differential distribution in any part of the IQ range. Gore (1966) studied records of those blind subjects who were aged 22 or less and who were registered with the New Jersey State Commission for the Blind in 1964. All RLF children for whom IQ scores were available constituted one group. The mean IQ (test unspecified) of these 233 cases was 98.2. Information about the lower limit of the age range was not given; nor was information about the age distribution across the sample. A subset of 28 RLF subjects was chosen on the basis of having matching subjects available from the non-RLF blind registrants. The non-RLF group was matched for sex, age, and degree of impairment, and onset of blindness was two years at the latest. Gore did not find a significant difference between the mean IQs of the two samples.

Other information on this question comes from two groups of children who have been studied longitudinally, those of Norris (and discussed by Cohen and others) and Parmalee. The Chicago sample, studied intensively by Norris, Spaulding, and Brodie (1957), consisted of a total of 295 children, of whom 209 (71 percent) were of RLF etiology.

Tests of intelligence used were the Cattell Intelligence Scale (up to 30 months) and the Interim Hayes-Binet. On both tests, the distributions of scores were virtually identical for the RLF and the non-RLF groups. Furthermore, the incidence of low scores was virtually identical for the two groups, and Norris et al. concluded that there was no evidence of a relationship between RLF and mental retardation. A subset of 66 children was selected from the larger sample for inclusion in an intensive study group. Important criteria for inclusion in the intensive group were a first observation before 15 months of age, absence of physical handicap, and relatively regular testing by the project psychologist. It is also worthy of note that children who had six months or more of continuous hospital or institutional care were excluded from the group. Thus it is likely that the intensive group was relatively free of several characteristics that may often be observed in institutionalized children, whether blind or not, such as emotional disturbance and lag in intellectual development. The intensive group consisted of 85 percent RLF children (all premature) and 15 percent non-RLF children (all full term). Therefore, the proportion of RLF etiology was somewhat higher in the intensive group than in the overall group. The mean Hayes-Binet score for the intensive group was 109.7, with a range of 65 to 175.

Cohen and his colleagues have reported several detailed follow-up studies of portions of the intensive group described by Norris et al. Cohen has been particularly concerned with the possibility that there are patterns of neurological abnormality associated with the RLF etiology. Cohen, Boshes, and Snider (1961) reported data from 28 of the 66 intensively studied children. All 28 showed varying signs of EEG abnormality. In addition, a neurologist made ratings of the children. There was a high correlation (0.75) between the neurological ratings (taken to indicate degree of brain damage) and Hayes-Binet IQ scores. The 28 children included in this study showed a distribution of intelligence scores that was substantially lower than the distribution reported by Norris et al. (1957) for the intensive group. Fifteen of the 28 children had IQ scores below 90, with six of the scores below 60. The relatively low distribution of IQ scores among the 28 children thus presents a striking contrast to the more positive picture presented by Norris et al. The contrast is especially striking in view of the fact that absence of additional physical handicaps was used as a criterion in the Norris study for inclusion in the intensive sample, from which the Cohen sample was apparently drawn. The relatively heavy incidence of neurological signs in the Cohen study is curious in this light. A partial resolution of the apparent conflict may be found in a longitudinal study reported by Gillman and Goddard (1974), who noted an age-related increase in the number of multiple handicaps within the group. That is, the intensive group of Norris et al. may have included some children with incipient neurological problems that appeared only as they became older.

In a subsequent report, Cohen, Alfano, Boshes, and Palmgren (1964) provided data on a further subset of 43 of the original intensive group of 66. The 43 included the 28 reported by Cohen et al. (1961). Hayes-Binet and verbal WISC IQ scores were available for 42 of the children. The scores for 17 of the 42 (40 percent) fell below 90, with six below 70. Again, the IQ picture appeared somewhat worse than that reported by Norris et al. (1957) for the intensive sample. And again, it should be noted that, although the original intensive group included no "additional physical handicaps," Cohen et al. (1964) found indications of neurological abnormalities in 35 percent of the sample, including a number of epilepsy and cerebral palsy cases.

Cohen (1966) provided an evaluation of a still larger subset (57) of the original children. Of the 57, four were not reliably testable, five were in institutions for the mentally retarded, and IQ scores were available for the remaining 48. Of the 48, 18 (38 percent) scored below 80, of whom 12 scored below 70. Thus again the IQ picture was worse than that presented by Norris et al., especially considering the probability that several of the nine children for whom IQ results were not reported would undoubtedly have been in the lower categories. Cohen noted in particular that lower IQ was more common for those subjects with lower birth weight and greater visual loss.

As noted, the apparent discrepancies between the original Norris report and the subsequent reports by Cohen and his colleagues are confusing. One possibility is that the apparent discrepancies may be attributable to developmental trends. That is, the tests reported in the various Cohen papers were all conducted subsequently to the tests reported by Norris et al., and it may be that a progressive decline with age occurred for a portion of the sample. Such a trend would, however, present a contrast to the general increase in IQ with age that has been reported by some investigators (Hayes, 1950; Hopkins & McGuire, 1967; Komisar & MacDonnell, 1955). It may also be that the various samples studied by Cohen were not chosen randomly from the original Norris et al. group. It seems unlikely that the differences in results may be explained by selective sampling, though, since the sequence of reports by Cohen included successively larger proportions of the original sample.

In sum, the weight of the Cohen studies would seem to require a substantial tempering of the optimism of the Norris et al. results. The IQ distributions in the various Cohen samples were clearly skewed toward the low end of the scale, although in each sample there were significant numbers of subjects who showed strong IQ scores. Of particular significance is the evidence of neurological abnormalities in the Cohen samples. It is not possible to attribute the skew in IQ distributions causally to RLF, since it is likely that the neurological abnormalities constituted a more direct cause of the lower IQ than did RLF. In any case, the conclusion that the distribution of IQ in samples of RLF children is the same as that in non-RLF blind or sighted samples would seem to be unwarranted on the basis of these data.

Parmalee and his colleagues have also been concerned with the IQ and other developmental testing of children with RLF and other types of blindness. Several reports are available (Parmalee, 1955; Parmalee, Fiske, & Right, 1959) for a group of 10 RLF children. Each child was selected for study within the first year of life. No child was included who was obviously mentally retarded. Thus the range of intelligence reported for the group (Parmalee et al., 1959) may not be taken as representative of RLF children as a group. Some useful points about developmental testing emerge, however. Parmalee (1955) successfully administered the Gesell tests to various groups of infants and found no differences between normal, RLF, and sighted premature groups. The lowest Developmental Quotient (DQ) reported for an RLF child was 94. In the subsequent study, however, Parmalee et al. (1959) found that three of the children showed Hayes-Binet scores of less than 80. The apparent lack of strong relation between the infant DQ scores and the later (age three to five years) IQ results should be taken in the context of the general agreement that there is not a strong empirical relationship between DQ and IQ. Furthermore, Parmalee et al. (1959) noted that the three cases of sub-80 IQ in their sample "have been considered by several observers to have normal mental potential that has been functionally suppressed because of severe emotional problems" (p. 203). This formulation seems reasonable in view of the evidence for a relatively high frequency of emotional problems in RLF children. IQ testing is a risky undertaking, especially when the child's total situation is such that there may be other factors, such as emotional maturity, that may interfere with valid testing. Such invalidly low IQ scores are appropriately referred to as pseudoretardation, a term that carries the implication that the low test score is more apparent than real. It may be that the downward IQ trend found in the Cohen samples, discussed earlier, was a result of just such a progressive pseudoretardation effect, although it must be noted that Cohen's samples did show a high frequency of neurological involvement.

In a larger-scale study, Parmalee, Cutsforth, and Jackson (1958) assessed IQ in samples of blind children in RLF and other etiological categories. The children were of school age (5.9 to 9.9), had varied current school placements and histories of school experience, but were apparently not selected on the basis of other criteria such as additional handicaps. The criterion of retardation was an IQ of less than 70 (several types of test had apparently been used, since the data were archival). By this criterion, there was no significant difference in incidence of retardation between the groups: 32 percent of the RLF and 41 percent of the non-RLF group were retarded. Unfortunately, the frequency of children in the retarded range was not reported for various age groups, and thus a test of the hypothesis that the incidence of pseudoretardation increases with age is not possible. There was also no difference between groups in the incidence of attendance in integrated schools programs (about a third were in such programs). Parmalee et al. noted a greater incidence of emotional disturbance in the RLF group and suggested that this factor may have contributed to the low IQ scores. On the other hand, several RLF children who were judged to be emotionally disturbed had IQ scores over 90. While emotional disturbance may be a contributing factor to low tested IQ, it apparently does not necessarily produce low IQ scores (although even these "average" children's IQ test scores may have been spuriously low).

The relationship between retardation and neurological factors should also not be neglected. The data reported by Cohen and his colleagues suggested such a relationship within the RLF group, and the Parmalee data provided further support in showing that several of the non-RLF group who had IQ scores below 70 had an optic-atrophy etiology, while others showed various evidence of CNS involvement, such as deafness.

Although Parmalee has found a generally higher incidence of mental retardation than that reported by Norris et al. (1957) (note the selection of the Norris intensive sample to exclude multiple handicaps), both researchers reached a similar conclusion about the possibility of a causal relationship between RLF and mental retardation. Both concluded that RLF is itself probably not a causal factor in retardation. Parmalee noted that retardation is generally found to be more frequent in premature children than in term children, whether blind or not. RLF blindness can be considered an indirect effect of prematurity (that is, RLF blindness is a result of the treatment for prematurity), and therefore retardation and RLF occur together with some frequency. Neurological factors also occur in children blind from other causes, though, and so neurologically based retardation occurs with some frequency in these children. A detailed consideration of the neurological correlates of visual deficit is beyond the scope of the present work. A comprehensive and detailed treatment of this question is available in a work by Novikova (1973).

Genn and Silverman (1964) reported a study that is useful in separating the effects of prematurity from those of RLF. A group of 53 children who had an RLF condition and birth weights less than 2400 gm were included in the RLF group. Ten of these children had "total visual handicaps." A comparison group of prematurely born infants without RLF was selected by matching birth weight, sex, and race. None of the control infants was blind. The IQ of each child was evaluated at about 7.5 years of age. Where standardized IQ tests could not be used, estimates were made by two experienced testers. Interrater agreement was very high (0.97). The mean IQ of the RLF group was 92.3, while that of the non-RLF group was 101.7. The difference was significant. There were some RLF children with IQ scores in the bright and superior categories, but 18 of the 53 RLF children scored below 90, whereas only 10 of the 53 non-RLF children scored below 90. Of the 10 totally blind children in the RLF group, four had IQ scores above 90, but five had scores of 60 and below. The results indicated that the IQ scores of RLF children (without reference to visual condition) tended to be somewhat lower than those of non-RLF children, although there were some high IQ scores in the RLF group. The existence of visual impairment did not necessarily produce low IQ scores, since there were some blind subjects with IQ scores in the normal range, but a disproportionate number of blind RLF children showed severely low scores.

In sum, the available evidence suggests that there is a somewhat greater proportion of RLF children who fall into the lower IQ ranges, and there has been some progress made in attributing the deficits to such factors as neurological dysfunction. It is probable that RLF is not itself a causal factor in retardation. Rather, prematurity would seem to be the culprit, especially with respect to the cases in which clear neurological involvement is found. At the same time, the fact should not be neglected that in every study on the incidence of retardation in RLF children, substantial proportions of children have been found to have IQ scores in the normal and superior ranges.

Blindness and Mental Retardation

Among the various types of "multiple handicap" involving blindness, the combination of blindness and mental retardation has received perhaps the greatest amount of attention. To a great extent, though, the attention has been directed to issues of incidence of retardation, of educational programs, and of the adequacy of evaluation and treatment of blind children in institutions for the retarded; there has been relatively little research on the abilities and potentials of blind retarded children.

There are various estimates of the incidence of retardation among blind children. Cruickshank (1964) assessed the incidence of multiple handicaps in a group of 2773 blind children (up to age 21) in New York State. New York State has a law requiring the registration of blindness, and thus the sample may be taken as reasonably representative. The results indicated that 42 percent of the 2058 children for whom IQ scores were available had scores below 90. (By contrast, a normal distribution of scores would produce about 25 percent below 90.) The 90-IQ level is certainly not an appropriate figure with which to make estimates of mental retardation, since retardation normally implies a much more severe deficit in IQ. Other estimates are available, and they range from the low figure of 4 percent by Walsh (1963) of the patients in a residential school for the mentally retarded who were totally or partially blind, to a higher figure of 15 percent of students in residential schools for the blind who are retarded (Paraskeva, 1959).

Some points made by Elonen and Zwarensteyn (1964) may serve to characterize the mentally retarded blind child. Severe deficiencies were noted in areas of self-help, such as feeding, dressing, and toilet training. Motor lags were seen, and locomotor and orientation abilities tended to be inadequate, as did language and communicative skills. Deficiencies in cognitive abilities were noted. The important point was made, however, that many of the children, while they showed generalized lags and abnormalities of development, did show areas in which they had acquired particular skills to a normal degree. Elonen and Zwarensteyn argued that these selected areas of normality may be taken as evidence that the general pattern of developmental lag is not representative of the child's potential. They noted, in connection with each separate area of possible retardation, a number of characteristics of the child's environment that may have produced selective lags. For example, the parents may not have encouraged feeding skills at all, or they may not have made serious attempts at toilet training. The spontaneous overprotectiveness of many parents of blind children creates a situation that encourages the child to show patterns of developmental lag that may make him seem quite retarded, whereas with appropriate encouragement and environmental structure relatively normal development might have taken place.

Guess (1967) also provided an overview picture of blind retarded children. In addition to poor performance on IQ tests and other tests of cognitive functioning, he noted deficiencies of speech development, with the speech that did occur being echolalic, perseverative, and egocentric; of motor development, involving both fine and gross motor skills; and of emotional behavior, which ranged from "passively negativistic withdrawing to aggressive hyperactivity, the former . . . more typical since the child is often fearful and anxious about his environment" (p. 473). In addition, as Guess (1966) has demonstrated, the blind retarded child shows a greater incidence of self-stimulatory behavior than the sighted child of comparable CA and MA levels.

Several writers have structured their descriptions and interpretations of the retarded blind child primarily around a cognitive deficit. Bachelis (1961), for example, discussed "a limit to the symbolic interaction which can be assimilated and put to use in understanding the environment, and, as a consequence, the differentiation of the environment from the individual" (p. 289). Bachelis suggested that the approprate environment for such children is one that is warm and stable, with a mild amount of variety to ensure that the child is not disturbed by his inability to cope with an environment that is too unpredictable. Similarly, Mattis (1967) advanced a theoretical framework involving the notion that "conceptual deficits of probable organic etiology result in inappropriate behavior and high anxiety" (p. 2). Inadequate conceptual ability may produce high anxiety levels because the child cannot understand the natural variability of the environment, and high anxiety may then lead to behavioral or emotional disturbances. The primary cause, then, of the personality and behavior disturbances often seen in these children is not thought by Bachelis or Mattis to be poor parent–child interaction (as Elonen and Zwarensteyn might argue) or extreme stress, but rather conceptual inability.

Rogow (1970) made the interesting and persuasive point, developing out of the theoretical framework of E. J. Gibson, that more demand is placed on the blind child's conceptual abilities than on those of the sighted child, since vision normally plays an important role in the differentiation and organization of the environment. Without vision, the blind child must "do more of it in his head," and thus even a mildly low level of conceptual ability may play a relatively debilitating role for the blind child, whereas it might not interfere substantially with the ability of the sighted child to organize and interpret his world.

However reasonable these formulations of the cognitive basis for various personality and behavioral disturbances in blind retarded children may be, Guess (1967) made a point that is well worth repeating. There simply has not been adequate research done on the various abilities and characteristics of the blind retarded child to allow confident statements about the extent to which other behavioral, language, and emotional disorders may be primarily attributed to cognitive deficiencies. The parental-interaction hypothesis of Elonen and Zwarensteyn makes a great deal of intuitive sense, especially in view of the similarities between the characteristics of the blind retarded child and those of nonretarded blind children who are raised by overprotective and restrictive parents. The two hypotheses produce obviously different implications for the handling of retarded blind children, and it is important to obtain research that adequately represents the complexity of the situation.

There is some evidence that mental retardation occurs more frequently in some blindness etiologies than in others. In the earlier section on retinoblastoma, it was pointed out that, while several investigators have found relations between high cognitive abilities and retinoblastoma, others have noted a higher-than-expected incidence of severe retardation in retinoblastoma samples. Taktikos (1964), for example, found nine cases of severe retardation in 300 cases of retinoblastoma blindness. The three-percent rate was about 10 times the rate of severe retardation in sighted children (the criterion for retardation was not given). Taktikos argued that the retardation should be considered the primary condition, rather than the retinoblastoma. That is, the blindness was not the cause of mental defect; rather, the cases were characterized by problems of the central nervous system, such as hydrocephalus and spasticity.

Dekaban (1972) reviewed the few studies in the literature dealing with the congenital retinal blindness syndrome and concluded that there is a higher incidence of mental retardation in this group than in other blind samples. Congenital retinal blindness is the term used to denote the hereditary condition characterized by the absence of or severe reduction in the numbers of rods and cones. The condition is present at birth in many cases, and in others vision is lost within the first several years. In the studies found by Dekaban, 18 of the 48 cases, or 37.5 percent, were mentally retarded or had neurological dysfunction. Of these 18, nine were retarded without additional deficiencies, while an additional seven cases were retarded in addition to having epilepsy or other neurological conditions. Unfortunately, a working definition of mental retardation was not provided by Dekaban.

Bachelis (1967) reported a study of 24 cases of blindness caused by bilateral congenital anophthalmos, a condition characterized by lack of eye-structure formation. Various IQ test scores were available for 15 of the 24 subjects. Eight of the 15 had IQ (various tests) below 50, while an additional three were in the 51-to-69 range. Three of the 15 had IQ of 110 or more. Of the nine for whom no information was available, descriptive reports characterized two as not retarded and six as retarded. Thus there was some evidence for a bimodal distribution of IQ within the sample of bilateral congenital anophthalmos cases, with a greater proportion showing IQ in the retarded range than in the above-average range.

Considerable concern has been expressed in the literature about the adequacy of treatment of blind children who are in institutions for the retarded. Guess (1967), for example, cited a study by Cawley and Spotts (1967), in which it was found that an extremely small number of qualified teachers of the blind were employed in these institutions. Another point about institutionalization concerns the tendency for the institutional environment to maintain the child's low level of functioning even if he might have progressed more normally in a normal environment. That is, a blind child might be committed to an institution for the mentally retarded on the basis of patterns of early developmental lag, and the environment would then fail to foster his development in many areas. The result would be that a normal child who was slow to develop in some areas would become a child who is severely retarded in many areas. Elonen, Polzien, and Zwarensteyn (1967) described the cases of six children who were drawn out of institutions for the retarded and placed in the Michigan School for the Blind, where almost all of them demonstrated marked advances in general behavioral level and measured IQ. The possible misdiagnosis as mentally retarded of blind children with moderate developmental lag seems especially insidious if it is generally the case that there is inadequate expertise in assessing the special developmental aspects of blind children in institutions. In any event, the case may be made very strongly for the need for a multidisciplinary diagnostic team to operate not only in residential centers for blind children but also in institutions for children with other handicaps who may also happen to be blind.

Elonen and Zwarensteyn (1963, 1964) described the results of a multidisciplinary diagnostic approach that was designed to assess whether more favorable diagnoses might be obtained for certain children who might otherwise be committed to institutions for the mentally retarded. Fifty-one "deviant" blind children were assessed, the criterion for acceptance being that the blind child had "been excluded from or refused entrance into educational programs on the basis of apparent inability to learn or to function adequately" (1964, p. 600). Many of the children scored below 50 on IQ tests, while others had shown such extreme behavioral characteristics that they had not even been tested. Of the group of 51, 11 were judged to be admissible to regular classes for the blind, while another 22 were judged to be potentially educable if they and their parents received appropriate therapy. Only four were judged to be so severely handicapped that no advantages were expected from therapy and educational placement.

An interesting clinical example of apparent misdiagnosis is provided by Burlingham (1968), who reported the course of therapy with a blind girl who was thought to be retarded. The girl was blind from birth with congenital cataracts. She suffered some early difficulties, not the least of which was "a raw and blistered skin" which made tactual contact aversive. Other characteristics of the case included a lack of exploration of the environment, failure to invite contact, walking at 2.5 years without crawling, an extreme sensitivity to sounds, especially strange sounds, feeding difficulties caused in part by a deformed mouth, no toilet training success, and garbled speech that communicated no social meaning. Such a complex syndrome of difficulties might well have led to the child's commitment to an institution for the retarded, but a therapist saw some hope for her and took her into treatment. The extensive therapy produced progress that occasionally showed serious setbacks that were usually attributable to a serious environmental upset. Over the course of several years, however, she made sufficient progress and was admitted at age nine to a private school. Here she made substantial progress in learning braille and other academic skills, in addition to learning to play the piano. The course of therapy described in the paper is not inexpensive, but it may serve as a striking example of the progress that may be made with a child who shows many characteristics of a seriously retarded blind child.

5
Language Development

The study of language and communication in blind children is important for several reasons. The adequacy of language ability is interesting in its own right, and developmental questions can be posed about various stages in the process of language acquisition from babbling to the production of complex sentences. Further, language is involved in other areas at very basic levels, such as the verbal mediation of problem solving, and both verbal and nonverbal aspects of interpersonal relations.

Aspects of Verbal Communication

Babbling

There is little evidence about the similarity of babbling in blind and sighted infants, but the evidence that does exist favors the view that there are no basic differences that can be attributed to blindness itself. Burlingham (1961) and Haspiel (1965) both noted that otherwise normal blind infants babble just as sighted infants do, although Haspiel pointed out that emotionally disturbed blind children may show a prolonged period of babbling, sometimes followed by a period of little vocal activity at all. Similar possibilities for the retarded blind were delineated by Elonen and Zwarensteyn (1964), who argued that the babbling stage may become especially pleasurable to some infants and thus be prolonged. Wilson and Halverson (1947) reported an intensive study of a single blind child. Developmental lag was noted in several areas, especially the motor and locomotor areas, but language behavior, and especially the babbling components, did not show any difference from sighted norms. A different result was reported by Maxfield and Fjeld (1942), who used the Vineland Social Maturity Scale on a large group of visually handicapped preschool children. On the single item from the test that is obviously related to babbling ("talks;" imitates sounds), the blind sample showed a small lag compared with sighted norms.

Thus the general pattern of results suggests that in the blind infant, babbling occurs much the same as for sighted infants. The question has not been studied in sufficient detail to state this conclusion definitively, however. The exact function of the babbling stage for sighted infants is not completely understood, although it has been widely noted that in the later phases of babbling, the set of sounds produced by the child gradually comes to approximate the set characteristic of the language environment to which the child is exposed. Reinforcement by parents for closer approximations of speech sounds is thought to be a vital part of this refinement, as is the child's ability to perceive similarities and differences between his productions and those of the language surround. Visual information must be involved in the refinement to some extent, and it seems possible that the blind child's inability to see the mouth of his parent makes it more difficult for him to refine his sound set as effectively as the sighted infant can. Although the issue is not clear, some writers (Berry & Eisenson, 1942; Elliott, 1938) have noted a general muting of the distinguishing characteristics of sounds in older blind children. It may be that this characteristic may be traced directly to the visual handicap, and a careful study of the later stages of babbling might reveal a similar muting of the sound set. Such information is not available at this time.

Post-babbling sound production and quality

Several studies have been made of the adequacy of sound production and the comparability of sound quality between blind and sighted children. Among the more extensive of these studies are ones by Miner (1963a), who studied elementary school children, and Brieland (1950), who studied children from 12 to 18 years of age. Brieland's congenitally blind subjects attended schools for the blind. Matching sighted control subjects were chosen from a public high school. Each subject was given a story to memorize. Then performance was filmed and tape-recorded. Speech teachers rated the performances on several factors, including vocal variety, pitch modulation, use of loudness, and degree of lip movement. There was no difference between blind and sighted subjects on vocal variety or use of loudness. The blind scored significantly better on pitch modulation, while the sighted were significantly better on lip movement. A supplementary measure of rate of speaking showed that the sighted spoke faster than the blind. On the basis of the vocal cues alone, the judges could not successfully tell the blind subjects from the sighted. In sum, then, there was no overall difference in favor of either group, and despite the evidence of greater lip movement by the sighted subjects, there was no difference in sound production factors. Further, subdivision of the blind group into totally blind and residual vision groups produced no consistent differences on the variables listed above.

Miner (1963a) studied somewhat younger children from schools for the blind. No sighted control group was used, although the overall incidence of speech deviations among the blind children was concluded to be four to five times that in public schools. A speech therapist conversed with each child and judged the presence or absence of speech deviations. Categories of speech deviation included articulation (sound substitutions, omissions, distortions), voice (pitch, loudness, or quality atypies), and stuttering. The most frequent speech deviation was articulation, which occurred in 25 percent of the sample, followed by voice (3.4 percent). Only one child of the 293 studied was found to stutter. The contrast between the conclusions of Miner and those of Brieland is striking. Brieland did not specify whether his sample was restricted. Miner excluded from consideration all children in deaf–blind classes, although he apparently included children with organic (aphasia) and nonorganic (delayed language) problems in the sample, along with some emotionally disturbed and mentally retarded children. (The percentage incidence of deviations in these latter two categories was not different from that in the remaining group.) Miner found no pattern of difference between subjects in sight-saving classes and those in braille classes. Stinchfield-Hawk (1944) surveyed the incidence of various speech defects in three large schools for the blind. Her estimates of the overall incidence of speech problems ranged somewhat higher even than those of Miner (1963a), although the categories of defect used were somewhat different from those of Miner. The large majority of the problems found by Stinchfield-Hawk were classified as dyslalia. No corresponding category was used by Miner. To the extent that comparison is possible, it appears that the percentages of blind children with voice defects were virtually identical in the two studies (about 3.5 percent). However, the incidence of articulation defects found by Miner was far greater than that reported by Stinchfield-Hawk, who reported that articulation scores among the blind were only "slightly lower" than those among sighted children. Of note in connection with articulation defects is the report by Sibinga and Friedman (1971) that articulation problems were frequently found in sighted childen who had been immobilized as infants for various reasons (such as splints or casts). Articulation problems and language delay were found more frequently among children who had been immobilized early (6 months or so) than among those who had been immobilized later. The possible relationship between sound production problems and motor behavior warrants further study, especially in view of the often cited delays in some areas of motor and locomotor behavior among the blind.

Mills (1983) reports a study which examines the potential role of vision in the refinement of articulation. Two-year-olds at the stage of two-word utterances were studied for their articulation of CV syllables. The two sighted subjects produced better articulation of those sounds whose production movements are external (/b/, /p/, /m/) than of those whose production movements are more internal (/d/, /t/). This finding suggests that vision plays a role in the refinement of articulation of the external category. If vision is involved in creating this difference in articulation, then the difference should not be found in blind children of comparable language level. This was borne out: the blind subject made more articulatory errors than the sighted, but the errors did not show the differential pattern based on the locus of articulatory movements. Although the data on which this conclusion is based are not extensive, they are clear in suggesting a key role of vision in the refinement of at least some articulatory movements.

Stuttering is an aspect of sound production about which there is substantial disagreement among investigators. Although the overall incidence of speech problems in his sample was quite high, Miner reported only one case of stuttering, and that was in a partially sighted child with neurological damage. Rowe (1958) also reported finding no cases of stuttering, although her sample appears to have been somewhat selective. Stinchfield-Hawk, on the other hand, reported an incidence of about 3 percent in her large blind sample, and Fladeland (1930) mentioned several cases of stuttering. Weinberg (1964) surveyed many schools for the blind and found a reported incidence of stuttering of about 2 percent. Although Weinberg provided numerical information about the breakdown of stutterers into totally blind vs. partially sighted and other categories, the information is of little use because of the absence of information about overall proportions of children in the various categories.

Although the weight of the evidence seems to favor the conclusion that there is a greater incidence of sound production and sound quality problems among the blind, it is impossible to make firm conclusions on the basis of the information contained in these studies. Part of the problem is that categories of speech defect are defined somewhat differently in each study, and comparability is questionable. The studies also vary widely in the ways in which defects were assessed. Finally, quite different methods of sampling subjects have been used. It is clear that additional well-gathered and well-reported information is needed before firm conclusions may be reached.

Although sex differences have not commonly been reported in the literature on the developmental effects of visual handicap, a notable exception occurs in the studies of the incidence of articulation or other motor production defects. In general, the adequacy of the reporting leaves much to be desired, and firm conclusions are not possible. Stinchfield-Hawk (1944), in her study of the incidence of speech defects in the students of several large schools for the blind, found results that varied substantially between schools. Boys showed a higher incidence of stuttering than girls, while the overall incidence of speech defects, including voice quality and associative difficulties as well as motor production difficulties, was higher (59 percent in one sample) for girls. Stinchfield-Hawk noted that studies of sighted samples have usually shown greater incidence of defects among boys. In Miner's (1963a) study of the incidence of various speech defects, articulation and voicing problems were the most frequently detected categories. The sample included 293 blind children between kindergarten and sixth grade. Of the 99 cases of speech defect identified, 57 (58 percent) were found in boys, with 42 in girls. The most common defect, articulation, was similarly divided, occurring in 43 boys and 30 girls. Miner's conclusion that speech defects are more common in boys than girls is not valid on the basis of his study, though, since 56 percent of the sample were boys and only 44 percent girls: the percentages of overall defect and articulation defect for boys and girls were almost identical to the percentages of boys and girls in the sample. Conclusions from the study of incidence of stuttering by Weinberg (1964) are also vague. Weinberg evaluated the incidence of stuttering among children in schools for the blind by means of questionnaires. Of the 43 identified stutterers whose sex was reported, 35 were boys and only eight were girls. Unfortunately, the distribution of boys and girls in the school samples studied was not reported. However, it seems quite unlikely that the proportion of boys to girls in the schools was as biased as 35 to eight, and so Weinberg's results, together with those of Stinchfield-Hawk (1944), allow a tentative conclusion that stuttering is a more common problem among blind boys than blind girls.

Brieland (1950) had observers rate films and tape recordings of blind children reciting a story. Although the specific results for sex were not given, it was reported that "all sex differences favored the girls" (p. 102). Brieland did provide an interesting specific in noting that the "greatest voice differences were shown by the totally blind girls compared to the totally blind boys" (p. 102). That is, the sex differences on voice were greatest in the totally blind sample, as compared with partially sighted and sighted groups. On the other hand, the sex-related bodily action differences were greater in the sighted group than in the other groups. Using a similar task and method of evaluation, Eisenstadt (1955) found a mixed pattern, in that visually impaired boys were better than girls in voice, language, and projection measures, while the girls were better in diction, self-projection, and "visible elements" (rated from films).

General conclusions about sex differences are unwise on the basis of the available data. The evidence for more articulation (motor production) difficulties among blind boys than girls seems to be reasonable and reflects the greater incidence generally found among sighted boys.

Early vocabulary

The evidence on the onset and growth of early word usage is mixed. Several investigators have noted no differences between blind and sighted children or even a superiority of the blind, while several have discussed lags in the production of the first words and the growth of vocabulary. In the Maxfield and Fjeld (1942) study using the Vineland Social Maturity Scale, only one item appeared related to early vocabulary, "uses names of familiar objects." On this item, the heterogeneous group of blind children scored marginally better than sighted norms. Haspiel (1965), in a study of language in emotionally disturbed blind children, noted that even in this group a few words are usually produced by 18 months or so, a figure quite comparable to that for sighted children. In their study of a single blind child, Wilson and Halverson (1947) found that, in spite of marked developmental lags in other areas, the 10- and 20-word vocabulary levels were reached by the child exactly at the norms for sighted children.

In contrast, reports by Keeler (1958) and Burlingham (1961, 1965) note that lags in productive vocabulary occur in blind children. Keeler was particularly interested in the apparently autistic symptoms of some RLF children, and one case report indicated severe delay of first word usage (3 years). Keeler reported that a larger sample of RLF children also showed language lags, presumably including first word usage. Burlingham (1961) wrote that mothers of congenitally blind children have reported that during the 16- to 18-month period, when sighted children are typically showing a marked vocabulary growth, the blind children add words to their vocabulary much more slowly, often showing regression from points once reached. Burlingham suggested that the mother's perception of the child's helplessness may cause her to anticipate his needs more than would be the case for sighted infants, and that the blind child may therefore have less demand for vocabulary growth placed on him. Burlingham (1965) expanded on the question of early vocabulary growth, noting that the blind child does not, contrary to what might be expected, easily begin to attach verbal labels to his tactual and auditory experiences. Burlingham attributed the subsequent inadequacy of vocabulary development to the fact that the sighted parent does not understand the nature of the child's experiences. That is, the parent may try to teach vocabulary that is based on visual experience, thus confusing the child, and at the same time the parent does not provide verbal labels for the experiences that the child does have. This situation might lead to the acquisition of idiosyncratic vocabulary items that fit the child's experience and to a lack of appropriate meaning for the "sighted" terms that the child does use.

The meaning of words

In 1932, Cutsforth published a report of a study in which he noted the tendency of blind children to use words for which they could not have a first-hand sensory base. Cutsforth's discussion of the implications of the use of such words, which he called verbalisms, touched off a continuing debate about the desirability of avoiding such usage in blind children. Cutsforth's procedure involved presenting an object name to the child and asking for a quality of the object. He found a considerable percentage (48 percent) of the responses of congenitally totally blind children to be visual qualities, while adventitiously blind children produced 65-percent visual responses. In a later discussion of these results (1951), he argued that such verbalisms must lead to "incoherent and loose thinking'' on the part of the blind child, since the words (and implicitly the concepts) used by the blind child are farther removed from a direct sensory referent than those of the sighted child. This conclusion was apparently taken very seriously by many people responsible for the education of blind children, with the result that some educational programs were structured to avoid the use of concepts that did not have direct sensory referents for the blind child. More recently there has been serious issue taken with Cutsforth's reasoning, and with the resultant educational practices. Dokecki (1966) provided an insightful review of arguments and research on the verbalism issue, including strong criticism of Cutsforth's conclusions and of the educational changes that they produced. Part of Dokecki's argument was made on logical grounds—there are many words that sighted people use that cannot possibly have sensory referents, and there is no indication that the concepts based on these words are meaningless or involve loose thinking.

There are several sources of data that bear on the notion that there are differences in word meaning, association, or usage between blind and sighted children. Several writers in the psychoanalytic literature (Burlingham, 1961, 1965; Nagera & Colonna, 1965) have treated the verbalism or parroting issue. Burlingham (1961) noted that the blind child's speech ''is less firmly connected with his sensory experience'' (p. 137). She pointed out that the blind child receives a great deal of praise for imitation of the (sighted) parent's speech, thus encouraging the use of words from the sighted person's vocabulary for which the blind child has less adequate sensory referents. Burlingham (1965) elaborated this argument in noting that the blind child develops a mixture of words, some of which refer (perhaps idiosyncratically) to his own sensory experience and some of which are verbalisms that parrot the usage of sighted persons. The distinction between the two types tends to become obscured with development. Nagera and Colonna (1965) also noted the tendency of the blind child to acquire vocabulary which is only a parroting of sighted words, and they echoed Cutsforth's notion that the use of such verbalisms may restrict the symbolic or cognitive capacities of the blind child to some unknown extent. They did, however, provide a somewhat positive note in pointing out that ''in spite of the absence of the visual contribution to many of these 'word symbols,' alternative compensatory means are finally found so that these symbols become useful elements in the performance of the complex mental processes for which these basic units are required'' (p. 280).

Schlaegel (1953) studied imagery in a heterogeneous group of 12- to 24-year-old blind subjects and a group of sighted controls. Test words and phrases were presented orally to the subject, who was asked to report whether the ''first mental image'' that he experienced was see, hear, muscle, touch, temperature, smell, or taste. Comparison of the overall frequency of imagery types did not differentiate the total group of blind subjects from the sighted group. For both groups, the rankings were, in order of decreasing frequency, visual, auditory, kinesthetic, tactile and temperature, and olfactory and gustatory. Interesting differences emerged from comparisons within the blind sample, however. The blind group was divided into three vision categories: none (up to LP), intermediate (movement to counting fingers at five feet), and "considerable" (better than 5/200). The group with "considerable" vision gave about 59-percent vision responses, compared to 42 percent for the intermediate group, 28 percent for the no-vision group, and 42 percent for the sighted control group. The high proportion of vision responses in the "considerable" group was especially interesting. Schlaegel suggested that "because of the importance of vision, the child may respond to the pressure of this importance by compensatory visual imagery" (p. 275). Whether Schlaegel meant to implicate social pressure, real dependence on vision, or some other more specific factor is not clear. In any case, the possibility that there were consistent differences between groups in perception of social pressure or in some other important factor detracts from the impact of the results. Tillman and Williams (1968) assessed the word associations of blind and sighted children. The blind sample consisted of severely blind residential school children, who were mostly blind before one year of age and of mixed etiology. Age ranged from seven to 11 years. Stimulus word categories included count nouns, mass nouns, adjectives, transitive verbs, intransitive verbs, and adverbs. The responses were scored for homogeneity, that is, whether the response word was of the same category as the stimulus word. The blind and sighted groups differed on only one category, the mass nouns, where the blind group showed significantly greater homogeneity than the sighted. This study, then, did not provide evidence that there is a consistent pattern of difference between the word associations of blind and sighted children.

As noted earlier, the negative implications of the use of verbalisms discussed by Cutsforth and others have come under considerable criticism. Nolan (1960b) conducted a replication and extension of Cutsforth's study of the frequency of visual responses in word association responses. Nolan's subjects were totally blind or had at most LP, included both boys and girls, ranged in age from nine to 20 years, and were mostly blind from birth. Two conditions were used, a controlled association task that was the same that Cutsforth had used, and a free association task. In each task, the subject was asked to respond to a stimulus word with a response word (association). In the controlled association condition, some examples of association words were given to try to produce a "set" in the child to respond in the same vein, while in the free association condition, no such set formation was attempted. The two conditions were conducted with separate groups of blind children. The percentage of visual responses was not significantly different for the free and controlled association groups. However, both percentages were significantly lower than the controlled association results reported by Cutsforth. To the extent that the performance of Nolan's blind subjects could be compared with free association norms for sighted children (such comparison was possible for four of the 39 words used), the blind subjects "closely resembled" sighted children. For these words, Cutsforth's subjects had made more visual responses than even the sighted norms. In discussing these findings, Nolan noted that educational methods have changed over the decades since Cutsforth's results were gathered, and that the real incidence of verbalisms may have been reduced.

Civelli (1983) compared early blind with sighted adolescents in their ability to cite definite and distinctive characteristics of a named object. No significant differences were found for words in the categories of material objects, animals, movements, or facial expressions. The negative results are not compelling, however, in that there are numerous factors, such as word difficulty, that could have masked any real differences.

Harley (1963) studied the incidence of verbalism and its relation to IQ, CA, experience, and personal adjustment. The subjects ranged in age from seven to 14 and were drawn from residential schools. All subjects had become blind very early (75 percent were RLF), and none had vision greater than LP. The procedure designed to establish verbalism scores involved two steps, definition of words and identification of the physical objects corresponding to the words. The verbalism score for a subject was the number of appropriate definitions minus the number of correct identifications. In addition, although the study was not primarily concerned with the use of visual terminology, a visual verbalism score was determined by counting the number of items for which the subject used visual terminology (presumably in the definition part of the procedure). Experience was scored by counting the number of objects with which the subject said that he had had direct contact, and personal adjustment was determined by use of the Tuddenham Reputation Test, which makes use of peer judgments of children. There were significant negative correlations between the verbalism score and CA, IQ, and experience, but the expected negative correlation between verbalism and adjustment score did not emerge. Thus, the younger, lower-IQ, and lower-experience children showed higher incidence of verbalism. Harley suggested that "the key to the reduction of verbalism among blind children is the increasing of interaction with their environments" (p. 32). Scores on the visual verbalism index tended to be low and did not show significant correlations with any of the other measures. The failure to find significant correlations must be viewed in the context of the relatively low visual verbalism raw scores—that is, the scores were low, and there was little variability among subjects.

In contrast to the object identification scoring, where "exactness was required for identification," Harley's scoring system for object definition seems quite lenient. During the definition portion of the test, the subject was asked for responses in a variety of ways if a response was not immediately forthcoming, and credit was given for synonyms, uses, attributes, general classification, correct use of the word, and descriptive features. Thus the verbalism score, which averaged 21.4 of a possible 39, was probably somewhat higher than would have been the case if more restrictive definition scoring or more lenient identification scoring had been used. Whether this apparent scoring bias may have affected the younger or lower-IQ subjects more than the older, thus leading to the significant negative correlations of verbalism with these variables, is not clear.

It is worth noting that Harley held quite a different view than Cutsforth about the possible direction of causality of verbalism. It is reasonably clear from Cutsforth's writing that he considered verbalism to be a *cause* of "incoherent and loose thinking." In stating his hypothesis, however, Harley suggested that "since verbalism may be caused by inaccurate and vague concepts resulting from insufficient sensory experience, verbalism may also vary with intelligence" (p. 12). If there is in fact a relationship between cognitive abilities and verbalism, the perspective provided by Harley would seem an important one to maintain. That is, the lack of sensory experience may be a cause both of verbalism and of cognitive difficulties, rather than being a cause of verbalism which in turn causes cognitive difficulties. The appropriate strategy of intervention, then, should be to concentrate on provision of the appropriate kinds of experience at the right time.

From the results of a study with congenitally blind and sighted adults, Tufenkjian (1971) also concluded that the verbalism issue is a more complex one than Cutsforth and others had thought. The "relevant question to ask is not the meaningfulness or meaninglessness of words to congenitally blind persons but rather to ask the nature of the meaningfulness of words in specific contexts. . . . The point is not that these subjects' understanding of these concepts are meaningless but that they demonstrate a different mode of experiencing some aspect of their world" (pp. 40–41).

DeMott (1972) provided some information about the relationship between verbalism and affective meaning in blind and sighted children. "Are verbalisms meaningless? If verbalisms do have meaning, are their meanings similar to the meanings they have for individuals who have had related sensory experiences?" (p. 1). DeMott's method involved two procedures, (1) comparison of meanings given for words varying in concreteness and visual connotations, and (2) comparison of responses to words by the use of the semantic differential. Two samples of visually impaired subjects were drawn from a residential school. The totally blind (LP or less) group, ranging in age from six to 19, had all become blind before one year of age. The "severely visually impaired" group had vision ranging from movement perception to 20/200 and ranged in age from seven to 20. The age at onset of impairment was not reported for this group. A sighted control group was also tested. For the evaluation of verbalism score, a group of 30 objects was used (from Harley's work). First the words were presented, and the subject's definition was (leniently) judged as correct or incorrect. Then the objects were presented for identification. Each subject's verbalism score was defined as the number of words correctly defined minus the number of objects correctly identified. The overall verbalism results for the three groups were unfortunately not reported. In the affective meaning part of the study, 15 words, representing concepts, were used as stimuli for the semantic differential. A five-point response scale was used, so that the subject could (for example, with the slow-fast pair) respond very slow, slow, neither slow nor fast, fast, or very fast. Fifteen adjective combinations were used for each of the 15 concept items. Factor analysis indicated that there were three main factors for each of the groups of subjects, and that there were no significant differences between groups in the characteristics of the factors. A subsequent analysis of variance produced interesting interaction effects, however. Specifically, there was evidence of differences between blind and sighted groups in the ways that some of the 15 concepts were evaluated on the semantic differential. In spite of these differences, DeMott concluded that there are no remarkable differences between blind and sighted subjects in the affective meaning of concepts. He thus supported the suggestion of Dokecki (1966) that, although blind children may use visually connoted words, they do not use them with a meaning that is less adequate than the meanings used by sighted children.

Although this conclusion may be basically sound, there are two qualifications that should be made. One is, as noted above, that there were some differences in the specific concepts. The second is the interesting result, reported by DeMott, that the use of the five-point adjective scale by the blind children was somewhat different from its use by the sighted children. Specifically, the blind tended to give more neutral or midscale responses than the sighted. Though DeMott suggested that the blind subjects may have been less confident or more cautious, it does seem possible that, while the average response was the same for blind and sighted, the concepts were in fact less strongly invested with affective meaning among the blind. This possibility is certainly worth further study, although it is a difficult issue from a methodological point of view.

Research on verbalism has thus served to clarify to some extent the issues involved and to raise serious question with the educational implications drawn by Cutsforth. It is not valid simply to assume that the use of visual terms and concepts is indicative of "loose thinking" on the part of the blind. As Dokecki (1966) pointed out in his review of research on verbalism, "it still remains to be demonstrated that associative and word-thing meanings are functionally different for the blind or for any other group" (p. 528). The question of the frequency of verbalisms must be sharply separated from the questions of meaning and usefulness. There is enough evidence that verbalisms are not words used without meaning by the blind that the educational implications seem clear enough—the use of visually related vocabulary should not be discouraged in the blind. It seems likely, as Dokecki has suggested, that the sheltering of the blind child from non-sensory-based language "might be producing a detrimental effect, since the scope of language is being curtailed" (p. 527). At the same time, though, there seems to be some substance to the possibility that somewhat different, or affectively weaker, meanings are attached to the visual vocabulary in the blind than in the sighted child. Certainly sighted children use terms for which they have no sensory referents. But they do have sensory referents for the visual terms that they use, and it stands to reason that these terms may be more meaningful at some level for the sighted than the blind, or at least that in order to acquire equivalent meanings, the blind child has to work harder.

A small number of studies have examined the usage by visually impaired children of more specific word classes, with respect to the issue of word meaning. McGuire and Meyers (1971) reported a long-term study of 27 totally blind children of mixed age and etiology. A substantial number (46 percent) of the children were found to refer to themselves in the third person, as he or she. The misuse of personal pronouns has also been noted and discussed extensively by Fraiberg and Adelson (1976). They distinguished, in particular, between two uses of "I," the syncretic "I" which is used with verb forms such as want or need, and the "I" which "is used inventively in new combinations." This second use, "which is freed from syncretic forms, requires a high level inference" (p. 137). The congenitally blind children (LP at most) studied by Fraiberg and Adelson did not differ from sighted children in their use of the syncretic "I." However, the use of the inventive "I" lagged markedly behind that of the syncretic "I" in the blind children. Three children who developed use of the inventive "I" between 2.9 and 3.5 had some LP, while one totally blind child showed the usage at 4.8 and the other had not shown it by age six. By contrast, in the one case study found by Fraiberg and Adelson (Zazzo, 1948), a sighted child developed use of the inventive "I" by age 2.7. Fraiberg and Adelson discussed the delayed use of the inventive "I," as well as other misuse of personal pronouns such as referring to the self in the third person, in terms of difficulties with self-representation in the blind child. They noted, for example, a delay in the child's ability to represent himself in play, citing Piaget's observation that levels of representation may be inferred from play in that objects may be used as symbolic representations of self. It may well be that the blind child has greater difficulty in differentiating the self-concept, since he does not have visual experience of the relationship of his body parts or of the similarity of the parts and whole of his body to those of other people. In this context, however, it is interesting that the same blind children who had difficulty with the use of personal pronouns did not apparently have any trouble with the concept of self as represented by their proper names.

Part of the cognitive difficulty in the use of personal pronouns seems to be with the concept that the same word, such as "I" or "he," may be applied to different people, depending on who the speaker is. Mulford (1980) proposed this linguistic uncertainty hypothesis as an alternative to the cognitive notion discussed above, although in fact Mulford's five-year-old subjects (thus older than those of Fraiberg and Adelson [1976]) did not show difficulty with pronouns.

Mulford's (1980) approach involved the study of five-year-old blind children interacting with an adult in a naturalistic setting. Spatial deictic terms (those which refer situationally to locations or location concepts) such as "this," "that," "here," and "there" have in common the characteristic that their meaning is situational: "here" has a different referent in an absolute sense than it does if the listener can take the relative viewpoint of the speaker. With such situational terms, Mulford found usage by the blind subjects to be worse than that of sighted children of comparable age.

Anderson (1979) and Anderson and Olson (1981) reported work in which the definitions and descriptions of "more tangible" and "less tangible" objects were assessed in a group of 10 congenitally blind children with at most LP, aged three to nine, and compared with those of a comparable group of sighted subjects. The "more tangible" objects were those which could be encompassed within the hand, whereas the "less tangible" ones were touchable, though not graspable (e.g., house, tree). The children's responses were classified as egocentric, functional, or perceptual. In general there were few consistent differences between groups, but several important comparisons did emerge that bear on the issue of the relationship of meaning to experience. The blind children's responses to the more tangible objects tended to be more egocentric than those of the sighted, and tended toward the more functional and less perceptual attributes. Overall, the blind clearly showed more use of tactually gained information, and they gave fewer attributes for the less tangible items than they did for the more tangible. Anderson and Olson (1981) suggested that the different patterns of the blind demonstrate that these children do not simply reflect usage of the language of sighted people, but rather reflect the experience-specific conceptualizations of objects that they are able to obtain via touch and the other nonvisual senses.

Bernstein (1978) compared the use of self-referent and external-referent locatives in congenitally blind and sighted children, ages two to four. For both blind and sighted children, the self-referent locatives were easier, and the sighted were generally better than the blind. Bernstein also studied, with the same groups, the usage of "same/different" and adjective pairs such as "big/little" and "thick/thin." Generally the usage of the blind was less adequate than that of the sighted children and suggested a simple developmental lag. Bernstein attributed the language lag primarily to a cognitive lag, although allowing that the acquisition of an appropriate language label may aid in the development and refinement of an immature concept.

Recent literature contains apparent disagreement about the semantic qualities of the speech of young visually impaired children. The issue has become livelier in recent years because of the use of methodologies that allow a more detailed evaluation of the child's word usage. The issue is far from settled.

Landau (1983) and Gleitman (1981) reported an intensive study of two early blind RLF children who began using single words at 23 and 26 months, later than the mean but within the range of sighted children, according to the Bayley Scales. The nature of the vocabulary acquired over the course of the succeeding several months was compared with Nelson's (1973) reports for sighted children. Under this approach, utterances (which averaged about 2 words in length) are classified into usage categories. Landau's blind children used all the categories used by the sighted children of Nelson's report, with only minor differences in distribution of frequencies. Landau concluded that there were no substantial differences between blind and sighted children, agreeing with the bulk of previous literature. Landau went on to look for any evidence of "empty meaning" of the words used by the blind. Do they simply repeat some words heard from others without understanding them? Landau examined one child in detail and concluded that there was no such evidence. Her conclusion was based on the blind child's interesting use of the verb "look" to refer to the active perceptual activities of the hands, in contrast to the verb "feel" to denote passive hand contact. The verb "look," as used by the child, was clearly meaningful and not devoid of content—furthermore, it meant something specific to the child, which could not simply have been borrowed from the language of the subject's sighted companions.

Although the phenomenon is provocative, it does not seem as compelling on the issue of meaning as Landau suggests. In the linguistic sense, "meaning" implies more than just association of a sound pattern (a spoken word) with a referent. It implies a cognitive basis with appropriate generalization, and a network of relationships to other related words. Dunlea (1982) and Andersen, Dunlea, and Kekelis (in press) report work that illustrates the contrast. They studied children at roughly the stage of the 100 word vocabulary. Their basic data, like those of Landau (1983), show similar distributions of word types for blind, sighted, and partially sighted youngsters. However, there were some important differences between the groups (each of which contained a pair of subjects—the detailed analysis required for this type of close analysis necessarily limits the number of subjects, unfortunately). First, there were very few idiosyncratic word inventions by the visually impaired child. In contrast, sighted children frequently invent their own words, which then drop out of their vocabulary as they go reinforced by their language environment. Such forms are evidence of the child's lexical inventiveness, and the absence of such forms in visually impaired children suggests that they simply "borrow" terms from the vocabularies of those with whom they interact verbally. Although such words may be meaningful in the narrower sense of denoting an unambiguous referent (the Landau usage of the term), they do not necessarily become part of the larger network of meaning in relation to other words. Corroborating this point, Dunlea (1982) and Anderson and et al., (in press) found that the sighted subjects "extended" the meanings of the vast majority of their vocabulary words to apply to related referents, whereas the visually impaired showed far fewer such extensions. To be sure, children typically "overextend" referents, as for example when they use the term "dog" to refer to all four-legged animals for a period before they refine the concept and recognize that dogs are but a subcategory of all animals. This overextension is an abnormal part of lexical development, though, and the finding that visually impaired children do far less of it suggests that they are simply accepting limited meanings for words rather than actively operating on them within a larger cognitive structure.

Dunlea (1982) and Anderson et al. (in press) found another pattern of difference as well, one which has also been reported by other researchers (e.g., McGinnis, 1981). The visually impaired childrens' use of action words was highly self-directed, rather than directed to external objects. Further, their use of relational terms such as "more" was largely centered on themselves rather than on external events, in contrast to the sighted children.

Like Landau (1983) and others, Anderson et al. (in press) found similar distributions of word types in the vocabularies of visually impaired and sighted children. Their more detailed analysis, however, led them to the conclusion that "behavioral and linguistic evidence are consistent in suggesting that the process which enables young sighted children to abstract criterial features of a referent and to extent the domain of application of early words is not functioning at the same level for blind children at the onset of language."

In some reasonably regular and predictable ways, then, the word meaning and usage of visually impaired children is different from that of the sighted. In virtually all of the instances reported, specific experiential factors seem capable of accounting for the observed differences. The evidence supports the notion that visually impaired children should *not* be shielded from words or concepts that are normally based on visual experience. Harley's (1963) conclusions are instructive on this point. Early exposure to concrete experiences, in connection with vocabulary, is desirable, and is even more important for lower intelligence children than higher. Children from more limited experiential backgrounds, further, need structured experience more than those from richer backgrounds. The goal should be to bring the blind child to the point of maximal use of the language used by the surrounding culture so that language can aid in meaningful and useful social interaction, in behavioral self-direction, and in progress within the educational system. The role that effective language use plays in the school-related education of the blind child is particularly important, since as Kenmore (1966) has noted, the reliance of instruction on verbal behavior becomes progressively greater in the higher grades. Finally, although it may be a self-evident point, it would seem necessary to begin this special attempt as early as possible in the child's life, so that experience and verbal usage may grow together. It seems clear that any program of early experience for the blind child should include a commitment to providing experiential referents for words as those words are being added to the child's vocabulary.

Sentences, syntax

There has been relatively little research on sentence characteristics in blind children. On the face of it, the available research generally supports the notion that there is no consistent pattern of difference between blind and sighted children. Wilson and Halverson (1947), in their study of a child who showed severe developmental lags in nonlanguage areas, reported the three-word sentence to appear according to sighted norms. Maxfield (1936), in an extensive study of the language production of eight totally blind (LP or less) children from three to six years of age, found no consistent pattern of differences from sighted norms in the production of complex and compound sentences or in sentence length. Maxfield and Fjeld (1942), using the Vineland Social Maturity Scale with children from one to seven years, found a heterogeneous group of blind children to score marginally better than sighted children on the item "talks in short sentences." Finally, from a different approach, Burlingham (1961) noted that while the early stages of vocabulary acquisition proceed somewhat more slowly in the blind, there is typically a spurt following the toddler stage, such that by the time the children are nursery school age they have approximated the sighted children in vocabulary and fluency. Thus with respect to the early production of sentences, the evidence does not support the notion of a general developmental lag.

Another important issue concerns the production of various types of sentences such as questions. There is very little evidence available comparing blind and sighted children. A noteworthy exception is the study by Maxfield (1936). Maxfield did not include sighted children in this study, but she references several earlier normative studies of sighted children. she found that the blind children produced somewhat fewer statements and negatives, about an equal number of commands, and somewhat more questions.

In a study that has been discussed in an earlier section, Tillman and Williams (1968) included a word usage task that was similar to those used by Brown and Berko (1960) with sighted children. The child was presented with two sentences in which a nonsense word occurred in a specific syntactical context. He was then required to make a verbal response, from which it could be determined if he understood what part of speech the nonsense word was. Six parts of speech were studied, count nouns, mass nouns, intransitive and transitive verbs, adjectives, and adverbs. The seven to 11 year old early blind children, who were exclusively braille users of mixed etiology, were significantly better than the sighted in the use of count nouns and transitive and intransitive verbs, while the sighted group was not significantly better in any category. Although the results of Tillman and Williams supported the notion that the comprehension of parts of speech by blind children is equal to or better than that by sighted children, the results were obtained from children in age range where syntactical development is virtually complete.

For the most part, the research reported through 1970 was conducting using word counts and other similarly molar measures. And in general, the cumulative impact of this research is that there is little difference in the language usage of blind and sighted children. However, a distinctly different conclusion is necessitated by more recent research, which has tended to employ more molecular levels of analysis. Urwin (1978), Andersen, et al. (in press), and McGinnis (1981) have studied in detail the nature of the interactive language patterns between a blind child and another speaker, and a close analysis of the effectiveness of the children's contributions to such conversations reveals considerable usage problems. Andersen et al. (in press), as noted earlier, found the typical pronoun misuse reported in previous research, and advanced the interpretation that such errors "are but one manifestation of a more general problem: a general lack of *perspective-taking* ability." Also in their analysis of detailed verbal interchange between child and adult, they noted many instances in which the child strayed from the thread of conversation to embark on another line of thought entirely. Further along these same lines, they noted a strong tendency to make more self-references than is characteristic of sighted children, an observation also reported by McGinnis (1981). A related observation, made by Urwin (1978) as well as Andersen et al. (in press), is that blind children are more likely to "parrot" the phrases of others, or in Urwin's (1978) terms, to use "ready-made phrases," both in self-speech and in conversation. Wills (1979) characterizes this as a tendency to echolalia.

All of these results bespeak a certain failure on the part of the blind child to engage in what might be called the *functional* aspects of language use. Andersen et al. (in press), as noted, interpret these phenomena as evidence of a general lack of perspective-taking ability, which in turn is at least indirectly a result of lack of visual information. Vision is important to "the processes underlying acquisition in the semantic and pragmatic aspects of language. Blind children have difficulties in just those areas of language acquisition where visual perception, combined with context-based linguistic input, can provide information about the world (e.g., shared features, reciprocity) and be a stimulus for forming hypotheses about the nature of certain aspects of the linguistic system."

The phrase "context-based linguistic input" is important to an understanding of this viewpoint. In fact, it is the study of the linguistic context in which the child acquires language that elucidates the specific elements that may lead to the differences reported. Kekelis (1981) and Kekelis and Andersen (1983) report a detailed study of the language patterns of mothers of blind and sighted children, in which they have found remarkable differences which form a logical basis for the differences observed between the blind and sighted children's own usage. In brief, Kekelis and Andersen examined the videotaped interactions between mother and child over a several-month period, concentrating particularly on the form (sentence type) and focus (topic type) of the mother's speech. The blind children's mothers tended heavily to ask questions requiring the children to answer or carry out a request. They provided fewer descriptions of the objects, people, and events which the child encountered, instead tending to provide labels for immediate objects or actions. Topics were more usually centered on the child rather than on the environment.

Thus the language environment of the blind children was quite different from that of the sighted children, and can generally be characterized as attempting (appropriately enough) to take the restrictions imposed by the child's lack of vision into account. The major differences between blind and sighted children's *own* language behavior, described earlier, can be seen as logically related to these differences in the language context. Examples are the blind child's tendency to center his language upon himself (since he is more often exposed to language with himself as the object), and to use language less extensively (since objects are more often labeled than described).

The blind child is, thus, apparently at a double disadvantage in the development of rich linguistic behavior. First, as Andersen et al. (in press) note, he lacks visual information about such things as the similarities and dissimilarities among objects and events. Second, though, the tendency of the parent is to use language forms that are apparently intended to help the blind child deal with language effectively but which in fact fail to provide the linguistic richness that might help to overcome the disadvantages of the lack of vision.

The research of the past few years has used methodologies which allow a more detailed picture of both the child's language use and the linguistic environment available to him. In contrast to the more global methodologies that have characterized the language area in the past, these techniques have led to the identification of some serious problem areas in the language development of the blind. These problems are not unsolvable, but their solution has been brought much closer by the implementation of more effective research techniques.

Language Remediation

Although a fuller review of language remediation procedures belongs properly in a full-length treatment of language development, there have been enough reports of language remediation procedures geared specifically to visually impaired children to warrant at least brief mention here. Curtis (1966), in discussing the verbal performance evaluation procedure used at the Syracuse Center for Multiply Handicapped Children, made a point that is applicable to children without additional handicaps as those with them. Detailed and specific examination and evaluation are necessary as a basis for effective intervention. This maxim is clearly true for visually impaired children with additional handicaps: it would be unreasonable to expect a hard-of-hearing child to respond to the treatment approaches that are needed by an emotionally disturbed child. Within the area of language dysfunction, it is clearly necessary to make a careful evaluation of the individual child's area of strength and weakness and to apply procedures that are designed to repair the weaknesses while maintaining any extant strengths.

Egland's (1955) paper on the treatment of speech difficulties in blind cerebral palsy children serves as an example of this differentiated approach. Similarly, Stinchfield-Hawk (1944) suggested specific techniques for use in cases where the difficulty is in motor production of speech. The "moto-kinaesthetic" training procedure advanced by Stinchfield-Hawk makes use of the child's ability to feel, with his hands, his own as well as his teacher's lips, throat and jaws, and to evaluate the relationship between his own produced sound and facial movements and those of his teacher.

At least three papers might be classified as advancing an "educational" approach to language remediation in the blind child (Cicenia, Belton, Myers, & Mundy, 1965; Miner, 1963b; Reich, 1968). These papers may be classified together because of their apparent common assumption that language difficulties occur because of inadequate opportunties for learning about language and its uses. The paper by Cicenia et al. is concerned primarily with blind mentally retarded children, although the approaches suggested might well be generalized to nonretarded children as well. The material on the nonverbal and the preverbal groups is of particular relevance to this section. Children in the nonverbal group were exposed to play therapy techniques, where the teacher "uses a running, verbal commentary to describe each object in the environment in detail. Simultaneously with the dialogue, the child is helped to experience objects tactually with the teacher" (p. 108). The approach was based on the notion that the child has been exposed to a large variety of sounds, and that he will acquire a set of associations between experiences and those words that describe or refer to them. The child was, of course, encouraged to use the words (associations) that he was acquiring, both in conversation and in music. Children were placed in the preverbal group if they produced words but did not understand them or use them correctly. The general thrust of the educational approach for these children was, like that with the nonverbal group, to provide the child with associations between experiences and the appropriate words for those experiences, so that the words may come to be used in context and with correct meaning.

Miner (1963b) described an educational program for the speech improvement of visually impaired children. The goals of the program were numerous, ranging from improvement in articulation and phonics to the recognition of sounds and the appropriate use of words for communication. Miner considered auditory discriminative abilities to be basic to other speech-related abilities, and time was spent on pitch, quality, intensity, location, and rhythm discrimination before going on to speech sounds and word use. Reich (1968) suggested the use of puppetry as a tool in language development for "disadvantaged" blind children. Reich considered one of the major problems in language deficiencies to be inappropriate or insufficient motivation, and she suggested that the use of puppet play may help in this area because it "demands active speaking and listening participation." It should be noted that the children for whom Reich found the technique to be useful were more advanced than children in the nonverbal or preverbal categories of Cicenia et al. Their "speech was characterized by incomplete words, sound substitutions, and poor syntactical structure. These poor speech patterns carried over into their reading, writing, and spelling" (p. 621). Reich noted several specific instances of improvement, particularly in areas of oral language such as phonetic use and speech volume.

By way of contrast to these examples of educational approaches to speech remediation at various levels of development, two quite different and more clinically oriented approaches may be noted. Kass, Gillman, Mattis, Klugman, and Jacobson (1967) described a psychodynamic approach to the remediation of a selective mutism in a six-year old girl. The procedure involved meetings with clinical personnel and placing the child in a regular first grade classroom. During the course of a year, her language developed from a simple exclamatory mode to "animated discussion of problem areas." Milstead (1972) described the use of a "contingency management" program to decrease the relative frequency of echolalic speech in an eight-year old blind child. The parents served as the primary agents of contingency manipulation —the child was required to produce acceptable, that is, nonecholalic, speech in order to receive his food at mealtimes. The significant decrease in echolalic responses apparently persisted for several weeks, although longer term follow-up assessment was not reported.

The drastic differences in the programs used by Milstead, Kass et al., and Miner illustrate the variety of remedial techniques that have been attempted. In part, this variety is undoubtedly appropriate to the variety of problems needing treatment. However, many of these techniques are characterized by a strong theoretical overlay on the specific problem framework. That is, the techniques used by the various workers apparently tend to reflect their theoretical biases. The variety of theoretical orientations and the resulting variety of procedural attempts bode well for the area of language remediation, but only if adequate evaluation of the methods is conducted. It is not sufficient to have faith that the behavior modification approach or the psychodynamic approach is the best— the field needs careful and objective evaluation of the relative effectiveness of the various approaches. It is undoubtedly true that one method is best suited for a particular type of problem while another method produces better results for another type of problem. At present, though, there does not seem to be an effective technology for matching remedial procedure to problem type.

Nonverbal Communication

Although the vast majority of the research on the communicative abilities of visually impaired children has been concentrated on verbal language, the question of nonverbal communication has received some attention. The work falls generally under the heading of "expressiveness," and it may be divided into two categories, facial and body expressions that accompany speech, and the facial expression of emotional states.

An example of the first category is a study by Brieland (1950), in which he assessed the expressiveness of body and face as well as the adequacy of verbal language itself. The subjects were congenitally blind children and sighted controls, age range 12 to 18 years. Expressiveness was rated from films that were taken while the child was telling a story. The blind children were significantly worse than the sighted in the degree of expressive bodily action. It should also be noted that although Brieland found the blind children to be significantly less expressive in lip movements, the ratings of general effectiveness of speech and voice were not significantly different.

McGinnis (1981), working with five-year-olds, also found differences. In conversation with others, the blind subjects used far fewer expressive hand gestures to accompany their speech than did sighted subjects. Nor did the blind children tend to use gestures such as nodding the head as a substitute for words. A contrasting finding was offered by Eisenstadt (1955), who reported that there was not a significant difference between visually impaired and sighted control children over a wide age range in "visible elements of speech."

Parke, Shellcross, and Anderson (1980) found a mixture of results, with visually impaired subjects from residential schools, age range five to 16 years. Each subject was engaged in videotaped conversation with the experimenter, and the tape was analyzed by raters with respect to the frequency and appropriateness of head nodding, smiling, and eyebrow raising. Interrater reliability was not impressive. In any case, there were moderate differences between the visually impaired and a matched group of sighted subjects on head nodding and eyebrow raising. For the most part, the visually impaired subjects showed these behaviors in appropriate situations.

Apple (1972) reviewed some literature on nonverbal expressiveness and communication and concluded that much nonverbal communication is learned. She suggested a list of "teachable" movements and expressions. No information was provided, however, about whether children actually can learn to produce these expressions, although Buchanan (1978) was able through training to improve the gesturing ability of visually impaired adolescents in the mobility setting. The question of the nonverbal analog of the "verbalism" might well be raised in connection with this issue — it may be that such educated gestures would serve merely a cosmetic purpose but not the purpose of true communication.

A study by Blass, Freedman, and Steingart (1974), while done with older adolescents, raises a set of interesting questions of the relationship between gestures and verbal behavior in young blind children. In previous work with sighted subjects, Freedman and others had found relationships between types of hand and body movements and verbal facility and difficulty. Specifically, well-articulated movements appeared together with verbal attributes which indicated verbal encoding facility, while less well organized gestures appeared with verbal attributes which indicated verbal encoding difficulty. In their work with blind subjects, Blass et al. made a primary distinction between object-focused and body-focused movements. In a five-minute segment of free verbal activity, there was significantly more body-focused gesture by the blind subjects than by a comparable group of sighted subjects. The primary body-focused activity was in "finger-to-hand" movements, although some "body-touching" occurred as well. In the blind sample, the finger-to-hand movements showed a substantial positive correlation with verbal fluency and the body-touching movements showed a negative correlation. The result for finger to hand gestures was opposite that for sighted subjects, where these gestures were associated with verbal nonfluency.

The significance of these patterns of results is by no means clear for adolescents, let alone for younger blind children. However, the phenomenon is an interesting one and deserves study within a developmental framework. Blass et al. discussed the relationships of these gestures to "blindisms" and suggested that a careful analysis of the relationships between hand gestures and cognitive and language processes is needed. The significance of their finding of significantly fewer object-oriented gestures also deserves developmental study. Finally, the apparent difference between blind and sighted people in the typical use of gestures in language may have implications for potential difficulties in the reception of the speech of the blind child by his sighted peers and adults.

The material on the expression of emotional states should be preceded by a word of caution. Care must be taken in interpreting the significance of possible differences between blind and sighted children. It is possible to compare the overt characteristics of the emotional expressions of blind and sighted children. From such results, however, it is probably not valid to draw conclusions about the relative strength of the emotions that are experienced by blind and sighted children, since overt expressiveness may not be an equivalent indicator of emotional experience for blind and sighted subjects.

In an early study, Dumas (1932) found that blind adults had some difficulty in producing appropriate facial expressions upon request. Foulke (1973) has made similar observations more recently. The question of the adequacy of facial expressions of emotional states is an interesting one in blind children, and it is important to the extent that effective communication with sighted people might be hampered by the production of inappropriate or insufficiently expressive facial configurations. There is some agreement in the literature (Goodenough, 1932; Thompson, 1941; Freedman, 1964) that important components of facial expressiveness are maturationally determined and are therefore not dependent on visually-mediated imitation of other people. Freedman, for example, found that the early course of smiling is identical for blind and sighted infants. The evidence from blind adults, though, suggest that imitation must play a part in either the refinement or the maintenance of appropriate facial expressions, and thus the question of the development of facial expressions of emotion in blind children becomes important.

Fulcher (1932) studied blind subjects ranging in age from six to 21, mostly totally blind from birth and of average intelligence. Sighted controls ranged from four to 16 years of age. Subjects were requested to produce facial expressions representing happiness, sadness, fear, and anger. Photographs were taken of each subject and were rated in three categories, adequacy, amount of facial activity, and movement of specific parts of the face. Apparently only one judge made ratings. On the measure of adequacy, the sighted subjects scored better than the blind. The sighted group showed age-related improvement while the blind group did not. For the measure of facial activity, the sighted showed more activity than the blind, and while the older sighted children showed more facial activity than the younger sighted ones, the older blind children showed less activity than the younger blind children. For both blind and sighted children, there was a tendency for the boys to show more facial activity than girls. On the measure of specific types of movement, there was evidence for more variety among the facial expressions of the sighted children than of the blind, although the types of movements were similar. A finding related to the age trends found by Fulcher was reported by Mistschenka (1933, cited by Thompson, 1941). Mistschenka found that blind children showed a decreasing ability to produce appropriate voluntary facial expressions over the age range from four to 18 years.

Thompson (1941) reported a study of the spontaneous expression of emotion in blind and sighted children. Emotional responses to naturally occurring situations were photographed and then rated on a series of criteria. The primary categories of response were laughing, smiling, and crying. The blind children had for the most part no more than LP, and many were totally blind. Most of the children had been blind from birth or early in the first year. The sighted children were of comparable age (seven weeks to 13 years) and intelligence. For the blind group, the amount of facial activity in smiling decreased with age, while there was no such trend for the sighted children. For both blind and sighted children, amount of facial activity in laughing decreased with age, although the developmental decrease was somewhat more rapid for sighted children. Finally, the facial activity in crying was found to increase for both blind and sighted groups up to about 3 years, beyond which there were no cases of crying. Although the data were less complete, Thompson also reported the incidence of anger, sulkiness, annoyance, and sadness in the blind group, and the responses were similar to those by sighted children. Furthermore, she noted that these emotions tended to be expressed in appropriate situations. Thompson also studied the facial expressions of four deaf–blind children ranging in age from seven to 14 years. To the extent that comparisons could be made on this small sample, the facial expressions were apparently not markedly different from those of the blind children. Thompson concluded that maturation plays a substantial part in the development of facial emotional expressiveness, but that mimicry or imitation in sighted children might allow a "voluntary" overlay on the maturational component.

Goodenough (1932) described the expression of emotions in a 10-year-old blind–deaf girl. Although the goal of the report was to argue for an innate componenet in the emotional expressions of children, the paper provides an interesting discussion of the particular expressions of a blind-deaf child. Goodenough argued that the circumstances in which the child had been raised had provided her with little feedback about her modes of emotional expression. Yet, in response to the action of the experimenter in putting a small doll down the child's dress, she exhibited successively: startled surprise, interest and attention, disappointment or displeasure (passive, pouting), exasperation and mild rage, and upon successfully retrieving the doll, delight, peals of hearty laughter, and pleased satisfaction. Apparently, each of these emotions was expressed at an appropriate point in the sequence of behavioral responses to the stimulus. Eibl-Eisbesfeldt (1970) made much the same point on the basis of evidence from two deaf-blind children, ages five and seven.

While the data on nonverbal exressiveness are not overwhelming, it does seem appropriate to conclude that early development is similar in blind and sighted children. However, there is some evidence for divergence in developmental patterns, and these differences can probably be accounted for by the unavailability of vision as a mediator of imitation in blind children. The question of the trainability of expressiveness remains open, and work should be initiated along the lines suggested by Apple (1972). Webb (1974) reported some success in training facial expressions in blind adults by a myoelectrical feedback system, but the suitability of such a system for blind children has not been studied.

Multiple Handicaps and Language

The foregoing material has been concerned primarily with the blind child without additional handicaps. Certain categories of additional handicap may make the task of language acquisition and use more difficult for the blind child. Egland (1955) discussed the possibility of various speech related difficulties in the blind with cerebral palsy (CP). The additional handicaps that CP imposes on the blind child are primarily motor in nature, and it seems fair to conclude from Egland's treatment of the subject that the language difficulties of the blind child with CP are not distinctly different from those of the sighted child with CP. That is, language difficulties do not necessarily increase with the addition of the motor handicap. This conclusion is perhaps not surprising, in view of the general absence of serious developmental language lags in blind children without additional handicaps. One of the areas which Egland discussed as bearing on the language of the blind child is the possible effect of CP on the muscles involved in the production of speech. He also pointed out that muscular difficulties may produce secondary effects on motivation, learning and adjustment. Another area where motor difficulties may compound the language problem of the blind child is locomotion, since there is evidence that blind children are slower to develop independent locomotion than sighted children (see Chapter 2). To the extent that locomotion is important in the child's acquisition of experiential basis for language, the language development of the blind child with CP or other motor disabilities may be adversely affected.

Several studies have dealt with problems of language development in the mentally retarded blind child (Cicenia et al., 1965; Elonen & Zwarensteyn, 1964; Rogow, 1972). Rogow suggested that the adequacy of social interaction may play a part in determining the language development of retarded blind children: "It has been this writer's experience that clinical evaluations of nonspeaking blind children tend to ignore the fact of social isolation and associated experiential deprivation" (p. 40). In a later paper, Rogow (1980) stressed the importance of the early establishment of basic interactive signals between parent and child, signals which can then be gradually differentiated to carry a variety of meanings. Elonen and Zwarensteyn noted that part of the speech difficulty in the retarded blind child may be attributed to the fact that "This type of child has always been able to indicate his needs satisfactorily through nonverbal methods which have been accepted by others and allowed to persist. Often the parents jump to the conclusion that the child is unable to speak and continue to respond to his nonverbal communication" (p. 606). The dangers of overprotection or oversolicitousness are apparent. Elonen and Zwarensteyn also noted that the retarded blind child is generally slower in progressing through the stages of language development. They pointed to an interesting dilemma that the therapist often encounters. On the one hand, the child should not be pushed too hard beyond his developmental level. On the other hand, there is considerable evidence suggesting that perhaps more than other areas of development, language development is characterized by critical periods. That is, if the child does not develop language appropriately within a certain period, development will be more difficult after that period. The resolution to this dilemma, if there is one, will depend on the convergence of several lines of research. Much more work needs to be done on the possibililty of critical periods in language development in sighted as well as nonretarded blind children. It is not known whether mental retardation might also retard the time course of critical periods in language development. Finally, of course, better and more detailed information is needed about the possible benefits, as well as the disadvantages, of "pushing" the retarded child faster than his spontaneous rate of development in any area, including language.

An additional handicap that has received somewhat more attention in the blind literature is the loosely defined area of emotional disturbance. Unfortunately this area has not been treated very rigorously. Often the term is used in a purely descriptive way to refer to children who show difficulty in establishing or maintaining social contacts. There has been very little attempt to study just how the emotional experience of such a child may differ from that of the child who does not give evidence of such difficulty. In any case, there has been some attention paid to the possibility that an "autistic-like" syndrome of social withdrawal may be characteristic of some blind children, and furthermore that the syndrome may be especially related to the RLF etiology. One marked characteristic of the syndrome involves, as autism does in sighted children, difficulty in interpersonal communication, especially via speech. Keeler (1958) discussed this situation in RLF children. The five subjects for whom he reported summary statements had all been prematurely born, had been placed in an incubator, and had developed RLF blindness. Characteristics of their social behavior included a resistance to physical contact, a lack of verbal response to speech by others, difficulties in toilet training and other trained skills such as eating, and notably, a pattern of rejection by the mother. (The last point seems especially interesting in relation to the material in other chapters which suggests that some of the early problems of the blind child may often be at least parly attributed to the parents' negative response to the fact of the child's blindness.) The pattern of auditory and language behavior by the children showed adequate understanding of spoken language but no verbal response to it, an exceptional liking for auditory stimuli and music in particular, excessive echolalia, and the impressive ability to hum and sing songs and to use the correct words in them. Thus there was apparently no auditory dysfunction that would prevent the intake of speech information of the understanding of the information, and not motor dysfunction that would prevent the child from speaking adequately. Rather, the difficulty was in the area of the appropriate use of speech in social contexts. The children simply did not produce the speech that was needed to maintain their end of a social interchange. Haspiel (1965) made similar points in discussing auditory and speech functions in the emotionally disturbed blind child (etiology unspecified).

It seems reasonable to suggest that the language and communication dysfunction in these children is not primarily an aspect of language itself, but rather that the language dysfunction is a symptom of a larger syndrome, the primary characteristics of which involve difficulties in social interactions. Keeler noted that "the mothers were greatly disturbed by finding their children blind and tended literally to put them out of their minds by leaving them in cribs and playpens off in a back room of the house or in the back yard for long periods of time, attending only in a minimal way to the most imperative of their physical needs... A few of these mothers repeatedly made the statement that they would rather see their children dead than the way they are" (p.66). Such statements clearly indicated emotional difficulties on the part of the parent, and it would be surprising not to find disturbances in the social behavior of children raised in such a situation. It does seem justified to attribute at least part of the blame to the parental environment. Such effects may occur directly from the absence of social interaction, or indirectly from the failure to provide appropriate perceptual and language stimulation for the child. For perspective, it seems important to point out that there is undoubtedly more to the difficulties than inadequate emotional response on the part of the parents. If the child's emotional disturbance were due solely to the parental response, one would expect to find a comparable incidence of reports of "autistic-like" behavior among children who were blind from birth but not premature. This is not the case, though, and thus it seems likely that some characteristics of the prematurity are implicated in producing emotional disturbance. This issue will be developed more fully in Chapter 7.

The deaf-blind child

A brief section on the deaf-blind child is more appropriate in a chapter on language than in any other chapter, since the literature on such children has concentrated primarily on problems of language acquisition. In absolute numbers of cases, the combination of blindness and deafness is a relatively rare situation, but in terms of the special problems of development that occur with the combination, it is one that is particularly worthy of attention. Burns and Stenquist (1960) estimated that there were almost 400 deaf-blind children below age 21 in the United States, of whom between one-fourth and one-third were totally blind and deaf, and of whom 40 percent had additional disabilities. Definitions of the deaf-blind syndrome vary depending on the primary orientation of the writer. Those who are primarily interested in deafness tend to view such children as deaf with the additional handicap of visual loss, while those primarily interested in blindness tend to regard the hearing impairment as secondary. Neither orientation necessarily precluded the realization of the severity of the problem—for the educator of the deaf, for instance, it is the additional handicap of blindness that makes the child largely unresponsive to the methods normally used with the deaf. Similarly, blind children normally depend heavily on auditory information to aid their locomotor, communicative, and other skills, and it is their inability to use auditory information in useful ways that brings deaf-blind children strongly to the attention of people who work with the blind. In either case, the individual methods for each single handicap are not generally applicable, and the child with the dual handicap may fail to receive a program that is geared optimally to his capabilities. One reason for this failure is that there are not many workers trained specifically to deal with the dual handicap. This lack may in turn be traced primarily to the fact that there is relatively little information to be communicated to potential workers with the deaf-blind. Compared to the volumes of material available on the blind or the deaf, research material on the deaf-blind is extremely limited.

Several writers, have stressed the necessity for a more detailed breakdown of the deaf-blind dual handicap. Jordan (1964), for example, argued for a tripartite distinction including the deafened blind, who is a blind person who subsequently loses his hearing, the blinded deaf, who lacks both hearing and vision from early childhood. Dinsmore (1967) suggested a further subdivision to take development into account. The five groupings are (1) those children who have had vision and hearing for several years, so that verbal and visual memory are available, (2) those who have been deaf from early in life but have had vision for some years, (3) those who have been blind from very early in life but have had auditory function for some years, (4) those who have been both visually and auditorily impaired from early in life, and (5) those who have variously combined partial losses.

Although there have been cases of blind-deaf persons reported and publicly known for decades (Salmon & Rusalem, 1966 provide an interesting historical account), it is only relatively recently that sufficient notice has been taken of the dual handicap to produce detailed approaches to evaluation and prescription for deaf-blind children. A major step forward was made possible in 1957 by the establishment of the diagnostic clinic at Syracuse University. The early history of this clinic with respect to the deaf-blind child was discussed by Root and Riley (1960), who described the multidisciplinary approach to evaluation in which medical personnel, psychologists, teachers, pediatricians and others participated in an extensive evaluation of the particular problems of the individual child. The child's parents were involved in the evaluation session, as was a caseworker from the family's town. Both Donlon (1964) and Dinsmore (1967) described the Syracuse program at later stages, and Dinsmore provided information about the program at the Perkins School. Stein and Green (1972) also provided a general discussion of the problems of evaluating individual deaf-blind children

Much of the published work with deaf-blind children has centered on problems of language and communication. When problems are discussed in other areas of development, such as socialization or interpersonal relations, they are often attributed to the primary deficits in communicative abilities. There can be no doubt that the development of language is an almost overwhelming task for the deaf-blind child. The language problems of the blind child are not severe, as has been discussed earlier in this chapter. Deaf children experience a great deal more difficulty than blind children in acquiring language, but considerable success has been reported by the advocates of both oral and manual language approaches. Both general approaches with the deaf depend heavily on the use of visual materials, though, and so the language problem for the deaf-blind child is truly one where the separate handicaps are not additive but multiplicative. It is certainly a positive note that very few children are both totally blind and totally deaf, but even for partially handicapped children the problems are immense.

Most of the techniques used in teaching language made the assumption (although usually only implicitly) that the deaf-blind child does not have a lesser cognitive potential than other children. There is little good evidence one way or the other on the question of cognitive capacity (and some would argue that, at least operationally, it is difficult if not impossible to assess cognitive or learning capabilities without making use of language). Salmon and Rusalem (1966), among others, have discussed the problems involved in the evaluation of cognitive abilities of deaf-blind adults. The evaluation problems with children are even more difficult, and many writers express a dissatisfaction with the effectiveness of evaluation in noting that there are many deaf-blind children who have been inappropriately assigned to institutions for the mentally retarded.

Elioseff (1971) discussed various guidelines for the expectation that a deaf–blind child may be responsive to language instruction. Although an IQ level of 50 has sometimes been used, she noted that a more appropriate index may be the attainment of a minimum mental age such as 18 months. Different expectations should probably be held for deaf–blind children who fall below some such criterion (given that the problem of reliability of evaluation can be solved), and different teaching methods are undoubtedly required. Even within the range specified by Elioseff and others as "language educable," there is good evidence to support the notion that different instruction methods may be optimal for different children. It has been reported (Umezu, 1972) that deaf– blind children who have been found unresponsive to one method do respond more favorably to another technique. It is likely that individual variation in cognitive ability patterns accounts for at least some of this selectivity. J. van Dijk (1971), for example, cited evidence on the relative occurrence of dyspraxia (impairment in motor coordination) and dysrhythmia (impairment in ability to sequence events rhythmically over time) in deaf children, and she suggested that selectivity in the use of training approaches is necessary if an adequate match is to be made between the child's characteristics and the characteristics of the training. It is not sufficient simply to have different methods available. It is equally important to have an effective way of matching an appropriate method to the individual child's characteristics. Although the technology of this matching process is not well developed, diagnostic tools such as the "manual-sign" approach described by Robbins (1971) provide a good indication that the goal is not an unreasonable one. Robbins argued that

> If we were to apply this model of relationship of retardation, cognitive and gross motor development to deaf–blind children, we should then be able to predict level of communication and/or language learning participation possible at a given time for a child by evaluating his physical and cognitive development. . . There are prerequisite cognitive levels for certain stages of language; however, attainment of the cognitive or motor level does not necessarily assure the language development. If, in addition to cognitive adequacy, the basic components related to language acquisition are present . . . language acquisition may take place with a general "naturalness" and the help of sensory aids and teacher-communication. Without the innate components, language acquisition seems to take a different route in a process which might be described as more like the "intellectual" process in learning to read than the totally unconscious process of learning to speak (p. 77).

There is clearly much research to be conducted on deaf–blind children, on language development as well as other aspects of development. Some perspective on the format that such research might take will be provided in Chapter 9.

6
Social Development

Infancy

Aspects of the social development of visually impaired infants were discussed in Chapter 1. A brief recapitulation of that section is appropriate here. Socialization is the process by which the child moves from the neonatal state, in which he is essentially an asocial being, to the state in which he takes appropriate account of the need to fit into the social structure of which he is a part. This social structure includes parents and siblings, as well as peers and others outside the family setting. Their demands range from the basic self-help skills such as eating, dressing, and toilet training to play and a variety of other social interactions. Early in infancy, one of the most critical processes involves the development of emotional bonds with significant others, especially parents and siblings. These "attachments," as they are called, form an important emotional security base for the child as he ventures beyond the confines of his immediate and well-known world, and therefore form a critical basis for his willingness to explore the physical environment and thereby gain the experience on which much of cognitive development is based. As well, it is necessary to have a strong positive relationship between parents and child, so that when the inevitable conflicts in the socialization process occur (such as in matters of obedience), they occur within a supportive and positive emotional context.

The impairment of vision may interfere with normal development in each of two areas, then. First, vision is an important interpersonal vehicle supporting the development of emotional bonds. Second, vision provides useful information about the specifics of the tasks which the young child is asked to learn about, such as dressing and eating. There is little direct research on the specifics of early socialization in the visually impaired infant, although what there is bears out expectations based on a common-sense evaluation of the role of vision in these tasks. The report by Reynell (1978) of the evaluation of young sighted, partially sighted, and blind children on the Reynell–Zinkin

Mental Development Scale bears this out. On the "social adaptation" part of the scale, groups of partially sighted and blind infants did not differ, but both showed a delayed course of development compared with the sighted group.

Childhood Social Maturity and Competence

Van Hasselt (1983) makes the point that in general the social competence of blind children and adolescents is not as strong as that of sighted children. The research evidence tends to bear out his conclusion. The Vineland Social Maturity Scale, developed by Doll in the 1930s has enjoyed some use as an indicator of general social development in blind children, although it was designed for use with sighted children. Part of the impetus for the development of the Vineland, and of subsequent modifications designed specifically for blind children, was apparently the need for an indicator of intelligence at younger ages than those for which IQ tests are useful. However, an important difference in orientation between tests of social maturity and intelligence should be noted. Intelligence tests are, at least theoretically, designed to assess intellectual potential. The progeny of the Vineland that were developed for blind children, the Maxfield–Fjeld and Maxfield–Buchholz scales, on the other hand, are specifically designed to assess actual performance rather than potential. Maxfield and Buchholz (1957) cautioned that "it is important to keep in mind that this is not a test of intelligence. Its level of expected performance is based on what blind children are *actually found to do* at different age levels. *Capacity to do* is not measured except indirectly" (p. 11). Nevertheless, social maturity or competence (represented as Social Quotient, or SQ, by some investigators) undoubtedly shares some commonality with IQ. Doll (1953) noted significant correlations between SQ and IQ, and Gillman (1974) and Gillman and Goddard (1974) found some significant correlations between SQ (administered before age six) and IQ (verbal WISC, administered after age six) in a longitudinally studied group of blind children.

McKay (1936) described the Vineland evaluation of several young blind children. The cases definitely showed lags in social maturity, but the results cannot be taken as normative for blind children since the subjects were drawn from an institutional setting that accepted only problem children. Bradway (1937) used the Vineland scale to compare the social levels of blind, deaf, and crippled children with standardization norms for sighted children. The blind subjects ranged in age from five to 20 years. Their Hayes–Binet IQ scores were "within average normal limits," and all had been blind since four years or earlier and had a maximum Snellen acuity of 5/200. Overall, the Social Quotient (SQ) of the blind children was 62, as compared with a standardization of 100 for sighted children (the average for the deaf children was 80). The SQ for the blind group showed a tendency to decrease with age, indicating a progressive decline in social competence relative to sighted norms. The pattern of deficit by the blind children was not apparently a result of inappropriateness of the items, since there were few items that were not passed at some age level. Rather, the blind subjects simply showed a lag, passing items at ages somewhat later than sighted children.

In a more recent study, McGuinness (1970) used the Vineland to compare the social maturity of blind children who had been exposed to itinerant teacher, integrated school, and special school educational settings. The subjects were drawn from the fourth through sixth grades, were totally blind or had at most LP, and had for the most part been blind since birth. About 85 percent of the children were of RLF etiology. McGuinness reported that the scores of all three groups were "generally lower" than sighted norms. However, the children from the itinerant teacher and integrated school settings showed higher social maturity scores than those from the special school setting. McGuinness discussed the latter result in the context of the relative lack of contact of children in the special school with age-appropriate social behavior, and of the greater availability of special help in the special school setting which might lead to reduced need by the children to "work out problems for themselves."

The use of the Vineland allows the comparison of the social maturity scores of blind children with norms for sighted children. However, the increasing numbers of blind children during the 1930s emphasized the need for a social maturity scale normed on blind children (Maxfield & Buchholz, 1957). Consequently, Maxfield and Fjeld (1942) undertook to study in depth the usefulness of the Vineland scale for blind children and to design a modification that would be optimally appropriate for blind children. The blind children studied by Maxfield and Fjeld were quite varied, ranging in age from nine months to almost seven years and in mental ability from very low to very high. Mental ability was roughly categorized by experienced workers as superior, normal, or retarded. Degree of visual loss ranged from total to minimal. The mean SQ for the blind children was 83.5, compared to the norm of 100 for sighted children. The standard deviation of the scores for the blind was almost 30, and the range was from 26 to 163. The pattern was not consistently in favor of the sighted, however, since there were 15 items that were relatively easier for the blind group, as compared to 14 which were relatively easier for the sighted group. Age-matched subgroups of totally blind and partially sighted subjects were compared, and although statistical tests were not reported, the results favored the partially sighted group, 87.7 vs. 80.2. The pattern of item differences between the two groups was interesting. "The results suggest that the blind children in this study tend to be more docile, have less initiative, are less active and outgoing, are more introverted, and possibly more cooperative than the partially seeing children . . . on the whole, the differences found to exist between the blind and the partially seeing children follow the pattern of behavior which appeared in the comparative study of the totally visually handicapped group and the normal seeing children" (p. 13). Maxfield and

Fjeld proposed a modified Vineland, later referred to as the Maxfield–Fjeld scale (MF) for use with visually handicapped children.

Norris, Spaulding, and Brodie (1957) used the MF scale in their extensive study of a large sample of blind children. They divided the item pool into seven separate developmental areas and reported quartile results within each of the areas. In general, the results of the Norris et al. study showed blind children scoring somewhat better on the MF scale than had been found by previous investigators: the mean SQ for the intensive group was 91.9. They noted that the scale did not effectively differentiate children above the age of three years.

The successor to the Maxfield–Fjeld scale was the Maxfield–Buchholz (MB) scale, described in 1957 (Maxfield & Buchholz, 1957) after extensive normative work. The MB included a relocation and rewording of some of the MF items, as well as an extension of the scale at the upper age ranges (five to six years). In describing the use of the test, the authors stressed that it is not considered a test of potential social maturity, but rather of actual or habitual social maturity.

Bauman (1973) noted that the usefulness of the MB scale may be diminished by virtue of the large weighting (60 percent) of RLF children in the norm group. In part because of this potential problem with the MB scale, a modification of the Levine–Elzey Social Competency Scale was prepared in the late 1960s. Although the scale was used in pilot work on various samples of blind children, it was not further developed because of inconsistencies in the results (Hatlen, personal communication).

Bauman (1973) described preliminary work on the development of the Overbrook Social Competency Scale. Children from six to 18 years were studied in the initial stages of the work. Although Bauman strongly qualified the usefulness of the test because of its relative newness, a striking (but not surprising) finding emerged from the preliminary work: children with some useful vision developed many skills significantly earlier than totally blind children. Further, boys without useful vision were rated considerably better than girls without useful vision on several skills. By contrast, sighted girls generally show more advanced social skills than boys of the same age.

Schindele (1974) used the Self-Concept Adjustment Score (Cowen, Underberg, Verillo, & Benham, 1961) to compare the social adjustment of fifth- and sixth-grade blind and sighted children. Two groups of blind subjects were used, one from residential schools and one from regular (integrated) schools. There were no differences in social adjustment between the residential and integrated school blind samples, or between either blind group and the sighted group. Closer analysis, however, revealed some interesting points. The residential school group showed a negative relationship of adjustment to age (the older children were less well adjusted), while the relationship was positive for the integrated school blind group. Schindele suggested that "while the social adjustment of visually handicapped students in regular schools has developed in a realistic surrounding the social adjustment of the visually handicapped in a residential school is mainly the result of being brought up in a sheltered and unrealistic environment. In this case the good social adjustment of these children might be seriously affected as they grow older and especially when they have to leave the residential school'' (p. 141). Further, for the integrated school blind group there was a strong positive correlation between social adjustment and intelligence. Schindele proposed that ''integrated visually handicapped students have to make special efforts to achieve a high level of social adjustment . . . more intelligent children are more likely to be successful in these efforts'' (p. 142).

The results of Schindele (1974) and of McGuinness (1970), discussed earlier, make it clear that a simple index of social maturity or adjustment does not provide an adequate picture of the situation. Although Schindele found overall mean scores to be equivalent for the various groups, the more detailed findings suggest that there are different sets of dynamics at work in the different environmental settings, both in the situation to which the child is required to adjust and in the factors that determine the adequacy of the adjustment.

''Social cognition'' refers to the individual's understanding of social relationships and the roles of self and others in the social context. The concept is not a particularly new one, although the terminology reflects the fascination of psychology in the past decade with the role of cognitive processes in a wide variety of areas. Such reconceptualizations are useful and often productive inasmuch as they help researchers break out of previous modes of thinking which may have become constraining. Whether or not this will be the case in the visual impairment literature is yet to be seen, but a positive example may be seen in a study by Gelber (1980). Congenitally blind and sighted children aged five to 11 were studied on three tasks. Sensory perspective-taking involved presenting the child with common objects to be manipulated and placed appropriately in the experimenter's hand, hypothetical dilemmas involved stories about socal conflict situations, and projective perspectives involved a hypothetical story setting in which the child was asked to describe the perspective of each of several characters in the story. Three hypotheses were confirmed: There was a similar progression from the preoperational to the operational stage in each group, there was a ''developmental lag'' of the blind children compared with the sighted, and the lag decreased with increasing age.

Schwartz (1981), similarly, explored the differences between legally blind and sighted children, age range seven to nine, in role-taking tasks, and in the relationships between role-taking behavior and degree of parental control. The results were essentially negative with respect to differences between visually impaired and sighted samples. As always, conclusions based on negative results must be guarded, since (and the Schwartz study is a case in point) it is always possible that the measures used may have simply been insensitive to real differences that may exist. Nonetheless, the importance of the social cognition approach should not be underplayed: again, the concept is not a novel one, but the casting of the variables in a different mode may, one hopes, lead to new perspectives on the conceptualization of research questions.

Questions about the use of appropriate norms have recurred from time to time in the social competency literature, and some discussion of the issues may be useful. Most generally, the question asks whether the social competency of blind children should be evaluated with respect to norms for blind children or for sighted children. As such, the question is similar to that considered earlier for the use of tests of intelligence. The question is sometimes considered in the context of the environment to which the blind child must adapt. That is, if the blind child is expected to adapt to the social world of the sighted, then he should be evaluated against norms for sighted children, whereas if he is expected to adapt to the social world of the blind, then blind norms should be used. Although the answer to this question is undoubtedly that the blind child should be able to adapt to the social world of the sighted, the specification of norms does not follow directly. The question of norms must be examined in its own right.

The use of sighted norms would seem to be justified for some research purposes, but not for the purpose of making prescriptive statements about individual blind children. Sighted norms may constitute a useful reference against which to evaluate groups of blind children in order to provide information about the areas of social development where lags do and do not occur. That is, in which areas does visual handicap impede progress, and to what specific aspects of the handicap and its interaction with development may lags be attributed? Individual differences should not be neglected in research on these questions, since knowledge may be generated about antecedent conditions (types of social interaction between parent and child) that tend to optimize development.

In two other classes of situation, however, the availability of norms for blind children would be desirable. One has to do with the evaluation of an individual blind child for the purpose of assessing his progress and prescribing possible interventions. In this case norms for blind children are clearly required, since it is with respect to the "normal" expectations for blind children that the progress of an individual child must be gauged. The other situation is the study of the effectiveness of programs provided by schools and other organizations concerned with groups of blind children.

Explanations for social maturity lags

Two types of explanation have been advanced to account for the social maturity lags of blind children. One may be characterized as involving the emotional, and the other the social aspects of interpersonal behavior.

On the emotional side, Hallenbeck (1954a) noted that one of the significant factors associated with the absence of emotional disturbance in a group of residential school blind children was "whether the child had established a good relationship with some person" before entering the school. Often it was found, in the histories of children who might otherwise have been expected to show emotional problems and did not, that the child had enjoyed a close emotional bond with a significant other. A similar question was studied by Barry and Marshall (1953). Thirty blind children, aged five to seven, were rated on a set of characteristics, such as "cooperative" and "ability to carry on simple conversations," that may be taken as a rough summary of social adequacy. Ratings of maternal rejection were also made in the family situation by a social worker. A strong negative relationship was found between the social adequacy of the children and the maternal rejection rating of the mother. Although this relationship was apparently somewhat stronger within the subgroup of 17 RLF children, it also appeared for the subgroup of children who had become blind from other causes. Tait (1972e), in discussing these and other results, suggested that such relationships may involve an intermediate step of play and exploratory behavior. As was pointed out earlier, the adequacy of exploratory behavior seems to be related to the degree of social attachment experienced by the child. To the extent that exploratory behavior is a significant and necessary step for the infant away from investment in himself and toward investment in the external world, it is reasonable to argue that exploratory behavior is also a step toward the establishment of social independence as well as adequate social relationships with people other than the parents.

Thus the importance of adequate early emotional relationships for later social adequacy is apparent. There are theoretical questions still in need of answers, however. It may be, as Tait (1972d,e) and others have suggested, that exploratory behavior and play constitute an important intermediate step on the way from early social attachment to later social competence. On the other hand, it seems reasonable to interpret the situation in terms of habits. The infant may learn that his relations with his parents are not dependable, and may thus generalize that expectation to his later social relationships with other people.

A somewhat different perspective on social competency or maturity is provided by writers whose orientation is to social role. Van Hasselt (1983), for example, cited several possible factors such as the absence or inappropriateness of feedback about social skills, adverse reactions by others to the handicap, and the difficulties experienced by blind and visually impaired children in social settings such as games. Czerwinski and Tait (1981) provided evidence that blind children do not show the same sort of developmental progression in the evaluation of abnormal social behaviors. They found in particular that the older (up to 17 years) children did not tend to regard external social influences as playing a significant part in such behaviors, whereas sighted children, increasingly with age, emphasized external social influences as determinant of abnormal social behaviors. Thus there are evidently differences between blind and sighted children in the perceptions of the casuality of social behaviors, and such differences may translate into their perspective on their own social behaviors.

Although the social role approach has not been well elaborated with respect to blind children and their socialization, Scott (1968) discussed the approach for blind adults and touched on some of the developmental issues involved in this interpretation. The notion of self-concept is basic to Scott's approach: "By 'self-concept' I mean an individual's perception of himself. A man's self-concept consists of the attitudes, feelings and beliefs he has about the kind of person he is, his strengths and weaknesses, his potentials and limitations, his characteristic qualities, and so forth. These things are expressed both in his actions and in his responses to the questions, 'Who am I?,' 'What kind of a person am I?' " (pp. 14-15). Scott went on to suggest that the self-concept is acquired in large part through interactions with other people. The expectations that other people hold play a major role in the development of self-concept. Applied to the blind, then, Scott's approach places substantial emphasis on the perceptions and expectations that other people hold of the blind person. The implications are clear that the nature of social development, and thus of the social competence or maturity, of a blind child is influenced to a large extent by the expectations that other people hold for the child. If they expect him to behave with certain limitations that they believe (whether justifiably or not) to be characteristic of blind children, then these limitations will come to be a part of the child's self-concept and thus will tend to find expression in his behavior. The implications are also clear that the blind child need not show social maturity lags—to the extent that people expect of the child that he will not differ from a sighted child, the tendency for the blind child's self-concept to be different from that of the sighted child will be decreased, and the blind child will thus behave and develop much as the sighted child does.

As discussed here, the hypothesis that blind children need not necessarily differ from sighted children in social development is clearly oversimplified. While blindness probably does not impose an overall limitation on social development, certain aspects of the tasks of social development are clearly more difficult for the blind child than they are for the sighted child. In a very real sense, the blind child has to do more with less (sensory) information than does the sighted child.The lesson from Scott's formulation, however, lies in the role of expectations in influencing the course of development. It is undoubtedly a strong tendency for the parents of blind children to expect less, or to expect differences, and these expectations may well result in lesser accomplishments and slower development.

Lairy and Harrison-Covello (1973) provided a very useful report of the developmental characteristics of a group of about 50 children with total or severe visual impairment. All were under six years of age and were presumably blind since birth or very early in life. Study was concentrated on a scale of development (a modification of the Maxfield–Buchholz scale) and on interviews with the parents and observations of the parent–child interactions. The development scale was arranged in five categories: posture, sensory-motor, sociability, speech, and autonomy. Interview and observation sessions were designed to provide information about the parents' attitudes toward the child and his handicap, and the nature and quality of the parent–child interaction. Effort was also devoted to reconstructing the history of the parents' reactions to the child's handicap.

The cases were roughly categorized into four types. Group I included those children whose developmental patterns were most nearly normal, with relatively homogeneous patterns of adequate scores in the five scale areas. About one-third of the total sample fell into this group. Less than half of these children were totally blind, and the authors noted that the children with some residual vision tended to make active use of it. The characteristics of the parental attitudes were interesting: in general, they showed a realistic acceptance of the child and his handicap. The fact that many of them had had additional children, born after the subject child, was taken as an indication of the adequacy of their responses. Group IV included children with a homogeneous low pattern on the development scale. Many had additional handicaps, and the etiology of handicaps was typically related to pervasive neurological factors. Groups II and III represented intermediate groups with mixed patterns of developmental characteristics. Group II included a disproportionate share of prematurely born children. They were characterized by low scores on the autonomy, sensory-motor, and sociability sectors and by normal scores on the postural and verbal scales. They were typically extremely passive, a behavioral mode that was apparently encouraged by parental overprotection. The authors interpreted the low scores in the selected areas as representing true developmental delays, rather than pathological arrest of development. The parental overprotective response was seen as based on an underestimation of the child's abilities. The parents typically responded well to the interviewer's analysis of their attitudes and approaches to the child, and the prognosis for the Group II children was quite positive. Group III children were characterized by good scores on the posture and autonomy scales, and by low scores on the sociability, language, and particularly the sensory-motor scales. Many had disturbances related to feeding. The low scores were interpreted as truly pathological, rather than as representing delayed normal development. Lairy and Harrison-Covello noted the similarity of the Group III syndrome to Fraiberg's characterization of "ego deviations." The developmental abnormalities were attributed largely to the parents' inability to accept the handicap and respond adequately to it. They had experienced lengthy periods of depression early in the child's life, and most of them still showed inadequate response to the child and his handicap. "Thus the child seems to be trapped in the maternal falsehood which consists of her apparent wish that he should be 'like a sighted child' and her prohibition of his existence as a blind child" (p. 12). The prognosis for these children was generally bad, and the authors anticipated that most of them would eventually become institutionalized. Thus unlike the Group IV children, whose development was hindered by neurological constraints, the Group III children had the potential for normal development but were faced with a pattern of parental response that precluded adequate development.

Collins (1982) evaluated the reactions of parents to the diagnosis of visual impairment in their children (who ranged from 0 to 8 years of age), hypothesizing that the pattern of reaction would parallel the stages in traumatic reactions to loss described by Kubler-Ross (1969). Although the suitability of the Kubler-Ross model for reaction to visual loss was not supported, Collins found similar factors of reaction, including depression, bargaining, blame, stress and burden, and acceptance. There was no regular progession of these reactions as a function of time since the diagnosis of visual impairment, and Collins concluded that the grief-and-mourning paradigm may be too limited to describe parents' reactions. The results serve to underscore the complexity of parental reactions, and to caution that any simplified manner of dealing with these reactions would surely not succeed.

As noted, the "social expectation" approach has not been developed in detail for blind children. There is, however, some evidence that suggests that this model holds promise and should be further developed. McGuinness (1970), in a study discussed earlier, found higher social maturity scores for fourth- to sixth-grade blind children who had experienced integrated school and itinerant teacher educational settings than for those who had been exposed to special schools. In discussing this result, McGuinness suggested that the fact that the integrated school and itinerant teacher children "have less opportunity to receive special help may force them to learn how to work out problems for themselves. The significantly lower scores of children from the special school setting may perhaps reflect the lowered expectations resulting from lack of competition with sighted children their own age" (p. 40). This explanation is clearly couched within the "social expectation" framework.

Lukoff and Whiteman (1970) summarized some of the socialization factors related to special school attendance. In discussing the factors that influence the choice to send the blind child to a special (usually residential) school, they noted that the earlier the onset of blindness, the more likely was attendance at a school for the blind. An interesting relationship was found between school attendance and the family's expectations for the child's independence. The pattern was different for congenitally and later blind groups. For the congenitally blind, there was relatively little difference in proportion of special school attendance for low, medium, and high expectations for independence, although a somewhat lower proportion attended special schools when family expectations for independence were low. For the youthfully blinded, however, the highest proportion (64 percent) attended special schools when there were low family expectations for independence, an intermediate proportion (45 percent) with medium expectations, and a lower proportion (35 percent) when family expectations for independence were high. The complexity of this pattern was also mirrored in the resultant social role categories into which the children fell. In general, and especially for the later blind, attendance at special schools lessened the likelihood of the child's achieving the most independent social role category. Lukoff and Whiteman discussed this and other results within the environmental context that the residential school provides: since virtually all the child's peers, as well as a fair proportion of his teachers, are visually handicapped, "The organization of the entire curriculum . . . is adapted to the vision problems of the students. . . . The entire education of these children in these schools, then, is attuned to their handicap'' (p. 92). They also argued that the pattern of friendships of blind people tends to reflect this socialization process, suggesting that ''Whether blindness serves as a sufficient basis for choosing friends, along with such factors as ethnic group and social class, hinges on the significance that the identification of blindness has for the individual'' (p. 99). In fact, they did find that attendance at a residential school increased the likelihood that a majority of the person's friends were reported also to be blind.

Mayadas (1972) conducted a study of the synchrony, or congruence, between the role expectations held by various ''significant others'' and the actual behavior of blind adolescents from a school for the blind. In addition, the subjects' self-expectations and their perception of the expectations of significant others were assessed. Synchrony was found between the social performance of the subjects and (1) the expectations of significant others (including parents, teachers, etc.), (2) the subjects' perception of the expectations of significant others, and (3) the subjects' self-expectations. There was asynchrony between the subjects' behavior and the expectations of a group of people who were ''strangers to the blind.'' The results strongly supported the notion of congruence between role expectations, both of the child himself and of those close to him, and actual behavior. A subsequent report by Mayadas and Duehn (1976) confirmed these basic conclusions, but placed somewhat more emphasis on the subject's self-expectations, while not downplaying the importance of those of significant others.

A study by Imamura (1965) also bears on the question of social behavior and the extent to which social maturity lags on the part of blind children may be a product of the social environment. The study is a useful one in that it provides a model for the study of the child's social behavior in settings involving interactions with other people, rather than simply administering an indicator test such as a social maturity scale. The blind subjects were 10 children from three to six years of age, with at most LP. Twelve sighted subjects were selected from archival files to serve as controls. The archival data were taken from a major study on cross-cultural patterns of child rearing, in which an extensive behavioral observation technique was used. The same technique was applied to the blind subjects. Several categories of behavior were observed, including dominance, nurturance, succorance, submission, sociability, self-reliance, responsibility, and sociable and nonsociable aggression. Similar categories were used to encode the mother's social behavior toward the child, including various categories of aggression, and dominance, succorance, sociability, and noncompliance. Each child was observed in social interactions in a number of five-minute periods, and the protocols were then scored by use of the behavioral categories.

Several interesting results emerged from a comparison of the social behavior of blind and sighted children. The blind children showed less initiative in initiating social contacts with the mother and with other children and adults. Of the contacts that did occur, though, the blind children made a greater proportion of sociability and succorant contacts. These contacts were generally characterized as "monotonous and repetitious." One possibility to account for the higher rate of succorant (i.e., asking for help in some way) contacts is that this is a result of maternal overprotection. This suggestion gained some support from the finding that the mothers of the blind children instigated far more contacts with the child than did the mothers of sighted children. A related suggestion was that blind children really do need help more often than sighted children. While this is undoubtedly only a partial explanation, Imamura noted that the blind children initiated "many succorant acts which are not directed toward seeking physical assistance" (p. 24). The analysis of maternal behavior in response to succorant requests from the child was also interesting: the mothers of blind children showed more frequent responses in the categories "noncompliance," "refusal," and "ignoring." When assessed in the light of the more frequent requests for succorance from blind children, the differences in rate were not striking, although the mothers of blind children did show a probability of ignoring succorant approaches that was about three times that of the mothers of sighted children, who almost never ignored their children's requests for succorance. While the mothers of blind children showed a higher probability of ignoring attention-getting succorant requests, they were somewhat less likely than the mothers of sighted children to refuse a request for real help.

Further analyses of the interactions between maternal and child behavior produced several additional patterns of difference between the blind and the sighted groups. The sighted children tended to respond to maternal dominance by a relative nonacceptance of the dominance, while the blind children tended to accept the dominance. In response to the mother's aggression, however, the blind children rejected the aggressiveness by being less submissive and more socially aggressive in return. The sighted children were more likely to show acceptance of maternal aggression. Differences also were found in the children's pattern of response to compliance by the mother. Blind children tended to show more sociable and less dominant responses, while the sighted children tended to assume a dominant role.

Imamura concluded that there are definite patterns of difference in the social interactive behavior of mothers with blind children and mothers with sighted children. The major differences were summarized as follows:

> The blind children of more dominant mothers accept the role of follower and submit, while the sighted children show no such tendency. This may be due to the fact that the more dominant mothers of the sighted children, besides being dominating, tend to be less sociable and more rejecting. The more dominant mothers of the blind children, on the other hand, have none of the negative tendencies associated with the

> more dominant mothers of the sighted children. Furthermore, they tend to ask their children for help. This act of asking for help, we suggested, may be seen as an act of inclusion (Schutz, 1958) by the mother, hence satisfying to a young child, particularly one who is blind (p. 45).

The research of Imamura is very useful in several respects. First, the subjects were younger than those studied in most other work on social interaction. Second, behavior was examined in real-life situations. The categories of behavior were carefully defined, and the reader is not confronted with the problem of inferring the validity of an indicator index such as a social maturity scale. Third, it provided an analysis of the social behavior of the child within a broader social context. Social behavior does not occur in a social vacuum, and it is necessary to consider the wider context in making comparisons between blind and sighted children.

Caution must be exercised in interpreting both the Mayadas (1972) and the Imamura (1965) work. It is unfortunately not possible to conclude a causal relation from this type of research. In Mayadas's work, it is possible that the subjects' behavior was caused at least in part by their perception of the expectations of others, but it is also possible that the expectations, both of the subjects and of the significant others, were shaped partly in response to the subjects' patterns of behavior. Research with younger children helps somewhat to clarify the causality picture. Even in the Imamura study, however, the causality situation is somewhat blurred, since it is not clear whether, for example, the greater incidence of succorant behavior among blind children is a result of or a cause of the greater incidence of the ignoring of that behavior by the mother. The problem lies not with the specific studies themselves, but rather with the descriptive research paradigm. The descriptive paradigm can be very useful, as demonstrated by the wealth of hypotheses generated in the study by Imamura. But care must be exercised not to make stronger conclusions than are warranted. The question of causality can only partly be answered, since true experimental research is out of the question in these areas. Careful longitudinal research, using the detailed analytic format exemplified by Imamura, may provide the best set of answers to questions of social development.

Sexual knowledge and behavior

One of the most severely understudied areas of social development in the blind child concerns sexual knowledge and behavior. Several writers (Cutsforth, 1951; Gendel, 1973; Scholl, 1974) have discussed the specific problems that blindness creates for the child's acquisition of knowledge about physical and behavioral aspects of sex, but there is very little evidence about just what blind children do know and how they acquire their knowledge. A study by Foulke and Uhde (1974) serves as a preliminary attack on the question of sexual knowledge at the adolescent level, but similar work is needed on younger children. It may be assumed, from the paucity of veridical information that Foulke and Uhde's adolescent informants had, that such a study would reveal quite incomplete or false notions among young children as well. Numerous writers agree that the problems of sex learning for the blind child are more difficult than those of the sighted child. Perhaps the most important fact is that the blind child's primary mode of learning, his tactual sense, is taboo when the topic of learning is sex. Both blind and sighted children are largely enjoined from gaining information about sex via tactual experience with others. Thus probably the most severe aspect of the sex-learning problem with blind children involves access to information. Of course, many blind as well as sighted children have access to information conveyed verbally by their parents, siblings, or peers. Two factors seem relevant here. One is that many parents, whether the child is blind or sighted, are hesitant to discuss sex-related matters with their children. Their recourse to the stork or cabbage-leaf explanations may be even more puzzling to the blind child than to the sighted child. The other is that often the stimulus for parental explanation is the child's question, and the child's question may often be stimulated by visual experience. Thus the blind child, lacking visual stimulation, may request fewer explanations from the parent or other informant.

Foulke and Uhde (1974) characterized the blind child's situation: "He knows about his own body because he can explore it freely. He is fairly well informed about the bodies of playmates of the same sex. He is less well informed about the bodies of playmates of the opposite sex. He is almost completely uninformed about adult bodies of either sex. By the time he reaches adolescence, he has been brought under the control of the taboos of his society, and is no longer free to explore any body but his own" (p. 194). At the same time, though, "In the course of growing up, the blind child becomes aware of the emphasis on sexuality in our culture, and a reasonable consequence of this combination of ignorance and curiosity is the creation of bizarre theories concerning the anatomy and the functions of sex" (p. 194).

Recognition of this situation has produced concern with the issue of sex education for blind children. Cutsforth (1951) discussed the issues of sex learning and behavior at some length. His approach to the issue may be fairly characterized as viewing sexual development as an integral part of social development. He noted the tendency of residential school personnel to "let sleeping dogs lie" with respect to sex, and to assume that the less made of it, the better. Cutsforth pointed out, though, that this approach probably has the effect of relegating sex primarily to fantasy life, with the corresponding loss of grounding in reality. The result is that the blind individual is ill-prepared for social–sexual interaction in the noninstitutional context into which he may enter. Cutsforth argued that an increased heterosexuality is needed in institutions, and that the potential problems attendant to integration of the sexes are minimal compared to the potential problems of individuals whose opportunities for normal social interaction are severely restricted. He reasoned that the child's sexuality would become enmeshed in a normal way in his larger social context, and that sexual behavior might thus take its proper perspective as part of the social functioning of the individual.

In recent years there has been a strong trend toward educating children actively about sex, in contrast to the relatively passive stance of responding to questions posed by the child. More active education requires that at least an implicit basic philosophy or set of goals exist. Questions may be answered on the spur of the moment without an overall plan, but a sex-education program requires a more structured approach and a set of goals. The issue for blind children is a complex one, since the question of goals is compounded by questions about how to do the teaching. It seems quite reasonable (although one could hardly expect unanimous agreement) to set the same goals for blind children as for sighted children, that knowledge about sexual functions and sexual behavior should be integrated with the larger picture of social development. Sexual knowledge should not be given undue weight, and it should not be segregated from the rest of what the child is learning. Gendel (1973) expressed this goal well: "Sexual growth and development cannot be separated from the other elements of physical, mental, social, and intellectual growth. They occur simultaneously and interdependently . . . a basic facet of sex education is to be sure that throughout the life cycle the factual as well as the philosophical aspects of the expectations of sexuality and growth are brought to the learner in the same manner as other subject areas" (p. 4).

How may this goal be accomplished specifically for the blind child? Programs have been proposed with increasing frequency, and it is not within the scope of this work to review them in detail. An example cited from Gendel (1973) may serve to provide a flavor:

> Young children may be introduced to their own bodies by feeling them. With help, ears, elbows, and knees are named as body parts while the child seeks them out on his own person. The previously neglected "missing parts" and the missing middle of the body can be felt and also be identified by their correct names—penis and vagina and urethra, etc., discussed as private, covered parts of the body. The use of accurate terminology is not the point of the activity—but rather the recognition of the respect implied in these terms . . . and the provision of a cushion against the impact of peer expressions which imply disrespect and contempt for sexual anatomy and activity. . . . Reproduction and the concept of all life coming from life is also introduced in the preschool or older program, to the level of the child's objective curiosity and delight in growth itself (p. 8).

Within the context of an institutional setting, van 'T Hooft and Heslinga (1968) suggested that sex education take place in groupings that approximate as closely as possible the family situation. (The "family situation" should probably not be held up as an ideal one, though, if the preliminary interview results of Foulke and Uhde [1974] are representative. Of the 18 boys and three girls interviewed, only nine reported having discussed sex with at least one parent. However, "The reports of six of these subjects suggest that they were misinformed by their parents" [p. 196].) Specifically, they suggested that the group should be coeducational and should include various levels of children and staff. "In this way, the institute offers children the chance to learn to get along with each other in a natural way. Older girls can be helpful in bathing little boys. Older boys and girls may sit together in the evening in a pleasant and normal way" (p. 18). Sussman, in response to Gendel's paper, also suggested the use of a peer-group model in sex education, to "go to the sources of action by finding out what the young people themselves want to know about sex, what they would like to know about their sexuality and to use that group situation as the basic socialization system" (p. 8).

The prospects for improving the situation represented in the interview results of Foulke and Uhde and discussed by many other writers would seem to be good. There is a general concern being expressed among those who work with blind children that the area of sexual knowledge should not be neglected. Bidgood (1971) reported the results of a questionnaire sent to numerous schools for the blind, agencies that work with the blind, and public schools that have programs for blind children. The vast majority of respondents indicated that they saw sex education as a responsibility of their institution, and a substantial majority reported that they either were providing sex education or were developing plans to do so. It may be hoped that future research, done perhaps a decade from now, would be able to document a good level of understanding of sex by blind children. It does seem important, though, to plan for evaluation of sex-education programs. There will undoubtedly be a wide variety of attempts at sex education for the blind, and some methods will be more successful than others. In order to make wise long-range plans for sex education, appropriate evaluation of programs must occur. The completed work of Foulke and Uhde (1974) and others currently working on the same evaluative problem may serve as a comparison against which to assess the effects of programs.

7 Personality Development

Definitions of personality are almost as numerous as writers on personality. No attempt will be made here to define the term rigorously, although a very simple definition (*Psychology Today, An Introduction*) may provide a working framework: personality is "an individual's characteristic pattern of behavior and thought." Personality is considered to include intrapersonal behavior and thought patterns as well as those patterns that are characteristic of an individual's social interactions.

There have been various attempts to characterize the personality of the blind. Some writers (Carroll, 1961) clearly consider the "blind personality" to be qualitatively different from that of sighted persons, while others (Foulke, 1972) argue that there are no necessary differences. Cutsforth (1966) also maintained that it is not productive to postulate a separate "psychology of the blind." Nevertheless, Cutsforth identified two types of reactions to blindness, both of which he saw as attempts to establish ego-importance in a social group and to maintain or regain feelings of security and self-assurance. One is the pattern of compensation, in which "the individual attempts to prove to himself and to the group that the inadequacy does not exist." The other pattern is one of retreat, "wherein the individual accepts his feelings of inadequacy as a valid evaluation of his ego-importance and establishes a false security by failing to meet life aggressively" (p. 55). However, he argued strongly that such patterns are not a necessary result of blindness itself, but result rather from the interaction of the blind individual with his social environment, including the attitudes and expectations of others and his own reactions to those attitudes and expectations. It seems reasonable, in support of this position, to suggest that the same dynamics affect the personality development of the blind child as affect that of the sighted child. There are, though, clearly important differences in the physical and social environments of blind and sighted children that may produce characteristic patterns of personality difference.

Muhl (1930) provided the results of a study on 105 blind children. The report is at best of historical interest since ages, residual visual characteristics, and etiologies were not reported for the subjects. The children, from a residential school for the blind, were tested on a series of intelligence, personality, and motor ability tests. Quantitative data were not in general reported. Nevertheless, a quote may give a flavor of the conclusions. "The personality studies revealed some remarkable characteristics, among which may be mentioned; suggestibility, acceptance without bitterness of handicap, tremendous phantasies, a feeling of inferiority, many fear reactions, good sense of humor, great curiosity, practically no hatred or suspiciousness, as general characteristics. The phantasies indicate a definite sadistic trend" (p. 568). Muhl noted, in particular, that certain characteristics need careful attention by those who work with the children, among them "the marked suggestibility, the lack of initiative (due to emotional blocking), the tendency to get discouraged" (p. 572). Despite the fact that there are apparently some contradictions contained within the results reported by Muhl, the picture that she presented was primarily a positive one. By contrast, a more recent picture presented by McGuire and Meyers (1971) was more negative. Based on their study of a sample of 27 children, they found "no evidence of a typology of personality of any kind," but common occurrence of three types of problems—"(1) an elective autistic type of behavior which was apparently not so much a withdrawal as a purposeful passive aggression; (2) defiant and upsetting behavior seeming to be a continual demonstration of power; and (3) verbalized self-concept of badness" (p. 139). The subjects included in the sample were not selected to be representative, but rather were those who "were conveniently available for observation and who otherwise met criteria of age, sufficiency of information, and absence of primary retardation or transcendent problem other than the visual" (p. 138). However, 12 of the children were drawn from an institutional setting, and despite the argument by McGuire and Meyers that the institutionalization was based on questionable criteria, it seems unlikely that the sample on which the conclusions were based was representative. Nevertheless, the picture presented by McGuire and Meyers serves as a contrast to that drawn by Muhl, and the two studies taken together underscore the difficulty of generalizing about personality in the blind child.

Personality in the Very Young Child

While there is virtually no true research on the personality characteristics of the very young blind child, there are several papers, primarily in the psychoanalytic literature, that conclude from case reports that there are various differences between blind and sighted children. Much of this material is subject to several criticisms. First, conclusions are typically based on very few cases and therefore have questionable generality. The value of the case report should not be denied, but caution must always be used in generalizing from very few cases. The second difficulty involves a frequent looseness in definitions of terms. An example may illustrate the difficulty. Burlingham (1961), in writing about anger in young blind children, stated "In the nursery our teachers are familiar with a form of anger characteristic of all children who feel under the impact of continual frustration. Alan (six years eleven months) tries to snap his belt shut which he has never been able to do alone. While doing this he repeats to himself in a whisper: 'Do it myself, do it myself,' although he is still unable to do it. The whispered words seem to express anger toward the teacher who finally comes to his help" (p. 130). The "anger" referred to in this segment is not apparent from the behavioral description, and the objectivity of the interpretation is questionable. Terms such as anger must be defined, and where subtle interpretations of overt behavior are made, the principles on which the interpretations are based must be made explicit.

Several key papers may be discussed as examples of the treatment of personality development in the young child. Burlingham (1961) suggested a framework in which both parental reactions to blindness and the experience of the child may contribute to personality development, or "the ego functions of the child." Mothers, upon discovering the handicap, may experience "feelings of injury, of hurt pride, of guilt, and of the depression which make them withdraw emotionally from the child and sometimes unconsciously or rationally wish for his death. It is only natural that the baby in this most vulnerable period reacts on his side to the mother's withdrawal and in his turn answers with passivity and withdrawal far beyond the degree caused by the visual defect itself" (p. 122). Burlingham further discussed specific areas of personality which may be affected by this mutual withdrawal of mother and infant. In the dependency area, Burlingham noted "Since vision is one of the important factors contributing to orientation and mastery of the surroundings, the blind child finds himself longer in the state in which need satisfaction is dependent on the objects which substitute in this respect for the function of his eyes. The mother on her part adds to this dependency . . . because of her sorrow, and her guilt over her death wishes, she will protect and keep the child near her, thus encouraging dependency"(p. 126-7). Nevertheless, the blind child has "the normal urge" for independence, and he may often become frustrated in his attempts to do things for himself where he really needs assistance. Burlingham made an additional point about the balance between dependence and independence: "the children do not find their dependence equally restricting if they can initiate it themselves" (p. 128). At the same time that the child fiercely tries to accomplish something by himself, he seems to be supported in his attempts by having a dependency figure available. "Often children are observed to say, 'I want to do it myself' and simultaneously to hold on to the person to whom they have directed this remark. To give expression to the double feeling: 'Don't hold me, but let me take hold of you, let me be the active one,' seems to be an intermediary step toward independence" (p. 129).

Burlingham (1961, 1979) also discussed anger briefly, although, as was mentioned earlier, it is not entirely clear just what was intended by the term. In any case, the episodes of anger that occur in six-year-old blind children "could be taken as well from seeing children, but they would then occur at an earlier age, between two to three years. The phase of conflict between dependence and independence, which is comparatively short with seeing children, has to be immeasurably longer with the blind" (p. 130). Burlingham suggested even deeper conflicts in blind children in pointing out that at the same time that they are "resentful and angry" when they compare themselves with the seeing person, they realize the extent of their real dependence on the seeing person and "merely control their anger because they realize how much they need the seeing" (p. 131). Curson (1979) made a similar point, observing that "generally, blind children are unaggressive. It is as though they cannot afford angry feelings for fear of losing the favor and love of the people on whom they are so dependent" (p. 62). While the dynamics proposed in this formulation may occur, the picture seems unnecessarily pessimistic. In any case there do not appear to be any data that support this formulation.

In writing about aggression, Burlingham noted a "comparative scarcity of free aggressive expression, as least so far as our nursery group of the blind are concerned" (p. 131). Two reasons were given for the scarcity of aggression, one the general muscular lag and the other a great dependence on other people. Blind children also show more fear of their own aggression, being "excessively sorry for every aggressive act." Two further aspects of the relative lack of aggression may be noted. First, blind children "are made uneasy by their inability to check on the consequences of an aggressive action . . . imagination at times leads them to believe that what they have done has had catastrophic results" (p. 132). If this is true, then appropriate communication from other people might serve to remove the inhibition. Second, an excessive concern on the part of the mother that the child's aggression may produce damage to others may be communicated to the child. Regarding this second point, it is difficult to see why the mothers of blind children should be more concerned than those of sighted children; comparative supporting data are apparently not available.

Burlingham (1965) argued that the passivity seen in many blind children has its roots in infancy. She cited several examples where young children were able, given appropriate motivation, to perform behaviors that they would not normally perform and of which they might therefore be judged incapable. Burlingham discussed this reluctance to perform possible behaviors in the context of competing emotions—the child realizes that certain things are much more difficult for him to do than for sighted children, he dislikes situations that remind him of his deficiency, and the combination creates inaction. Whether the dynamics of passivity as suggested by Burlingham are correct or not, the implication of the formulation seems reasonable enough. The child should not be encouraged in his passivity by oversolicitous parents, but he should rather be encouraged whenever possible to accomplish a goal on his own.

An extension of Burlingham's formulations was provided by Sandler (1963), who noted a characteristic passivity on the part of children at the blind nursery, expressed as "the tendency of these children, no matter how much they are stimulated by their teachers, to lack any sort of real creative drive toward, or interest in, the progressive mastery of the outside world" (p. 345). This lack was seen as a necessary concomitant of blindness—that is, "the present hypothesis is that the ego deformation resulting from the blindness occurs in its own right, and is linked with a path of development which basically cannot be reversed by the environment, although its outcome can be modified to a large extent by suitable mothering" (p. 346). The position is clear: the differences are seen as relatively unavoidable consequences of the lack of vision, rather than as the result of conditions that might be avoided.

Sandler argued that there are not significant developmental differences between blind and sighted infants until the fourth month or so, when the developmental patterns begin to diverge. At that time the sighted child begins to reorient from himself to the outside world, while this reorientation is retarded for the blind child. In an earlier chapter the implications of this type of difference for cognitive as well as for motor and perceptual development were discussed. The implications for personality development are also important and were couched by Sandler in terms of ego development: "The blind child may be limited . . . not only by his immediate sensory handicap, but by the lack of satisfaction he can achieve from the outside world. When he does relate to the things and people around him, his relationship seems colored by his drive to bodily gratification. In the face of frustration he will often tend to resort to repetitive self-stimulating behavior, or to lapses into passivity, and he will have the greatest difficulty in sustaining activities which do not lead to immediate somatic stimulation and discharge" (p. 355). Sandler stressed the infant's failure to turn outward as a key to the development of personality problems. This position presents a contrast to the discussion of Burlingham (1961), who placed greater emphasis on the dependence-independence conflict and on the blind child's perceived need for sighted persons. Burlingham's discussion was oriented more to the four- to six-year-old child than to the infant, though, and an argument could be made that the basis for later dependency problems lies in the earlier failure to turn outward adequately. The possibility of such a causal sequence has not been analyzed, however, and the formulation seems somewhat tenuous.

Both Wills (1970) and Fraiberg (1968) have noted the lack or suppression of aggression in the blind child. Both authors added the notion that this lack may be partly formulated in terms of the cognitive development of the child. According to Fraiberg, "A blind baby may be well endowed with aggression, but in the second or third year and even later, we will see a very different pattern of discharge from that of the sighted child. We have almost no examples from our blind young children of 'fighting back.' . . . The pattern is one of gross discharge of rage, without aim or object. . . . And how, in fact, does the child without vision construct a causal sequence in which he can attribute to someone outside of himself an action or a sequence of actions that have affected him and frustrated his own wishes?'' (p. 297). This conceptual difficulty was echoed by Wills (1970), who also provided a link in her formulation to the dependence-independence situation. She noted that the blind child may have more difficulty in realizing that the mother is the same person in situations where she is angry and where she is loving. ''In fact, the blind child may be in serious trouble if he does not have a sufficiently stable inner representation of his mother as a basically loving person by the time he clashes with her'' (p. 473). Wills' suggestion for ameliorating this potential problem seems reasonable enough: ''Encourage mothers to give such children as much positive experience in the early years as they can. For instance, they should keep the child in close contact and try to avoid further separations; they should look for enjoyable experiences for him, and so on. This would . . . enable him to make some compromise, some fusion, in his feelings and their expression'' (pp. 478–479).

Fraiberg (1968) pointed to another possible result of the blind infant's difficulty in turning outward to other people and the external world. She cited evidence to the effect that the ''blind child is slow in achieving a stable mental representation of the mother and a belief in object permanence'' (p. 296). For the sighted child, the ''consistency'' of the parent allows him to incorporate the parent's characteristics into his play, thereby serving a function in the developing identification of the child with the parent. ''The variety of imitative and imaginative games which a sighted child in the second year demonstrates tells us how he incorporates the qualities and characteristics of his human protectors and makes them his own. We have no parallels for the blind child in the second year and we begin to see fragmentary forms of such identifications only in the third and fourth years'' (pp. 296–297). The lag cited in this quote is especially impressive since the subjects were those from Fraiberg's longitudinal group which is thought to be relatively advantaged by the ''educational program'' as well as, for the most part, more than adequate parents.

Fraiberg and Freedman (1964), like Sandler, pointed to divergent development in the early part of the first year as a basis for patterns of personality disturbance in some blind children. The seven children under consideration in the paper ranged in age from three to 13 years, but the material is appropriate to this section on infancy because of the heavy stress on infant etiological factors. The emotional disturbance in these children was more severe than that of the children discussed by Sandler and others: ''The child may be two years old, five years, nine, or even thirteen years old and the picture is almost unvarying. Typically the deviant child spends hours in bed or in a chair or lying on the floor, absently mouthing an object. . . . Contact with human objects is often initiated by biting and even more often by a primitive clutching and clawing with the hands. For all these children the mouth remains the primary organ of perception'' (p. 115). In interpreting this pattern of behavior, Fraiberg and Freedman noted that ''The deviant blind children showed a uniform developmental arrest and a freezing of personality on the level of mouth primacy and nondifferentiation. These and certain details in the retrospective histories suggested that the process of ego formation had been impeded during the critical period nine to eighteen months'' (p. 113). Fraiberg and Freedman discussed two interdependent factors as being implicated in the problems: ''(1) blindness as a communications barrier between mother and infant with extraordinary demands upon the mother's own adaptive capacity; (2) blindness as an impediment during critical phases of ego formation with extraordinary demands upon an infant's adaptive capacity'' (p. 152). The second point is analogous to that discussed by Sandler, but Fraiberg and Freedman placed much more emphasis on the role of the parent in influencing the course of the infant's ''ego development.'' It should be noted that the children considered by Sandler were not cases of severe developmental arrest, like those discussed by Fraiberg and Freedman, and it seems reasonable to suggest that it is the combined effect of the two factors that may produce severe difficulties in ego development. Fraiberg and Freedman also noted that the blindness factor itself does not necessarily produce developmental arrest: ''We must assume from the evidence presented by large numbers of healthy and educable blind children that other sensory modalities can substitute for vision in the process of ego formation'' (p. 114).

Severe emotional disturbance will be treated at more length in a later section. In this section on infancy, it suffices to say that the observational data are persuasive that severe emotional disturbance often has its roots in early infancy, and that it is undoubtedly the result of a complex interaction of perceptual, cognitive, and interpersonal factors. The desirability of counseling for parents of blind infants is obvious.

Personality Assessment of Blind Children

Even more than of intelligence testing, it may be said of personality testing that there has been insufficient attention to the adequate personality assessment of the blind child. There have been few attempts to standardize instruments on blind samples.

Lebo and Bruce (1960) reviewed the uses of projective tests with the blind. The bulk of the studies that they cited did not deal with children. The relative scarcity of projective test data with blind children has continued since 1960, although there are exceptions (Chase & Rapaport, 1968). One of the most serious problems with the use of projective tests with the blind, as discussed by Lebo and Bruce, applies equally to adults and children. There is an unfortunate tendency for each new researcher to develop his own test, adding to the substantial number of tests about which little is known. A good example is the large number of auditory projective tests, all somewhat different and having similar names. It is no less true of the projective test approach than of the inventory approach to personality assessment, that effective use of a test requires an extensive norming basis. Well-known tests such as the Rorschach derive their usefulness from the availability of a vast quantity of prior information about how the tests work. Certainly the skill of the tester is important, but test-interpretation skill depends heavily on an accumulation of use of the test, so that the results for one subject may be compared with those of many other previous subjects. In order for projective assessment with the blind to become effective, attention will have to be channeled to relatively few tests so that an adequate interpretive base may be built.

There has been more concentration on a smaller number of personality inventories. Perhaps the greatest amount of testing of the blind child has been done using the California Personality Inventory, although other inventories have been adapted for use with the blind, especially adolescents. It is apparent, however, that extreme care must be taken in interpreting the test results of blind children when the test was designed and standardized for sighted samples. Simply omitting items that make direct reference to or use of sight is an inadequate approach to the adaptation of a test for the blind. The meaning of a particular inventory scale depends on the composite of items that form the scale, and it is not clear that the results on a modified scale (with a subset of items deleted) would have the same meaning as those from the entire scale. Bateman (1965) stated these issues clearly:

> [We] must ask 'How meaningful is it to administer, in unmodified form, an item which isn't entirely suitable or relevant for a blind child?' On the other hand, 'How appropriate is it to modify an item without such modification being explicitly in line with the standardization procedure?' The problems . . . suggest that total reliance on standardized procedures is perhaps impossible and/or foolhardy. But the alternative of clinical interpretation and informal testing and observational techniques should be based on 'built-in' standards for blind children's behavior. . . . In short, heavy reliance on clinical judgment alone does not seem much more feasible than does mechanical applications [sic] of standardized measures (p. 193).

The most desirable approach would be to develop personality assessment instruments specifically for use with blind children. The development of a new instrument requires a substantial investment of resources if a sufficient usage base is to be built. Bauman, Platt, and Strauss (1963) have made an impressive start on the development of the Adolescent Emotional Factors Inventory (AEFI). The instrument is unfortunately not useful for preteen children. It is clear that before adequate evaluation of personality characteristics can be conducted with blind children, a great deal of focused attention must be devoted to the development and norming of suitable instruments.

Personality Characteristics of Blind Children

Despite the difficulties in administering and interpreting standardized personality tests for blind children, there has been considerable effort directed to the comparison of various groups of blind children, and to the comparison of blind with sighted children. The results of this research will be reviewed in this section. It should be noted at the outset that there is little evidence available on young blind children. Many of the studies have used adolescent subjects, and there is even a wider age gap in the personality literature than there is in the perceptual and cognitive areas.

It is convenient to make a rough distinction between those personality characteristics that involve interpersonal functioning and those that are intrapersonal characteristics. The two categories will be considered in turn.

Interpersonal personality characteristics

Social adjustment. Several studies have provided information about the relative "social adjustment" of blind and sighted children. The term social adjustment, however, has been used quite generally, and it is often not clear what the implications for prevention or treatment of social adjustment problems are. Hastings (1947) found no differences, as measured by the California Test of Personality, in social adjustment between blind and sighted children in grades one to 12. Brieland (1950), on the other hand, did find differences in favor of sighted children, age 12 to 18, on the social adjustment measure of the Bell Adjustment Inventory. Petrucci (1953) reported that blind high school students "felt the need for sociability" 78 percent more than sighted norms. The Bernreuter Personality Inventory was used for assessment. Pintner and Forlano (1943) compared partially sighted children with sighted norms and found little difference in either home or school adjustment. There was evidence of a greater lag among the partially sighted children in the group comprised of fourth grade and below, but there is some question whether the Pupil Portraits Test, used in the study, is valid below the fourth grade. Sommers (1944) administered the California Test of Personality orally to braille-reading adolescents, age 14 to 21. Although the scores were somewhat lower than sighted norms for the test, Sommers concluded that the administration to blind children of a personality test designed for and normed on sighted subjects is inappropriate.

The studies of social adjustment leave much to be desired. It is not clear just what form social "maladjustment" takes, and therefore preventive and remedial procedures are not apparent from the research. Furthermore, much of the work does not provide detailed information about possible age differences in social adjustment. There are important changes in the social environment and the social demands placed on the child over the school-age range, and research is needed that distinguishes carefully the social adjustment that occurs in the various periods of social growth.

Introversion–extroversion. Several investigators have reported results from measures of introversion–extroversion. Petrucci (1953) administered the Bernreuter Personality Inventory, which includes an introversion–extroversion scale, to 32 high school students. Comparison of their results with sighted norms showed 67 percent more introversion in the blind group. Unfortunately, no information about the characteristics of the blind sample was provided. Brown (1938) compared adolescents, ranging in age from 16 to 22 and drawn from schools for the blind, with a group of sighted high school seniors on the Neymann–Kohlstedt Diagnostic Test for Introversion–Extroversion. The overall differences between blind and sighted samples was not significant, but the comparison may be invalid since the age range of the blind sample, 16 to 22 years, was probably much wider than that of the sighted sample, who were all high school seniors. In addition, the blind subjects were from residential schools, and Brown pointed out that they may thus not have had as much exposure to "home life" as the sighted sample. Comparison of blind males with blind females showed the males to be more extroverted. A somewhat similar result was found by Pintner and Forlano (1943) in their comparison of partially sighted subjects with sighted norms on the Extroversion–Introversion scale of the Aspects of Personality Test. The age range of the children was not precisely identified, although it apparently extended from below fourth grade to above seventh grade. The degree of loss of the partially sighted children was not given, but the subjects were in "sight saving" classes and performed on the test using large print. Partially sighted males scored very close to the sighted norm for extroversion throughout the age range. The partially sighted girls, by contrast, were far below the sighted norms on extroversion through the sixth grade. At seventh grade and above, the partially sighted girls were about equal to the partially sighted males, but still somewhat below the sighted norm. Zahran (1965) administered, among other tests, the Junior Maudsley Personality Inventory to blind and sighted nine- to 14-year-olds and did not find significant differences in extroversion, athough the blind were somewhat more introverted. There were no sex differences for blind or sighted subjects.

Thus, although there is some disagreement among studies, blind children generally show somewhat lower extroversion scores than sighted children. The relationship of extroversion to age has not been well studied. Several results converge on the conclusion that blind males show higher extroversion scores than blind females. It is an interesting but unanswered question whether the differences that emerge from personality inventory results would also appear if behavior were evaluated directly. In particular, it would be interesting to know for both sexes now extroverted behavior varies within predominantly male, predominantly female, and mixed-sex social situations.

Assertiveness–submissiveness. Factors apparently related to this dimension appear under several other names, such as dependency (Wilson, 1967) and succorance (Imamura, 1965). Petrucci (1953), in the study mentioned earlier, found blind high schoolers to be 22 percent more submissive, 71 percent less self-confident, and 73 percent less self-sufficient than sighted norms, according to results from the Bernreuter Personality Inventory. Greenberg and Jordan (1957), also using the Bernreuter, did not find a difference in dominance between totally blind (including LP) and partially sighted adolescents. They did, however, find the totally blind group to be less authoritarian as assessed by the California "F" Scale. Greenberg, Allison, Fernell, and Rich (1957) cited results from the Bernreuter showing that both boys and girls in grades six through 10 in a residential school scored low on dominance, while the 11th and 12th graders averaged near the 50th percentile. Children at all grade levels from six to 12 were low on the self-sufficiency scale, and all showed weaknesses on the self-confidence scale. Wilson (1967), in discussing psychological factors in mobility, noted that the self-confidence needed for effective mobility may be lacking in the blind child, and he attributed much of the fear on which the child's low self-confidence is based to parental fear that is communicated to the child.

A useful study of several aspects of dependency was provided by Imamura (1965), who compared blind children ranging in age from three to six with a comparison group of sighted children. Among the types of behavior evaluated were several related to dependency, including dominance, succorance (requesting help), submission, and self-reliance. The children were rated on these characteristics in series of observational sessions. The blind children showed a significantly higher rate of succorant acts than the sighted controls, but there were no differences on the other categories relating to dependency.

Pintner and Forlano (1943) assessed the ascendance–submission of partially sighted grade school children. The boys showed steadily increasing quartile scores for ascendance as compared to sighted norms, while the scores for the girls indicated about average ascendance except in the group at fourth grade and below, where the scores were generally lower than sighted norms.

In sum, the evidence points to somewhat greater dependency or submissiveness among blind children, although the pattern is by no means clear. Attention should be drawn to a previous section in which findings on dependency and assertiveness in blind infants were discussed (Burlingham, 1961, 1965; Sandler, 1963; Wills, 1970). There is a great need for careful study of age-related changes. The research model presented by Imamura is a useful one in that it does not depend on the comparison of blind children to sighted on tests that are designed for the sighted.

Aggression, hostility. Several reports provide information about indices of interpersonal aggressiveness and hostility. Imamura (1965), in her study of blind three- to six-year-old children, found no differences in frequency of occurrence of either sociable aggression (aggression with the intent of being sociable) or nonsociable aggression (aggression with the intent of harm) between blind and sighted samples. McGuire and Meyers (1971), on the other hand, found a strikingly high incidence of various kinds of aggressiveness directed toward the mother, including hostility toward mother doll or mother figure in therapy (73 percent of cases), negative or hostile verbalization toward mother (87 percent), and physically punitive behavior toward the mother (73 percent). The 27 blind children ranged in age from middle childhood through adolescence. The sample included 12 children who were in a program for the blind–retarded, but McGuire and Meyers raised doubt as to whether these children were appropriately classified as retarded: they were ''ablebodied other than the blindness, young, and with histories of creating difficulty because of being withdrawn or acting out'' (p. 138). The inclusion of these 12 subjects in the sample of 27 makes it doubtful that the sample could be taken as representative of blind children in general, at least on dimensions relating to aggressiveness and hostility, and so the extremely high frequencies of aggressive behaviors must be viewed with caution.

Jervis and Haslerud (1950), in their study of adolescent responses to frustration, categorized the responses of blind, sighted, and blindfolded sighted subjects in frustrating game situations as extrapunitive, intropunitive, or impunitive. The blind subjects, all blind before the age of two and from schools for the blind, showed more intropunitive and fewer extrapunitive and impunitive responses than the sighted subjects. That is, the blind subjects did not attribute their failure to external sources as much as did sighted subjects. Rather, the blind expressed more self-blame than the sighted.

Aggression and hostility are difficult factors to assess even in the best of situations. It is generally agreed that intent must be considered in judging whether or not a given behavior is to be classified as aggressive, and intent is at best an ephemeral variable. Further, aggression should ideally be subcategorized as verbal or physical, and as self- or other-directed. Neither of these factors has been effectively studied in blind children. ''Passive'' aggression has not been well differentiated in research on the blind child. In view of these definitional problems, it is not surprising to find apparent contradictions between, for instance, McGuire and Meyers' excessively high aggression frequencies and Jervis and Haslerud's relatively low extrapunitive scores in blind subjects. Further, age is again an important factor, since it is widely accepted that modes of aggressive behavior are highly subject to socialization influences. Although some discussion of aggressiveness is found in the psychoanalytic literature on infants (Burlingham, 1961; Fraiberg, 1968; Wills, 1970), no information is available on which to base conclusions about the developmental continuity of aggressiveness.

Intrapersonal personality characteristics

Moral development. In the same study in which they evaluated the reasoning abilities of blind children, Stephens and Simpkins (1974) assessed the moral judgment and the moral conduct of blind children ranging in age from six to

18. Moral judgment was assessed from the child's responses to a series of hypothetical situations involving rules, transgressions, and punishments. Moral conduct was assessed from the child's behavior in structured test situations. In general, there were no marked differences between the blind children and a control group of sighted childen. On moral judgment, the sighted children made more mature judgments where differences did occur, but the blind children gave evidence of generalizing moral judgments more than the sighted. There were virtually no differences between blind and sighted groups on the moral conduct phase.

Self-concept. The term self-concept has been used in two apparently unrelated contexts. One is the cognitive context where self-concept refers to the child's ability to distinguish conceptually between himself and other objects and people in the world. The other context has to do with self-evaluation, or how well the child thinks of himself. The distinction of self from world has been discussed in Chapter 1, and the self-evaluation aspect of self-concept will be considered here.

Jervis (1959) reported a study of the self-concepts of totally blind and sighted residential school adolescents, aged 15 to 19. Data were gathered from an interview and from a card-sorting task. On the card-sorting task, in which the subject selected cards containing statements which he considered applicable to himself, there was no significant difference in self-concept between the blind and sighted groups, although there were more blind subjects with extreme scores (both highly positive and highly negative). The interview was structured around a series of stimulus questions, and the responses were rated by two psychologists. Unfortunately, the reliability of the interview scoring was very low (0.65). There was no significant difference between the interview results of the blind and the sighted groups. One interesting difference did emerge from the interview results, however. Most of the blind subjects expressed concern or uncertainty about their future, while most of the sighted subjects were quite positive about their future.

Zunich and Ledwith (1965) administered Lipsitt's (1958) self-concept scale to sighted and blind boys and girls in the fourth grade. Each child judged how well or poorly adjectives such as friendly, trusted, lazy, and jealous applied to himself. There were no overall differences between blind and sighted groups. There was some indication that blind girls showed more positive self-concepts than their sighted controls, and blind boys more negative. Given the number of items, however, the number of significant differences on individual items was not greater than would be expected by chance. A finding similar to that of Jervis (1959) emerged in that the blind children tended to use the extremes of the scales more frequently than did the sighted.

More recently, Meighan (1971) studied self-concept in adolescents, using the Tennessee Self Concept Scale (TSCS). The subjects, who ranged in age from 14 to 20, all attended schools for the blind. Compared to the norm sighted group for the TSCS, the 120 totally blind and 83 partially sighted subjects fared significantly more negatively on all subscales. Although there is no direct basis on which to question the findings, the validity of the results seems questionable on two counts. First, Meighan noted an "extraordinary homogeneity" in the results of the visually impaired sample on the TSCS. This finding contradicts the generally higher variability normally found for most variables in most samples of visually impaired subjects, and more specifically it contradicts the findings of Jervis (1959) with respect to variability in self-concept measures. Second, the absence of significant correlations between TSCS scores and Stanford and other achievement test scores, which were also taken by Meighan (1971), is bothersome and suggests lack of TSCS validity for the sample. Head (1979) also used the TSCS with a sample of low vision and blind adolescents, grade range seven to 12, and varying in school placement (residential school, resource room, and itinerant teacher settings). The sample, like that of Meighan (1971), was varied with respect to race, sex, and academic performance. TSCS scores were analyzed with respect to two factors, visual status (blind vs. low vision) and educational setting. Neither variable accounted for significant variance in the TSCS scores. Coker (1979), using the Piers-Harris Self Concept Scale, also found no difference between integrated school and residential school samples of visually impaired children, grades three to six.

As is the case for many of the variables of personality, the work on self-concept is less than fully satisfying. Cook-Clampert (1981) pointed out that the research is often methodologically flawed, and, as noted above, some of the results do not fit well with expectations based on other research. Further, and perhaps most fundamentally, one may question the value of studying in the first place whether self-concept is higher or lower in visually impaired or sighted children, or in residential school or integrated school children, unless the research also studies the functional importance of such differences.

A study by Jervis and Haslerud (1950) on response to frustration was discussed earlier, but it bears on this section as well. Blind adolescents, aged 15 to 18, showed a much greater frequency of intropunitive verbalizations in response to frustrating puzzle situations than did sighted control subjects. Intropunitive responses may be interpreted as self-deprecating, or as indicative of a less good self-concept. Both extrapunitive (attributing blame to others) and impunitive (intellectualization of blame, thought to be more emotionally mature) responses were proportionately less frequent among the blind.

Locus of control is a term used to describe a person's perception of whether he is in command of the events that affect his life, and as such it is related to self-concept. Internal locus of control describes the individual who sees himself as exercising substantial control over his life, while external locus of control describes the individual who sees himself as being relatively highly controlled by other people or by situational variables. Land and Vineberg (1965) administered the Bialer-Cromwell Children's Locus of Control Scale to two groups of blind children and one group of sighted children. One group of blind children was drawn from residential schools and the other from the public school system. Ages ranged from six to 14 years, and the blind subjects had been blind since before the age of five. The two blind groups did not differ from one another, but both blind groups showed significantly less internal locus of control than the sighted control group. There were no differences attributable to the severity of the visual loss. With increasing mental age, locus of control was found to become more internal. This trend occurred for both blind and sighted children: both higher MA blind children and higher MA sighted children gave more indication of internal locus of control. Thus the developmental trend was similar for blind and sighted children, but the blind children showed a developmental lag rather than a general failure to acquire internal locus of control. There was also greater variability within the blind groups: some blind children scored as high on internal locus of control as did the highest sighted children. Land and Vineberg suggested that their results showed an "overprotest on the part of some blind subjects in respect to their ability to handle the world" (p. 259). They also discussed the importance of the environment in producing internal locus of control, however, and in particular the important role that parents play. The developmental dynamics of this personality variable deserve much more intensive study. In addition to the evaluation of locus of control itself, attention should be devoted to the degree to which children actually do exercise control over events, since this degree undoubtedly varies widely both within and between groups of blind and sighted children.

Tait (1972e) also discussed some implications of locus of control. The sighted child has some degree of control over the frequency of his interactions with other people in that he can make use of eye contact. He can determine when the parent's attention is oriented elsewhere and direct his own behavior accordingly. The relative inability of the blind child to make this determination may lead, as the data of Imamura (1965) suggest, to a greater proportion of nonresponse by the parent to the child's requests for attention or help. As Tait pointed out, this difference produces a relatively lesser degree of control by the blind child over his social interactions, and it may contribute to the blind child's tendency, noted in various contexts, to keep his attention turned inward rather than turning it outward to the world.

A dimension somewhat related to the self-concept material is level of aspiration. McAndrew (1948a,b) assessed level of aspiration in groups of blind and sighted children between 10 and 15 years of age by asking for estimates of how firmly the child thought he could squeeze a hand dynamometer. There were no striking differences between the blind and sighted groups, although there was some indication of a greater sensitivity to failure to meet the estimated level in the blind.

Self-concept is clearly a complicated issue. Studies that have measured a general self-concept (Jervis, 1959; Zunich & Ledwith, 1965) have found no overall differences between blind and sighted children, although Meighan (1971) is an exception. However, differences have been found in some studies of components of self-concept, such as locus of control (Land & Vineberg, 1965). It is certain that the dynamics that influence aspects of self-concept are complex. It is desirable to study these variables from both the inventory approach (e.g., Lipsitt's self-concept scale) and the behavioral approach (i.e., observing behavioral indicators of aspects of self-concept), and to evaluate their functional importance. Assuming that a positive self-concept is demonstrably advantageous, careful evaluation of variables that affect aspects of self-concept is needed in order to make suggestions about ways to enhance the self-concept of the blind child.

Temperament. A dimension that has received very little attention in blind children is temperament. Chess and Fernandez (1976) discussed the usefulness of the temperament concept in accounting for variations in the behavior of a variety of normal and clinical cases, and they described the use of their nine-category typology with a group of rubella children, including some with varying degrees of visual loss. Thus their findings were not specific to visually impaired children in general, but the typology of aspects of temperament should prove useful in future work. Although the notion of the innateness of temperamental differences among sighted children has waxed and waned in the history of child development, the position that there are important interactions between the infant's temperamental "style" and parental responses to it seems almost indisputable. Careful study of temperament in blind children should prove interesting and useful.

Neuroticism. Brown (1939) and Petrucci (1953) both reported greater tendencies toward neuroticism in blind adolescents than in sighted controls. Brown administered the Clark Revision of the Thurstone Personality Schedule to blind subjects drawn from residential schools, age range 16 to 22, and to a group of sighted high school seniors. The attempt was made to exclude items that were inappropriate for the blind, or to change them to suit the blind. The overall comparison of blind and sighted samples showed a significantly greater neuroticism score for the blind. Analysis by sex, however, showed that most of the overall difference between blind and sighted groups was attributable to the highly neurotic scores for the blind girls. The sighted females were also significantly more neurotic than the sighted males, but the sex difference was much greater in the blind group. The sighted males showed the least neurotic scores, while the blind males were about equal to the sighted females. Petrucci (1953) reported that blind high school students were 70 percent more neurotic than sighted controls, as assessed by the Bernreuter Personality Inventory. Sex differences were not reported. Greenberg et al. (1957), also using the Bernreuter, found blind adolescents from grades six to 12 in a residential school to score high on the neuroticism scale. Zahran (1965) used the Junior Maudsley Personality Inventory with blind and sighted children, age nine to 14. Although the blind showed somewhat higher neuroticism scores, the difference was not significant. Similarly Greenberg and Jordan (1957) found no differences in neuroticism between partially sighted and totally blind adolescents on the Bernreuter scale.

Overall scores on neuroticism scales are somewhat unsatisfactory, since the term neuroticism applies to a range of more specific difficulties. One such aspect of neuroticism is anxiety. Hardy (1968) described the development of the Anxiety Scale for the Blind (ASB), which he designed to provide a more suitable instrument for the blind than the traditional Taylor Manifest Anxiety Scale (TMAS). Items were written and subjected to intensive screening by panels of clinicial experts. The ASB and the TMAS were each administered twice to 122 adolescents ranging in age from 13 to 22 and varying in intelligence and degree of remaining vision. Teacher ratings of students were also solicited. The correlations between teacher ratings of anxiety and the ASB results were statistically significant but not impressive (0.20 to 0.30 range). On the other hand, the correlation between the ASB and the TMAS was 0.74. The group was divided, on the basis of severity of visual loss, into groups of totally blind, LP blind, and those with "relatively useful vision." There were no marked variations in anxiety scores across the three subgroups, although there was a tendency for the LP group to score somewhat higher in anxiety. Finally, anxiety scores increased somewhat with increasing age. Some interesting relationships among degree of vision, sex, intelligence, and anxiety scores were also reported.

Miller (1970) found similar results using the ASB: no differences emerged between partially sighted and blind samples of ninth through twelfth graders, or between special class (EMR) and the regular residential school sample. Like Hardy (1968), Miller found an increase in anxiety with increasing grade placement. Miller attributed the increased anxiety to the older children's impending departure from the relatively secure residential school environment.

Studies such as those of Hardy (1968) and Miller (1970) are of much more potential value than studies using a more general neuroticism index. It is unfortunate that more has not been done with other aspects of neuroticism than anxiety, since it is from the more specific work that useful approaches to the handling of these problems will come.

Emotional adjustment. Several writers have reported evaluations of the comparative emotional adjustment of blind and sighted children. It should be noted at the outset that the term emotional adjustment is a difficult one to define, and it is more difficult yet to operationalize and measure. Rarely in the literature is specific information given about what is intended by emotional maladjustment. The usage of some writers clearly implies a component of adjustment in social situations, while that of others implies some characteristic that is not dependent on a social context for its expression. The notion of emotional adjustment should undoubtedly be separated into various facets. Intrapersonal adjustment should be distinguished from interpersonal adjustment. Types of emotion (joy, anger) should be distinguished from the strength or frequency of occurrence of emotions.

Given the vagueness of the term emotional adjustment, it is not surprising that much of the work that has studied it is not very satisfying. An example is a study by Morgan (1944), who administered the Personal Index, by Loofbourow and Keys (n.d.), to a group of 128 children, aged 12 and older (average 15.8) from a residential school. The test consisted of three scales, False Vocabulary, Social Attitudes, and Adjustment Questionnaire. The Adjustment Questionnaire was designed to assess emotional instability. The responses of the blind sample were compared to norms for normal sighted boys as well as for delinquent boys. The tests had not, however, been normed on blind children. The results were not broken down by subtest. The distributions of scores for the blind boys and girls did not differ markedly, but the blind overall tended to score lower than the norm for sighted boys. In fact, the incidence of maladjustment in the blind children was more similar to that for a group of reform school boys than to that of the normal boys. This result should be viewed with caution, since norms for blind children were not available. There is also no evidence that an attempt was made to adapt the tests to the blind, aside from requiring the responses to be made in braille. In fact, the total testing time for the blind was over two hours, as compared with 35 minutes for the sighted children, and so the validity of the test for blind children is in serious question. Hastings (1947, cited by Barker, 1953) compared the emotional adjustment, as measured by the California Test of Personality and Mental Health Analysis, of blind and sighted children in grades one through 12. Since vital characteristics such as age, intelligence, and method of test administration differed between the blind and sighted samples, the results should be evaluated cautiously. However, the blind were found to be more disturbed on the self-adjustment scale and to have more mental health liabilities, but not to score worse on the social adjustment scale. Brieland (1950), in a study primarily concerned with speech characteristics, administered the Bell Adjustment Inventory by tape recording to blind and sighted subjects, age range 12 to 18. The overall difference on the inventory was significantly in favor of the sighted group. Subscales involving health, social, and emotional adjustment were in favor of the sighted, while there was no significant difference in home adjustment.

Sommers (1944) administered the California Test of Personality to 143 students, aged 14 to 21 and drawn from residential schools. The mean percentile score for the blind on the self-adjustment scale was 46.5, while on the social adjustment scale it was 41.7. Sommers argued, however, that tests that are normed on sighted samples may not be appropriate for blind samples. She conducted subsequent work using an interview format. Of the 50 adolescent subjects, only seven were classified as having "wholesome compensatory reactions," while the remaining 43 were divided among categories including hypercompensatory, denial, defensive, withdrawing, and nonadjustive reactions. Sommers found substantial relationships between the degree of maladjustment and the attitudes of the parents toward the child and his disability.

The work of Sommers deserves special mention from a methodological point of view. In particular, it is noteworthy that in addition to the use of a standardized personality test (although it was standardized on sighted samples), Sommers used a questionnaire format with both the blind children and their parents as well as a structured interview situation. With such a research design, it is possible to gain some picture of the validity of any one of the measures by comparing its results with those from the other measures. The inclusion of a behavioral observation level, such as that used by Imamura (1965), would have given a still fuller picture. As it was, the interview and questionnaire results provided a useful background against which to evaluate the results of the California Test of Personality.

Bauman (1964) investigated differences between residential and nonresidential blind students using the Adolescent Emotional Factors Inventory (AEFI). Partially sighted subjects were also compared to subjects without useful vision. Considerable detail was given about specific items that differentiated effectively between subgroups. In general, though, the residential school group showed more problems of social and emotional adjustment. Further, the partially sighted group was less well adjusted than the totally blind group: the partially sighted "reflect a greater sense of tension and pressure . . . are definitely more suspicious, give more of the mildly paranoid responses . . . feel less able to meet the demands of family and school . . . lack self-confidence" (p. 105). Morgan (1944) had found a similar difference in favor of totally blind over partially sighted adolescents. Pintner and Forlano (1943), on the other hand, did not find remarkable differences between partially sighted school children and sighted norms for the Emotional Stability index from the Aspects of Personality Test.

This sampling of work on emotional adjustment does present a picture of differences between blind and sighted children, with blind children showing more maladjustment. However, there are serious difficulties with the set of results, the most important of which is that it is not clear what emotional maladjustment is, or what should be done about it, or whether "adjustment" might be an entirely different variable for blind and sighted children. Studies that have used standardized tests are subject to the criticism that in general these tests are not normed for blind children and therefore may not be valid for the blind. Perhaps more important yet is that the concept of emotional adjustment is so global as to be of little use. That is, we are not aided in helping a particular child, or in designing a suitable environment for blind children in general, by knowing that blind children are more likely to be "emotionally maladjusted." Much more work is needed with adequate definitions of concepts and adequate ways of measuring the variables in question.

Serious emotional disturbance

The incidence of serious emotional disturbance in blind children is high enough that the blind–emotional disturbance category is regarded by some as a multiple handicap. In his review of the Study of Services to Blind Children in New York State, Cruickshank (1964) found that in the group of 2236 children for whom reports of emotional characteristics were available, emotional problems were reported in 790, or about one-third of the sample. The use of numbers to represent the incidence of emotional disturbance should not be allowed to hide the fact that there is no clear set of criteria for defining the handicap. In particular, there is no clear distinction between "emotional maladjustment" as discussed in the previous section and "serious emotional disturbance." The distinction is at best one of degree of severity. In this section, the more serious aspects of emotional maladjustment will be discussed.

A working characterization of what is meant by serious emotional disturbance may emerge from descriptions of cases. Blank (1959), for example, presented a case report of a young girl who was "unresponsive to teachers and other children. . . . Kicking and screaming were her characteristic responses to stimulation. . . . . Her enunciation was defective almost to the point of incomprehensibility and her speech served no function of communication" (pp. 242–243). Three major points are represented in the quote, social unresponsiveness, abnormal responsiveness to perceptual stimulation, and language dysfunction. These points have received repeated mention by various authors. Green and Schechter (1957), in their presentation of several case reports, stressed the lack of effective verbal communication. They suggested that an important part of the etiology of such disorders is an extreme symbiosis that may develop in the relationship between mother and blind child: the mother develops the ability to anticipate the needs of the child and therefore does not give the child opportunity to develop effective broader communication. Maintenance of the symbiosis then serves the needs of both mother and child, with the result that the child is unprepared for communication with other people. Haspiel (1965) also noted a high incidence of speech and communication disorders in a group of emotionally disturbed blind children. The auditory potential of these children appeared to be normal, but the functional use of audition was severely limited.

Keeler (1958) described the commonality among a group of five preschool children, all blind due to RLF, and noted the similarity of the syndrome to autism. The children showed "self-isolation and . . . lack of the use of language for the purpose of interpersonal communication . . . showing no effort to initiate any activity whatsoever. When spoken to they would not respond. . . . They appeared to make the same type of contact with complete strangers as they would with their own mothers. Two of them became very disturbed if any physical contact was made with them whatsoever. These children manifested autistic patterns of activity such as rhythmically rocking back and forth, usually to music. They . . . preferred playing with things which would make a noise or were of a mechanical nature'' (p. 65). In discussing possible reasons for the behavior syndrome, Keeler noted that the maternal response was quite similar to that of neglect and rejection often associated with parents of sighted autistic children.

Omwake and Solnit (1961), in their description and analysis of one case history, stressed the sensory aspects of emotional disturbance. They argued that the function that vision normally serves in organizing and interpreting sensations received via the other modalities is absent, with the result that the child is overwhelmed by those sensations. Effective treatment of the child hinged on the role of the therapist as a perceptual ''guide,'' and her help in putting sensory experience into perspective was viewed as enabling the child to develop adequate control of sensory input.

Klein (1962) provided an interesting elaboration of some of the ideas of Omwake and Solnit. He pointed out that it is important to distinguish between a specific sensory deficit and general isolation from the environment, that is, ''a drastic reduction of opportunities for assessing environmental facts and signals having serious consequences for adjustment'' (pp. 82–83). The latter situation may occur as a consequence of blindness, but it may occur for other reasons as well and need not necessarily occur as a result of blindness. According to Klein, the more general deprivation has to do with ''impairing the organism's opportunities of building up and sustaining intrapsychic structures that subserve cognition, affect, action, and motivation'' (p. 85). Continuing, he argued that blindness does not necessarily produce this deprivation: ''The essential factor here is not the blindness, but maladjustive consequences of a vacuum created by inadequate ego surrogates . . .[what is required instead is] a continuing feedback-evaluation process by means of which the child develops ideas of anticipatable and predictable reality. . . . Surely the mother, as the environment's representative who ordinarily affords the most secure opportunities of trial contacts, is an important ancillary of the child's ego in this process'' (pp. 87–88). Thus Klein took the position that the development of an adequate adjustment to the demands of the world requires consistency, organization, and meaningfulness in the environment. Blindness creates a situation in which maladjustment may have a greater tendency to occur, specifically because of the absence of vision as an organizer of experience. Thus a greater burden is placed on those responsible for the child, since they are charged with providing an integrative or organizational framework for the child's experience. Realistically, it should be noted that this added burden of responsibility is placed on the parents in situations which also tend to create other pressures on them. Hallenbeck (1954b) provided a useful perspective on the RLF syndrome in particular: ''Without exception . . . each mother was repeatedly told by professional personnel and by others who saw her child, that the child was mentally deficient or that the child had brain disease, and would not live long. All factors, a fearful delivery followed by separation, a slowly developing child, the diagnosis of retrolental fibroplasia, and finally a diagnosis of mental deficiency—progressively interfered with the relationship between the mother and child'' (p. 302). Blank (1959) also discussed parental reactions to the RLF situation, and he noted that the first year may not even be the most difficult time for the parent. It is when the child enters the second-year defiance syndrome that ''the parent, confronted with loss of control and frustrated by having an obviously unusual child, becomes anxious, alternately hostile and overprotective'' (p. 240).

Although the similarities between these patterns of emotional disturbance in blind children and those associated with autism are obvious, there are also apparently some differences that make it unwise to conclude that the syndrome seen in these blind children is in fact autism. Fraiberg and Freedman (1964) described the characteristics of a group of emotionally disturbed children as follows: ''Typically the deviant child spends hours in bed or in a chair or lying on the floor, absently mouthing an object. There is no interest in toys or any objects that are not in themselves need satisfying or stimulating to the mouth. Contact with human objects is often initiated by biting and even more often by a primitive clutching and clawing with the hands'' (p. 115). However, they also noted ways in which the syndrome differs from that of sighted autistic children. ''The mouth has remained the center of this primitive personality; perception is largely mouth-centered and those qualities that we call 'aggressive' and 'erotic' remain mouth-centered and appear to be undifferentiated. Tactile perception is minimal; in fact, the hand appears to have no autonomy from the mouth. These characteristics of the blind deviant child have no parallel among sighted autistic children'' (p. 151). Elonen and Cain (1964) similarly noted differences between a ''pseudo-autistic'' syndrome and the true autistic child. The children that Elonen and Cain described did show autistic-like behaviors such as communication difficulties, extremes of tantrum and withdrawal, and self-destructive behaviors. Although for the most part the children had been previously diagnosed as retarded and/or autistic, Elonen and Cain found highly beneficial effects of therapeutic personal and environmental stimulation. These successful efforts were described as being far less intensive than would normally be required for similar progress in truly autistic children. Furthermore, a close analysis of their speech indicated that, rather than being bizarre, it tended to be characterized by ''fixation to and prolongation of the normal stages of speech development'' (p. 629). Since the children tended to have histories of environmental and social isolation, the therapy program involved both sensory stimulation and active involvement by the therapist in the child's motor and verbal activities. They noted that, although a sensitivity to the child's individual personality problems was critical to the treatment, relatively untrained graduate students were just as successful as trained therapists in producing progress in the child's behavior. However, they also stressed the need for simultaneous parent counseling, since ''unless the parents can give up older pathological ways of reacting to these children and are able to utilize the emerging skills and readiness of the child, the therapeutic progress will be minimal'' (p. 630).

Emotional Disturbance and RLF

Many writers have noted a striking incidence of emotional disturbance in children with blindness due to RLF. Case reports range from those of children who are only slightly withdrawn to ones who show symptoms that are apparently similar or identical to those characteristic of autism in sighted children. Chase (1972) provided an excellent review of the bodies of literature on autism, RLF, and prematurity. Two major questions arise in connection with the RLF–emotional disturbance issue. First, is emotional disturbance in general more frequent in RLF children than in other blind children, and are the more severe instances in particular more frequent? Second, what are the causes of emotional disturbance in the RLF child, and are they different in important respects from the causes in other children?

Relative incidence

Several studies provide evidence that symptoms of emotional disturbance are more prevalent in RLF children than in other children who are blind from birth. Keeler (1958) studied intensively the communicative abilities and emotional characteristics of five severely disturbed RLF children who showed definite autistic symptoms. These children did not constitute a random sample, since they were studied because of their referral for ''strikingly abnormal behavior and mental development.'' However, Keeler also studied a group of 35 RLF children who had not been brought for psychiatric evaluation and who therefore were assumed to be a representative sample of RLF blind children. Keeler noted marked similarities in the behavior patterns of these children to those of the five severely disturbed children, although the symptoms were much less intense in the larger group. Further comparison was then made with a group of 18 children who had been blind from birth from other causes. Referring to the non-RLF group Keeler reported that ''one did not see the same degree of autistic patterns of behavior, although some of these children were somewhat withdrawn. Abnormalities in motility were noted but were not so prevalent and not so severe'' (p. 73). Thus Keeler concluded that there was a greater incidence of autistic patterns of behavior in the RLF group than in the non-RLF group. A note of reservation should be made, however, since while all subjects had less then 20/200 vision in the better eye, the amount of remaining vision was ''much greater'' in the non-RLF group than in the RLF group.

Blank (1959) also reported that ''the incidence of severe ego defects and autistic and motility disturbances is far higher among children with retrolental fibroplasia than among congenitally blind children without brain damage who were born full-term'' (p. 237). He also noted, however, that ''severe personality problems among the blind prematurely born with brain damage, but without retrolental fibroplasia, is probably as high as among those with retrolental fibroplasia'' and that ''the incidence of these problems among visually normal children with brain damage, e.g., cerebral palsy, and with a history of two- to three-months premature birth is almost as high as among the blind with retrolental fibroplasia'' (p. 237). Blank cited brain damage and prematurity as factors that, together with visual loss, may account for the relatively high incidence of emotional disturbance among RLF children.

Finally, Parmalee, Cutsforth, and Jackson (1958) reported a study of 60 children from six to 10 years of age, 39 of whom were RLF children and 22 of whom were blind from other causes. For the non-RLF group, the age at onset of blindness was not specifically noted, although the reported etiologies suggest that a large majority of the cases were blind from birth. The total sample included all cases in the geographic area known to the Field Service who fell within the specific age range in the study year, and thus it may be considered a representative sample for that year (1955). It was thought that the selection procedure, which required the parent's initiative, might reduce the incidence of emotional disturbance. However, while the overall sample may have included smaller incidence of emotional disturbance than a truly random sample, there is no reason to suppose that the relative incidence in the RLF and otherwise blind groups differed by virtue of the selection procedures. Although the primary concern of the study was with mental development, data on emotional disturbance were gathered and reported. Of the 38 RLF children, seven were reported to be significantly emotionally disturbed. Of the 22 non-RLF children, only one was so classified. Parmalee et al. suggested that ''some special factor is operative, unique either to children of premature birth or to children with blindness due to retrolental fibroplasia or both'' (p. 645).

Thus, although the weight of the evidence is not great, data from several sources indicate that there is a somewhat higher incidence of serious emotional disturbance in RLF children than in children blind from birth from other causes.

Causes of emotional disturbance in RLF children

To what may the greater incidence be attributed? Several variables have been noted in connection with the results from the studies cited, and other variables also seem potentially important. The list includes the parent- (or caretaker-) child relationship, early sensory deprivation, prematurity and variables associated with prematurity such as birth weight and duration of gestation, oxygen ''poisoning,'' brain damage, and mental retardation. Two points are obvious from scanning this list. One is that some of the variables are not independent of others, and may therefore operate in an interactive fashion to affect emotional disturbance. An obvious example is blindness and the parent-child relationship, since it may often be the case that the parent's role in the relationship is adversely affected by his reactions to the fact of blindness. The second point, related to the first, is that while one factor might operate as an initial cause, it may have its effect partly directly and partly through its effect on another causal factor. For example, brain damage might affect emotional disturbance directly, and it might exercise an effect indirectly by acting as a contributory cause of mental retardation, which then might affect emotional disturbance directly. It is difficult if not impossible to separate these complex relationships. Some of the variables will thus be discussed in clusters that seem especially interrelated in their possible effects.

Prematurity factors. RLF almost always involves prematurity, although there are occasional cases of RLF in full-term infants. Prematurity itself must be regarded as a possible contributing cause of emotional disturbance, as must such factors as brain damage and low birth weight that are statistically associated with prematurity. Does prematurity itself produce emotional disturbance? Chase (1972), in her detailed study of a large number of RLF case histories, found very little relationship between the degree of prematurity and the incidence of emotional disturbance. Only one index of the gestational age–emotional disturbance relationship showed a correlation in a direction suggesting that shorter gestational age was related to greater emotional disturbance. Other indices showed correlations in the opposite direction. Chase also found that lighter birth weight was associated with a smaller, rather than a larger incidence of emotional disturbance symptoms in those correlations that were significant. However, none of the correlations that showed statistical significance were impressive. Fraiberg and Freedman (1964) similarly reported a failure to find significant relationships between birth weight or gestational age and degree of "developmental arrest" (a syndrome involving various types of difficulty, but strongly characterized by emotional disturbance). Thus the conclusion seems reasonable that there is little relationship between degree of prematurity or birth weight and incidence or severity of emotional disturbance.

It is undoubtedly an oversimplification to speak of a possible direct effect of prematurity on emotional disturbance. Instead, it may be that factors such as brain damage that are statistically associated with prematurity influence emotional factors. Such evidence is available from several sources. Parmalee, Cutsforth, and Jackson (1958) and Knobloch, Rider, Harper, and Pasamanick (1956) cited various evidence that brain damage is more frequent in prematurely born infants regardless of their visual status. Blank (1959) noted that symptoms of emotional disturbance occur in premature sighted children with brain damage with a frequency similar to that in RLF children, and Cohen (1966) found significant correlations between the incidence of neurological signs and incidence of emotional disturbance. Keeler (1958) discussed the possibility that brain damage may be implicated in the greater incidence of emotional disturbance in RLF children: "Such a factor could account for the differences in severity of the condition within the group of children with retrolental fibroplasia, i.e., those with a marked psychiatric syndrome may have marked cerebral involvement and those without much symptomatology may have cerebral involvement either to a very mild degree or perhaps not at all" (p. 75). However, Keeler noted that the clinical picture of emotional disturbance is not typically like that found in other brain-damaged children, and that the factor of brain damage may interact with other factors such as visual loss to produce the peculiar symptomatology of some RLF children. Hallenbeck (1954b) also argued that brain damage could not by itself account for the patterns of emotional disturbance in RLF children.

The question also arises whether the brain-damage factor may affect emotional disturbance indirectly via the route of mental retardation. Although this possibility deserves some attention, it seems unlikely as a major causal sequence. Several summaries of RLF case studies (Parmalee et al., 1958) have noted instances where severe emotional disturbance occurs in spite of quite adequate IQ scores. It does seem plausible, though, that brain damage and its effects, such as motor problems, produce cases where other situational factors (e.g., inadequate emotional response of parents to a child with physical handicaps) may interact to produce emotional disturbance.

It is widely accepted that the RLF condition is a direct result of the administration of oxygen-rich environments to prematurely born infants. Thus the question occurs whether it might be the oxygen factor itself that is implicated in the greater incidence of emotional disturbance in RLF children. Parmalee et al. (1958) discussed this possibility but found no evidence to support it. Chase (1972) studied the relationship of degree of oxygenation to several indices of emotional disturbance and found only one correlation that was significant. However, the correlation was in the opposite direction, suggesting that those children who had received more intensive oxygen treatment showed less evidence of emotional disturbance. Fraiberg and Freedman (1964) also reported a failure to find a relationship between developmental arrest and the duration of oxygen treatment. There is, therefore, no evidence to suggest that emotional disturbance is caused by more intensive oxygen treatment.

In sum, the evidence on the prematurity factors suggests that none of these factors exercises a direct effect on emotional disturbance. However, both brain damage and prematurity may set the stage for indirect effects via their interaction with subsequent factors such as inadequate parental response and sensory deprivation.

Sensory deprivation. An extensive discussion of the effects of early sensory deprivation on development has been presented in Chapter 2, and the evidence will not be repeated in detail here. In brief, though, it may be suggested that, because of the restrictions of the incubator environment and the relative isolation that typically accompanies prematurity, there is a greater likelihood that RLF children will have experienced a period of early sensory deprivation than non-RLF children. To the extent that early sensory deprivation may be a causal factor in emotional disturbance, then, RLF children might be characterized by more emotional disturbance. There are several lines of evidence and argument that do implicate sensory deprivation in emotional disturbance. The strongest argument is based on comparative data. Hebb (1949), and others following him, have found a greater range of adaptive responses in rats that received early (first 10 days) somatosensory stimulation via handling. Denenberg (1964), among others, has found striking differences on indices of emotional reactivity in rats as a result of early handling experience. Prescott (1976) emphasized that kinesthetic-*vestibular* sensory stimulation was of primary importance for motor-mental and social-emotional adjustment. Proceeding to arguments and data bearing more directly on humans, Freedman (1971) suggested that the coenesthetic (relatively diffuse, including primarily somatosensory and vestibular) stimulation is critical: "In its effect on later physical and psychological development, early coenesthetic deprivation may be more devastating than either congenital blindness or the melange of troubles that affects thalidomide and some rubella babies" (p. 117). Provence and Lipton (1962) found early and marked differences between two groups of sighted infants in responsiveness to handling: an institutionalized group that received little direct personal stimulation was less responsive than a "home reared" group. The analogous behaviors in some emotionally disturbed RLF children may be variously described as a dislike of cuddling (Keeler, 1958) or fear of handling (Hallenbeck, 1954b). More generally, the emotional withdrawal syndrome among some disturbed RLF children has been characterized as an aversion to affection, or an emotional coldness and withdrawal from human contact. Even granting that the attribution of these tendencies to early somatosensory and vestibular deprivation is based largely on indirect evidence, the formulation does seem reasonable. One piece of evidence does apparently contradict the indictment of sensory deprivation in causing emotional disturbance. In her archival study of factors in emotional disturbance in RLF children, Chase (1972) assessed the effects of both duration of incubation and duration of hospitalization. Contrary to her hypothesis, Chase found that the longer an infant has been in the incubator, the less likely was the occurrence of emotional disturbance. Similarly, although the relationships were not strong, Chase found that the children who had spent a longer period of initial hospitalization were less likely to show signs of emotional disturbance.

Parent-child interactions. Because true experimental investigation of early deprivation variables with human infants is not possible, there is some argument about whether these aspects of emotional disturbance are a result of sensory deprivation or of some more general parental or social deprivation. The two possible causes are difficult to separate. Writers such as Spitz (1945, 1946) have attributed the problems to maternal deprivation. Others (e.g., Schaffer & Callender, 1959) have suggested that social deprivation is not really involved until the second half of the first year, and that during the first six months, separation has effects only in the sensory-perceptual area. A complicating factor in the issue is the frequent description of parents of autistic children as having been emotionally cold and rejecting of their infants. Kaplan and

Mason (1960) found patterns of maternal emotional response to be less adequate for premature than for full-term infants. Thus maternal handling of premature infants may be less warm and adequate than normal. This situation may be partly caused by the parent's response, but also partly by the infant's own predilections: Fraiberg et al. (1969) noted that the three infants from their sample of 10 that were "non-cuddlers" were all prematurely born infants and had spent several weeks in the hospital before coming home.

Parental inadequacy may in many cases produce situations of sensory deprivation. For example, numerous instances appear in published case histories where the parents of early blind children left the infant in the crib without attention for as much of the time as was possible, either because of a fear of damaging the child through inappropriate stimulation or because of a more active emotional rejection of the child. In either case, sensory deprivation results. (It may be noted that many clinicians [Blank, 1959, for instance] interpret the overprotectiveness as a form of rejection or compensation for rejection.)

There is no reason to think that emotional rejection by the parent should necessarily accompany RLF blindness any more than it does blindness from other causes. There are concomitants of the RLF situation, though, that may produce a straining of the emotional relationships beyond that normally attendant on blindness from other causes. A quote from Blank (1959) illustrates the possible complications. "The mother who has to leave the hospital without her baby feels inadequte, cheated, and anxious even before she knows the child is blind. The news of the child's blindness is therefore superimposed on the trauma of separation and produces anxious rumination. Moreover the 'preemie' joining the mother at home at two or three months of age is not as well developed, active, or responsive as the baby the mother had expected" (p. 239). Cohen (1966) suggested several possible types of parental response to this situation: "Some parents feel a deep guilt which interferes with their ability to love the child. Others bear the burden of the child as a 'cross,' which brings them no closer to real love for the child. Parental anxiety may result in either of the following damaging attitudes: perpetual overprotection; or expectation of more from the child than is realistic" (p. 152). Another pattern of response was noted by Keeler (1958): mothers "tended literally to put them out of their minds by leaving them in cribs and playpens off in a back room of the house or in the back yard for long periods of time, attending only in a minimal way to the most imperative of their physical needs" (p. 66). To the extent that other physical problems (e.g., cerebral palsy) exist in addition to the blindness, the picture of parental rejection might be expected to be intensified. Seashore, Leifer, Barnett, and Leiderman (1973) reported a related finding from a study of mothers of sighted premature infants. Two groups were established, one of mothers who were denied physical interaction with their infants for several weeks after birth and the other of mothers who were allowed physical contact. In general, those mothers with low self-confidence in their mothering skills tended to maintain a lower degree of self-confidence if they were in the former group than if they were in the latter. Further, the degree of self-confidence was a moderately good predictor of observed skill at mothering a week after the infant was discharged from the hospital.

Summary. There are situational factors surrounding RLF blindness that may account for the greater incidence of emotional disturbance in this group. It is apparent, though, that with the possible exception of the sensory deprivation associated with incubation, the factors are not ones that are found only for RLF children. In fact, some factors, such as separation due to hospitalization in cases of retinoblastoma, may operate more strongly in other etiologies. It should also be noted that, in all likelihood, none of the factors operates independently of all the others. The interdependence of various factors is stressed in many papers: parental neglect may be a response to the blindness itself, to the early separation, to additional physical handicaps, or to some combination of these factors. It is undoubtedly the convergence of the several factors in the RLF situation that produces the greater incidence of emotional disturbance in this group. It may be that parent–child emotional relationships play a greater part than the other factors, but even this relationship is not "clean," in the sense that damaged parent–child relationships may often be precipitated by other factors, such as early separation. Finally, the obvious point should be made that the various factors, either in isolation or in combinations, do not necessarily produce emotional disturbance. There are many RLF blind people whose physical, cognitive, language, and emotional characteristics are outstanding.

Treatment of Emotional Problems

As is the case for sighted children, there have been various approaches to therapy for emotional problems in the blind. One approach that has received some attention with blind children is play therapy. Axline (1947) has been a major figure in the development of the approach with sighted children. As a non-directive therapy, play therapy "is based on the assumption that the individual has within himself, not only the ability to solve his own problems satisfactorily, but also the growth impulse that makes mature behavior more satisfying than immature behavior" (p. 15). Briefly, the procedure involves allowing the child to become engaged in play situations in which he may feel relatively unconstrained by parent, peer, or therapist. His play serves the function of expression, where he may, for example, engage in aggressive behavior that would not occur around other people. In addition, the therapist may be able to gain insights into the nature of the child's problems by observing his play and listening to his verbalizations. Therapists tend to differ in degree of directiveness — some intervene fairly actively in the play and suggest "leading" situations for the child, while others eschew interference in the ongoing activity.

There are some differences in the use of play therapy for blind and sighted children. Jones (1952) noted that toys should be as realistic as possible for the blind child, and that special attention must be given to bringing the child repeatedly into contact with the range of materials that are available for his play. Rothschild (1960) expanded this point in noting that the blind child may not be as used to expressing himself in play as the sighted child; therefore more attention is needed to establish the blind child's feeling of comfort with the play materials and situation. More ongoing reintroduction to the variety of playthings is also important, since what may be an interesting and effective toy in one situation may not be as effective in a different situation. Several writers also mention the need for the therapist to provide a more directive role than is needed with sighted children. Rothschild discussed this need in connection with the greater difficulty of the blind child in sustaining play, while Avery (1968) noted that often more language supportiveness is needed, since the blind child cannot see that the therapist is attending and accepting of his behavior.

There has not been sufficient evaluation of the effectiveness of play therapy as compared with other approaches for blind children. However, excerpts from case studies reported by Jones (1952) and Avery (1968) may serve to illustrate areas in which the approach is thought to be effective. Jones noted the expression of aggressive behavior in play situations that was in striking contrast to the child's passivity in everyday life. This point is especially interesting in view of the literature, reviewed earlier, that suggests that blind children experience conflict in the expression of aggression. Jones also noted progress in the areas of attention span, bladder control, social unease, independence, and language. Avery cited an example of substantial progress in interpersonal relations, where the child initially placed severe demands on other people but gradually came to assume responsibility for his own actions and needs. Avery also noted a decrease in the anxiety that had produced withdrawn behavior: the child became more able to engage in social relationships, including effective communication.

Play therapy is undoubtedly a useful procedure with younger children, since it depends very little on effective verbalization. There is, as yet, very little differentiating information on the types of problems for which it may be more or less effective. Progress in the effective use of play therapy with blind children will depend on its more extensive use, and on the willingness of investigators to make careful assessments of the particular problems of their subjects, of the nature of the activities occurring during play therapy, and of the detailed outcomes of the approach, including the failures as well as the successes.

Rothschild (1960), in his discussion of play therapy for blind children, noted that play therapy tends to be most successful in cases where the parent simultaneously undergoes therapy. Similar stress on the need for involvement of the family in therapy appears in the literature on counseling approaches to emotional disturbance in blind children. Cerulli and Shugerman (1961), for example, emphasized the need for family counseling for parents of blind infants as a preventative measure, in advance of any possible expression of emotional disturbance on the part of the infant. Numerous authors advise family counseling approaches for older children. Group counseling approaches may be especially effective for parents who see their own situation as markedly different from that of other families. Exposure of such parents to examples of successfully developing older blind children may serve a useful function in helping them to form a perspective on their own situation.

Group counseling may be of benefit for older children. Manaster and Kucharis (1972) described a successful group approach with congenitally blind adolescents. Substantial progress was reported for one boy who was "emotionally disturbed," and useful exploration of feelings about blindness was reported for the group as a whole.

The use of behavior modification techniques with emotional disorders has not been as prevalent as might be expected on the basis of the recent popularity of the method. An example of a behavior control approach is provided by Greene and Hoats (1971), who used aversive tickling as a means of decreasing unwanted behaviors in two retarded 13-year-old girls. One girl showed self-destructive behavior, while the other showed a variety of undesirable interpersonal behaviors such as biting and kicking. The administration of aversive tickling upon performance of these behaviors produced some decreases in the behaviors over a period of weeks in both cases, although in neither case was the undesired behavior extinguished completely. The authors noted that the episodes that tended to disappear were those which were "not highly motivated," while the episodes accompanied by emotional responses remained. Success cannot be claimed on the basis of this work, but the potential of behavior modification approaches has not been adequately explored.

There are numerous accounts available of intensive psychotherapeutic approaches with blind children. Examples are papers by Green and Schechter (1957) and Kass et al. (1967). The former paper described therapy with several children with autistic-like symptoms such as language disorders and social withdrawal, while the latter described work with a case of selective mutism. Although such papers typically do not provide very much detail about the psychotherapeutic process, there are common themes that may be drawn out. One theme is a careful handling of the relationship of the child to his sensory world. This concern grows out of the notion that the child's withdrawal may in large part be due to a sensory overload rather than to social factors. That is, without the interpretive and organizational functions of vision, the child experiences and withdraws from a bombardment of confusing sensory impressions. With respect to the child's gaining contact with the sensory world, the therapist's role is typically seen as a mediator, organizer, and clarifier of sensory experience. A second theme is that intensive psychotherapeutic contact is often coupled with a gradual involvement of the child in a social environment of peers. Kass et al. (1967), for example, coupled psychotherapy with the placement of the child in a normal public school class with sighted peers. A third theme is involvement of the parents. Blank (1959) and Green and Schechter (1957) have particularly stressed the inadequacy of the parents' sponse to the blindness situation as a major factor in the child's symptoms, and both papers noted the need for intensive work with the parents as well as with the child.

The most detailed description of intensive psychotherapy is found in a paper by Omwake and Solnit (1961). Extensive discussion of the paper cannot be provided here, and the interested reader is referred to the original. Ann was first seen at age 3.5 years, at which time "she was tyrannizing her family with a demand for the constant physical contact and undivided attention of her mother. She refused to talk, walk, or move about, to handle toys, or to become involved in any kind of play either of a manipulative, dramatic, or social nature. When the mother moved out of reach of Ann's hand or hearing, the child screamed, flung her body about, and bumped her forehead on the floor. She ate poorly, did nothing for herself, and no one had been able to attempt toilet training" (p. 356). Ann was thought to have an inability to engage in repression in defense of the ego. Much of the problem was seen as being grounded in perceptual and sensory processes: "The eruption of fragmentary sensorimotor memories under the influence of the primary process occurred when deficits in the stimulus barrier and in the capacity to form a visual psychic image were combined with the understimulation and lack of protective guidance Ann received in the first three years of her life. This formulation could explain Ann's inability to erect repressive barriers as an adaptive mechanism available to her ego" (p. 403). The therapist gained sufficient trust that he "was gradually permitted to provide leadership in organizing the perceptual experiences, especially those dependent upon a visual component" (p. 402). It is interesting that one of the major breakthroughs in Ann's therapy occurred when she realized her blindness and became able to ask about it and discuss it.

The questions of when congenitally blind children realize that their blindness somehow sets them apart, what the adult's response to this realization is, and whether he should encourage it to occur earlier, have been discussed in the literature. Speaking primarily of partially sighted but legally blind children, Winton (1970) stressed the need for informing the child as early as possible of his handicap, so that he "can thus adjust to his difficulties by making appropriate indications to himself. He can answer his questions about why he cannot do all the things that other children can do" (p. 21). In view of the desirability of a stable self-concept, this advice seems wise. If the child has to make a relatively sudden change in his self-concept when blindness is realized, he is probably more likely to experience difficulties in adjusting. On the other hand, there is reason to avoid overemphasizing the fact of blindness. For example, in their study of vocationally successful and unsuccessful blind adults, Bauman and Yoder (1966) found that the more self-sufficient and mobile individuals tended to come from families which did not make a big issue of the fact of blindness: "The pattern of family relationships is more likely to be the pattern it would have been had the individual had normal vision" (p. 69).

Thus some compromise must be made between shielding the child from the realization of his blindness and overstressing the fact of the blindness.

By way of summary of the available literature on therapeutic approaches to emotional disturbance in blind children, it is clear that many approaches are available and have been used. As yet there has been little attempt to make a comparative evaluation of the effectiveness of the various approaches. The evaluation of therapy is difficult enough for sighted children, and it is no easier for the blind. Evaluation is necessary, though, if the goal is to provide the optimal approach for any given case of emotional disturbance. Review of the available literature produces the strong impression that the particular therapeutic approach used in any given case was chosen more on the basis of the predilections of the therapist than on the basis of an attempt to match a particular therapeutic mode to the individual characteristics of the case. It is likely that the various therapeutic approaches (behavior modification, play therapy, psychodyamic, counseling) are differentially effective for different types of problems. Effective matching cannot be possible until there is a concerted effort to gather detailed information about patient characteristics, types of therapy attempted, and outcome evaluations. Not the least important aspect of this venture is the careful reporting of cases where particular therapeutic attempts have not been successful.

8
What is Known and What Needs to Be Studied

In the Introduction four questions were outlined as a framework within which to consider and organize the research literature on visual impairment and development. The four are as follows:

1. In what ways is development the same in blind children and in sighted children, and in what ways does development differ? How does development differ among various types of blind children?
2. Where there are differences, what variables can be identified as producing or influencing the differences?
3. What procedures may be identified as producing optimal development, or minimizing developmental lag?
4. What are the possibilities for the remediation of developmental lag once it has occurred?

I also noted that I am uncomfortable with them as a way of structuring our knowledge about visual impairment, because as they are posed the questions tend to direct us too much to comparison of visually impaired with sighted children. The danger lies in the easy conclusion that developmental norms for the sighted population should be set as goals for the visually impaired population. For the reasons that I discussed in the Introduction, I believe this to be a faulty conclusion. It is far more important to ask the question "How can the developmental progress of the visually impaired child be optimized?" than the question "How can the visually impaired child be made to achieve sighted age norms?"

Therefore I want to add a fifth question to the set of four, and to stress its importance beyond that of the others. The first four may be a reasonable framework for the organization of the literature, but the fifth is the paramount question that we should be asking in our research. It is simply:

5. How can the developmental progress of the visually impaired child be optimized?

There has been substantial research attention devoted to the description of the characteristics and abilities of blind children, and to the comparison of blind children with sighted children. However, while comparative *description* is possible in several topical areas (particularly perceptual and motor development), the literature does not provide a very satisfying picture of the *development* of the blind child, or of the comparative *development* of blind and sighted children. There are at least two reasons for this shortcoming. First, much of the evaluative work on blind children has included children over a wider age range than is typically the case in the developmental literature on sighted children. This inclusiveness is attributable to the relative unavailability of blind subjects, but it is unfortunate in that it sometimes precludes thorough treatment of age-related changes. Second, most research with visually impaired children has been restricted to the description of abilities and behavior and has stopped short of investigating developmental *process*. Thus, while the differences between three- and six-year-olds may be known, little is known about the nature of and reasons for the changes that the three-year-old undergoes in becoming a six-year-old. The relative lack of attention to developmental process means, of course, that we cannot claim much knowledge about why there are differences between the blind and sighted, or why the development of the blind child may be less than optimal. (For perspective, it may be noted that research in child development can be generally criticized for a relative lack of attention to developmental process—for example, one of the most persuasive and widely influential theories of development, Piaget's theory of cognitive development, is often criticized for its lack of attention to the processes that cause development to proceed from one stage to another.)

The lack of information about the variables that produce developmental differences also necessitates an incomplete set of answers to the third question. If the variables that produce suboptimal development or developmental differences are not understood, then it is not possible to incorporate those variables into maximally effective developmental intervention programs. There are intervention programs reported in the literature, but it is extremely questionable whether they are optimal programs, since there simply is not the research available on which to build optimal programs. In general, too, it is not possible to make strong statements about the effectiveness of these programs because adequate evaluation research has not been done. Answers to the fourth question, concerning remediation, are not as dependent on an understanding of developmental process as are the answers to the third question. That is, remediation of developmental problems once they have occurred may require a different set of approaches than does the structuring of experience to avoid the problems in the first place. The literature on remediation is characterized by a heavy concern for diagnosis, but remedial programs have not in general been effectively described, compared with other programs, or evaluated in their effectiveness.

What is Known?

The following is a set of very general answers (to the extent that they can be formulated) to the questions to which this review is directed.

Perceptual-motor development

Perceptual discrimination abilities, such as perception of texture, weight, or sound, do not typically show differences between visually impaired and sighted children, or between groups of visually impaired children with various characteristics. In more complex or integrative categories of perception, such as form identification, spatial relations, intermodality relations, and perceptual-motor integration, there are some areas where blind children have substantial difficulties. There are also marked differences between various groups of blind children. For instance, a period of early vision produces an advantage in some areas. Some statements may be made about the variables that produce the differences. The variables about which statements *can* be made tend to be self-selected variables such as duration of early vision, and there is much less material available about variables that might be suitably manipulated in a program designed to optimize acquisition of these perceptual abilities. There has been little *systematic* attempt to structure the young child's environment in such a way as to optimize development, and programs that have attempted to do this have not been effectively evaluated. With respect to the question of remediation, there have been few programs reported, and these too have not been effectively evaluated or compared with other programs.

Cognitive development

There are several types of cognitive abilities that show differences between blind and sighted children, or between various groups of blind children. These abilities range from relatively specific (understanding spatial concepts) to relatively general ones (understanding the properties of the world, as assessed by Piagetian tasks). Historically, cognitive development has been understudied in comparison with perception, but in recent years there has been a great deal of interest in cognitive development and the picture is changing rapidly. Until the past decade, the research on cognitive development had, like that in perceptual development, been characterized primarily by descriptive work, and there had been relatively little attention to the variables that influence the developmental course. There is preliminary evidence on some promising leads, however. For example, several researchers have noted impressive differences between residential school and integrated school samples. Some of the variables that differentiate these two environments are amenable to manipulation. Therefore, there is a strong possibility that well-designed research on the antecedents of cognitive differences will be forthcoming and will provide important information about the experiences to which blind children should be exposed in order for them to do their best. There has as yet been little research on ways of structuring the environment in order to meet this goal. The few studies that are available on remediation do show some promise. Great care must be taken in such research, however, for two reasons. First, improvements may be produced by a remedial program that are only temporary and that do not continue much beyond the end of the special program. The permanency of effects must be evaluated well beyond the termination of the program. Second, to the extent that the slower developmental acquisition of cognitive abilities is characteristic of blind children in general, avoidance of the lags would produce development that is *accelerated* compared to the normal rate for blind children. Any occurrence of accelerated development must be carefully assessed with respect to the question of whether the abilities that are acquired are as stable and flexible as they would have been under the normal course of development. Acceleration of development (avoidance of lag) may, in such situations, actually be to the child's disadvantage. The danger of taking sighted developmental norms as a frame of reference for the development of the blind child is obvious. The more appropriate frame of reference is the optimal development of the blind child himself, difficult as this is to determine. Researchers must guard against oversimplified goals and inadequate long-term evaluation.

Language development

For blind children without additional handicaps, there is little evidence of developmental difference from sighted children in some areas of language development. The production and refinement of sounds, the acquisition of early vocabulary, and the acquisition of grammatical forms are not apparently different in important ways. The area where the question is still quite wide open is that of meaning (including "verbalism"). The new work of the past several years strongly suggests that, while blind children may use words with the same frequency counts as sighted children, the meanings of words for the blind are not as rich or as elaborated. It is not yet clear whether any such differences have implications for the adequacy of thought. In this same recent work there has been more effective attention to the variables that might produce differences, specifically the linguistic content provided for the blind child by parents and others. There have been some promising approaches to the question of the trainability of language in such functional categories as general and spatial relations vocabulary, but the long-term effectiveness of these attempts has not been adequately evaluated, nor has the extent to which any demonstrated improvements find expression in functional behavior that depends on vocabulary.

Social development

There is substantial evidence that the course of social development is different in blind and sighted children. For example, the indicators of social attachment and identification follow a slower developmental course in blind children, and the acquisition of social skills such as eating, toilet training, and dressing proceeds more slowly. It is not clear that the lags in indices of social development denote a less adequate socialization process for the blind child, however, since there is reason to think that the indicators are not equivalent for blind and sighted children. There has, appropriately, been some consideration of the important role that parents and other people play in the socialization of the blind child and particularly the possible impact of negative reactions to the fact of the child's handicap. This work has been primarily descriptive and has not effectively concentrated on ways of preventing or ameliorating the potentially negative influences that these "significant others" may have. In the area of social maturity, the weight of the research suggests that there are substantial developmental lags shown in various areas by blind children. The significance of tested lags on indices of social maturity is not clear; it is not well understood just how a lag as measured by a social maturity scale translates into inadequate social behavior. A gap also exists in the understanding of the causes of particular lags. More adequate theoretical treatment of social development may help by providing a structure for useful research.

Personality development

In the area of personality development, there are some reasonably well- established differences between blind and sighted children, although the bulk of the research has been concerned with adolescents. There have been reports of differences between blind and sighted infants in characteristics such as aggressiveness and passivity, but these reports have not been based on large numbers of infants and must, therefore, be taken with some reservation. Of more importance is the lack of research that draws lines of continuity between the characteristics imputed to infants (and the variables that are thought to affect those characteristics) and the characteristics that have been noted for older children. Personality does not develop in a vacuum, and there is much to be learned about the determinants of personality characteristics in blind children. The questions of prevention or "remediation" of certain characteristics quickly begin to take on serious value judgments. At present the field is far from having to deal with these judgments because there is so little known about the determinants of personality development in the blind child. A characteristic that has received some concentrated attention is locus of control, and here the value judgments would seem to be less critical since it may be hypothesized that internal locus of control bears significantly on the independence and self-sufficiency of the blind child (and adult). In general, there is relatively little known about either the determinants of or the functional signifiance of personality characteristics in blind children.

In the area of emotional disturbance, there has been some success in tracing disturbance to etiological factors such as the parent's emotional stability and interaction with the child. This work has been primarily descriptive in nature, and it has not tended to generate effective (or effectively evaluated) modes of treatment or intervention.

What Needs to Be Studied?

The brevity of the foregoing section implies that there is much work to be done on the effects of visual impairment on the development of children, and there is, indeed. The purpose of the following sections is to draw attention to some of the areas in which there is inadequate information to construct a picture of the development of the blind child.

Perceptual and motor development

Audition. As noted in Chapter 1, there has been little information gathered about the development of responsiveness to auditory stimulation. The information that is available is based on small samples and case studies, and there is not a sufficient normative data base against which to evaluate the development of any particular infant. This lack is unfortunate in view of the desirability of identifying multiple handicaps involving visual and auditory deficits as early as possible. It is also unfortunate that not more is known about the normative development of the blind infant's use of auditory information in mediating his perception of the identity and location of objects in the world. The development of various motor responses to auditory stimulations is also an important area of study, including the possibility of head, eye, and body orientation to sounds as well as the development of manual reaching to sounds. Reaching for objects on the basis of auditory cues has received intensive attention from Fraiberg and others, but as yet the sample on which such study is based is quite limited and a firm picture cannot be drawn. There are indications in this literature that there are marked differences among individual infants, and it is important to establish the range of normal behavior as well as to study the extent to which differences might be traced to differences in early experience.

The study of auditory functioning in early and middle childhood has also been relatively neglected, despite the obvious importance that auditory perception has for the blind child. The sparseness of the work in auditory localization is perhaps the most obvious lack in this area, but the even more neglected area of auditory information selection and use is just as important.

The blind child is, even more than the sighted child, dependent on the effective selection, processing, retention, and use of auditory information, and the careful and systematic study of these topics would allow immediate applications in the areas of mobility, interpersonal behavior, and education. Finally, there has been no study of the continuity of auditory abilities between infancy and childhood.

Motor development. There is basic agreement from several sources that in general gross motor development is not retarded in blind infants and young children. Selective lags occur in certain aspects of manual (midline bimanual coordination) and locomotor development (crawling, walking). Writers such as Norris et al. (1957) have argued that the selective lags may be attributed to specific environmental characteristics. While this suggestion seems quite reasonable, there is little direct evidence either for or against it. Formulations about causality have been too general to serve a prescriptive function for those who work with young blind children. There have been enough reports of individual variation among blind infants to suggest that a study of individual variation and the specific environmental antecedents of such variation would be very rewarding. In such research, attention should also be given to social interactive factors such as parental overprotection, inasmuch as such factors may play a major part in motor development.

With the exception of evaluative studies such as that of Buell (1950) and experiential programs such as those of Cratty (1970), there has been insufficient attention devoted to motor development in school-age children. The development of mobility readiness scales such as that of Lord (1969) is an important step in this area, but even the impressive work of Lord has been directed primarily to readiness screening rather than to evaluation for the purpose of remediation. The published reports of motor remediation programs have suffered from a lack of adequate evaluation. This lack is especially unfortunate in view of the substantial effort that must be put into such programs.

As is the case for many other areas of research with blind children, the age range between late infancy and school age is notably unstudied. It is important to study individual variation among infants and to attempt to trace differences to environmental conditions. It is just as important to study the continuity of individual patterns of motor development between infancy and childhood. Careful longitudinal research is needed here. Longitudinal research is tedious and expensive, but it is critical to determine whether infants showing relatively precocious motor behavior are those children who later exhibit better mobility readiness or achievement. Longitudinal approaches are also required to determine whether environmental adjustments which produce relatively more advanced infants continue to have a noticeable effect on four-, six-, and eight-year-old children.

Mobility success, both in the sense of response to formal mobility training and in the more informal sense of the general ability to "get around," deserves more intensive study, since successful mobility is one of the key prerequisites for the independence of the blind child or adult. Warren and Kocon (1974) have provided an extensive review of factors in successful mobility. A summary statement of the review is that there are several avenues but many potential obstacles to successful mobility. The relevant variables are by no means restricted to motor and perceptual areas, though: parental overprotection (a "social" variable) may be one of the potentially most limiting experiential characteristics. Only careful, inclusive (with respect to range of variables), and critically evaluative research will produce the progress needed in this area. Welsh and Blasch (1980) treat the orientation-and-mobility area in all its facets.

Stereotypic behaviors. The etiological picture of stereotypic behaviors is not clear, and there are competing theories based on sensory deprivation and social deprivation/emotional disturbance formulations. While the available evidence would seem to support the sensory deprivation formulation, it may be that the etiological question, while important, is not the most critical one. Other important questions have to do with the specific situational stimuli (such as stress) for the occurrence of stereotypic behaviors, the desirability of decreasing such behaviors, including both pros and cons, and the ways that a decrease might be effected. The argument by Guess (1966) that the child's stereotypic activity may decrease his attention to the external environment is a convincing one, and it argues strongly that ways should be studied to decrease the incidence of stereotypies. On the other hand, researchers must be sensitive to the possibility that stereotypie provides a behavioral mode to which the child can adaptively regress in situations of extreme stress. Attempts to prevent the child from engaging in stereotypic behaviors in such situations may only make the child's dilemma more severe, especially when such attempts take on aspects of punishment.

Tactual perception. The study of tactual discrimination (texture, pattern, length, size, etc.) has enjoyed a long history, and there is continuing research on these questions now. Much of this work has been directed to questions of the comparability of the abilities of blind and sighted children. While this work is interesting, it is probably not the most important direction for research in this area to take. Three orientations should receive more attention in new research. First, the role of experience in the development of tactual discrimination abilities is important. There is some provocative work comparing the abilities of good and poor braille readers and non-braille readers, but the questions of causality have not been handled adequately. Given that good braille readers are better at tactual discrimination than poor readers, is the additional experience involved in becoming a good reader a cause of the better tactual sensitivity, or do these children become good braille users because of their better tactual sensitivity? What role does intelligence play? The answers to these questions are not clear, and the questions are only representative of the larger question of the role of experience in the development of tactual sensitivities. The second important direction has to do with the functional significance of good or poor tactual discrimination for more complex functions that depend on discrimination abilities. For example, discrimination of texture should not be studied in isolation. It should be studied along with the role of tactual discrimination in more complex activities such as braille perception, map reading, and pattern identification. The simple discriminative abilities are of little use in isolation, but they are critical to many more complex skills which blind children must use every day. Third, studies of manual search strategies (e.g., Davidson, Gunn, Wiles-Kettenmann, & Appelle, 1981) hold great promise for a better understanding of tactual perception as well as other abilities that depend on it, such as areas of cognition.

Spatial relations. Much of the research on tactual perception beyond simple discrimination has been taken as bearing on spatial relations. However, spatial relations abilities are complex, involving several levels, and care must be taken not to overgeneralized about spatial relations on the basis of tactual tasks. Aspects of motor abilities, auditory, and even visual perception are involved in spatial relations in blind children. Given this complexity, it is appropriate to study functional levels of performance in research on spatial relations. For example, in studies of tactile maze learning where reference is made to spatial relations, tests might also be made of the relationships between tactile maze learning and map use for mobility. If some aspect of auditory-motor spatial relations is under consideration, the goal might be to ascertain how variations in auditory-motor abilities become expressed as variations in functional spatial behavior. The point is simple: it is not sufficient to study an ability in isolation from its functional significance for behaviors that may depend on it.

In their review of early vision and its significance for various aspects of spatial behavior, Warren, Anooshian, and Bollinger (1973) noted the need to consider the specific task requirements of any given "spatial relations" task. In particular, they concluded that the advantage of blind subjects who had a period of early vision is more marked for more complex tasks than for relatively simple tasks. Similar evidence was reviewed in the spatial relations section of Chapter 2. In research on spatial relations, then, special care must be taken to analyze and report adequately the nature of the task being used. In addition, as spatial relations tasks become more complex, various subject characteristics such as duration of early vision, degree of residual vision, and time since blindness onset become more important. The issue of whether residual vision use should be encouraged or not is an important one, and research is needed on the relative spatial relations and mobility success of children who have and have not been encouraged to rely on residual vision.

Another issue deserving more attention in the spatial relations area is the nature of spatial representation. Do some children conceptualize space topologically while others "construct" space by learning a set of verbal rules or S-R links? If there are such differences, what are the antecedent conditions that influence the type of representation that develops? The occurrence of a period of early vision may be an important factor, but it is undoubtedly not the whole answer. For congenitally blind children, is a verbally mediated representation of space more or less effective than a topological representation that might be built up on the basis of an integration of appropriate motor, tactual, and auditory experience? These are complicated questions, and their answers will not be found from simple research paradigms. It may well be that the most effective way to study this area is through an analysis of the individual differences in spatial relations abilities that seem to occur spontaneously in blind children. It may be that a large proportion of this apparently spontaneous variation between individuals may be traced to differences in their early experience.

The new work on spatial cognition represents an important step forward in our understanding of spatial behavior. This work attempts to address the issue of the nature of spatial representation as it is related to the issue of mobility itself. Although this area has emerged rapidly over the past few years and has shown considerable progress, there remains much to be done.

Cognitive development

The Piagetian approach has proved valuable in structuring research on the child's understanding of the properties of the physical world. Some significant gaps remain in this area, however, and considerably more research is needed even in those areas (e.g., conservation) which have received the most attention. A major gap in the research appears in the early stages of cognitive development, specifically the sensorimotor period (first two years). A careful theoretical analysis of the development of the blind infant is needed, and considerable data will have to be gathered before the theoretical accounts may be tested adequately. Even in the later preoperational and concrete operations stages, the research to date has been primarily concerned with generating comparisons between blind and sighted children, and there has been relatively little effective analysis of the differences that have been found. This area would benefit from a concentration not only on what happens normatively over developmental levels, but also on the variations that occur within each level. Hierarchically organized research is needed to include consideration not only of the cognitive tasks but also of sensory factors (see Gottesman, 1976) and learning environment factors (Norris et al., 1957). Higher order levels should also be included in this research, including consideration of the various ways that cognitive abilities can help or hinder the child's adaptation to the tasks that he encounters in his everyday life. The need for hierarchically organized research is especially acute in areas where patterns of results from laboratory-type criterion tasks are complex (classification, abstract reasoning). Here the nature of the criterion task, and the extent to which a given criterion task may be generalized to statements about functional abilities, must be carefully analyzed.

There is a major need for studies of the effectiveness of various types of training in cognitive abilities that involve understanding of the physical world.

Training studies are particularly valuable in areas where there is a fairly regular developmental course of acquisition of abilities. Research on training techniques must also be appropriately hierarchical, including attention to subject characteristics (and their antecedents) and a careful assessment of training-related improvements in the criterion tasks as well as those abilities which the criterion tasks are assumed to represent.

The imagery question arises in several areas within the cognitive realm, such as spatial behavior and learning abilities. There is a need for research on types of imagery and on the functional importance of imagery. Hall's (1981a,b; 1983) work provides welcome progress in this area. Given the implicit difficulties in defining imagery and the multiplicity of ways the term has been used, it is especially important to devote careful attention to definitions. One way of ensuring this attention is to maintain an orientation to the functional tasks in which imagery is thought to be required. Another requirement of research in this area is to provide a careful analysis of the imagery tasks, and to avoid the assumption that all possible tasks defined to tap "imagery" are equivalent.

The work in cognitive style is potentially very important in its implications for educational approaches with blind children. The possibility that blind children in general are characterized by different cognitive styles than sighted children deserves more attention, as does the likelihood that there is at least as great a range of individual variation in cognitive style among blind children as there is among the sighted. Research on these questions has potential relevance for the issue of individualization of residential educational instruction for blind children, as well as for the issue of the integrated classroom.

Intelligence. A primary point of concern with the area of intelligence testing of blind children has to do with validity. The fact that a particular test has enjoyed wide use with sighted children constitutes no ground for the assumption that it must therefore be a valid test for blind children. In fact, the popularity of the intelligence testing movement with sighted children should not be used to argue that the intelligence testing of blind children should enjoy similar importance. The usefulness of standardized testing for any population must be determined with reference to that population. If it is found that intelligence tests are useful predictors of some areas of adaptation (e.g., school achievement) for blind children, then testing should be done. The uses to which such tests are put should always be carefully evaluated, and the use of a test for purposes for which it was not specifically designed should be avoided. Before any test is used for purposes that have implications for what will happen to the child as a result of his performance (e.g., placement), the test should be studied in considerably more detail than has been done for most of the tests currently used with the blind. In particular, such evaluation should be directed to the predictive validity of the test for the specific purpose for which it is to be used. It simply is not justified to use the verbal WISC, for example, for purposes of educational placement or prognosis of blind children simply because the test has been shown to have good predictive validity with respect to the educational achievement of sighted children. Furthermore, the demonstration of the predictive validity of a test with respect to one class of criterion behaviors (e.g., educational achievement) cannot be taken as demonstration of the validity of that test for another class (e.g., readiness for formal mobility instruction), even if the test was developed for and normed on blind children. The validity issue cannot be stressed heavily enough. Standardized tests are simply handy indicators of abilities or characteristics, and the behaviors required by the tests often bear little similarity to the behaviors of which the tests are thought to be indicators. The tendency to place such tests on pedestals is most insidious, and should be conscientiously held in check.

There has been a substantial effort devoted to studying the relationships of status variables, such as degree of residual vision, duration of early vision, and chronological age, to performance on tests of intelligence. While this sort of research is useful, it should be kept in careful perspective. Specifically, the relationship between these variables and tested IQ should not be of primary concern. Rather, the relationships between these variables and the abilities or behaviors of which the IQ tests are taken to be indicators are important. A general point that has been repeatedly stressed elsewhere in this and other chapters should again be repeated here. The most beneficial research is that which is concerned with hierarchically related sets of variables. Antecedents such as the status variables mentioned above, along with others such as the nature of the learning environment, should be studied in conjunction with intelligence test performance and with aspects of functional behavior such as actual success in school situations. The primary concern, in fact, should be with the relationships between the antecedents and the functional behaviors, and the indicators, IQ tests, should not be allowed to interfere with that primary goal.

It has been stressed in many papers that there are variables that act as "suppressors" of intelligence as evaluated by standardized tests. This point appears in several papers on the intelligence of emotionally disturbed children, for example, and it is often suggested that the emotional problems have suppressed the expression of intelligence as assessed by the intelligence test. This point is typically made on the basis of "clinical intuition," however, and it is important to develop more reliable ways than are presently available for assessing and excluding such depressor effects. The acquisition of a larger data base about these situations is an important step in the direction of the goal of more effective evaluation, and concentrated attention should be devoted to the acquisition of such data.

A final point should be made about the research that has been devoted to the evaluation of the intelligence characteristics of various "special groups," such as retinoblastoma or RLF children. To the extent that such evaluation aids in the understanding of the characteristics of these groups, the research is valuable. There is an attendant danger, however, and it should be carefully weighed. Findings about the characteristics of a group should never be allowed to stand in the way of individualized evaluation of a member of that group. Overgeneralization should be avoided. This point is particularly important for, although not limited to, groups such as retinoblastoma where the literature contains apparent contradictions. It may well be the case that retinoblastoma children are bimodally distributed with respect to intelligence, and thus the application of a group characteristic to an individual member of the group would be especially inappropriate.

Language development

There are a number of questions in the language area that were identified in Chapter 5 as lacking definitive resolution. Several of these questions, although their answers would be interesting and informative, are less demanding of research attention. An example is the nature of the transition from babbling to initial word sounds and whether the relationship between these two categories of behavior is different for blind and sighted children. A variation of this question has to do with the possibility that the sounds produced by blind children are more muted, or less well defined. There is some evidence that there may be such differences. However, there is also evidence that any such differences do not produce functional deficits in the comprehensibility of the blind child's speech (Brieland, 1950). Comprehensibility, as a vehicle to communication, is the critical functional aspect of sound production, and since there are apparently no differences in comprehensibility, the issue of differences in sound quality becomes less important. Another question on which there is relatively little evidence is that of the growth of early vocabulary. Although there is some argument for temporary lags in vocabulary acquisition in blind children (Burlingham, 1961, 1965), the lags are apparently not marked. In any case, the more important issue concerns possible deficiencies in the meanings carried by words. A reasonable question is whether the proportion of the words in the child's vocabulary that are functionally effective is lower in blind children, and more importantly, whether any delay in effective vocabulary is functionally involved in other abilities that depend on language, such as self-instructed behavior, cognitive development, and interpersonal communication. The verbalism issue arises here, and there has been a very low ratio of reliable information and careful analysis to total pages written on this question. The review by Dokecki (1966) is an important exception—in this paper the issues are discussed clearly and logically. In discussing the functional aspect of word meaning, Dokecki concluded: "It still remains to be demonstrated that associative and word-thing meanings are functionally different for the blind or for any other group" (p. 528). Results from subsequent research (DeMott, 1972) supported Dokecki's scepticism with regard to the verbalism issue as discussed by Cutsforth and others. The study by DeMott was an important one, and since the issue is a vital one in a functional sense, it would be useful to have the same question studied from different approaches.

A valuable approach involves the study of the relationship between the child's early language environment and his subsequent use of "visual" as well as other categories of words. It may be that two blind children might use visual words equally frequently, but that the usage of one child might be more adequate in a functional sense than that of the other child. It would be valuable to generate a research approach that would allow relationships to be drawn between functional usage differences and types of verbal interaction such as "elaborative" vs. "restrictive" usages, or special attempts to provide experiential bases for words. The recent work by Andersen and her colleagues (Andersen et al., in press; Kekelis & Andersen, 1983) and by Urwin (1978) serves as an important demonstration that these issues can be effectively addressed by close attention to the details of the child's language use and to the linguistic context in which it occurs.

The self-instructive function of language was mentioned above, and since there has been little or no research on this aspect of language function in blind children, the issue bears some elaboration. Luria (1959) detailed stages in the development of the sighted child's ability to control his behavior according to either his own verbal instruction or that of an adult. The sighted child is able to initiate behavior by a verbal command, but until at least the age of three he is much less able to inhibit his behavior selectively upon either his own or an external verbal command. One aspect of the difficulty in inhibiting behavior by verbal command is apparently the relative strength of perceptual cues, and it is only gradually that the child can free his behavior from dependence on perceptual cues and bring it under the control of verbal cues. Although this area of language development has not received concentrated attention in sighted children, research on verbal control of behavior might prove quite productive in the understanding of the development of blind children. Fraiberg and Adelson (1976) provided evidence from the case report of a two-year-old congenitally blind girl that self-instructed behavior may be effective in the blind child. The child "employed parental admonitions to inhibit forbidden actions. 'Don't put your finger in your eye,' she said to herself, imitating her mother's voice when she pressed her eye, and sometimes succeeded in inhibiting the act" (p. 138). Other writers have noted that, though the interpersonal, shared aspects of verbal behavior may be deficient, the blind child does sometimes effectively use a personal system of communication. Such a system may effectively mediate the self-direction of behavior even though it is not adequate for interpersonal communication. The issues involved here certainly deserve research attention.

Another issue discussed in Chapter 5 that merits some perspective is nonverbal communication. Several researchers and more casual observers have noted that, with increasing age, blind children and adults become less elaborative in the use of facial, manual, and body expressions and gestures, and some of these writers (e.g., Apple, 1972) have suggested that expressions and gestures might be taught. While there is undoubtedly benefit to be gained from such instruction, the matter should be kept in careful perspective. The purely "cosmetic" purpose of facial expressions and gestures should probably be separated from the communicative purpose, although the two are not completely separable since the use of inappropriate gestures or expressions can interfere with communication. But blind children should not be taught to make gestures and expressions simply to make them look like sighted children. The effectiveness of gestures and expressions in enhancing communication should be examined, as should methods of teaching them.

A general point may be made with respect to potential research on language in blind children. Where language differences are found between blind and sighted children, care must be taken to assess whether the language difference is primarily an issue of language, or is attributable to some other, and possibly more basic, difference. For example, language development is closely related to and interdependent with cognitive development. It may be that certain differences in language ability may be a direct product of differences in cognitive abilities. To the extent that language is an overt manifestation of underlying cognitive functioning, it would be of little use to attempt to eliminate the language lag without prior or simultaneous attention to the cognitive area. The use of personal pronouns may be a case in point: several investigators (e.g., Fraiberg & Adelson, 1976) have noted differences between blind and sighted children. To the extent that the blind child is delayed in establishing a firm distinction between himself and other people, differences in pronoun usage would be expected. A full understanding of the issue requires attention to both cognitive and language aspects.

Social development

Within the area of social development, there is a clear need for research on the phenomenon of attachment and on the variables that affect it. In this usage, attachment is considered in a relatively limited sense to denote the first emotional ties that occur typically in the first year for sighted children. As such, attachment is considered to be the basis for the subsequent establishment of emotional ties with other people, and is a very important phenomenon. There is a great need for research on the factors influencing the onset and strength of attachment, as well as on the factors affecting the subsequent broadening of the social and emotional responsiveness to and relationships with a wider set of people. As assessed by the indicators typically used with sighted children, such as stranger fear and separation anxiety, there apparently are lags shown by blind children. It is not clear that these indicators are equivalent for blind children, though, and effort should be devoted to this question, as well as to the question of whether there are more valid indicators for blind children. The question cannot stop simply with the establishment and study of suitable indicators—it is even more important to determine what functional significance any developmental differences might have for the blind child. It is likely that multivariate approaches will be required for effective treatment of these questions, since attachment is surely as multiply determined in blind children as it is in sighted. Further, it is apparent that, besides the social factors that are involved, there are aspects of cognitive functioning that must be considered as an integral part of social attachment.

A related issue needing further study is the role of social attachment in nonsocial behaviors such as exploration of the environment. There is convincing evidence that a good "emotional security base" is critical for the development of effective exploratory behavior. An important component of this issue is to maintain the blind child's ongoing awareness of the parent's presence, since vision apparently serves an important function in this regard for the sighted child.

More research is needed on the factors influencing the effects of separation from the parents or other people who are important to the blind child. Periods of forced separation are an almost inevitable concomitant of early blindness, and there is abundant evidence for the potentially harmful results of such separation. It is unfortunate that most of the reports on the effects of separation have concentrated on negative cases. There are undoubtedly cases in which separation has occurred, but where the effects have not been serious. It would be of benefit to the literature in this area to have reports of such cases, accompanied by a careful analysis of the factors that seem to have mitigated the potential harmful effects.

Identification has been almost totally neglected in the blindness literature. Identification is the process that is hypothesized to account for the child's acquisition of sets of characteristics of the parents or other important people. There are several theoretical formulations of the dynamics of the identification process, most notably the psychodynamic and the social learning approaches. The social learning formulation, involving imitation, modeling, and social reinforcement, seems especially useful in approaching the identification question in the blind child, since testable predictions about the effects of the lack of vision should be easily generated within this framework. There has apparently been no careful and thorough attempt to analyze the identification of blind children within this framework, though, and there is virtually no research on the process of identification. This is one of the most substantial and unfortunate gaps in the literature on the social development of the blind child.

The question of the social maturity or social competence of blind children has received some attention, but there are major questions yet to be answered. Apparently, few practitioners or researchers are satisfied that a suitable test of the social maturity of young blind children exists. The Maxfield-Buchholz Scale is considered by many to be very difficult to administer to preschool children, but an adequate substitute has not been developed. The Reynell-Zinkin Developmental Scales (Reynell & Zinkin, 1975) are promising, but they have not as yet been adequately evaluated for their reliability or validity characteristics. Many practitioners prefer the "seat of the pants" method of assessing social competence, and claim a high degree of validity and reliability for their judgments. As good as an individual's judgments may be, though, research using such approaches is less than satisfying, and program evaluations and comparisons are suspect when the validity and reliability of evaluation cannot be demonstrated. The substantive questions of social maturity also need attention. While most studies and informal observations agree that the blind child is socially less mature than his sighted peer, the reasons for the lags are generally not specified. Useful formulations have been made in terms of interpersonal emotional processes and social expectations, but at present these formulations are for the most part restricted to explanatory function and are not generally useful in predictive, ameliorative, or preventive contexts. Analyses of social maturity have in large part been directed to descriptions of the blind child who shows substantial lags. Two supplementary lines of research should prove useful. First, more attention should be paid to the antecedent conditions of social immaturity. That is, an intensive attempt should be made to identify these social environmental situations that produce children with lags in social maturity. Second, far greater attention should be paid to those blind children who do not show lags, and their social environments should be carefully studied for clues to the etiology of their maturity. Research paradigms such as that of Imamura (1965), who studied the social interactive characteristics of both children and parents, should prove useful, particularly if they can be conducted within a longitudinal framework.

Knowledge about sexual characteristics and functions is a clearly identifiable aspect of the social maturity question, and this area has only recently begun to receive careful attention. There is important research to be done here. The need for evaluation of sex-education programs cannot be stressed heavily enough.

Finally, there is a major need for research on the dynamics of the integration of blind children into various social groups beyond the immediate family, whether these groups include primarily blind children, primarily sighted children, or both. An obvious and important social situation that falls under this topic is the child's integration into and adjustment to the school situation. There has been some work on assessment of the attitudes both of the blind child and of the receiving group, but there is little such research that would prescribe how such social situations might be structured in order to lead to a smoother socialization process.

Personality development

Several large areas of need can be identified in the literature on personality development. An obvious gap occurs in the younger age ranges: the case-report material on children up to several years of age, coming as it does from the study of relatively small samples of children, cannot be considered normative or representative in any strict sense. The gap between this age range and middle school age is even more severe, since there are few case reports available.

Research with standardized instruments is almost nonexistent for blind children through the middle school years.

Another major gap exists in the availability of personality-assessment instruments for blind children. The problems stem partly from the inappropriate adaptation of tests normed for sighted children, and partly from the failure of investigators to agree on a limited number of instruments to be used with the blind. This second point is particularly applicable to projective tests, and the result is that there is not sufficient accumulated evidence about any of the tests in use to allow them to be used effectively.

The fact that a given test probably cannot be administered to blind and sighted children with equivalent validity means that the goal of comparing blind with sighted children on personality characteristics or profiles is an impossible one. It may even be an inappropriate goal. Rather than comparing blind with sighted children, research should be concentrated on more intensive evaluation of blind children. To date, much of the work on blind children has been simply evaluative, producing statements that blind children are more or less aggressive, or introverted, for example. Such conclusions are interesting, but not really useful, and the research should be expanded in two directions. One is toward discovering the etiological factors that produce variation in some of the more important personality dimensions, and the other is toward discovering the manner in which various personality characteristics are functionally expressed. Ideally, all three levels of inquiry, etiology, description, and functional expression, should be included in any piece of research. Investigation of etiological factors clearly requires a multivariate approach, including both multiple determining variables and multiple personality characteristics. The issue of the functional expression of personality characteristics deserves brief elaboration. We do not advance very far by describing the characteristics of a sample, or by comparing the characteristics of several samples. Beyond description, we need to know how those personality characteristics become expressed in real-life situations, and what advantages or disadvantages a person with certain characteristics might have in certain situations. Among others, locus of control is a dimension that deserves concentrated research attention, with respect to both the etiology and the functional expression questions. The functional questions are important since they bear on characteristics of motivation for achievement, mobility, independence, and other related variables.

The relationship between the assessment of personality characteristics and functional expression is even more important in the area of emotional adjustment. The vagueness of definitions in this area was noted in Chapter 7. Better-defined concepts, and particularly definitions that draw relationships between measured personality characteristics and the characteristics of behavior in real situations, would be of great benefit.

More attention has been devoted to the etiological question in the area of the more severe emotional disturbances, but the issues are by no means resolved. One unresolved question is whether the syndrome noted particularly in some RLF children is in fact autism or is rather some other condition that simply has several characteristics in common with autism. However, this question is probably not the most important one. A negative answer to the question would leave the blind child no further ahead than he is now. An affirmative answer might not help much either, since it is by no means clear either that the causal factors would work in the same ways for blind and sighted children or that the remedial approaches would be similarly effective. The question of the parallel between sighted autistic children and emotionally disturbed blind children may not be a useful one in any practical sense. Attention should instead be concentrated on the etiological factors in blind children, with regard for social and sensory factors as well as the particular role that visual loss might play in exacerbating the situation. An approach that has not been explored very much but that might provide useful information involves the study of children who are not emotionally disturbed. For example, if a particular constellation of factors is found to be correlated with the occurrence of serious emotional disturbance, then the discovery that the same constellation does not typically occur in nondisturbed children would provide a useful additional corroboration. The finding that the constellation does occur in nondisturbed children would necessitate reevaluation of the hypothesized relation between those factors and emotional disturbance. In any case, it is clear that the effective study of the etiology of emotional disturbance demands a multivariate approach. The interactions among classes of sensory, social, and birth-situation factors are undoubtedly complex, and univariate approaches are simply not powerful enough.

Finally, with respect to the question of therapeutic approaches, it is sufficient simply to reiterate a point made in Chapter 7. There is a clear need for the careful evaluation of the effectiveness of the various therapeutic approaches for the various types of problem encountered. One of the strongest conclusions from outcome research with sighted clients is that various therapies are differentially effective with different problems. The situation can be no less complex for blind children. To the extent that therapists are strongly committed to a particular therapeutic school, they will probably be less totally effective than if they were able to choose a therapy to fit the specific case. Such effective selection cannot be made without an evaluation basis, and so the need for objective assessment of outcomes is critical to progress in the field.

Age at onset of blindness

An area that deserves intensive attention does not fit into any of the foregoing sections, since it applies to the research in each of the areas covered in those sections. There has been relatively little effort devoted to the study of the reactions of children who become blind at various ages, or of the effects of "later blindness" on the various areas of ability and behavior. Age at blindness has been included as a variable in research in some areas, notably perception, but it has typically been used as a "control variable" rather than as a variable worthy of study in its own right. The proportion of the blind population that is blind from birth is relatively small, yet a large proportion of the available research has effectively disregarded the age-at-onset variable. There is reason to suspect that varying durations of early vision have substantial effects on the nature of subsequent development, and much more direct study of these effects should be made.

Multiple handicaps

The term "multiple handicap" is used to refer to the coincidence of any of a variety of conditions with blindness, conditions which if they were not accompanied by blindness would in themselves constitute areas of concern. Writers differ in their specificity of classification of multiple handicaps, but several obvious categories may be identified: emotional disturbance, physical handicap, mental retardation, and deafness. There is often overlap among these categories, and they should not be regarded as mutually exclusive.

Some of the research work on various categories of multiple handicap has been described in the preceding chapters, but there is not a large enough research literature on any of the categories to warrant a special chapter. The relative neglect of the multiply handicapped child in research contexts is remarkable in view of the high incidence of multiple handicaps in the population of blind children. The incidence is in fact difficult to estimate. Probably the best information is contained in a paper by Cruickshank (1964), who assessed the incidence of multiple handicaps (excluding deaf-blind) in a group of 2773 blind children in New York State. Of the 2058 children for whom IQ scores were available, 42 percent had IQ below 90. According to the expectations of IQ scores based on the normal distribution, 25 percent of any random sample should score below 90. However, IQ data were not available for 715 children, and it seems likely that low intelligence children may have been overrepresented in the nontested part of the sample. In any case, there are substantial numbers of blind children who fall into the low-IQ categories. Of the 2236 children for whom incidence of emotional adjustment was available, 35 percent showed evidence of emotional disturbance, while 65 percent were "within normal limits for their chronological age." Of the total group, 21 percent were classified as brain-injured, although Cruickshank noted that some of the 4.5 percent who were classified as hyperactive or aggressive may have been brain-injured as well. Of the total group, 31 percent were classified as having one or more of a variety of physical disabilities. Of these 31 percent, 24 percent showed cerebral palsy, while 14 percent had epileptic symptoms. Data are available from other sources for deaf-blind children. For example, Burns and Stenquist (1960) estimated that there were almost 400 deaf-blind children in the United States below the age of 20.

Thus it is clear that the problem of multiple handicap is a serious one from the point of view of incidence, and the figures cited above make it all the more striking that only a very small proportion of the research reported with blind children has concerned the multiply handicapped. There are undoubtedly several reasons for this relative neglect. Cruickshank (1964) noted one such reason: "They remain almost completely ignored because insufficient numbers exist in a single agency either to bring the problem forcibly to the attention of professional personnel or to permit professional personnel to become sophisticated regarding its nature" (p. 74). Another difficulty is certainly that the multiply handicapped blind child is an even more difficult subject for whom to design valid indices of various abilities than is the blind child, since the problem of visual impairment is compounded by limitations in other areas of performance. Still another reason for research neglect of multiply handicapped children is the extreme heterogeneity of the children within any of the various definitional categories. Even within a reasonably specifiable dual handicap such as blindness–deafness, the range of both visual and auditory abilities is extreme, and thus any limited sample of such children cannot be reliably regarded as representative of the entire group.

Much of the literature on multiple handicaps stresses the need for adequately detailed evaluation of and differential prescription for these children. The multiple handicaps program at Syracuse University, for example, generated several papers (Dinsmore, 1967; Root & Riley, 1960) that described in some detail the evaluative procedures that were used. Far less emphasis was placed, in these papers, on the details of how programs were prescribed for individual children, and almost no mention was made of any evaluation of the success of the programs that were prescribed. Therefore, it is virtually impossible to make any objective conclusion about the effectiveness of the diagnosis, the prescription, or the success of the prescribed program. It is not at all clear at what point the system may have been especially strong or weak, or even whether the children were better off for having been exposed to the process.

There is a great need for research on two levels with the multiply handicapped blind child. First, the evaluation of abilities has been almost totally neglected, so that it is not possible to evaluate the abilities and behavior of a given child against a background of data. Thus it is almost impossible to make a determination of the level at which a remedial program should be directed for any given ability area. Second, there is a great need for evaluation to be conducted on the effectiveness of various remedial or program approaches. Several approaches are used in connection with any of the types of multiple handicap, and it would be useful to have information about the relative effectiveness of the various approaches. Without effective program evaluation, the field of intervention with multiply handicapped blind children cannot move very far forward.

It may well be possible to combine these two research goals into a single research format, in which normative and descriptive information about various aspects of development is gathered at the same time that evaluation is conducted of programs to which the children are exposed. Several of the larger centers would have to engage in close cooperation in order to ensure the successful conduct of this research, since there are, as Cruickshank pointed out, relatively small numbers of children in any given multiple-handicap category available at any single location. Over a period of several years, however, pooled evaluative data could become available from substantial numbers of multiply handicapped children. In addition, if effective program evaluation were conducted, a pool of information on the relative effectiveness of various diagnostic and prescriptive procedures would become available.

Themes

Throughout the preceding sections, several themes have appeared repeatedly and bear some elaboration.

Theoretical bases

There is a need for a theoretical basis for research in many areas of blindness. Individual studies often seem to have been conducted "in isolation" from a larger body of related literature. This isolation is sometimes apparent from the author's failure to cite and review related studies, but often from failure to relate the research question to a larger framework and/or discuss the findings in this relation. It is partly because of this relative isolation of studies on blindness that the research in some areas seems so disjointed. The research on tactual perception is a good example: while there are as many good research papers available in this area as in any other, they do not fall easily into a framework out of which summary statements emerge, or out of which it is possible to generate practical applications. Tactual perception may be the best example of an area for which the argument can be made that there is enough research to allow identification of the important parameters so that the area is ready to be systematized and to have larger-scale, intensive, and integrated intervention projects conducted. To date there has been little such work done. A contrast to the relatively atheoretical body of research in tactual perception is the recent surge of interest in cognitive development within the Piagetian theoretical framework. Although there is far less cognitive than tactual perception research available, the cognitive development area is in a better position to make major advances. The reason is that the various findings may be tied together into a system such that research on one aspect of the system has implications for other aspects. By contrast, the disjointed nature of the tactual perception field almost necessarily restricts the implications of a given piece of research to a small area.

Following the cognitive-development example briefly, it should be noted that, although the Piagetian theoretical framework has helped to define research questions and has provided a common methodology, it has not as yet helped substantially in the integration of the various results into a common framework. In part this failure is attributable to the fact that the Piagetian system is itself more a descriptive than a process approach to development. The theory has been criticized for failing to propose change mechanisms that are amenable to experimental test. Another reason that Piagetian interpretation has not been as helpful as possible is that most researchers on cognitive development in blind children have not paid careful enough attention to those variables that may be particularly implicated in producing differences among blind children, or between blind and sighted children. Variables such as degree of remaining vision, history of early vision, and learning environment have not been effectively studied.

Although I am making the argument for using theoretical systems in organizing knowledge about blindness and development, I do not suggest that theoretical systems should be borrowed from the sighted literature without regard to suitable modification for use with the blind. The role of vision in some areas of development may be so important that the lack of vision would force an almost total reorganization of the other variables in the explanatory or predictive system. However, the point should not be lost: careful attention to the integration of research findings into a systematic organization would be of benefit to the field both in providing meaningful direction for research and in allowing meaningful interpretation of the results of research.

Another aspect of the need for a more broadly based approach to the study of blind children has to do with the interrelations among various aspects of development. It is perhaps unfortunate that a review such as this has to be organized into chapters, each dealing with a "separate" area of development. The areas are not, in fact, separate. The interrelations among the areas are too numerous to list exhaustively, but several examples may serve to emphasize the point. Cognitive development does not proceed independently of language or perceptual development. Language development is closely interrelated with perceptual development, as is exemplified by the verbalism issue. Social and personality development are not independent of cognitive, perceptual, and language development. The development of communication is an important component of socialization, and cognitive development (object constancy) is heavily implicated in the development of social and emotional ties. These are merely some of the more obvious examples of interrelationships among the various areas of development, and pages could be devoted to elaborating these and other interdependencies. Studies of development should not be constrained to or interpreted within narrow areas of development.

Functional emphasis

In virtually every area of research on the development of blind children, there is a need for research to be concentrated on functional behaviors and abilities. In blindness research, just as in most psychological research, the tendency has been to concentrate on those abilities and behaviors that are amenable to study in the laboratory or the structured situation. This level of inquiry is important, but it is not sufficient. Researchers must not stop short of evaluating the relationships between those laboratory behaviors and the real-world behaviors of which the laboratory behaviors are thought to be representative. It is simply not sufficient to study, for example, the relative finger-maze learning abilities of early and later blind children. At the same time that maze learning is evaluated, researchers should also study the abilities of the children to perform real-world behaviors, such as mobility map use, which the laboratory behaviors are thought to represent. Children do not, after all, have to perform finger-mazes very often. I do not want to argue that the laboratory refinements are not important—it is often only in the laboratory that adequate control over relevant variables may be exercised. But the laboratory is not enough.

Individual differences

The need for attention to individual differences has been stressed repeatedly. Although many areas of psychology, such as personality, have devoted considerable attention to the investigation of the ways in which individuals differ from one another, some areas have taken the approach of studying primarily the commonalities among people. This orientation can be identified by the concentration of results sections on group means, and by the relative neglect of within-group variation. I argue that this approach is not a suitable one for the study of blindness, and particularly for the developmental aspects of blindness. The study of commonalities is most suited for populations which are characterized by little variation or by homogeneous characteristics. Blindness is nothing if it is not heterogeneous. Researchers on the blind cannot indulge in the luxury of studying the group mean and neglecting variation from it, since it is just that variation that contains the potential for the effective individualization that is needed for a heterogeneous population. Substantial variability almost always occurs in sets of research results, and a large proportion of that variability can almost certainly be traced to determinant factors if the effort is made. Early experience has become a banner carried by developmental psychologists, and certainly some of the variability in the abilities and behavior of blind (and sighted) children is produced by variations in their early experience. The human development literature has not been very successful in tracing the causality of individual variation to specific aspects of early experience, however. One reason for this lack of success is that adequate ways of characterizing and quantifying aspects of experience have not been developed. This point is just as true of the sighted literature as it is of the blindness literature, but if anything it is more important to develop effective ways of studying the effects of experience for blind children than it is for sighted children, since the implications are more directly obvious for the blind. In research on every aspect of development far more attention must be devoted to assessment of the characteristics of the environment in which the blind child functions and develops. A strong orientation to the importance of the "learning environment" was provided by Norris et al. 20 years ago. Other writers have stressed the importance of the environment in affecting development in other areas, such as social-emotional or mobility. Despite these writings, there has been little organized effort devoted to the study of the characteristics of the environment and their effects on various aspects of development. People who work with blind children (including educators, parents, and other providers of services) have a great deal of potential and obligation for structuring the child's environment in such a way as to provide the opportunity for optimal development. The fulfillment of this potential and obligation will be possible only if research is conducted with adequate attention to the etiology and significance of individual differences.

9
Issues in Research Methodology

Technical Issues

I have become somewhat disappointed with the body of literature on blind children. The disappointment centers around my conclusion that the sum of real knowledge that can be distilled from this literature seems small in relation to the effort that has gone into producing it. There are two major reasons for this situation. The first concerns the research models that have been used extensively with the blind child. Most of the models have been borrowed with little or no modification from research with sighted children and are therefore not ideally suited for research with a population that is both extremely heterogeneous and relatively scarce. Later in this chapter, I will propose a model that I think is a much more suitable one for research with blind children. The second reason has to do with quality. Much of the work on blindness is characterized by various types of methodological weakness that decrease the value of the research. The purpose of the first section of this chapter is to point out some of the more common of these weaknesses and to suggest ways in which they might be avoided or ameliorated. Some of the problems are inherent in the study of any heterogeneous group of events, and these problems cannot be totally avoided. They can, however, often be handled in ways that minimize the researcher's disadvantage, and in fact some aspects of heterogeneity may be effectively exploited to the researcher's advantage. Another category of problems involves those difficulties that could and should be avoided by conscientious and well-informed researchers. Good research is difficult to do, but bad research is not worth doing at all. It would be of benefit to the field to have far fewer studies done each year, but to have them done as well as is possible within the constraints of the subject matter. Just as discouraging as reading poorly executed research is reading about research that might well have been good work, but is reported in such a way that one does not know whether it was good or bad, or what may be safely concluded from it.

Subject selection and description

Perhaps the most serious, and at the same time the most common, shortcoming of research on blindness is the failure to specify and adequately analyze certain important characteristics of the samples. The characteristics that will be discussed undoubtedly have more influence on the results in some areas of research than in others. Even so, it is rarely if ever justified to omit consideration of these characteristics. The variables in question here include chronological age (CA), IQ or mental age (MA), residual vision, cause of blindness, age at onset of blindness, and duration of blindness. Sex might also be included in this list, although it probably has a critical effect on results less often than the other variables. All these are "status" or "self-selected" variables. That is, they are characteristics that the subject brings with him to the research setting; they are not under the potential control of the researcher. The researcher's most important responsibility with respect to these variables is to record and report them. The characteristics of the research sample simply must not be omitted in published reports. Although this point may seem self-evident, far too many of the research papers reviewed in this work have some type of shortcoming in this area. Beyond the recording and reporting of these characteristics, the researcher has the further obligation to deal with the variables in both the research design (subject selection) and the statistical analysis portions of the work. The notion of heterogeneity of the blind population was introduced above, and it is particularly with respect to these self-selected variables that heterogeneity becomes an important issue. The sample available to any researcher almost certainly contains individuals who differ widely from one another on several or all of these variables. The researcher has two general approaches available to deal with this heterogeneity. First, he can select a sample carefully to ensure homogeneity with respect to all the variables that might possibly influence the dependent variables in which he is interested. (If this approach is chosen, the researcher incurs an important responsibility to describe the selection procedures and the characteristics of the resultant sample.) In general, this approach is extremely uneconomical with respect to use of potential subjects, since in order to obtain a homogeneous sample the researcher may have to exclude a large proportion of the potential subjects on the grounds of their "status" on one or more of these variables. The second approach to the heterogeneity problem is to integrate the variation into the research design and the statistical analysis. Statistical procedures for treating heterogeneous samples are available, and their increasing use in conjunction with computerized treatment of data makes it quite possible to "control" these variables statistically rather than by subject selection. Thus, the researcher may consider such variables as part of the research design, in that he can plan from the outset to evaluate the variation in results attributable to these variables, in much the same way that he evaluates the effect of a particular experimental "treatment."

There are several significant advantages to be gained from this second approach to heterogeneity. One is the increased economy of use of potential subjects. A second advantage is the possibility of evaluating, rather than simply ignoring, the effects of these variables. Such evaluation makes possible comparative conclusions about various subgroups or subjects, rather than requiring a restriction of the conclusions to a limited and homogeneous sample. Third, to the extent that these variables are found not to exert a significant effect on the dependent variables, more generalized conclusions may be drawn from the research than if a restricted homogeneous sample had been used. In connection with the situation where such variables are found not to have an effect on the dependent variables, these "negative" results should definitely be reported. In experimental research, there is often a concern with the interpretation of negative results. That is, when a particular experimental manipulation is not found to produce a difference in comparison to a control condition, the negative result always leaves open the possibility that the chosen experimental manipulation was not an adequate way of making the variable in question operational, and that with a different approach a significant difference would have emerged. This conservatism, while fully in order for experimentally manipulated variables, is generally not warranted for self-selected variables. The difference is simply that these self-selected variables are not under the experimenter's control, and thus, barring his failure to categorize his subjects adequately on these variables or to measure the dependent variable in an appropriate way, there is nothing in the research itself on which to blame the failure to find differences. Thus the "no difference" result may be much more confidently represented as the true state of affairs.

There are several ways that statistical evaluation of self-selected variables may be done, and the method must be carefully selected on the basis of the nature of the variable and the distribution of the subjects on the variable. For the "nature of the variable," the key distinction is whether the variable is a discrete or a continuous variable. A discrete variable is one where there is not a gradual progression from one category to another. A good example is cause of blindness, where it is not meaningful, for example, to speak of a gradation from retinoblastoma to RLF. For discrete variables, analysis should usually be done by separating the subjects into appropriate groups and comparing the groups on the dependent variable. All the variables having to do with either time (CA, age at onset, duration of blindness) or amount (IQ, residual vision) are continuous variables. If a key condition is met by the sample, correlational analysis, is usually the best method of evaluating the effects of these variables. That is, the dependent variable is correlated with the self-selected variable and the statistical significance of the correlation is evaluated. The key condition, and it is a very important one, is that in order to conduct correlational analysis there must in fact be a reasonably continuous distribution of the subjects in the sample with respect to the self-selected variable. Thus, if the sample is reasonably distributed with respect to CA, then correlation of the dependent variable with CA may be conducted. If the sample shows clustering on the self-selected variable, though, correlational analysis may be inappropriate. This situation would occur, for example, if the researcher chose samples of first- and fourth-graders. The CA of the combined sample would be discontinuous, and the subjects would be bimodally distributed with concentrations in the six- and nine-year ranges. In such a situation, two types of analysis should usually be conducted. First, the samples of first- and fourth-graders should be compared with each other by means of a *t*-test or other statistic designed for the comparison of groups. Second, correlational analysis should be conducted between CA and the dependent variable within each of the two CA clusters. A second, somewhat different, example may serve to round out this picture. Consider a situation where the age at onset of blindness ranges from birth to four years, and where the subjects (a group of six-year-olds) are tested on a task involving texture discrimination. In most such samples there would be a cluster of subjects, perhaps half the total sample, who have been blind since birth. The others might have become blind at some time between birth and four years of age. Although age at onset is technically a continuous variable, it would not be appropriate in this case to correlate age at onset with texture performance using the entire example, since the relative concentration of subjects in the blind-from-birth end of the continuum would tend to suppress the possibility of discovering a significant correlation between the two variables. The appropriate procedure in such a case is to exclude the subjects who have been blind from birth, and then to correlate age at onset with the dependent variable only for the remaining subsample.

In general, when the characteristics of the sample allow it, the effects of these self-selected variables should be evaluated by correlational analysis rather than by comparing subgroups. There is a statistical basis for this argument. Consider a situation where some characteristic is studied in a group of children ranging in CA from five to 10. If the children are distributed in CA across the entire CA range from five to 10, then it would be inappropriate to divide the children into groups (five through seven and eight through 10). Such a procedure would combine seven-year-olds with five-year-olds and eight-year-olds with ten-year-olds, despite the fact that the seven- and eight-year-olds are more similar to one another than either is to the other extreme in its group. The effect of such a grouping would be to constitute groups with a high degree of "built-in" CA variability, and the variability would artificially decrease the possibility of finding a significant relationship between CA and the dependent variable. Correlational analysis, on the other hand, is specifically designed to make use of the variability in CA, and is therefore the appropriate procedure for allowing a relationship between CA and the dependent variable to be discovered, if in fact the relationship exists.

To complicate the matter of evaluation of self-selected variables still further, it is often the case that two or more of these variables should appropriately be considered in conjunction with one another, since their potential effects are not independent of each other. An example is the relationship between age at onset and cause at blindness. RLF children almost all become effectively blind very early in the first year, while retinoblastoma children range much more widely in age at onset. Thus, the two variables have an interactive relation with one another; that is, they are not independent. If both retinoblastoma and RLF children are included in the same sample, then a simple correlational assessment of age at onset should not be made. Rather, the sample should be subdivided on the basis of cause of blindness. Correlational analysis of age at onset with the dependent variable should be conducted for the retinoblastoma group, but such an analysis would not be appropriate for the RLF group because of the extremely small variability in age at onset. There are several other examples of interdependencies among the self-selected variables under consideration, but they need not be detailed. Suffice it to say that sophisticated and useful multivariate data analytic techniques are available for the treatment of such interactive relationships, and these methods should be used whenever appropriate.

In working with sighted children, the researcher typically selects a sample or samples at random. That is, he chooses children to participate in the research in such a way that each child in the population theoretically has an equal chance of being included in the sample. The purpose of this procedure is to ensure, insofar as is possible, that the sample chosen for participation will not be nonrepresentative of the population with respect to any characteristic that might affect the outcome of the experiment. While random selection is just as desirable in research with the blind, it is often not practical to use random subject selection procedures. There are usually relatively few children available in a given geographical area who belong to the population under study, and the researcher typically must, in order to obtain a large enough sample for adequate statistical analysis, use all the children who are available. Often, in fact, he must travel considerable distances in order to obtain a sufficiently large sample. Thus, random selection of blind children for research samples is typically not feasible. This fact does not necessarily decrease the value of the research, but it increases the burden on the experimenter to follow certain additional procedures, beyond those of the researcher who uses randomly selected groups, in order to make the research optimally useful to other workers. Above all, he must describe the characteristics of the children in the sample. There are several instances in the foregoing chapters where the results from two apparently similar studies stand in direct contradiction to one another. As often as not, it is probably the case that such discrepancies are attributable to the fact that the two researchers were working with samples that were not equivalent. Each may have selected subjects without using any special selection criteria, but the two samples may nevertheless have been different simply because of the immense heterogeneity of the population of blind children. In attempting to resolve such discrepancies, it would be of great benefit to the reader to have as full a description of each of the samples as possible. It is thus incumbent on researchers with blind children to provide such descriptions.

It is particularly important to describe the selection procedures in studies of the incidence of such phenomena as emotional distubance or language disorders. It is almost hopeless, in attempting to make comparisons of the incidence of such phenomena in blind and sighted children, to be certain that the samples studied were truly representative of their respective populations. I do not see the overriding benefit of conducting such comparisons anyway, but if they are done, extremely careful attention to the representativeness of the samples is critical.

The heterogeneity of the population of blind children also has implications for studies that use control groups of blind children. A good example is a simple training study in which the effectiveness of a certain method of teaching a skill is evaluated. Typically, two groups would be selected, and one group would be exposed to the training while the other would not. Then the performance of the two groups on a criterion test of the skill would be compared in order to determine whether the trained group performed significantly better. In order to attribute any superiority to the training procedures, it is critical to be sure that the groups were equivalent before the training began. Usually a pretest is conducted, and the groups are selected in such a way that the pretest performance is the same for the two groups. In training studies on blind children, however, this pretest matching may not be sufficient, since the two groups might be equivalent in pretest performance but still be significantly different in other ways that might influence the potential effect of the training and thus the posttest scores. A useful, but often very difficult, way of avoiding such group differences is to match the groups initially not only on the basis of the pretest but also on the basis of any other variables that might potentially create important incomparabilities between the groups. Often this procedure is not possible because of the limited pool of potential subjects. In this case, the effects of the variables for which matching was not possible should be evaluated in a post hoc fashion by appropriate means. Any differences between the groups would then require appropriate qualification of the results of the study. In general, researchers should be extremely careful not to induce a mismatching of comparison groups by equating them on one relevant variable, when equating on that variable then produces a difference on another relevant variable. This problem often occurs in studies where blind and sighted groups are matched on the basis of school grade, and where this matching produces a mismatch on CA. The danger of CA mismatching tends to increase as school grade increases, since there is a tendency for the range of CA to be wider for the blind than for sighted children in the higher grades. This general problem of group matching is a serious one, and researchers should give it adequate attention in any research paradigm.

Issues of methodology and research design

There are a number of potential problems in the selection of ways to evaluate dependent variables. A task or other measure of an ability or characteristic must be chosen to represent that ability or characteristic adequately. A great deal of care is required in this aspect of research design, since the results of a study are meaningful only to the extent that the characteristic being evaluated is validly represented by the method chosen to measure or test it. Although this point seems trivial, it bears some elaboration. First, adequate working definitions of variables must be provided. Two researchers may have quite different concepts of what "spatial relations" means, for example, and they may thus choose quite different ways of measuring spatial relations ability. One may use a finger maze, while the other may choose a verbal test. Spatial relations is an exceedingly complex issue, and unless adequate definitions are provided within each study it is not possible to fit the results of the study into an overall picture of spatial relations abilities. Second, it is valuable to provide an independent demonstration of the validity of the particular definition with respect to the characteristic being studied. Unless it is clear that a particular way of operationalizing a concept is in fact a valid representation of that concept, the results of the study will be limited in generality. It is not very satisfying to conclude from a study that early blind subjects are worse at finger-maze learning than later blind subjects, but a more general statement about differences in spatial relations abilities can only be made if it can be demonstrated that performance on the finger maze represents a valid aspect of spatial relations abilities. This is a difficult problem, and it has received insufficient attention. Later in this chapter a general approach to its solution will be suggested. The approach involves the inclusion of hierarchical levels of performance in the same study. For example, assessment of finger-maze performance may be accompanied by assessment of behavior in more functional, real-life spatial relations situations.

Careful attention must be devoted to the selection of measures that are sensitive to differences in the subjects under study. The use of a task that is too easy leads to "ceiling effects," where most of the subjects perform very well and therefore are not effectively differentiated by the task. The use of a task that is too difficult leads to similar problems. Task selection is especially difficult in research where the purpose is to assess the development of a characteristic over age. If a common task is used for all children, age effects may be depressed at both the low and the high ends of the CA range because the task is respectively too difficult and too easy for the extremes. Some progress has been made in the design of tasks that can be appropriately varied in difficulty in order to make the task sensitive for a wide range of ages. The model for this type of task is, of course, the IQ test, where items spanning a wide range of difficulty are included. The more difficult items are omitted for the younger children, on the assumption that very few of the children will answer them correctly, and the easier items are omitted for the older children.

Another key to the selection of appropriate measures applies especially in research where different groups such as blind and sighted children are to be compared on the same task. Care must be taken to ensure that the task is appropriate for all groups. The use of IQ tests without consideration of the appropriateness of the items for the blind subjects is an example. This is often a difficult problem, and ways of solving it are not immediately apparent. Sometimes a "commonsense" approach to the problem may be sufficient. A more rigorous, but also more difficult, approach is to conduct validation of the measure for each group. That is, the measure may be assessed, separately for each group, in the extent to which it predicts the characteristic under study. In any case, care must be taken, and if the researcher is not confident that the measure is appropriate for the various groups, then he must assess its appropriateness in a preliminary phase of the research.

In assessing performance on relatively complex tasks, it is important to consider the possibility that poor performance may occur not only as a result of the complex aspects of the task, but also as a result of inadequate ability to perform relatively simple individual components of the task. A good example is found in tasks involving intermodality relations. Consider a task that is designed to assess the ability to integrate auditory with tactual information. Poor performance on the integrative task may in fact be a result of poor integrative ability, but it may also be a result of poor ability to process either the auditory or the tactual information, regardless of the integrative demands of the task. In studies of performance on complex tasks, it is useful to include independent measures of performance on the simpler components of the task.

It is particularly important in studies of perceptual and cognitive abilities to be aware of possible warm-up effects, and to ensure that the subject fully understands the requirements of the task. The purpose of assessing performance on a controlled task is to enable statements to be made about the ability which the task is designed to represent. To the extent that a subject shows an improvement in performance during the course of the task, the conclusion about his ability will tend to err in the direction of underestimating the ability, if a warm-up effect is operating. The most accurate estimate of ability is obtained after performance on the task has stabilized. It is especially important to consider possible warm-up effects when the performances of two or more groups are compared. If one group for some reason shows a more prolonged warm-up effect, then its ability will tend to be underestimated in comparison with that of another group that shows a shorter warm-up effect. A good example of the danger of the warm-up effect may be found in the comparison of the performance of blind subjects with that of blindfolded sighted subjects. The blindfolded sighted subjects may show a more prolonged warm-up effect than the blind subjects, and unless care is taken to compare stabilized performance levels there will be a tendency to underestimate the ability of the sighted subjects. Useful information may be gained from the warm-up effect itself, and it is often instructive to record and analyze performance on warm-up trials independently of the analysis of the stabilized performance. Warm-up effects should not simply be controlled and then forgotten. Rather, their nature should be reported so that subsequent studies may be designed with that information available.

A final methodological point is directed to the use of a common pool of subjects in successive experiments. Because of the limited availability of blind subjects, it is sometimes necessary, either for the same researcher or different researchers, to use the same children in two or more successive studies. Caution must be used in such situations, since the child's participation in one experiment may have carryover effects on his performance in a subsequent experiment. When performance in the subsequent experiment is to be compared with that of a sample of sighted children, such a carryover effect may lead to invalid comparisons, since it is less likely that the sighted subjects would have participated in the previous experiment. It is often difficult or impossible to avoid using blind children in repeated experiments, and it is the researcher's responsibility to be familiar with the "experimental history" of his subjects, to consider the possibilities of carryover effects, and to discuss such issues in his report.

Statistical considerations

Some statistical issues related to the analysis of self-selected variables were discussed earlier, and they need not be repeated here. Aside from these points, there is little in the statistical area for research on blind children that does not also apply to research with sighted children, and it is not within the intent or scope of this work to make an exhaustive treatment of these issues. It remains only to point out that there are several statistical shortcomings occurring frequently enough in studies on the blind to warrant special mention. It is important to provide the reader with enough detail about the results of the research so that the pattern of results can be fully understood. Papers should simply not be accepted for publication without adequate descriptive statistics. Mean scores are important but not sufficient, and they are not useful at all without some information about the variability of the scores around the mean. In conducting tests of statistical significance, the researcher must be certain that the test selected is one that fits the nature of the data. As has been mentioned repeatedly, the samples with which researchers on the blind work tend to be heterogeneous, and the need for statistical expertise is correspondingly great. Few researchers are so well informed about statistics that they need not consult an expert from time to time.

Training studies

The need for studies of the effectiveness of training procedures is especially great in areas where substantial developmental lags occur in blind children. A word of caution is in order, however. The discovery of a developmental lag does not automatically call for the prescription of a remedial training program for those children who are old enough to show the lag, or a preventive training program for those children who do not yet show the lag. There may well be areas of development where it is to the blind child's advantage to proceed more slowly, or even where it would be to his disadvantage to proceed more rapidly. It might be, for example, that in order to produce "reaching to external objects" in blind infants earlier than normally occurs, so much of the infant's time and energy would have to be devoted to the training procedures that other areas of development would suffer. It is not the purpose of this section to explore this issue in detail, but some mention of the issue seems important in order to maintain an adequate perspective on training studies.

In general, the purpose of a training study is to evaluate the effectiveness of intervention methods that are designed to accelerate the acquisition of a set of abilities or characteristics. The training notion is not a narrow one; it includes attempts to structure the child's environment in such a way as to avoid the occurrence of developmental delays, as well as attempts to provide remedial experiences. Whether training is regarded as the use of a specific set of instructional experiences or as the structuring of the child's environment in a particular way, careful assessment of training procedures is critical if the best possible job is to be done in providing the blind child with an environment that is most appropriate for development to his greatest potential.

The most basic requirement of studies designed to assess the effectiveness of training procedures is that a group of children who are exposed to the training must be compared to an initially comparable group that does not receive the training, the control group. The control group is necessary in order for the researcher to be able to attribute any improvement shown by the training group to the training procedures rather than to maturation, general learning experience, or some other factor not related to the training itself. The only difference that should occur between the training group and the control group is the training. It is particularly important, in cases where improvement by the training group is assessed by comparison of its performance on a posttest to that of a pretest, to administer the pretest to the control group as well, so that any improvement shown by the training group cannot simply be attributed to experience with the pretest itself. Often the control group will show a significant improvement from pre- to posttest. To the extent that such improvement occurs without training, any gain shown by the training group from pre- to posttest must be qualified. Only the improvement by the training group that is significantly greater than that shown by the control group may be attributed to the training procedures. Although it is sometimes possible to reduce the potential carryover effect of the pretest experience on the posttest results by using different versions of an evaluative test for the pre- and posttests, this method does not eliminate the need for a control group or the need to administer the pretest to the control group as well as the training group.

In order to conduct a useful evaluation of a training procedure, it is necessary to choose a test that adequately represents the abilities to which the training is oriented. At the same time, though, the test should usually not include specific items that have been covered in the training procedures, since the goal of most training is to produce a general rather than a specific improvement. It is often necessary to use a range of assessment measures in order to study the generality of the training-related improvement adequately. In particular, it is desirable to assess whether any improvement that occurs on a criterion test also generalizes to functional behaviors that are thought to depend on the ability being trained. Further, the effects of training procedures should be evaluated, not only directly following the termination of the training phase, but also after some considerable delay, in order to determine whether any improvement is transient or permanent.

The necessity for studying individual variations in performance that may be attributable to self-selected variables has already been discussed, but this point bears repeating with respect to training studies. Even if a significant improvement occurs for the training group as a whole, it is important to assess the degree of improvement shown by types of subjects in the training group. It may be that the particular training methods chosen are effective for subjects only with certain characteristics (for example, those who had a period of early vision before becoming blind). Such relationships may be discovered by the use of appropriate post hoc analyses. Training procedures often involve a substantial commitment, not only of the time and resources of the trainer, but also of the time and effort of the child who is being trained. Therefore, it is important to assess the extent to which the training procedures are effective for all children, or only for children with certain characteristics.

A comment is in order about the individualization of training procedures. Certain training procedures may be effective for children with particular characteristics, while other training variations may be better suited to children with other characteristics. Ultimately, training techniques should be individualized in order to meet the needs of each child. Effective individualization is only possible in relatively refined training programs, however, and a great deal of caution must be exercised in building individualization of training into studies designed to evaluate the effectiveness of training. To the extent that the training procedures are varied from subject to subject, the researcher is constrained from making general statements about the effectiveness of any particular aspect of the training. There is a vitally important issue involved here, an issue of the relative emphasis on research and applications. They must be able to coexist. Applications are clearly needed because of the immediacy of the needs of blind children, children who exist now. For the sake of these children, we cannot afford to wait until an optimally effective set of intervention techniques is available. At the same time, research is needed on the effectiveness of specific intervention techniques in order that optimal progress may be made in the refinement of those techniques.

The appropriate balance is difficult, if not impossible, to define in the abstract. It is my own impression that training programs with blind children have tended to be characterized by more attention to immediate applications and less to the development of optimally effective techniques. The attention to immediate applications may easily be justified by recourse to humanitarian concern for the children who are with us now. Blindness is not likely to be eliminated in the foreseeable future, however, and so a concern with the development of optimally effective techniques may be easily based on a humanitarian concern for the blind children of the future. A balance is needed. An appropriate balance will be achieved only by investigators who are fully aware of the alternatives, and who are able on the basis of sophisticated evaluation to weigh one benefit against the other within the context of the nature of their own work.

Alternative Strategies

Given the difficulties with applying traditional research strategies to the visually impaired population, it is appropriate to review two alternatives that are also available to researchers. One is the single-case design, which under the proper circumstances is useful with the visually impaired, particularly to evaluate changes as a result of training or other intervention strategies. The other, called "synthesizing outcomes," is less a matter of research format than a strategy for trying to bring together results from several studies on the same issue, the combination of which may give a fuller picture than any of the studies taken alone.

Single-case designs

Although single-case studies have been reported for many years, particularly in behaviorally oriented research, their use with special populations such as the visually impaired has not been stressed. The researcher who wishes to use single-case designs is referred to several treatments of the general issues in such research, such as Hersen & Barlow (1976) and Kratochwill (1978). Van Hasselt and Hersen (1981) have provided an overview of single-case designs for use with visually impaired subjects. The underlying premise of such designs is that a single subject can serve as his own control, such that the effectiveness of some intervention can be evaluated by comparing the subject's behavior before and after the intervention. In essence, a baseline measure of the subject's pre-intervention behavior is established, and then is used for comparison with the subject's behavior once the intervention is applied. In the straightforward A–B design, phase A refers to the baseline measure, while B refers to the measure (s) taken during and/or after the intervention. If the baseline measure is relatively stable, reliably denoting preintervention behavior, then substantial change from that baseline as a result of the intervention can be taken as evidence of the effectiveness of the intervention.

There are difficulties with this simple A–B design, however. Foremost among them is that there is no assurance that any change in behavior from A to B can confidently be attributed to the intervention itself, rather than to some extraneous factor that may have been operating at the same time to produce the change. Thus results from the simple A–B design may be provocative, but they are rarely conclusive.

More confidence may be gained from variations on this simple design, for example, the design that may be represented by A_1–B–A_1. Here, the baseline A_1 is established, then the intervention B is delivered and the behavior measured, then the intervention is removed and the behavior measured again in its absence (A_2). If the intervention is indeed producing the change from A_1 to B, then its cessation in A_2 should produce a return to the original baseline A_1. Assuming such an effect occurs, it is typically desirable to reinstate the intervention to reintroduce the behavioral improvement, so that the design often becomes A_1–B_1–A_2–B_2, with B_2 representing the reintroduced intervention.

The logic of the A_1–B–A_2 design fails, however, if the intervention B in fact does produce a *lasting* change in the behavior. In this case, the behavior would remain at the higher level when measured in A_2. When this result occurs, the researcher does not necessarily know whether A_2 is high because some extraneous variable, rather than B, has made a difference, or because the intervention has had an effect that endures even when the intervention has ceased. There are two possible solutions to this problem. First, if the intervention has a lasting effect the first time it is applied, then it may well have additional effect if it is applied again. Thus the A_1–B_1–A_2–B_2 design finds another use: when the intervention is applied again in B_2, additional improvement will be seen. Extension of the design to include additional segments of intervention and nonintervention leads to the general model A–B–A–B–A–B–A . . . , which is particularly useful when the intervention divides into natural segments that can be successively evaluated as they are completed.

Second, the uncertainty about whether a continued high A_2 score represents lasting improvement or the operation of an extraneous variable can be reduced by replication of the single-case design with another subject or subjects. If A_2 behavior remains high for each replication, then the researcher can have more confidence that the intervention created a lasting effect, unless he has unwittingly introduced a consistent extraneous variable for each of the subjects.

In any case, the desirability of replication of single-case designs should be stressed. While it is true that a properly done A–B–A–B design can demonstrate the effectiveness of an intervention, it is not true that such a demonstration for one subject carries generality for the population from which that subject was drawn. Generality can be gained from successful replication of the design with a succession of subjects, and it is rarely acceptable to omit this step. Why, then, if the researcher is going to have to test a number of subjects, does he not simply start off with a more traditional "group" design? It is true that in very simple cases a set of single-subject replications can turn out to be the same as a group design. However, in most cases the replicated single-case design has distinct advantages. It allows each subject to be evaluated with respect to his own baseline, a fact that carries the advantage of allowing individual differences to emerge rather than becoming hidden in error variance. It also allows for flexibility in the administration of the intervention: if a behavioral criterion is set such that during the intervention the subject must reach that criterion before being returned to the baseline (A) evaluation, then the differing acquisition rates of different subjects can be allowed for and evaluated, rather than again becoming part of a group error variance.

Clearly the single-case design, with replications, holds some advantages over traditional groups designs. However, it is not a panacea, and indeed it is not useful for research in which no intervention occurs. The measurement of a particular subject's score on a test of classification ability, for example, does not lend itself to such a design, and in fact it is virtually worthless to know what a single subject's score is. Further, despite the apparent simplicity of the method, there are many pitfalls that await the researcher. These are well outlined in various places, and particularly for the field of visual impairment research by LaGrow (in press). Nonetheless, use of the design should be more widely considered in situations where it is appropriate. Even in a study, such as a training study, which lends itself to the traditional groups model because of the use of a number of subjects, it may often be valuable to consider the use of a single-case design with as many replications as there are available subjects. As noted above, this approach has the advantage of saving rather than losing potentially valuable information about individual differences.

Synthesizing outcomes

Pillemer and Light (1980) described procedures for the synthesizing of results from several studies on the same topic. Briefly, the notion is that if there are several similar studies, no one of which serves sufficiently to define an outcome, then it may be possible to combine their separate outcomes conceptually, or even statistically, and arrive at a confident conclusion collectively where no such conclusion was possible from any one of them. At the level of conceptual synthesis, this process may in reality be no different from what the research reviewer does when he attempts to make overall sense of a group of similar studies. True statistical synthesis, in which results from various studies are placed in a common statistical analysis, is rarely warranted because of the almost inevitable differences between methodologies employed in the various studies. Nonetheless, the concept of outcome synthesis is worth elaborating.

Unruh and Barraga (1981) provided a description of the basic approaches specifically with regard to research with the visually impaired. Four techniques are described. The first, called "increasing power," refers to the fact that the statistical analysis done with a small group of subjects has only weak statistical power; that is, it is unlikely to produce statistically significant results. If there are several such similar studies, then the results may be combined to yield, in effect, a larger sample size for whose results greater statistical power would obtain. Unruh and Barraga correctly pointed out that such statistical combination of results from separate studies depends on the assumption that the methodologies of the separate studies were sufficiently alike to make the combination of their results suitable. It should also be noted, though, that combination across studies with minor differences in methods can lead to a set of results with greater generality than if the larger number of subjects had been used in a single study with a consistent methodology.

The second technique is called "effect size estimate." Essentially, the notion is that instead of the traditional measures of statistical significance, the magnitude of an effect in one group (say an treatment group) is evaluated with respect to the mean of a control group. This rough gauge of the size of a treatment effect may give better guidance for policy determinations than the traditional statistical analysis—in essence, one asks whether the effect is *important,* rather than whether it is *statistically significant*; or, to use Van Hasselt and Hersen's (1981) terminology, whether it is clinically significant, as opposed to statistically significant.

The third technique, called "describing the form of a relationship," refers to the process of drawing conclusions about the larger form of a relationship between variables from several studies, whereas each study taken alone examines only the smaller form of the relationship between these variables. Unruh and Barraga used the example of the variation of mobility skills with chronological age: if each of three studies examines the relationship in a different section of the CA spectrum, and if the studies are sufficiently similar in methodology, then the relationship between mobility skills and CA can be constructed over the larger age range represented by the three studies taken collectively. A word of caution is in order here, however: If the combination seems to yield a nonlinear relationship, as in the case given by Unruh and Barraga, one must be very careful before concluding that the relationship is indeed nonlinear, since even small methodological differences between the studies may make an actually linear relationship look nonlinear.

The fourth technique, called "using information from conflicting results," is not so much a matter of pooling results from several studies as an attempt to resolve discrepancies between their findings. The technique describes what the research reviewer attempts to do when he finds studies of apparently the same phenomenon in conflict with one another. He examines the methodologies carefully to determine whether there may have been important though minor differences, and whether there may have been different sets of extraneous variables operating in the different studies.

Researchers who use a very heterogeneous and typically small-sample population such as the visually impaired must depend on such approaches to make larger sense of small and sometimes conflicting pieces of evidence. This is the essence of constructing a system of knowledge out of many pieces of evidence, and it is what the reviewer's task is all about!

Perspectives

A note of perspective is needed on the way that researchers interpret their work and represent that work to others via their contributions to the blindness literature. The researcher-author is the person who is in the single best position with respect to providing interpretation of and perspective on his work to others in the field. As the occupant of that position, he incurs a most significant responsibility. He is absolutely obligated to provide an objective view of his work. That objectivity includes the enumeration and discussion of any alternative explanations to the one that he prefers. Too often (and this point is by no means restricted to the blindness literature!) it is apparent that research has been conducted with the goal of providing support for a particular preconceived belief, rather than of adding objectively to a system of knowledge. It is not difficult to understand a researcher's commitment to his own interpretation. He is often trained in, or otherwise committed to, a certain theoretical position, and at the very least he has invested substantial energy and other personal resources in his work. This commitment, whatever its sources, does not constitute absolution from objectivity. The researcher's primary and overriding commitment is to the acquisition of knowledge, and knowledge in any meaningful sense goes well beyond the confines of any one individual's personal orientation, whether it be theoretical or otherwise.

I should also like to contribute a word of perspective on the issue of "basic" vs. "applied" research and their relationship to practice. The distinction between "basic" and "applied" research is one that cannot and should not be clearly drawn. "Applied" research is initiated with the goal of providing an answer to an immediate problem. Such research should take its direction not just from the specific problem, but also from the wider set of issues and knowledge that bear on the problem. If the research is so directed, it should be effective in generating a solution to the immediate problem, and at the same time it should contribute effectively to the growth of the general system of knowledge. "Basic" research is not research that is conducted in a vacuum. Rather, it is research that is done with the primary goal of contributing to the general system of knowledge, without being constrained by the nature of an applied problem that needs an immediate solution. Such research, insofar as it does add to the general system of knowledge, will necessarily add to the potential of the field to provide answers to applied problems, present and future.

Thus it is important for "applied" research to be designed and conducted with a basis in the general system of knowledge. It is equally important for "basic" research to be done by researchers who are aware of and have a healthy respect for the immediate and potential problems of the field.

The success of the practitioner is critically dependent on the adequacy of the knowledge that he has at his disposal. Effective solutions to problems simply cannot be generated without a basis in a system of factual knowledge. We may hope that, some number of years in the future, a complete system of knowledge about visual impairment will be available that will allow an effective answer to be given to any applied question. Such a system is not available now, and it will not arrive in the near future. For the present, then, we will continue to need research that is directed to specific applied questions. But, at the same time, we cannot afford to lose sight of the goal of the complete system of knowledge, and so "basic" research must continue. Both types of research orientation are important, and neither should be allowed to overwhelm the other. It is my impression, from reading the recent literature and speaking with many people who are now doing research with the blind, that there has been a shift toward an overriding concern with research that will generate immediate applications, and away from a concern for research that will contribute to the general system of knowledge. Further, it is my impression that the responsibility for this shift lies not so much with the people who do the research as with those who control the resources that are available for research. The support that is available for nonapplied research is insufficient, and it is apparently decreasing. This is a most unfortunate trend, and it must be reversed. Resources must be made available for research that will contribute to the generation of a system of knowledge, or else the potential of the field for generating solutions to present and future problems will wither. These words were originally written in 1976—they are no less true in 1984.

A Research Model for the Future

In the preceding chapter, three themes were identified that recurred in the summary of research needs. In the first part of this chapter, it was noted that much of the research with blind children has been conducted within models borrowed from research with sighted children, and that these models may not be ideally suited for research with the blind. In this section, I would like to propose a research model that I believe will allow effective attention to the three themes as well as to some of the difficulties discussed in the present chapter. The model may be characterized as a hierarchical model. Most briefly, the principle behind the model may be stated as follows: research on a characteristic should not only involve evaluation of that characteristic, but should also include attention both to the etiology of the characteristic and to the ways in which the characteristic is expressed in real-life behavior. For example, the study of a cognitive ability (such as a classification skill) should not just measure that ability. It should include evaluation of present and past factors that might produce variations in the ability, such as contributing sensory and perceptual factors and characteristics of the learning environment, and it should include evaluation of the ways in which the ability is expressed in the child's behavior, such as his ability to understand his world and to succeed in school. If some aspect of tactual perception, such as form discrimination, is studied with the goal of using the ability in a functional behavior, such as map use for mobility, then the research should not stop with evaluation of the tactual ability. It should evaluate variables that may contribute to the tactual ability, such as fingertip sensitivity, memory for sequentially scanned items, and experiential factors on which these component abilities may depend, and it should evaluate the ability of the subjects to translate the tactual skill into the functional behavior of map use. The study of personality characteristics should not stop at simple evaluation of the characteristics. It should include attempts to identify those factors that may have led to individual variation in the characteristics, and it should assess the relative advantages or disadvantages that the characteristics confer on the subjects in adapting to various real-world situations in which the characteristics may play a part.

The hierarchical research format is not as easy to design, conduct, analyze, or interpret as the simpler format that has primarily been used in research on handicapped as well as nonhandicapped populations. It is necessary to spend more time with the subjects, to use more imagination in designing ways of gathering data and assessing possible relationships, and, in general, to handle many more variables in any given study. Perhaps the most severe stumbling block at the present time is the relative unavailability of methods for studying etiological factors, and intensive research effort should be devoted to the development of such methods. The research design and data analytic requirements present no great problem: multivariate research design and data analysis have become increasingly popular, useful, and sophisticated. The potential advantages of this research format are immense and well worth the additional difficulties. Multivariate approaches are far better suited to the evaluation of individual differences than are univariate approaches. Use of the hierarchical model would constitute a major step toward providing the structure that is needed for the integration of findings in various areas of the blindness literature. Finally, the inclusion of the level of functional behavior would serve to facilitate an orientation to important problem areas.

There are two major remaining problems that cannot be solved solely by the hierarchical model for research. One problem is the need for the coordinated study of the various areas of development such as perceptual, cognitive, language, social, and personality development. For the most part, any given piece of research has been concentrated on one area of development or another, without consideration of how the results contribute to a total picture of development. (There are some exceptions to this generality—the extensive longitudinal study by Norris et al. [1957] is one, and the set of relatively intensive, long-term case studies by Fraiberg and her colleagues is another. The intensive case study approach has typically used very few subjects, and cannot therefore reliably be taken as providing normative information about development. The Norris et al. study was concerned primarily with RLF children, and therefore the findings are not optionally appropriate for today's blind children.) The second problem is that, because of the extreme heterogeneity of the blind population, the sample chosen for any given piece of research may be quite nonrepresentative. If the researcher knew to what extent and in what ways his sample was nonrepresentative, he could provide appropriate qualification of his results. The potential contradictions between different studies using different samples might be kept in appropriate perspective. At present most researchers have no way of assessing whether their samples are representative, and therefore the generality of their results is unknown.

There is need for a major coordinated research effort that would allow these two important problems to be solved, and that would, if its component projects were conducted within the hierarchical model discussed earlier, provide for the collection of research data that would contribute to a much more complete and useful picture of the development of the blind child than is now available. Most basically, the intent of the coordinated effort is to gather various categories of information about a large number of visually impaired children, so that the particular sample that is available to any given researcher may be compared with a large population whose important characteristics are known. The categories of important information are the following:

1. Description of the environment. Key characteristics of various aspects of the child's environment should be assessed, including the sensory, learning, language, and social aspects. In each of these areas the environment should be evaluated and quantified in general but useful ways. Attention should be devoted not only to the child's current environment, but also to any major environmental changes that may have occurred in the past.
2. Self-selected status characteristics. Information about the most important self-selected characteristics of the children should be gathered. The most important of these variables, as discussed earlier, are sex, intelligence (or learning aptitude), residual vision, history of early vision, and etiology of blindness. Two additional variables are also important but change over time, CA and duration of blindness.
3. Acquired characteristics and abilities. A small number of key indicators should be chosen that may represent the child's acquired characteristics and abilities in a range of areas. These should include perceptual and perceptual-motor, cognitive, language, social, and personality characteristics. The purpose of the information in this category is to provide a "synopsis" of the child's important characteristics.

The availability of these types of information for large numbers of blind children would serve several purposes. The information from the first category, environmental description, would aid in the adequate treatment of the etiological aspects of research within the hierarchical model. That is, the researcher would be able to assess the extent to which the characteristics and abilities of the children in his sample can be accounted for by factors in the children's experiential histories. As argued earlier, this level of analysis is critical in generating knowledge about the experiential determinants of development, and about implications for the effective structuring of the environment as well as effective attention to individual differences in development. The information in the third category, acquired characteristics and abilities, would allow the researcher to place his own research results in the perspective of a broad set of developmental characteristics of a large population of blind children. If a research study is directed to some aspect of cognitive development, for example, the detailed findings of the research with respect to cognitive development may be grounded within the total picture of the characteristics of the sample. Such a perspective would be of great benefit in helping to keep general developmental questions in mind, and in generating a system of knowledge about the "whole child." Most important, the information from the second category in particular, but also from the first and third categories, would allow the researcher to make well-based statements about the degree to which his sample is representative of the population of blind children. The availability of information about the population, as well as about each sample, would allow apparently discrepant results (or similar ones, for that matter) to be resolved or at least considered within a systematic framework.

If the researcher were committed to the goal of the generation of an integrated body of knowledge about blind children, he would take steps to gather these categories of information about his sample. He could then contribute that information to the growing pool of normative data about the population of blind children, and he would be able to make careful assessment of the particular characteristics of his sample and of the degree to which it is representative of the general population of blind children. Significantly, he would be able to interpret his own research results within the perspective of a systematized and growing body of information about blind children.

About the Author

David H. Warren is Professor of Psychology and Dean of the College of Humanities and Social Sciences, University of California at Riverside. He holds a degree in psychology from Yale, and in child development from the University of Minnesota, and is a member of the Psychonomic Society. Dr. Warren is on the editorial advisory board of the *Journal of Visual Impairment & Blindness* and has published extensively on vision, blindness, child development, perception, and cognitive psychology. In September 1984 Dr. Warren served as director of a NATO conference on visual-spatial prostheses for blind persons.

References

Adelson, E., & Fraiberg, S. (1974). Gross motor development in infants blind from birth. *Child Development,* **45,** 114–126.

Adi, H., & Pulos, S. (1977–78). Conservation of number and the developmental lag among the blind. *Education of the Visually Handicapped,* **9,** 102–106.

Adkins, S. D. W. (1965). Effects of visual deficit on acquisition of classification concepts. *Dissertation Abstracts,* **26,** 1769A, Vol. ix, No. 4. (University Microfilms No. 65–08567)

Aitken, S., & Bower, T. G. R. (1982a). Intersensory substitution in the blind. *Journal of Experimental Child Psychology,* **33,** 309–323.

Aitken, S., & Bower, T. G. R. (1982b). The use of the Sonicguide in infancy. *Journal of Visual Impairment & Blindness,* **76,** 91–100.

Als, H., Tronick, E., & Brazelton, T. B. (1980a). Stages of early behavioral organization: The study of a sighted infant and a blind infant in interaction with their mothers. In T. M. Field (Ed.), *High-risk infants and children, adult and peer interactions.* New York: Academic Press.

Als, H., Tronick, E., & Brazelton, T. B. (1980b). Affective reciprocity and the development of autonomy: The study of a blind infant. *Journal of the American Academy of Child Psychiatry,* **19,** 22–40.

Andersen, E. S., Dunlea, A., & Kekelis, L. S. Blind children's language: Resolving some differences (In press). *Journal of Child Language.*

Anderson, D. W. (1979). *A descriptive analysis of language and cognition in congenitally blind children ages 3 through 9.* Unpublished doctoral dissertation, University of North Dakota.

Anderson, D., & Olson, M. (1981). Word meaning among congenitally blind children. *Journal of Visual Impairment & Blindness,* **75,** 165–168.

Anderson, R. P. (1961). *Modification of the Raven Progressive Matrices for the blind.* Unpublished progress report, Project 670–61–1, U.S. Office of Vocational Rehabilitation.

Apple, M. M. (1972). Kinesic training for blind persons: A vital means of communication. *New Outlook for the Blind,* **66,** 201–208.

Aronson, E., & Rosenbloom, S. (1971). Space perception in early infancy: Perception within a common auditory-visual space. *Science,* **172,** 1161–1163.

Avery, C. (1968). Play therapy with the blind. *International Journal for the Education of the Blind,* **18,** 41–46.

Axelrod, S. (1959). *Effects of early blindness.* New York: American Foundation for the Blind [Research Series, No. 7].

Axline, V. (1947). *Play therapy.* Boston: The Riverside Press.

Ayres, A. F. (1966). *A comparison of selective perception among early blinded and sighted adolescents.* Dissertation Abstracts, **27,** 1256A. (University Microfilms No. 66-12061)

Bachelis, L. A. (1961). Some characteristics of sensory deprivation. *New Outlook for the Blind,* **55,** 288–291.

Bachelis, L. A. (1967). Developmental patterns of individuals with bilateral congenital anophthalmos. *New Outlook for the Blind,* **61,** 113–119.

Baird, A. S. (1977). Electronic aids: Can they help blind children? *Journal of Visual Impairment & Blindness,* **71,** 97–101.

Barker, R. G. (1953). *Adjustment to physical handicap and illness: A survey of the social psychology of physique and disability.* Social Science Research Council Bulletin, 55.

Barraga, N. C. (1964). *Increased visual behavior in low vision children.* New York: American Foundation for the Blind [Research Series, No. 13].

Barraga, N. C. (Ed.). (1970). *Visual efficiency scale.* Louisville, KY: American Printing House for the Blind.

Barraga, N. C. (1976). *Visual handicaps and learning: A developmental approach.* Belmont, CA: Wadsworth Publishing Co.

Barraga, N. C., & Collins, M. E. (1979). Development of efficiency in visual functioning: Rationale for a comprehensive program. *Journal of Visual Impairment & Blindness,* **73,** 121–125.

Barraga, N. C., Collins, M. E., & Hollis J. (1977). Development of efficiency in visual functioning: A literature analysis. *Journal of Visual Impairment & Blindness,* **71,** 387–391.

Barry, H., Jr., & Marshall, F. E. (1953). Maladjustment and maternal rejection in retrolental fibroplasia. *Mental Hygiene,* **37,** 570–580.

Bartholomeus, B. (1971). Naming of meaningful nonverbal sounds by blind children. *Perceptual and Motor Skills,* **33,** 1289–1290.

Bateman, B. (1965). Psychological evaluation of blind children. *New Outlook for the Blind,* **59,** 193–196.

Battacchi, M. W., Franza, A., & Pani, R. (1981). Memory processing of spatial order as transmitted by auditory information in the absence of visual cues. *Memory & Cognition,* **9,** 301–307.

Bauman, M. K. (1947). Mechanical and manual ability tests for use with the blind. In M. W. Donahue & D. Dabelstein (Eds.), *Psychological diagnosis and counseling of the adult blind*. New York: American Foundation for the Blind.

Bauman, M. K. (1964). Group differences disclosed by inventory items. *International Journal for the Education of the Blind,* **13,** 101–106.

Bauman, M. K. (1973). The social competency of visually handicapped children. Paper presented at conference on The Blind Child in Social Interaction: Developing Relationships with Peers and Adults, New York.

Bauman, M. K., Platt, H., & Strauss, S. (1963). A measure of personality for blind adolescents. *International Journal for the Education of the Blind,* **13,** 7–12.

Bauman, M. K., & Yoder, N. M. (1966). *Adjustment to blindness—reviewed.* Springfield, IL: Charles C Thomas.

Berg, J., & Worchel, P. (1956). Sensory contributions to human maze learning: A comparison of matched blind, deaf, and normals. *Journal of General Psychology,* **54,** 81–93.

Berkson, G. (1973). *Animal studies of treatment of impaired young by parents and the social group.* Paper presented at Conference on The Blind Child in Social Interaction: Developing Relationships with Peers and Adults, New York.

Berla', E. P. (1972). Effects of physical size and complexity on tactual discrimination of blind children. *Exceptional Children,* **39,** 120–124.

Berla', E. P. (1974). Tactual orientation performance of blind children in different grade levels. *American Foundation for the Blind Research Bulletin,* **27,** 1–10.

Berla', E. P. (1981). Tactile scanning and memory for a spatial display by blind students. *Journal of Special Education,* **15,** 341–350.

Berla', E. P. & Butterfield, L. H., Jr. (1977). Tactual distinctive features analysis: Training blind students in shape recognition and in locating shapes on a map. *Journal of Special Education,* **11,** 335–346.

Berla', E. P., Butterfield, L. H., Jr., & Murr, M. J. (1976). Tactual reading of political maps by blind students: A videomatic behavioral analysis. *Journal of Special Education,* **10,** 265–276.

Berla', E. P., & Murr, M. J. (1974). Searching tactual space. *Education of the Visually Handicapped,* **6,** 49–58.

Berla', E. P., & Murr, M. J. (1975). Psychophysical functions for active tactual discrimination of line width by blind children. *Perception & Psychophysics,* **17,** 607–612.

Berla', E. P., Rankin, E. F., & Willis, D. H. (1980). Psychometric evaluation of the Low Vision Diagnostic Assessment Procedure. *Journal of Visual Impairment & Blindness,* **74,** 297–301.

Bernstein, D. K. (1978. *Semantic development in congenitally blind children.* Unpublished doctoral dissertation, City University of New York.

Berry, M. F., & Eisenson, J. (1942). *The defective in speech.* New York: F. S. Crofts & Co.

Bidgood, F. E. (1971). A study of sex education programs for visually handicapped persons. *New Outlook for the Blind,* **65,** 318–323.

Bitterman, M. E., & Worchel, P. (1953). The phenomenal vertical and horizontal in blind and sighted subjects. *American Journal of Psychology,* **66,** 598-602.

Blackhurst, A. E., Marks, C. H., & Tisdall, W. J. (1969). Relationship between mobility and divergent thinking in blind children. *Education of the Visually Handicapped,* **1,** 33-36.

Blank, H. R. (1958). Dreams of the blind. *Psychoanalytic Quarterly,* **27,** 158-174.

Blank, H. R. (1959). Psychiatric problems associated with congenital blindness due to retrolental fibroplasia. *New Outlook for the Blind,* **53,** 237-244.

Blasch, B. B. (1975). *A study of the treatment of blindisms using punishment and positive reinforcement in laboratory and natural settings.* Dissertation Abstracts International, **36,** 3558A. (University Microfilms DCJ 75-27236)

Blass, T., Freedman, N., & Steingart, I. (1974). Body movement and verbal encoding in the congenitally blind. *Perceptual and Motor Skills,* **39,** 279-293.

Block, C. (1972). *Developmental study of tactile-kinesthetic discrimination in blind, deaf, and normal children.* Dissertation Abstracts International, **33,** 1781B. (University Microfilms No. 72-25, 247)

Boehm. A. E. (1971). *Boehm Test of Basic Concepts: Test Manual.* New York: The Psychological Corporation.

Boldt, W. (1969). The development of scientific thinking in blind children and adolescents. *Education of the Visually Handicapped,* **1,** 5-8.

Bottrill, J. H. (1968). Locomotor learning by the blind and sighted. *Perceptual and Motor Skills,* **26,** 282.

Bower, T. G. R. (1974). *Development in infancy.* San Francisco: W. H. Freeman and Co.

Bower, T. G. R. (1977a). Blind babies see with their ears. *New Scientist,* **73,** 255-257.

Bower, T. G. R. (1977b). Babies are more important than machines. *New Scientist,* **73,** 712-714.

Bradway, K. P. (1937). Social competence of exceptional children: III. The deaf, the blind, and the crippled. *Exceptional Children,* **4,** 64-69.

Brekke, B., Williams, J. D., & Tait, P. (1974). The acquisition of conservation of weight by visually impaired children. *Journal of Genetic Psychology,* **125,** 89-97.

Brieland, D. M. (1950). A comparative study of the speech of blind and sighted children. *Speech Monographs,* **17,** 99-103.

Brown, C. E., Briller, S., & Richards, S. S. (1967). A new program for young blind children—A cornerstone for future services. *New Outlook for the Blind,* **61,** 210-217.

Brown, P. A. (1938). Responses of blind and seeing adolescents to an introversion-extroversion questionnaire. *Journal of Psychology,* **6,** 137-147.

Brown, P. A. (1939). Responses of blind and seeing adolescents to a neurotic

inventory. *Journal of Psychology,* **7,** 211-221.
Brown, R., & Berko, J. (1960). Word association and the acquisition of grammar. *Child Development,* **31,** 1-14.
Buchanan, D. R. (1978). Nonverbal communication for the congenitally blind: A review. *Journal of Visual Impairment & Blindness,* **72,** 81-84.
Buckman, F. G. (1965). Multiple-handicapped blind children (an incidence survey). *International Journal for the Education of the Blind,* **15,** 46-49.
Buell, C. (1950). Motor performance of visually handicapped children. *Exceptional Children,* **17,** 69-72.
Burlingham, D. (1961). Some notes on the development of the blind. *Psychoanalytic Study of the Child,* **16,** 121-145.
Burlingham, D. (1964). Hearing and its role in the development of the blind. *Psychoanalytic Study of the Child,* **19,** 95-112.
Burlingham, D. (1965). Some problems of ego development in blind children. *Psychoanalytic Study of the Child,* **20,** 194-208.
Burlingham, D. (1967). Developmental considerations in the occupations of the blind. *Psychoanalytic Study of the Child,* **22,** 187-198.
Burlingham, D. (1968). The re-education of a retarded blind child. *Psychoanalytic Study of the Child,* **23,** 369-390.
Burlingham, D. (1979). To be blind in a sighted world. *Psychoanalytic Study of the Child,* **34,** 5-30.
Burns, D. J., & Stenquist, G. M. (1960). The deaf-blind child in the United States: Their care, education and guidance. *Rehabilitation Literature,* **21,** 334-344.

Caetano, A. P., & Kaufman, J. M. (1975). Reduction of rocking mannerisms in two blind children. *Education of the Visually Handicapped,* **7,** 101-105.
Canning, M. (1957). *Exploring the number concept in blind children.* Unpublished manuscript, University of Birmingham.
Carpenter, P. A., & Eisenberg, P. (1978). Mental rotation and the frame of reference in blind and sighted individuals. *Perception & Psychophysics,* **23,** 117-124.
Carr, H. (1921). The influence of visual guidance in maze learning. *Journal of Experimental Psychology,* **4,** 399-417.
Carroll, T. J. (1961). *Blindness.* Boston: Little, Brown.
Casey, S. M. (1978). Cognitive mapping by the blind. *Journal of Visual Impairment & Blindness,* **72,** 297-301.
Caton, H. (1977). The development and evaluation of a tactile analog to the Boehm Test of Basic Concepts, Form A. *Journal of Visual Impairment & Blindness,* **71,** 382-386.
Cawley, J. F., & Spotts, J. V. (1967). *Survey of treatment and educational facilities and programs for retardates with accompanying sensory defects: Auditory and visual impairments.* Storrs: University of Connecticut.
Cerulli, F., & Shugerman, E. E. (1961). Infancy: Counseling the family. *New*

Outlook for the Blind, **55**, 295–297.
Chase, J. B. (1972). *Retrolental fibroplasia and autistic symptomatology.* New York: American Foundation for the Blind [Research Series, No. 24].
Chase, J. B., & Rapaport, I. N. (1968). A verbal adaptation of the Draw-A-Person techniques for use with blind subjects. *International Journal for the Education of the Blind,* **18**, 113–115.
Chess, S., & Fernandez, P. (1976). Temperament and the Rubella child. In Z. S. Jastrzembska (Ed.), *The effects of blindness and other impairments on early development* (pp. 186–207). New York: American Foundation for the Blind.
Cicenia, E. F., Belton, J. A., Myers, J. J., & Mundy, G. (1975). The blind child child with multiple handicaps: A challenge. *International Journal for the Education of the Blind,* **14**, 105–112.
Civelli, E. M. (1983). Verbalism in young blind children. *Journal of Visual Impairment & Blindness,* **77**, 61–63.
Cleaves, W. T., & Royal, R. W. (1979). Spatial memory for configurations by congenitally blind, late blind, and sighted adults. *Journal of Visual Impairment & Blindness,* **73**, 13–19.
Cohen, J. (1966). The effects of blindness on children's development. *New Outlook for the Blind,* **60**, 150–154.
Cohen, J., Alfano, J. E., Boshes, L. D., & Palmgren, C. (1964). Clinical evaluation of school-age children with retrolental fibroplasia. *American Journal of Ophthalmology,* **47**, 41–57.
Cohen, J., Boshes, L. D., & Snider, R. S. (1961). Electroencephalographic changes following retrolental fibroplasia. *Electroencephalogical Clinical Neurophysiology,* **13**, 914–922.
Cohen, P. C. (1964). The impact of the handicapped child on the family. *New Outlook for the Blind,* **58**, 11–15.
Coker, C. (1979). A comparison of self-concepts and academic achievement of visually handicapped children enrolled in a regular school and in a residential school. *Education of the Visually Handicapped,* **11**, 67–74.
Collins, M. E., & Barraga, N. C. (1980). Development of efficiency in visual function: An evaluation process. *Journal of Visual Impairment & Blindness,* **74**, 93–96.
Collins, M. S. (1982). *Parental reactions to a visually handicapped child: A mourning process.* Unpublished doctoral dissertation, University of Texas, Austin.
Colonna, A. B. (1968). A blind child goes to the hospital. *Psychoanalytic Study of the Child,* **23**, 391–422.
Cook-Clampert, D. (1981). The development of self-concept in blind children. *Journal of Visual Impairment & Blindness,* **75**, 233–238.
Correa, V. I., Poulson, C. L., & Salzberg, C. L. (1984). Training and generalization of reach-grasp behavior in blind, severely/profoundly mentally retarded young children. *Journal of Applied Behavior Analysis,* **17**, 57–69.
Corsini, D., & Pick, H. L., Jr. (1967). *The effect of texture on tactually per-*

ceived length. Paper presented at the meeting of the Midwestern Psychological Association, Chicago.

Coveny, T. E. (1972). A new test for the visually handicapped: Preliminary analysis of the reliability and validity of the Perkins-Binet. *Education of the Visually Handicapped,* **4,** 97–101.

Coveny, T. E. (1976). Standardized tests for visually handicapped childen: A review of research. *New Outlook for the Blind,* **70,** 232–236.

Cowan, M. K. (1972). Sex role typing in the blind child as measured by play activity choices. *American Journal of Occupational Therapy,* **26,** 85–87.

Cowen, E. L., Underberg, R. P., Verillo, R. T., & Benham, F. G. (1961). *Adjustment to visual disability in adolescence.* New York: American Foundation for the Blind.

Craig, E. M. (1973). Role of mental imagery in free recall of deaf, blind, and normal subjects. *Journal of Experimental Psychology,* **97,** 249–253.

Crandell, J. M., Hammill, D. D., Witkowski, C., & Barkovich, F. (1968). Measuring form-discrimination in blind individuals. *International Journal for the Education of the Blind,* **18,** 65–68.

Cratty, B. J. (1967). The perception of gradient and the veering tendency while walking without vision. *American Foundation for the Blind Research Bulletin,* **14,** 31–51.

Cratty, B. J. (1969). *Perceptual-motor behavior and educational processes.* Springfield, IL: Charles C Thomas.

Cratty, B. J. (1970). *Some educational implications of movement.* Seattle: Special Child Publications.

Cratty, B. J., Peterson, C., Harris, J., & Schoner, R. (1968). The development of perceptual-motor abilities in blind children and adolescents. *New Outlook for the Blind,* **62,** 111–117.

Cratty, B. J., & Sams, T. A. (1968). *The body-image of blind children.* New York: American Foundation for the Blind.

Critchley, M. (1952). Tactile thought, with special reference to the blind. *Proceedings of the Royal Society of Medicine,* 27–30.

Cromer, R. F. (1973). Conservation by the congenitally blind. *British Journal of Psychology,* **64,** 241–250.

Cruickshank, W. M. (1964). The multiple-handicapped child and courageous action. *International Journal for the Education of the Blind,* **14,** 65–75.

Curson, A. (1979). The blind nursery school child. *Psychoanalytic Study of the Child,* **34,** 51–83.

Curtis, W. S. (1966). The evaluation of verbal performance in multiply handicapped blind children. *Exceptional Children,* **32,** 367–374.

Cutsforth, T. D. (1932). The unreality of words to the blind. *Teachers Forum,* **4,** 86–89.

Cutsforth, T. D. (1951). *The blind in school and society.* New York: American Foundation for the Blind.

Cutsforth, T. D. (1966). Personality and social adjustment among the blind.

American Foundation for the Blind Research Bulletin, **12,** 53–67.

Czerwinski, M. H., & Tait, P. E. (1981). Blind children's perceptions of normal, withdrawn, and antisocial behavior. *Journal of Visual Impairment & Blindness,* **75,** 252–257.

Dauterman, W. L. (1973). A study of imagery in the sighted and the blind. *American Foundation for the Blind Research Bulletin,* **25,** 95–168.

Dauterman, W. L., Shapiro, B., & Suinn, R. M. (1967). Performance tests of intelligence for the blind reviewed. *International Journal for the Education of the Blind,* **17,** 8–16.

Davidson, P. W. (1976). Haptic perception. *Journal of Pediatric Psychology,* **1,** 21–25.

Davidson, P. W., Dunn, G., Wiles-Kettenmann, M., & Appelle, S. (1981). Haptic conservation of amount in blind and sighted children: Exploratory movement effects. *Journal of Pediatric Psychology,* **6,** 191–200.

Davis, C. J. (1964). Development of the self concept. *New Outlook for the Blind,* **58,** 49–51.

Davis, C. J. (1970). *New developments of the intelligence testing of blind children.* Proceedings of the Conference on New Approaches to the Evaluation of Blind Persons. New York: American Foundation for the Blind.

Davis, C. J. (1980). *Perkins–Binet Tests of Intelligence for the Blind.* Watertown, MA: Perkins School for the Blind.

Dekaban, A. S. (1972). Mental retardation and neurologic involvement in patients with congenital retinal blindness. *Developmental Medicine and Child Neurology,* **14,** 436–444.

DeMott, R. M. (1972). Verbalism and affective meaning for blind, severely visually impaired, and normally sighted children. *New Outlook for the Blind,* **66,** 1–8.

Denenberg, V. H. (1964). Critical periods, stimulus input, and emotional reactivity: A theory of infantile stimulation. *Psychological Review,* **71,** 335–351.

DeNelsky, G. Y., & Denenberg, V. H. (1967a). Infantile stimulation and adult exploratory behavior: Effects of handling on tactual variation seeking. *Journal of Comparative and Physiological Psychology,* **63,** 309–312.

DeNelsky, G. Y., & Denenberg, V. H. (1967b). Infantile stimulation and adult exploratory behavior in the rat: Effects of handling upon visual variation seeking. *Animal Behavior,* **15,** 568–573.

Deutsch, E. (1928). The dream imagery of the blind. *Psychoanalytic Quarterly,* **15,** 288–293.

Deutsch, F. (1940). The sense of reality in persons born blind. *Journal of Psychology,* **10,** 121–140.

Dinsmore, A. (1967). Services for deaf–blind adults and children. *New Outlook for the Blind,* **61,** 262–266.

Dodds, A. G., Howarth, C. I., & Carter, D. C. (1982). The mental maps of the blind: The role of previous experience. *Journal of Visual Impairment & Blindness,* **76,** 5–12.

Dokecki, P. C. (1966). Verbalism and the blind: A critical review of the concept and the literature. *Exceptional Children,* **32,** 525–530.

Doll, E. A. (1947). *The Vineland Social Maturity Scale: Manual of directions.* Educational Test Bureau.

Doll, E. A. (1953). *A measurement of social competence: A manual for the Vineland Social Maturity Scale.* Educational Test Bureau.

Donlon, E. T. (1964). An evaluation center for the blind child with multiple handicaps. *International Journal for the Education of the Blind,* **13,** 75–78.

Drever, J. (1955). Early learning and the perception of space. *American Journal of Psychology,* **68,** 605–614.

Duehl, A. N. (1979). The effect of creative dance movement on large muscle control and balance in congenitally blind children. *Journal of Visual Impairment & Blindness,* **73,** 127–133.

Dumas, M. G. (1932). Mimicry of the blind. *And There Was Light,* **2,** 30–33.

Duncan, B. K. (1934). A comparative study of finger-maze learning by blind and sighted subjects. *Journal of Genetic Psychology,* **44,** 69–95.

Dunlea, A. (1982). *The role of visual information in the emergence of meaning: A comparison of blind and sighted children.* Unpublished doctoral dissertation, University of Southern California.

Duran, P., & Tufenkjian, S. (1970). The measurement of length by congenitally blind children and a quasiformal approach for spatial concepts. *American Foundation for the Blind Research Bulletin,* **22,** 47–70.

Eaves, L., & Klonoff, H. (1970). A comparison of blind and sighted children on a tactual and performance test. *Exceptional Children,* **37,** 269–273.

Egland, G. O. (1955). Teaching speech to blind children with cerebral palsy. *New Outlook for the Blind,* **49,** 282–289.

Eibl-Eibesfeldt, I. (1970). Behavior of children born blind or deaf-blind. In I. Eibl-Eibesfeldt, *Ethology: The biology of behavior* (pp. 403–408). New York: Holt, Rinehart & Winston.

Eichel, V. J. (1978). Mannerisms of the blind: A review of the literature. *Journal of Visual Impairment & Blindness,* **72,** 125–130.

Eichel, V. J. (1979). A taxonomy for mannerisms of blind children. *Journal of Visual Impairment & Blindness,* **73,** 167–178.

Eichorn, J. R., & Vigaroso, H. R. (1967). Orientation and mobility for preschool blind children. *International Journal for the Education of the Blind,* **17,** 48–50.

Eisenstadt, A. A. (1955). The speech status and the speech ability of visually handicapped children. *Speech Monographs,* **22,** 199–200.

Elioseff, J. (1971). Training or education learning patterns of younger deaf-blind children. In Fourth International Conference on Deaf-Blind Children, Perkins School for the Blind, Vermont Printing Co.

Elkind, D. (1961). Children's discovery of the conservation of mass, weight and volume: Piaget replication, study II. *Journal of Genetic Psychology,* **98,** 219–227.

Elliott, R. (1938). Spoken English at the Oklahoma School for the Blind. *Teachers Forum,* **9,** 1–8.

Elonen, A. S., & Cain, A. C. (1964). Diagnostic evaluation and treatment of deviant blind children. *American Journal of Orthopsychiatry,* **34,** 625–633.

Elonen, A. S., Polzien, M., & Zwarensteyn, S. B. (1967). The "uncommitted" blind child: Results of intensive training of children formerly committed to institutions for the retarded. *Exceptional Children,* **33,** 301–307.

Elonen, A. S., & Zwarensteyn, S. B. (1963). Michigan's summer program for multiple-handicapped blind children. *New Outlook for the Blind,* **57,** 77–82.

Elonen, A. S., & Zwarensteyn, S. B. (1964). Appraisal of developmental lag in certain blind children. *Journal of Pediatrics,* **65,** 599–610.

Endress, D. T. (1968). *Developmental levels and parental attitudes of preschool blind children in Colorado.* Unpublished doctoral dissertation, Colorado State College.

Erikson, E. H. (1950). *Childhood and society.* New York: W. W. Norton.

Ewart, A. G., & Carp, F. M. (1962). Recognition of tactual form by sighted and blind subjects. *American Journal of Psychology,* **76,** 488–491.

Fernald, M. R. (1913). The mental imagery of two blind subjects. *Psychological Bulletin,* **10,** 62–63.

Ferrell, K. A. (1980). Can infants use the Sonicguide? Two years experience of Project VIEW. *Journal of Visual Impairment & Blindness,* **74,** 209–220.

Ferrell, K. A. (1983). Environmental sensors, spatial orientation, and mobility. Address presented at the Annual Meeting of the American Printing House for the Blind, Louisville, KY.

Fladeland, S. V. (1930). Some psychological effects of blindness as indicated by speech disorders. *Journal of Expression,* **9,** 129–134.

Fletcher, J. F. (1980). Spatial representation in blind children. 1: Development compared to sighted children. *Journal of Visual Impairment & Blindness,* **74,** 381–385.

Fletcher, J. F. (1981a). Spatial representation in blind children. 2: Effects of task variations. *Journal of Visual Impairment & Blindness,* **75,** 1–3.

Fletcher, J. F. (1981b). Spatial representation in blind children. 3: Effects of individual differences. *Journal of Visual Impairment & Blindness,* **75,** 46–49.

Foster, E. L. (1977). *Cognitive development and mental imagery in congenitally and adventitiously blind children.* Unpublished doctoral dissertation, City University of New York.

Foulke, E. (1962). The role of experience in the formation of concepts. *International Journal for the Education for the Blind,* **12,** 1–6.

Foulke, E. (1964). A multi-sensory test of conceptual ability. *New Outlook for the Blind,* **58,** 75–77.

Foulke, E. (1972). The personality of the blind: A non-valid concept. *New Outlook for the Blind,* **66,** 33–37.

Foulke, E. (1973). Panel discussant, Conference on The Blind Child in Social Interaction: Developing Relationships with Peers and Adults, New York.

Foulke E., Amster, C. H., Nolan, C. Y., & Bixler, R. H. (1962). The comprehension of rapid speech by the blind. *Exception Children,* **29,** 134–141.

Foulke, E., & Uhde, T. (1974). Do blind children need sex education? *New Outlook for the Blind,* **68,** 193–200, 209.

Fox, J. (1965). Improving tactile discrimination of the blind. *American Journal of Occupational Therapy,* **19,** 5–7.

Fraiberg, S. (1968). Parallel and divergent patterns in blind and sighted infants. *Psychoanalytic Study of the Child,* **23,** 264–300.

Fraiberg, S. (1970). Smiling and stranger reaction in blind infants. In J. Hellmuth (Ed.), *Exceptional infant.* New York: Brunner-Mazel.

Fraiberg, S. (1972). Separation crisis in two blind children. *Psychoanalytic Study of the Child,* **26,** 355–371.

Fraiberg, S. (1975). The development of human attachments in infants blind from birth. *Merrill-Palmer Quarterly,* **21,** 315–334.

Fraiberg, S. (1977). *Insights from the blind.* New York: Basic Books.

Fraiberg, S., & Adelson, E. (1976). Self representation in young blind children. In Z. S. Jastrzembska (Ed.), *The effects of blindness and other impairments on early development* (pp. 136–159). New York: American Foundation for the Blind.

Fraiberg S., & Freedman, D. A. (1964). Studies in the ego development of the congenitally blind child. *Psychoanalytic Study of the Child,* **19,** 113–169.

Fraiberg, S., Siegel, B., & Gibson, R. (1966). The role of sound in the search behavior of a blind infant. *Psychoanalytic Study of the Child,* **21,** 327–357.

Fraiberg, S., Smith, M., & Adelson, E. (1969). An educational program for blind infants. *Journal of Special Education,* **3,** 121–142.

Freedman, D. A. (1971). Congenital and perinatal sensory deprivation: Some studies in early development. *American Journal of Psychiatry,* **127,** 115–121.

Freedman, D. A., Fox-Kolenda, B. J., Margileth, D. A., & Miller, D. H. (1969). The development of the use of sound as a guide to affective and cognitive behavior — A two-phase process. *Child Development,* **40,** 1099–1105.

Freedman, D. A., & Cannady, C. (1971). Delayed emergence of prone locomotion. *Journal of Nervous and Mental Disease,* **153,** 108–117.

Freedman, D. G. (1964). Smiling in blind infants and the issue of innate *vs.* acquired. *Journal of Child Psychology and Psychiatry,* **5,** 171–184.

Freeman, R. D. (1974). A study of blind and partially sighted children with special reference to "mannerisms." Paper presented to the International Study Group on Child Neurology & Cerebral Palsy, Oxford, England.

Freides, D. (1974). Human information processing and sensory modality:

Cross-modal functions, information complexity, memory, and deficit. *Psychological Bulletin,* **81,** 284–310.

Friedman, J., & Pasnak, R. (1973a). Attainment of classification and seriation concepts by blind and sighted children. *Education of the Visually Handicapped,* **5,** 55–62.

Friedman, J., & Pasnak, R. (1973b). Accelerated acquisition of classification skills by blind children. *Developmental Psychology,* **9,** 333–337.

Fulcher, J. S. (1942). "Voluntary" facial expression in blind and seeing children. *Archives of Psychology,* **272.**

Furuta, N., Homma, K., & Muranaka, Y. (1977). Tactile pattern recognition with the Optacon of four-year-old blind children. *Bulletin of the Tokyo Metropolitan Rehabilitation Center for the Physically and Mentally Handicapped,* **7,** 21–29.

Garry, R. J., & Ascarelli, A. (1960). Teaching topographical orientation and spatial orientation to congenitally blind children. *Journal of Education,* **143,** 1–49.

Gelber, A. H. (1980). *The development of social cognition in blind children.* Unpublished doctoral dissertation, City University of New York.

Gendel, E. S. (1973). Sex education of the blind child. Paper presented at Conference on the Blind Child in Social Interaction: Developing Relationships with Peers and Adults, New York.

Genn, M. M., & Silverman, W. A. (1964). The mental development of ex-premature children with retrolental fibroplasia. *Journal of Nervous and Mental Diseases,* **138,** 79–86.

Gerhardt, J. B. (1982). The development of object play and classificatory skills in a blind child. *Journal of Visual Impairment & Blindness,* **76,** 219–223.

Gesell, A., Ilg, F., & Bullis, C. E. (1949). *Vision, its development in infant and child.* New York: Hoeber.

Gibbs, S. H., & Rice, J. A. (1974). The psycholinguistic characteristics of visually impaired children: An ITPA pattern analysis. *Education of the Visually Handicapped,* **6,** 80–87.

Gibson, E. J. (1969). *Principles of perceptual learning and development.* New York: Appleton-Century-Crofts.

Gibson, E. J., Gibson, J. J., Pick, A. D., & Osser, H. A. (1962). A developmental study of the discrimination of letter-like forms. *Journal of Comparative and Physiological Psychology,* **55,** 897–906.

Gibson, J. J. (1979). *The ecological approach to visual perception.* Boston: Houghton Mifflin.

Gilbert, J. G., & Rubin, E. J. (1965). Evaluating the intellect of blind children. *New Outlook for the Blind,* **59,** 238–240.

Gillman, A. E. (1973). Handicap and cognition: Visual deprivation and the rate of motor development in infants. *New Outlook for the Blind,* **67,** 309–314.

Gillman, A. E., & Goddard, D. R. (1974). The 20-year outcome of blind children two years old and younger: A preliminary survey. *New Outlook for the Blind,* **68,** 1–7.

Gipsman, S. C. (1979a). The ability to assume the upright position in blind and sighted children. Unpublished report. (ERIC Document Reproduction Service No. EC 130158)

Gipsman, S. C. (1979b). *Factors affecting performance and learning of blind and sighted children on a balance task.* Unpublished doctoral dissertation, University of California, Berkeley.

Gipsman, S. C. (1981). Effect of visual condition on use of proprioceptive cues in performing a balance task. *Journal of Visual Impairment & Blindness,* **75,** 50–54.

Gleitman, L. R. (1981). Maturational determinants of language growth. *Cognition,* **10,** 103–114.

Gliner, C. R. (1966). *A psychophysical study of tactual perception.* Unpublished doctoral dissertation, University of Minnesota.

Goldman, H. (1970). Psychological testing of blind children. *American Foundation for the Blind Research Bulletin,* **21,** 77–90.

Gomulicki, B. R. (1961). *The development of perception and learning in blind children.* Cambridge: The Psychological Laboratory, Cambridge University.

Goodenough, F. L. (1932). Expression of the emotions in a blind-deaf child. *Journal of Abnormal and Social Psychology,* **27,** 328–333.

Gore, G. V. (1966). Retrolental fibroplasia and I. Q. *New Outlook for the Blind,* **60,** 305–306.

Gore, G. V. (1969). A comparison of two methods of speeded speech. *Education of the Visually Handicapped,* **1,** 69–76.

Gottesman, M. (1971). A comparative study of Piaget's developmental schema of sighted children with that of a group of blind children. *Child Development,* **42,** 573–580.

Gottesman, M. (1973). Conservation development in blind children. *Child Development,* **44,** 824–827.

Gottesman, M. (1976). Stage development of blind children: A Piagetian view. *New Outlook for the Blind,* **70,** 94–100.

Graham, M. D. (1965). Wanted: A readiness test for mobility training. *New Outlook for the Blind,* **59,** 157–162.

Green, M. R., & Schecter, D. E. (1957). Autistic and symbiotic disorders in three blind children. *Psychiatric Quarterly,* **31,** 629–646.

Greenberg, H. M., Allison, L., Fewell, M., & Rich, C. (1957). The personality of junior high school students attending a residential school for the blind. *Journal of Educational Psychology,* **48,** 406–410.

Greenberg, H. M., & Jordan, S. (1957). Differential effects of total blindness and partial sight. *Exceptional Children,* **24,** 123–124.

Greene, R. J., & Hoats, D. L. (1971). Aversive tickling: A simple conditioning technique. *Behavior Therapy,* **2,** 389–393.

Guess, D. (1966). The influence of visual and ambulation restrictions on stereotyped behavior. *American Journal of Mental Deficiency,* **70,** 542-547.

Guess, D. (1967). Mental retardation and blindness: A complex and relatively unexplored dyad. *Exceptional Children,* **33,** 471-480.

Hall, A. (1981a). Mental images and the cognitive development of the congenitally blind. *Journal of Visual Impairment & Blindness,* **75,** 281-285.

Hall, A. (1981b). A developmental study of cognitive equivalence in the congenigenitally blind. *Journal of Mental Imagery,* **5,** 61-74.

Hall, A. (1983). Methods of equivalence grouping by congenitally blind children: Implications for education. *Journal of Visual Impairment & Blindness,* **77,** 172-174.

Hallenbeck, J. (1954a). Two essential factors in the development of young blind children. *New Outlook for the Blind,* **48,** 308-315.

Hallenbeck, J. (1954b). Pseudo-retardation in retrolental fibroplasia. *New Outlook for the Blind,* **48,** 301-307.

Halpin, G. (1972). *The effects of visual deprivation on creative thinking abilities of children.* Dissertation Abstracts International, **33,** 3381A. (University Microfilms No. 72-34, 082)

Halpin, G., Halpin, G., & Tillman, M. H. (1973). Relationships between creative thinking, intelligence, and teacher-rated characteristics of blind children. *Education of the Visually Handicapped,* **5,** 33-38.

Halpin, G., Halpin, G., & Torrance, E. P. (1973). Effects of sex, race, and age on creative thinking abilities of blind children. *Perceptual and Motor Skills,* **37,** 389-390.

Hammill, D. D., & Crandell, J. M., Jr. (1969). Implications of tactile-kinesthetic ability in visually handicapped children. *Education of the Visually Handicapped,* **1,** 65-69.

Hammill, D. D., Crandell, J. M., & Colarusso, R. (1970). The Slosson Intelligence Test adapted for visually limited children. *Exceptional Children,* **36,** 535-536.

Hammill, D. D., & Irwin, O. C. (1966). An abstraction test adapted for use with mentally retarded children. *American Journal of Mental Deficiency,* **70,** 807-812.

Hammill, D. D., & Powell, L. S. (1967). An abstraction test for visually handicapped children. *Exceptional Children,* **33,** 646-647.

Hampshire, B. (1977-78). Language and cognitive development in the blind child. *Education of the Visually Handicapped,* Vol. ix, No. 4, 97-101.

Hanfmann, E., & Kasanin, J. (1937). A method for the study of concept formation. *Journal of Psychology,* **3,** 521-540.

Hanninen, K. A. (1970). The effect of texture on tactual perception of length. *Exceptional Children,* **36,** 655-659.

Hanninen, K. A. (1971). Review of the educational potential of texture and tactually discriminable patterns. *Journal of Special Education,* **5,** 133-141.

Hanninen, K. A. (1976). The influence of preference of texture on the accuracy of tactile discrimination. *Education of the Visually Handicapped,* **8,** 44–52.
Hapeman, L. (1967). Developmental concepts of blind children between ages 3 and 6 as they relate to orientation and mobility. *International Journal for the Education of the Blind,* **17,** 41–48.
Hardy, R. E. (1968). A study of manifest anxiety among blind residential school students. *New Outlook for the Blind,* **62,** 173–180.
Hare, B. A., Hammill, D. D., & Crandell, J. M. (1970). Auditory discrimination ability of visually limited children. *New Outlook for the Blind,* **64,** 287–292.
Harley, R. K., Jr. (1963). *Verbalism among blind children.* New York: American Foundation for the Blind [Research Series, No. 10].
Harley, R. K., Jr., & Merbler, J. B. (1980). Development of an orientation and mobility program for multiply impaired low vision children. *Journal of Visual Impairment & Blindness,* **74,** 9–14.
Harley, R. K., Jr., & Spollen, J. (1973). A study of the reliability and validity of the Visual Efficiency Scale with low vision children. *Education of the Visually Handicapped,* **5,** 110–114.
Harley, R. K., Jr., Spollen, J., & Long, S. (1973). A study of the reliability and validity of the Visual Efficiency Scale with preschool children. *Education of the Visually Handicapped,* **5,** 38–42.
Harley, R. K., Jr., Wood, T. A., & Merbler, J. B. (1975). Programmed instruction in orientation and mobility in multiply impaired children. *New Outlook for the Blind,* **69,** 418–423.
Harley, R. K., Jr., Wood, T. A. & Merbler, J. B. (1980). An orientation and mobility program for multiply impaired blind children. *Exceptional Children,* **46,** 326–331.
Harlow, H. F. (1958). The nature of love. *American Psychologist,* **13,** 673–685.
Hart, V. (1983). Characteristics of young blind children. Paper presented at the Second International Symposium on Visually Handicapped Infants and Young Children: Birth to 7. Aruba.
Hartlage, L. C. (1968). Deficit in space concepts associated with visual deprivation. *Journal of Learning Disabilities,* **1,** 21–23.
Hartlage, L. C. (1969). Verbal tests of spatial conceptualization. *Journal of Experimental Psychology,* **80,** 180–182.
Hartlage, L. C. (1976). Development of spatial concepts in visually deprived children. *Perceptual and Motor Skills,* **42,** 255–258.
Haspiel, G. S. (1965). Communication breakdown in the blind emotionally disturbed child. *New Outlook for the Blind,* **59,** 98–99.
Hastings, H. J. (1947). An investigation of some aspects of the personality of the blind. Unpublished manuscript, University of California.
Hatwell, Y. (1966). *Privation sensorielle et intelligence.* Paris: Presses Universitaires de France.
Hatwell, Y. *Sensory privation and intelligence*, Eng. ed. New York: American Foundation for the Blind. (In press, 1984)

Hayes, C. S., & Weinhouse, E. (1978). Application of behavior modification to blind children. *Journal of Visual Impairment & Blindness,* **72,** 139–146.

Hayes, S. P. (1929). The new revision of the Binet Intelligence Tests for the blind. *Teachers Forum,* **2,** 2–4.

Hayes, S. P. (1930). *Terman's Condensed Guide for the Stanford Revision of the Binet–Simon Tests,* adapted for use with the blind. Watertown, MA.: Perkins Publication, No. 4.

Hayes, S. P. (1933). New experimental data on the old problem of sensory compensation. *Teachers Forum,* **5,** 22–26.

Hayes, S. P. (1935). Where did that sound come from? *Teachers Forum,* **7,** 47–51.

Hayes, S. P. (1942). Alternative scales for the mental measurement of the blind. *Outlook for the Blind,* **36,** 225–230.

Hayes, S. P. (1950). Measuring the intelligence of the blind. In P. A. Zahl (Ed.), *Blindness* (pp. 141-173). Princeton, New Jersey: Princeton University Press.

Hayes, S. P. (1952). *First Regional Conference on Mental Measurements of the Blind.* Watertown, MA.: Perkins Publications. No. 15.

Head, D. (1979). A comparison of self-concept scores for visually impaired adolescents in several class settings. *Education of the Visually Handicapped,* **11,** 51–55.

Hebb, D. O. (1949). *Organization of behavior.* New York: John Wiley & Sons.

Hepfinger, I. M. (1962). Psychological evaluation of young blind children. *New Outlook for the Blind,* **56,** 309–315.

Herman, J. F., Chatman, S. P., & Roth, S. F. (1983). Cognitive mapping in blind people: Acquisition of spatial relationships in a large-scale environment. *Journal of Visual Impairment & Blindness,* **77,** 161–166.

Herman, J. F., Herman, T. G., & Chatman, S. P. (1983). Constructing cognitive maps from partial information: A demonstration study with congenitally blind subjects. *Journal of Visual Impairment & Blindness,* **77,** 195–198.

Hermelin, B. M., & O'Connor, N. (1971a). Right and left handed reading of braille. *Nature,* 231, 470.

Hermelin, B. M., & O'Connor, N. (1971b). Spatial coding in normal, autistic and blind children. *Perceptual and Motor skills,* **33,** 127–132.

Hermelin, B. M., & O'Connor, N. (1975). Location and distance estimates by blind and sighted children. *Quarterly Journal of Experimental Psychology,* **27,** 295–301.

Hersen, M., & Barlow, D. H. (1976). *Single case experimental designs: Strategies for studying behavior change.* New York: Pergamon Press.

Higgins, L.C. (1973). *Classification in congenitally blind children.* New York: American Foundation for the Blind [Research Series, No. 25].

Hill, B. E. (1951). Social treatment of the young blind child. *Social Casework,* **32,** 381–388.

Hill, E. W. (1970). The formation of concepts involved in body position in space. *Education of the Visually Handicapped,* **2,** 112–115.

Hill, E. W. (1971). The formation of concepts involved in body position in space. *Education of the Visually Handicapped,* **3,** 21–25.

Hill, E. W., & Blasch, B. B. (1980). Concept development. In R. L. Welsh & B. B. Blasch (Eds.), *Foundations of orientation and mobility* (pp. 265-290). New York: American Foundation for the Blind.

Hill, E. W., & Hill, M. M. (1980). Revision and validation of a test for assessing the spatial conceptual abilities of visually impaired children. *Journal of Visual Impairment & Blindness,* **74**, 373-380.

Hollyfield, R. L., & Foulke, E. (1983). The spatial cognition of blind pedestrians. *Journal of Visual Impairment & Blindness,* **77**, 204-210.

Hopkins, K. D., & McGuire, L. (1966). The validity of the Wechsler Intelligence Scale for Children. *International Journal for the Education of the Blind,* **15**, 65-73.

Hopkins, K. D., & McGuire, L. (1967). IQ constancy and the blind child. *International Journal for the Education of the Blind,* **16**, 113-114.

Hoshmand, L. T. (1975). "Blindisms": Some observations and propositions. *Education of the Visually Handicapped,* **7**, 56-60.

Huckabee, M. W., & Ferrell, J. G., Jr. (1971). The Tactual Embedded Figures Test as a measure of field dependence-independence in blind adolescents. *Education of the Visually Handicapped,* **3**, 37-40.

Humphrey, G. K., Harris, L., Muir, D. M., & Dodwell, P. C. The use of the Canterbury Child's Aid in infancy and early childhood: A case study. (In press). *Journal of Visual Impairment & Blindness.*

Humphrey, G. K., & Humphrey, D. E. The use of binaural sensory aids by blind infants and children: Theoretical and applied issues. In F. Morrison, C. Lord, & D. P. Keating (Eds.), *Applied developmental psychology,* (Vol. 2). (In press.) New York: Academic Press.

Hunter, W. F. (1964). An analysis of space perception in congenitally blind and in sighted individuals. *Journal of General Psychology,* **70**, 325-329.

Imamura, S. (1965). *Mother and blind child.* New York: American Foundation for the Blind [Research Series, No. 14].

Irwin, O. C., & Hammill, D. D. (1964). An abstraction test for use with cerebral palsied chldren. *Cerebral Palsy Review,* **25**, 3-9.

Irwin, O. C., & Jensen, P. J. (1963). A test of sound discrimination for use with cerebral palsied children. *Cerebral Palsy Review,* **24**, 5-11.

Jankowski, L. W., & Evans, J. K. (1981). The exercise capacity of blind children. *Journal of Visual Impairment & Blindness,* **75**, 248-251.

Jastrow, J. (1900). *Fact and fable in psychology.* Boston: Houghton Mifflin.

Jastrzembska, Z. S. (1973). Social and psychological aspects of blindness: A sampling of the literature. *American Foundation for the Blind Research Bulletin,* **25**, 169-174.

Jervis, F. M. (1959). A comparison of self-concepts of blind and sighted children. In C. J. Davis (Ed.), *Guidance programs for blind children* (pp. 19-31). Watertown, MA: Perkins Publications. (No. 20)

Jervis, F. M., & Haslerud, G. M. (1950). Quantitative and qualitative difference in frustration between blind and sighted adolescents. *Journal of Psychology,* **29,** 67–76.

Johnson, R. A. (1979). Creative imagery in blind and sighted adolescents. *Journal of Mental Imagery,* **3,** 23–30.

Johnson, R. A. (1980). Sensory images in the absence of sight: Blind versus sighted adolescents. *Perceptual and Motor Skills,* **51,** 177–178.

Jones, B. (1972). Development of cutaneous and kinesthetic localization by blind and sighted children. *Developmental Psychology,* **6,** 349–352.

Jones, B. (1975). Spatial perception in the blind. *British Journal of Psychology,* **66,** 461–472.

Jones, J. W. (1952). Play therapy and the blind child. *New Outlook for the Blind,* **46,** 189–197

Jordan, J. E., & Felty, J. (1968). Factors associated with intellectual variation among visually impaired children. *American Foundation for the Blind Research Bulletin,* **15,** 61–70.

Juurmaa, J. (1973). Transposition in mental spatial manipulation: A theoretical analysis. *American Foundation for the Blind Research Bulletin,* **26,** 87–134

Juurmaa, J., & Jarvilehto, S. (1965). On the obstacle sense of the blind. *Helsinki Institute of Occupational Health Monographs,* No. 28.

Kaplan, D. M., & Mason, E. A. (1960). Maternal reactions to premature birth viewed as an acute emotional disorder. *American Journal of Orthopsychiatry,* **30,** 539–552.

Kass, W., Gillman, A. E., Mattis, S., Klugman, E., & Jacobson, B. J. (1967). Treatment of selective mutism in a blind child: School and clinic collaboration. *American Journal of Orthopsychiatry,* **37,** 215–216.

Kay, L., & Kay, N. (1983). An ultrasonic spatial sensor's role as a developmental aid for blind children. *Transactions of the Ophthalmological Society of New Zealand,* **35,** 38–42.

Kay, L., & Strelow, E. R. (1977). Blind babies need specially-designed aids. *New Scientist,* **73,** 709–712.

Keeler, W. R. (1958). Autistic patterns and defective communication in blind children with retrolental fibroplasia. In P. H. Hoch & J. Zubin (Eds.), *Psychopathology of communication* (pp. 64–84). New York: Grune & Stratton.

Kekelis, L. S. (1981). *Mothers' input to blind children.* Unpublished master's thesis, University of Southern California.

Kekelis, L. S., & Andersen, E. W. (1984). Family communication styles and language development. *Journal of Visual Impairment & Blindness,* **78,** 54–65.

Kenmore, J. R. (1965). *Associative learning by blind versus sighted children with words and objects differing in meaningfulness and identifiability without vision.* Unpublished doctoral dissertation, University of Minnesota.

Kennedy, J. M. (1980). Blind people recognizing and making haptic pictures. In

M. Hagen (Ed.), *The perception of pictures* (pp. 263-303). New York: Academic Press.

Kennedy, J. M. (1982). Haptic pictures. In W. Schiff & E. Foulke (Eds.), *Tactual perception: A sourcebook* (pp. 305-333). Cambridge: Cambridge University Press.

Kennedy, J. M. (1983). What can we learn about pictures from the blind? *American Scientist,* **71,** 19-26.

Kennedy, J. M., & Domander, R. (1981). Blind people depicting states & events in metaphoric line drawings. Paper presented at meetings of The Psychonomic Society, Philadelphia.

Kephart, J. G., Kephart, C. P., & Schwarz, G. C. (1974). A journey into the world of the blind child. *Exceptional Children.* **40,** 421-427.

Kinsbourne, M., & Lempert, H. (1980). Human figure representation by blind children. *Journal of General Psychology,* **102,** 33-37.

Kirtley, D., & Cannistraci, K. (1974). Dreams of the visually handicapped: Toward a normative approach. *American Foundation for the Blind Research Bulletin,* **27,** 111-134.

Klein, G. S. (1962). Blindness and isolation. *Psychoanalytic Study of the Child.* **17,** 82-93.

Knight, J. J. (1972). Mannerisms in the congenitally blind child. *New Outlook for the Blind,* **66,** 297-302.

Knobloch, H., Rider, R., Harper, P., & Pasamanick, B. (1956). Neuropsychiatric sequelae of prematurity. *Journal of the American Medical Association,* **161,** 581-585.

Knotts, J. R., & Miles, W. R. (1929). The maze-learning ability of blind compared with sighted children. *Journal of Genetic Psychology,* **36,** 21-50.

Koch, H. L., & Ufkess, J. (1926). A comparative study of stylus maze learning by blind and seeing subjects. *Journal of Experimental Psychology,* **9,** 118-131.

Koehler, O. (1954). Das Lächeln als angeborene Ausdrucksbewegung [The Smile as an In-born Expressive Movement]. *Mensch. Vereb. und Konstitutionslehre,* **32,** 390-398.

Kohler, I. (1966). Vestibular guidance. In R. Dufton (Ed.), *International conference on sensory devices for the blind* (pp. 215-219). London: St. Dunstan's Press.

Komisar, D., & MacDonnell, M. (1955). Gains in IQ for students attending a school for the blind. *Exceptional Children,* **21,** 127-129.

Kool, V. K., & Rana, M. (1980). Tactual short term memory of blind and sighted children. *Psychologia: An International Journal of Psychology in the Orient.* **23,** 173-178.

Korner, A. F., & Thoman, E. B. (1970). Visual alertness in neonates as evoked by maternal care. *Journal of Experimental Child Psychology,* **10,** 67-78.

Kratochwill, T. R. (1978). *Single subject research: Strategies for evaluating change.* New York: Academic Press.

Kubler-Ross, E. (1969). *On death and dying.* London: Macmillan.

LaGrow, S., & Prochnow-LaGrow, J. E. (1983). Consistent methodological errors observed in single case studies: Suggested guidelines. *Journal of Visual Impairment and Blindness,* **77,** 481–488.

Lairy, G. C., & Harrison-Covello, A. (1973). The blind child and his parents: Congenital visual defect and the repercussion of family attitudes on the early development of the child. *American Foundation for the Blind Research Bulletin.* **25,** 1-24.

Land, S. L., & Vineberg, S. E. (1965). Locus of control in blind children. *Exceptional Children,* **31,** 257–260.

Landau, B. (1983). Blind children's language is not "meaningless." In A. E. Mills (Ed.), *Language acquisition in the blind child* (pp. 62–76). San Diego: College-Hill Press.

Landau, B., Gleitman, H., & Spelke, E. (1981). Spatial knowledge and geometric representation in the child blind from birth. *Science,* **213,** 1275–1277.

Lane, H., & Curran, C. (1963). Gradients of auditory generalization for blind, retarded children. *Journal of the Experimental Analysis of Behavior,* **6,** 585–588.

Larendeau, M., & Pinard, A. (1970). *The development of the concept of space in the child.* New York: International Universities Press.

Lebo, D., & Bruce, R. S. (1960). Projective methods recommended for use with the blind. *Journal of Psychology,* **50,** 15–38.

Lebron-Rodriguez, D. E., & Pasnak, R. (1977). Introduction of intellectual gains in blind children. *Journal of Experimental Child Psychology,* **24,** 505–515.

Leonard, J. A. (1969). Static and mobile balancing performance of blind adolescent grammar school children. *New Outlook for the Blind,* **63,** 65–72.

Leonard, J. A., & Newman, R. C. (1967). Spatial orientation in the blind. *Nature,* **215,** 1413–1414.

Levitt, E. A., Rosenbaum, A. L., Willerman, L., & Levitt, M. (1972). Intelligence of retinoblastoma patients and their siblings. *Child Development,* **43,** 939–948.

Lipsitt, L. P. (1958). A self-concept scale for children and its relationship to the children's form of the Manifest Anxiety Scale. *Child Development,* **29,** 463–472.

Lockman, J. J., Rieser, J. J., & Pick, H. L., Jr. (1981). Assessing blind travelers' knowledge of spatial layout. *Journal of Visual Impairment & Blindness,* **75,** 321–326.

Loofbourow, G. C., & Keys, N. (n.d.). *Personal Index Manual,* Educational Test Bureau, Minneapolis.

Lopata, D. J., & Pasnak, R. (1976). Accelerated conservation acquisition and IQ gains by blind children. *Genetic Psychology Monographs,* **93,** 3–25.

Lord, F. E. (1969). Development of scales for the measurement of orientation and mobility of young blind children. *Exceptional Children,* **36,** 77–81.

Lowenfeld, B. (1948). Effects of blindness on the cognitive functions of children. *Nervous Child,* **7,** 45–54.

Lowenfeld, V., & Brittain, W. L. (1964). *Creative and mental growth* (4th ed.). New York: Macmillan.

Lukoff, I. F., & Whiteman, M. (1970). Socialization and segregated education. *American Foundation for the Blind Research Bulletin,* **20,** 91–107.

Luria, A. R. (1959). The directive function of speech in development and dissolution. *Word,* **15,** 351–352.

Lydon, W. T., & McGraw, M. L. (1973). *Concept development of visually handicapped children.* New York: American Foundation for the Blind.

Manaster, A., & Kucharis, S. (1972). Experiential methods in a group counseling program with blind children. *New Outlook for the Blind,* **66,** 15–19.

Marmor, G. S., & Zaback, L. A. (1976). Mental rotation by the blind: Does mental rotation depend on visual imagery? *Journal of Experimental Psychology: Human Perception and Performance,* **2,** 515–521.

Martin, C. J., Boersma, F. J., & Cox, D. L. (1965). A classification of associative strategies in paired-associate learning. *Psychonomic Science,* **3,** 455–456.

Martin, C. J., & Herndon, M. A. (1971). Facilitation of associative learning among blind children. *Proceedings of the American Psychological Association,* 629–630.

Mattis, S. (1967). An experimental approach to treatment of visually impaired multi-handicapped children. *New Outlook for the Blind,* **61,** 1–5.

Maxfield, K. E. (1936). The spoken language of the blind preschool child. *Archives of Psychology,* No. 201.

Maxfield, K. E., & Buchholz, S. (1957). *A social maturity scale for blind preschool children: A guide to its use.* New York: American Foundation for the Blind.

Maxfield, K. E., & Fjeld, H. A. (1942). The social maturity of the visually handicapped preschool child. *Child Development,* **13,** 1–27.

Mayadas, N. S. (1972). Role expectations and performance of blind children: Practice and implications. *Education of the Visually Handicapped,* **4,** 45–52.

Mayadas, N. S., & Duehn, W. D. (1976). The impact of significant adults' expectations on the life style of visually impaired children. *New Outlook for the Blind,* **70,** 286–290.

McAndrew, H. (1948a). Rigidity and isolation: A study of the deaf and the blind. *Journal of Abnormal and Social Psychology,* **43,** 476–494.

McAndrew, H. (1948b). Rigidity in the deaf and the blind. *Journal of Social Issues,* **4,** 72–77.

McGuinness, R. M. (1970). A descriptive study of blind children educated in the itinerant teacher, resource room, and special school setting. *American Foundation for the Blind Research Bulletin,* **20,** 1–56.

McGinnis, A. R. (1981). Functional linguistic strategies of blind children.

Journal of Visual Impairment & Blindness, **75,** 210–214.

McGuire, L. L., & Meyers, C. E. (1971). Early personality in the congenitally blind child. *New Outlook for the Blind,* **65,** 137–143.

McGurk, H., & Lewis, M. (1974). Space perception in early infancy: Perception within a common auditory-visual space? *Science,* **186,** 649–650.

McKay, B. E. (1936). Social maturity of the preschool blind child. *Training School Bulletin,* **33,** 146–155.

McKinney, J. P. (1964). Hand schema in children. *Psychonomic Science.* **1,** 99–100.

McReynolds, J., & Worchel, P. (1954). Geographic orientation in the blind. *Journal of General Psychology,* **51,** 221–236.

Meighan, T. (1971). *An investigation of the self concept of blind and visually handicapped adolescents.* New York: American Foundation for the Blind.

Melzack, R. M., & Scott, T. H. (1957). The effects of early experience on the response to pain. *Journal of Comparative and Physiological Psychology,* **50,** 155–161.

Melzack, R. M., & Thompson, W. R. (1956). Effects of early experience on social behavior. *Canadian Journal of Psychology,* **10,** 82–90.

Menaker, S. L. (1966). *Perceptual development in blind children.* Dissertation Abstracts International, **27,** 1625B. (University Microfilms No. 66–11, 297)

Merry, F. K. (1932). A further investigation to determine the value of embossed pictures for blind children. *Teachers Forum,* **4,** 96–99.

Merry, F. K. (1933). An experiment in teaching blind children to recognize simple embossed pictures. *Teachers Forum,* **5,** 73–78.

Merry, R. V. (1930). To what extent can blind children recognize tactually, simple embossed pictures? *Teachers Forum,* **3,** 2–5.

Merry, R. V., & Merry, F. K. (1934). The finger maze as a supplementary test of intelligence for blind children. *Journal of Genetic Psychology,* **44,** 227–230.

Millar, S. (1975a). Effects of phonological and tactual similarity on serial object recall by blind and sighted children. *Cortex,* **11,** 170–180.

Millar, S. (1975b). Effects of tactual and phonological similarity on the recall of braille letters by blind children. *British Journal of Psychology,* **66,** 193–201.

Millar, S. (1975c). Spatial memory by blind and sighted children. *British Journal of Psychology,* **66,** 449–459.

Millar, S. (1975d). Visual experience or translation rules? Drawing the human figure by blind and sighted children. *Perception,* **4,** 363–371.

Millar, S. (1976). Spatial representation by blind and sighted children. *Journal of Experimental Child Psychology,* **21,** 460–479.

Millar, S. (1977a). Spatial representation by blind and sighted children. In G. Butterworth (Ed.), *The child's representation of the world.* London: Plenum Press.

Millar, S. (1977b). Tactual and name matching by blind children. *British Jour-*

nal of Psychology, **68,** 377–387.

Millar, S. (1978a). Short-term serial tactual recall: Effects of grouping on tactually probed recall of braille letters and nonsense shapes by blind children. *British Journal of Psychology,* **69,** 17–24.

Millar, S. (1978b). Tactual shapes. *Occasional Papers of the British Psychological Society,* **2,** 55–59.

Millar, S. (1979). The utilization of external and movement cues in simple spatial tasks by blind and sighted children. *Perception,* **8,** 11–20.

Millar, S. (1981a). Crossmodal and intersensory perception and the blind. In R. D. Walk & H. L. Pick, Jr. (Eds.), *Intersensory perception and sensory integration.* London: Plenum Press.

Millar, S. (1981b). Self-referent and movement cues in coding spatial location by blind and sighted children. *Perception,* **10,** 255–264.

Millar, S. (1982). The problem of imagery and spatial development in the blind. In B. de Gelder (Ed.), *Knowledge and representation.* London: Routledge & Kegan Paul.

Miller, B. S., & Miller, W. H. (1976). Extinguishing "blindisms": A paradigm for intervention. *Education of the Visually Handicapped.* **8,** 6–15.

Miller, C. K. (1969). Conservation in blind children. *Education of the Visually Handicapped,* **1,** 101–105.

Miller, S. E. (1982). Relationship between mobility level and development of positional concepts in visually impaired children. *Journal of Visual Impairment & Blindness,* **76,** 149–153.

Miller, W. H. (1970). Manifest anxiety in visually impaired adolescents. *Education of the Visually Handicapped,* **2,** 91–95.

Mills, A. E. (1983). The acquisition of speech sounds in the visually-handicapped child. In A. E. Mills (Ed.), *Language acquisition in the blind child: Normal and deficient.* San Diego: College-Hill Press.

Mills, R. J. (1970). Orientation and mobility for teachers. *Education of the Visually Handicapped,* **2,** 80–82.

Mills, R. J., & Adamshick, D. R. (1969). The effectiveness of structured sensory training experiences prior to formal orientation and mobility instruction. *Education of the Visually Handicapped,* **1,** 14–21.

Milstead, J. R. (1972). Modification of echolalic speech in a blind, behaviorally-deficient child using parental contingency management. *Journal of Communication Disorders,* **5,** 275–279.

Miner, L. E. (1963a). A study of the incidence of speech deviations among visually handicapped children. *New Outlook for the Blind,* **57,** 10–14.

Miner, L. E. (1963b). Speech improvement for visually handicapped children. *New Outlook for the Blind,* **57,** 160–163.

Mistschenka, M. H. (1933). Ueber die mimische Gesichtsmotorik der Blinden. [On the Means of Facial Mimicry Among the Blind] *Folia Neuropathologica Estoniana,* **13,** 24–43.

Mommers, M. J. C. (1980). Braille reading: Effects of different hand and finger usage. *Journal of Visual Impairment & Blindness,* **74,** 338–343.

Morgan, D. H. (1944). Emotional adjustment of visually handicapped adolescents. *Journal of Educational Psychology,* **35,** 65–81.

Morris, J. E., & Nolan, C. Y. (1961). Discriminability of tactual patterns. *International Journal for the Education of the Blind,* **11,** 50–54.

Morris, J. E., & Nolan, C. Y. (1963). Minimum sizes for areal type tactual symbols. *International Journal for the Education of the Blind,* **13,** 48–51.

Morris, R. H. (1974). A play environment for blind children: Design and evaluation. *New Outlook for the Blind,* **68,** 408–415.

Morrissey, W. P. (1950). The fantasy life of the blind. *Outlook for the Blind,* **44,** 195–198.

Muhl, A. M. (1930). Results of psychometric and personality studies of blind children at the California State School for the Blind. *American Association of Instructors of the Blind, Proceedings,* 568–573.

Mulford, R. C. (1980). *Talking without seeing: Some problems of semantic development in blind children.* Unpublished doctoral dissertation, Stanford University.

Myers, J. (1978). Compressed speech increases learning efficiency. *Education of the Visually Handicapped,* **10,** 56–64.

Nagera, H., & Colonna, A. B. (1965). Aspects of the contribution of sight to ego and drive development. *Psychoanalytic Study of the Child,* **20,** 267–287.

National Institute for the Visually Handicapped. (1981). *A comparative study of the manneristic behavior of blind and sighted children.* Research Series No. 1, Ministry of Social Welfare, Government of India.

Nelson, K. (1973). Structure and strategy in learning to talk. *Monographs of the Society for Research in Child Development,* **38**(No. 149).

Newcomer, J. (1977). Sonicguide: Its use with public school blind children. *Journal of Visual Impairment & Blindness,* **71,** 268–271.

Newland, T. E. (1964). Prediction and evaluation of academic learning by blind children. *International Journal for the Education of the Blind,* **14,** 1–7.

Newland, T. E. (1970). Discussion following paper by C. J. Davis, *Proceedings of the Conference on New Approaches to the Evaluation of Blind Persons.* New York: American Foundation for the Blind.

Newland, T. E. (1979). The Blind Learning Aptitude Test. *Journal of Visual Impairment & Blindness,* **73,** 134–139.

Nolan, C. Y. (1960a). Roughness discrimination among blind children in the primary grades. *International Journal for the Education of the Blind,* **9,** 97–100.

Nolan, C. Y. (1960b). On the unreality of words to the blind. *New Outlook for the Blind,* **54,** 100–102.

Nolan, C. Y., & Morris, J. E. (1960). Further results in the development of a test of roughness discrimination. *International Journal for the Education of the Blind,* **10,** 48–50.

Norris, M., Spaulding, P. J., & Brodie, F. H. (1957). *Blindness in children.*

Chicago: University of Chicago Press.
Novikova, L. A. (1973). *Blindness and the electrical activity of the brain.* New York: American Foundation for the Blind [Research Series, No. 23].

O'Connor, N., & Hermelin, B. M. (1971). Inter- and intra-modal transfer in children with modality specific and general handicaps. *British Journal of Social and Clinical Psychology,* **10,** 346–354.
O'Connor, N., & Hermelin, B. M. (1972a). Seeing and hearing in space and time. *Perception & Psychophysics,* **11,** 46–48.
O'Connor, N., & Hermelin, B. M. (1972b). Seeing and hearing in space and time: Problems by blind and sighted children. *British Journal of Psychology,* **63,** 381–386.
O'Connor, N., & Hermelin, B. M. (1978). *Seeing and hearing in space and time.* New York: Academic Press.
Ohwaki, Y., Tanno, Y., Ohwaki, M., Hariu, T., Hayasaka, K., & Miyake, K. (1960). Construction of an intelligence test for the blind. *Tohoku Psychologia Folia,* **18,** 45–63.
Oi, H., Koyanagi, K., & Maehigashi, T. (1956). Experimental researches on the process of solving tactile block-design problems by blind children. *Tohoku Psychologia Folia,* **15,** 1–9.
Omwake, E. B., & Solnit, A. J. (1961). It isn't fair: The treatment of a blind child. *Psychoanalytic Study of the Child,* **16,** 352–404.

Paivio, A., & Okovita, H. W. (1971). Word imagery modalities and associative learning in blind and sighted subjects. *Journal of Verbal Learning and Verbal Behavior,* **10,** 506–510.
Paraskeva, P. C. (1959). A survey of the facilities for the mentally retarded blind in the United States. *International Journal for the Education of the Blind,* **8,** 139–145.
Parke, K. L., Shellcross, R., & Anderson, R. J. (1980). Differences in coverbal behavior between blind and sighted persons during dyadic communication. *Journal of Visual Impairment & Blindness,* **74,** 142–146.
Parker, J. (1969). Adapting school psychological evaluation of the blind child. *New Outlook for the Blind,* **63,** 305–311.
Parmalee, A. H. (1955). The developmental evaluation of the blind premature infant. *American Medical Association Journal of Diseases of Children,* **90,** 135–140.
Parmalee, A. H., Cutsforth, M. G., & Jackson, C. L. (1958). Mental development of children with blindness due to retrolental fibroplasia. *American Medical Association Journal of Diseases of Children,* **96,** 641–654.
Parmalee, A. H., Fiske, C. E., & Wright, R. H. (1959). The development of ten children with blindness as a result of retrolental fibroplasia. *American Medical Association Journal of Diseases of Children,* **98,** 198–220.
Parten, C. B. (1971). Encouragement of sensory motor development in the

preschool blind. *Exceptional Children,* **37,** 739–741.

Petrucci, D. (1953). The blind child and his adjustment. *New Outlook for the Blind,* **47,** 240–246.

Piaget, J. (1952). *The origins of intelligence in children* (2nd ed.). New York: International Universities Press.

Piaget, J., & Inhelder, B. (1969). *The psychology of the child.* New York: Basic Books.

Pick, A. D., & Pick, H. L., Jr. (1966). A developmental study of tactual discrimination in blind and sighted children and adults. *Psychonomic Science,* **6,** 367–368.

Pick, H. L., Jr., Klein, R. E., & Pick, A. D. (1966). Visual and tactual identification of form orientation. *Journal of Experimental Child Psychology,* **4,** 391–397.

Pick, H. L., Jr., & Pick, A. D. (1967). A developmental and analytic study of the size-weight illusion. *Journal of Experimental Child Psychology,* **5,** 362–371.

Pillemer, D. B., & Light, R. J. (1980). Synthesizing outcomes: How to use research evidence from many studies. *Harvard Educational Review,* **50,** 176–195.

Pintner, R., & Forlano, G. (1943). Personality tests of partially sighted children. *Journal of Applied Psychology,* **27,** 283–287.

Pitman, D. J. (1965). The musical ability of blind children. *American Foundation for the Blind Research Bulletin,* **11,** 63–80.

Prescott, J. W. (1976). Somatosensory deprivation and its relationship to the blind. In Z. S. Jastrzembska (Ed.), *The effects of blindness and other impairments on early development* (pp. 65–136). New York: American Foundation for the Blind.

Provence, S., & Lipton, R. C. (1962). *Infants in institutions.* New York: International Universities Press.

Psychology today: An introduction (1970). Del Mar, CA: CRM Books.

Rankin, R. J. (1967). The Ohwaki–Kohs Tactile Block Design Intelligence Test. *Journal of Educational Measurement,* **4,** 261–262.

Reich, R. (1968). Puppetry—A language tool. *Exceptional Children,* **34,** 621–623.

Renshaw, S. (1930). The errors of cutaneous localization and the effect of practice on the localizing movement in children and adults. *Journal of Genetic Psychology,* **38,** 223–238.

Renshaw, S., Wherry, R. J., & Newlin, J. C. (1930). Cutaneous localization in congenitally blind versus seeing children and adults. *Journal of Genetic Psychology,* **38,** 239–248.

Révész, G. (1950). *Psychology and the art of the blind.* New York: Longmans, Green.

Reynell, J. (1978). Developmental patterns of visually handicapped children.

Child Care, Health & Development, **4,** 291–303.

Reynell, J., & Zinkin, P. (1975). New procedures for the developmental assessment of young children with severe visual handicaps. *Child Care, Health & Development,* **1,** 61–69.

Reynolds, J. C. (1951). Suggestions for parents of visually handicapped babies. *New Outlook for the Blind,* **45,** 243–247.

Rhyne, J. M. (1982). Comprehension of synthetic speech by blind children. *Journal of Visual Impairment & Blindness,* **76,** 313–316.

Rice C. E. (1970). Early blindness, early experience, and perceptual enhancement. *American Foundation for the Blind Research Bulletin,* **22,** 1–22.

Rice, C. E. (1976). Data differences in two studies (Discussion following Spiegelman paper). In Z. S. Jastrzembska (Ed.), *The effects of blindness and other impairments on early development* (pp. 57–59). New York: American Foundation for the Blind.

Rich, C. C., & Anderson, R. P. (1965). A tactual form of the progressive matrices for use with blind children. *Personnel and Guidance Journal,* **43,** 912–919.

Riesen, A. H. (1947). The development of visual perception in man and chimpanzee. *Science,* **106,** 107–108.

Riesen, A. H. (1966). Sensory deprivation. In E. Stellar & J. M. Sprague (Eds.), *Progress in physiological psychology.* New York: Academic Press.

Rieser, J. J., Guth, D. A., & Hill, E. W. (1982). Mental processes mediating independent travel: Implications for orientation and mobility. *Journal of Visual Impairment & Blindness,* **76,** 213–218.

Rieser, J. J., Lockman, J. J., & Pick, H. L., Jr. (1980). The role of visual experience in knowledge of spatial layout. *Perception & Psychophysics,* **28,** 185–190.

Robbins, N. (1971). The teaching of a manual-sign as a diagnostic tool with deaf-blind children, *Fourth International Conference on Deaf-Blind Children*, Perkins School for the Blind, Vermont Printing Co.

Rogow, S. M. (1970). Retardation among blind children. *Education of the Visually Handicapped,* **2,** 107–111.

Rogow, S. M. (1975). Perceptual organization in blind children. *New Outlook for the Blind,* **69,** 226–233.

Rogow, S. M. (1980). Language development in blind multihandicapped children: A model of co-active intervention. *Child Care, Health & Development,* **6,** 301–308.

Rogow, S. M. (1981). The appreciation of riddles by blind and visually handicapped children. *Education of the Visually Handicapped,* **13,** 4–10.

Root, F. K., & Riley, B. G. (1960). Study of deaf-blind children: A developmental plan. *New Outlook for the Blind,* **54,** 206–210.

Rosencranz, D., & Suslick, R. (1976). Cognitive models for spatial representations in congenitally blind, adventitiously blind, and sighted subjects. *New Outlook for the Blind,* **70,** 188–194.

Rosenstein, J. (1957). Tactile perception of rhythmic patterns by normal, blind, deaf, and aphasic children. *American Annals of the Deaf,* **102,** 399–403.

Rothschild, J. (1960). Play therapy with blind children. *New Outlook for the Blind,* **54,** 329–333.

Rowe, E. D. (1958). *Speech problems of blind children.* New York: American Foundation for the Blind [Education Series No. 10].

Royster, P. M. (1964). Peripatology and the development of the blind child. *New Outlook for the Blind,* **58,** 136–138.

Salmon, P. J., & Rusalem, H. (1966). The deaf-blind person: A review of the literature. *Blindness 1966: American Association of Workers for the Blind Annual,* 15–63.

Sandler, A. M. (1965). Aspects of passivity and ego development in the blind infant. *Psychoanalytic Study of the Child,* **18,** 343–361.

Sandler, A. M., & Wills, D. M. (1963). Preliminary notes on play and mastery in the blind child. *Journal of Child Psychotherapy,* **1,** 7–19.

Santin, S., & Nesker Simmons, J. (1977). Problems in the construction of reality in congenitally blind children. *Journal of Visual Impairment & Blindness,* **71,** 425–429.

Sato, Y., & Anayama, T. (1973). Standardization of tactual perception for the blind. *Japanese Journal of Special Education,* **10,** 12–26.

Schaffer, H. R., & Callender, W. M. (1959). Psychologic effects of hospitalization in infancy. *Pediatrics,* **24,** 528–539.

Schaffer, H. R., & Emerson, P. E. (1964). The development of social attachments in infancy. *Monographs of the Society for Research in Child Development,* **29** [No. 1].

Schindele, R. (1974). The social adjustment of visually handicapped children in different educational settings. *American Foundation for the Blind Research Bulletin,* **28,** 125–144.

Schlaegel, T. F. (1953). The dominant method of imagery in blind as compared to sighted adolescents. *Journal of Genetic Psychology,* **83,** 265–277.

Schmitt, T. L. (1978). *Early experience and spatial functioning in the blind.* Unpublished doctoral dissertation, University of California, Riverside.

Scholl, G. T. (1974). The psychosocial effects of blindness: Implications for program planning in sex education. *New Outlook for the Blind,* **68,** 201–209.

Scholl, G., & Schnur, R. (1976). *Measures of psychological, vocational, & educational functioning in the blind and visually handicapped.* New York: American Foundation for the Blind.

Schutz, W. C. (1958). *Firo: A three-dimensional theory of interpersonal behavior.* New York: Rinehart.

Schwartz, A. W. (1972). A comparison of congenitally blind and sighted elementary school children on intelligence, tactile discrimination, abstract reasoning, perceived physical health, perceived personality adjustment and parent–teacher perceptions of intellectual performance. *Dissertation Abstracts International,* **33,** 5588A. (University Microfilms No. 73–9717)

Schwartz, T. J. (1981). *Role-taking and referential communication in visually-impaired and sighted children.* Unpublished doctoral dissertation, New School for Social Research, New York.

Scott, R. A. (1968). *The making of blind men.* New York: Russell Sage Foundation.

Scott, R. A. (1969). The socialization of blind children. In D. A. Goslin (Ed.), *Handbook of socialization theory and research.* Chicago: Rand McNally.

Seashore, M. J., Leifer, A. D., Barnett, C. R., & Leiderman, P. H. (1973). The effects of denial of early mother–infant interaction on maternal self-confidence. *Journal of Personality and Social Psychology,* **26,** 369–378.

Shurrager, H. C., & Shurrager, P. S. (1964). *Manual for the Haptic Intelligence Scale for the Blind.* Chicago: Psychology Research Technology Center, Illinois Institute of Technology.

Sibinga, M. S., & Friedman, C. J. (1971). Restraint and speech. *Pediatrics,* **48,** 116–122.

Siegel, A. W., Herman, J. F., Allen, G. L., & Kirasic, K. C. (1979). The development of cognitive maps of large- and small-scale spaces. *Child Development,* **50,** 582–585.

Siegel, I. M., & Murphy, T. J. (1970). *Postural determinants in the blind.* Final Project Report, Grant RD–3512–SB–700C2.

Simpkins, K. (1971). An auditory training program for kindergarten through third grade. *Education of the Visually Handicapped,* **3,** 70–73.

Simpkins, K. E. (1974). *Piagetian number concept in normal, retarded, and blind children.* Unpublished doctoral dissertation, Temple University.

Simpkins, K. E. (1979a). Development of the concept of space. *Journal of Visual Impairment & Blindness,* **73,** 81–85.

Simpkins, K. E. (1979b). Tactual discrimination of household objects. *Journal of Visual Impairment & Blindness,* **73,** 86–92.

Simpkins, K. E. (1979c). Tactual discrimination of shapes. *Journal of Visual Impairment & Blindness,* **73,** 93–101.

Simpkins, K. E., & Siegel, A. J. (1979). The blind child's construction of the projective straight line. *Journal of Visual Impairment & Blindness,* **73,** 233–238.

Singer, J. L., & Streiner, B. F. (1966). Imaginative content in the dreams and fantasy play of blind and sighted children. *Perceptual and Motor Skills,* **22,** 475–482.

Slosson, R. L. (1963). *Slosson Intelligence Test (SIT) for Children and Adults.* East Aurora, NY: Slosson Educational Publications.

Smith, M. A., Chethik, M., & Adelson, E. (1969). Differential assessments of "blindisms." *American Journal of Orthopsychiatry,* **39,** 807–817.

Smits, B. W. G. M., & Mommers, M. J. C. (1976). Differences between blind and sighted children on WISC verbal subtests. *New Outlook for the Blind,* **70,** 240–246.

Solntseva, L. I. (1966). Features peculiar to perception of the blind preschool children. In *Mental Development and Sensory Defects, 18th International Congress of Psychology,* 226–230.

Sommers, V. S. (1944). *The influence of parental attitudes and social environment on the personality development of the adolescent blind.* New York: American Foundation for the Blind.

Spiegelman, M. N. (1976). A comparative study of the effects of early blindness on the development of auditory-spatial learning. In Z. S. Jastrzembska (Ed.). *The effects of blindness and other impairments on early development* (pp. 29–63). New York: American Foundation for the Blind.

Spitz, R. A. (1945). Hospitalism. *Psychoanalytic Study of the Child,* **1,** 53–74.

Spitz, R. A. (1946). Anaclitic depression. *Psychoanalytic Study of the Child,* **2,** 313–342.

Stankov, L., & Spilsbury, G. (1978). The measurement of auditory abilities of blind, partially sighted, and sighted children. *Applied Psychological Measurement,* **2,** 491–503.

Stein, L. K., & Green, M. B. (1972). Problems in managing the young deaf–blind child. *Exceptional Children,* **38,** 481–484.

Stellwagon, W. T., & Culbert, S. S. (1963). Comparison of blind and sighted subjects in the discrimination of texture. *Perceptual and Motor Skills,* **17,** 61–62.

Stephens, B. (1972). Cognitive processes in the visually impaired. *Education of the Visually Handicapped,* **4,** 106–111.

Stephens, B., & Grube, C. (1982). Development of Piagetian reasoning in congenitally blind children. *Journal of Visual Impairment & Blindness,* **76,** 133–143.

Stephens, B., & Simpkins, K. (1974). *The reasoning, moral judgment, and moral conduct of the congenitally blind* (Report No. H23–3197). Office of Education, Bureau of Education for the Handicapped.

Stephens, B., Simpkins, K., & Wexler, M. (1976). A comparison of the performance of blind and sighted subjects age 6–10 years on the Rotation of Squares Test. *Education of the Visually Handicapped,* **8,** 66–70.

Stinchfield-Hawk, S. (1944). Moto-kinaesthetic speech training applied to visually handicapped children. *New Outlook for the Blind,* **38,** 4–8.

Stone, A. A. (1964). Consciousness: Altered levels in blind retarded children. *Psychosomatic Medicine,* **26,** 14–19.

Stone, N. W., & Chesney, B. H. (1978). Attachment behaviors in handicapped infants. *Mental Retardation,* **16,** 8–12.

Strelow, E. R. (1983). Use of the Binaural Sensory Aid by young children. *Journal of Visual Impairment & Blindness,* **77,** 429–438.

Strelow, E. R., & Boys, J. T. (1979). The Canterbury Child's Aid: A binaural spatial sensory for research with blind children. *Journal of Visual Impairment & Blindness,* **73,** 179–184.

Strelow, E. R., Kay, N., & Kay, L. (1978). Binaural sensory aid: Case studies of its use by two children. *Journal of Visual Impairment & Blindness,* **72,** 1-9.

Suinn, R. M. (1967). The theory of cognitive style: A partial replication. *Journal of General Psychology,* **77,** 11-15.

Swallow, R.-M. (1976). Piaget's theory and the visually handicapped learner. *New Outlook for the Blind,* **70,** 273-281.

Swallow, R.-M., & Poulsen, M. K. (1973). An exploratory study of Piagetian space concepts in secondary, low-vision girls. *American Foundation for the Blind Research Bulletin,* **26,** 139-150.

Swanson, L. (1979). Partially sighted children's conservation development. *Journal of Genetic Psychology,* **135,** 153-154.

Swanson, L., Minifie, D., & Minifie, E. (1979). Conservation development in the partially sighted child. *Psychology in the Schools,* **16,** 309-313.

Sylvester, R. H. (1913). The mental imagery of the blind. *Psychological Bulletin,* **10,** 210-211.

Tait, P. E. (1972a). Behavior of young blind children in a controlled play situation. *Perceptual and Motor Skills,* **34,** 963-969.

Tait, P. E. (1972b). A descriptive analysis of the play of young blind children. *Education of the Visually Handicapped,* **4,** 12-15.

Tait, P. E. (1972c). The implications of play as it relates to the emotional development of the blind child. *Education of the Visually Handicapped,* **4,** 52-54.

Tait, P. E. (1972d). Play and the intellectual development of blind children. *New Outlook for the Blind,* **66,** 361-369.

Tait, P. E. (1972e). The effect of circumstantial rejection on infant behavior. *New Outlook for the Blind,* **66,** 139-151.

Tait, P. E., & Ward, M. (1982). The comprehension of verbal humor by visually impaired children. *Journal of Visual Impairment & Blindness,* **76,** 144-147.

Taktikos, A. (1964). Association of retinoblastoma with mental defect and other pathological manifestations. *British Journal of Ophthalmology,* **48,** 495-498.

Teare, J. F., & Thompson, R. W. (1982). Concurrent validity of the Perkins-Binet Tests of Intelligence for the Blind. *Journal of Visual Impairment & Blindness,* **76,** 279-280.

Telson, S. (1965). Parent counseling. *New Outlook for the Blind,* **59,** 127-129.

Thompson, J. (1941). Development of facial expression of emotion in blind and seeing children. *Archives of Psychology,* **264.**

Thurrell, R. J., & Josephson, T. S. (1966). Retinoblastoma and intelligence. *Psychosomatics,* **7,** 368-370.

Thurrell, R. J., & Rice, D. G. (1970). Eye rubbing in blind children: Application of a sensory deprivation model. *Exceptional Children,* **36,** 325-330.

Tillman, M. H. (1967a). The performance of blind and sighted children on the

Wechsler Intelligence Scale for Children: Study I. *International Journal for the Education of the Blind,* **16,** 65–74.
Tillman, M. H. (1967b). The performance of blind and sighted children on the Wechsler Intelligence Scale for Children: Study II. *International Journal for the Education of the Blind,* **16,** 106–112.
Tillman, M. H., & Bashaw, W. L. (1968). Multivariate analysis of the WISC scales for blind and sighted children. *Psychological Reports,* **23,** 523–526.
Tillman, M. H., & Osborne, R. T. (1969). The performance of blind and sighted children on the Wechsler Intelligence Scale for Children: Interaction effects. *Education of the Visually Handicapped,* **1,** 1–4.
Tillman, M. H., & Williams, C. (1968). Associative characteristics of blind and sighted children to selected form classes. *International Journal for the Education of the Blind,* **18,** 33–40.
Tisdall, W. J., Blackhurst, A. E., & Marks, C. H. (1971). Divergent thinking in blind children. *Journal of Educational Psychology,* **62,** 468–473.
Tobin, M. J. (1972). Conservation of substance in the blind and partially sighted. *British Journal of Educational Psychology,* **42,** 192–197.
Tobin, M. J. (1978). An introduction to the psychological and educational assessment of blind and partially sighted children. *Occasional Papers of the British Psychological Society,* **2,** 9–17.
Totman, H. E. (1935). What shall we do with our blind babies? *Outlook for the Blind,* **29,** 52–60.
Tufenkjian, S. (1971). *A study of the meaningfulness of optical conceptions to congenitally blind persons.* Unpublished dissertation, The California School of Professional Psychology.
Turner, M., & Siegel, I. M. (1969). Physical therapy for the blind child. *Physical Therapy,* **49,** 1357–1363.

Umezu, H. (1972). Formation of verbal behavior of deaf-blind children. *Proceedings of the 20th International Congress of Psychology,* Tokyo, 58–74.
Unruh, D., & Barraga, N. C. (1981). Data synthesis: Alternative approaches to research with low incidence populations. *Journal of Visual Impairment & Blindness,* **75,** 317–320.
Urwin, C. (1978). The development of communication between blind infants and their parents. In A. Lock (Ed.), *Action, gesture and symbol: The emergence of language.* London: Academic Press.

Vander Kolk, C. J. (1977). Intelligence testing for visually impaired persons. *Journal of Visual Impairment & Blindness,* **71,** 158–163.
van Djik, J. (1971). Learning difficulties and deaf-blind children. In *Fourth international conference on deaf-blind children,* Perkins School for the Blind, Vermont Printing Co.
Van Hasselt, V. B. (1983). Social adaptation in the blind. *Clinical Psychology Review,* **3,** 87–102.

Van Hasselt, V. B., & Hersen, M. (1981). Applications of single-case designs to research with visually impaired individuals. *Journal of Visual Impairment & Blindness,* **75,** 359–362.

van 'T Hooft, F., & Heslinga, K. (1968). Sex education of blind-born children. *New Outlook for the Blind,* **62,** 15–21.

von Fieandt, K. (1966). *The world of perception.* Homewood, IL: Dorsey Press.

Vopata, A. E. (1978). Uses of the Sonicguide as a concept development device. *Education of the Visually Handicapped,* **10,** 24–28.

Walker, D. L. (1970). *The effects of training on the body image of blind children of elementary school age: A pilot study.* Unpublished manuscript, University of Virginia.

Walker, D. L. (1971). *The effects of training on the body image of blind children of kindergarten age.* Unpublished doctoral dissertation, George Peabody College for Teachers, Nashville, TN.

Walker, D. L. (1973). Body image and blindness: A review of related theory and research. *American Foundation for the Blind Research Bulletin,* **25,** 211–232.

Wallach, M. A., & Kogan, N. (1965). A new look at the creativity–intelligence distinction. *Journal of Personality,* **33,** 348–369.

Walsh, F. B. (1963). Blindness in an institution for the feeble-minded. *Archives of Ophthalmology,* **69,** 1965.

Walters, R. H., & Parke, R. D. (1965). The role of the distance receptors in the development of social responsiveness. In L. P. Lipsitt & C. C. Spiker (Eds.), *Advances in child development and behavior* (Vol. 2). New York: Academic Press.

Warren, D. H. (1970). Intermodality interactions in spatial localization. *Cognitive Psychology,* **1,** 114–133.

Warren, D.H. (1974). Early vs. late vision: The role of early vision in spatial reference systems. *New Outlook for the Blind,* **68,** 157–162.

Warren, D. H. (1977). *Early childhood research: Implications for orientation and mobility.* Address to California Association of Orientation and Mobility Specialists, San Francisco, CA.

Warren, D. H. (1978a). Childhood visual impairment: Sources and uses of knowledge. *Journal of Visual Impairment & Blindness,* **72,** 404–411.

Warren, D. H. (1978b). Perception by the blind. In E. C. Carterette & M. P. Friedman (Eds.), *Handbook of perception* (Vol. 10). New York: Academic Press.

Warren, D. H., Anooshian, L. J., & Bollinger, J. G. (1973). Early vs. late blindness: The role of early vision in spatial behavior. *American Foundation for the Blind Research Bulletin,* **26,** 151–170.

Warren, D. H., & Kocon, J. A. (1974). Factors in the successful mobility of the blind: A review. *American Foundation for the Blind Research Bulletin,* **28,** 191–218.

Warren, D. H., & Pick, H. L., Jr. (1970). Intermodality relations in localization in blind and sighted people. *Perception & Psychophysics,* **8,** 430–432.

Wattron, J. B. (1956). A suggested performance test of intelligence. *New Outlook for the Blind,* **50,** 115–121.

Webb, N. C. (1974). The use of myoelectric feedback in teaching facial expression to the blind. *American Foundation for the Blind Research Bulletin,* **27,** 231–262.

Webster, R. (1976). A concept development program for future mobility training. *New Outlook for the Blind,* **70,** 195–197.

Webster, R. (1983, February). What—No blindisms in African blind children? *Imfama,* **7,** 16, 18.

Weinberg, B. (1964). Stuttering among blind and partially sighted children. *Journal of Speech and Hearing Disorders,* **29,** 322–326.

Weiner, L. H. (1963). The performance of good and poor braille readers on certain tests involving tactual perception. *International Journal for the Education of the Blind,* **12,** 72–77.

Welsh, R. L., & Blasch, B. B. (1980). *Foundations of orientation and mobility.* New York: American Foundation for the Blind.

Wertheimer, M. (1961). Psychomotor co-ordination of auditory and visual space at birth. *Science,* **134,** 1692.

White, B. L. (1971). *Human infants: Experience and psychological development.* Englewood Cliffs, NJ: Prentice-Hall.

White, B. L., & Held, R. (1966). Plasticity of sensorimotor development in the human infant. In Rosenblith, J. F., & Allinsmith, W. (Eds.), *Causes of behavior: Readings in child development and educational psychology* (2nd ed., pp. 60–71). Boston: Allyn & Bacon.

Williams, C. E. (1968). Behaviour disorders in handicapped children. *Developmental Medicine and Child Neurology,* **10,** 736–740.

Williams, C. E. (1978). Strategies of intervention with the profoundly retarded visually-handicapped child: A brief report of a study of stereotypy. *Occasional Papers of the British Psychological Society,* **2,** 68–72.

Williams, M. (1956). *Intelligence test for children with defective vision.* Birmingham, England: University of Birmingham.

Williams, M. (1968). Superior intelligence of children blinded from retinoblastoma. *Archives of Diseases of Childhood,* **43,** 204–210.

Wills, D. M. (1965). Some observations on blind nursery school children's understanding of their world. *Psychoanalytic Study of the Child,* **20,** 344–363.

Wills, D. M. (1968). Problems of play and mastery in the blind child. *British Journal of Medical Psychology,* **41,** 213–222.

Wills, D. M. (1970). Vulnerable periods in the early development of blind children. *Psychoanalytic Study of the Child,* **25,** 461–480.

Wills, D. M. (1979). Early speech development in blind children. *Psychoanalytic Study of the Child,* **84,** 85–117.

Wilson, E. L. (1967). A developmental approach to psychological factors which may inhibit mobility in the visually handicapped person. *New Outlook for the Blind,* **61,** 283–289, 308.

Wilson, J., & Halverson, H. M. (1947). Development of a young blind child. *Journal of Genetic Psychology,* **71,** 155–175.

Winton, C. A. (1970). On the realization of blindness. *New Outlook for the Blind,* **64,** 16–24.

Witkin, H. (1965). Cognitive patterning in congenitally blind children. Paper presented at the American Psychological Association Meeting, Chicago.

Witkin, H. A., Birnbaum, J., Lomonaco, S., Lehr, S., & Herman, J. L. (1968). Cognitive patterning in congenitally totally blind children. *Child Development,* **39,** 767–786.

Witkin, H. A., Oltman, P. K., Chase, J. B., & Friedman, F. (1971). Cognitive patterning in the blind. In J. Hellmuth (Ed.), *Cognitive studies* (Vol. 2). New York: Brunner/Mazel.

Wolff, P. (1963). Observations on the early development of smiling. In B. M. Foss (Ed.), *Determinants of infant behavior II.* New York: Methuen.

Wolff, P. (1966). Developmental studies of blind children: II. *New Outlook for the Blind,* **60,** 179–182.

Worchel, P. (1951). Space perception and orientation in the blind. *Psychological Monographs,* **65,** 1-28.

Worchel, P., Mauney, J., & Andrew, J. G. (1950). The perception of obstacles by the blind. *Journal of Experimental Psychology,* **40,** 746–751.

Zahran, H. A. S. (1965). A study of personality differences between blind and sighted children. *British Journal of Educational Psychology,* **35,** 329–338.

Zazzo, R. (1948). Image du corps et conscience de soi. *Enfance,* **1.**

Zunich, M., & Ledwith, B. E. (1965). Self-concepts of visually handicapped and sighted children. *Perceptual and Motor Skills,* **21,** 771–774.

Zweibelson, I., & Barg, C. F. (1967). Concept development of blind children. *New Outlook for the Blind,* **61,** 218–222.

Index